Mastering ESL and Bilingual Methods

Mastering ESL and Bilingual Methods

Differentiated Instruction for Culturally and Linguistically Diverse (CLD) Students

Socorro G. Herrera
Kansas State University

Kevin G. Murry
Kansas State University

PEARSON

Boston ■ New York ■ San Francisco
Mexico City ■ Montreal ■ Toronto ■ London ■ Madrid ■ Munich ■ Paris
Hong Kong ■ Singapore ■ Tokyo ■ Cape Town ■ Sydney

Senior Editor: Aurora Martínez Ramos
Series Editorial Assistant: Erin Beatty
Editorial-Production Service: Omegatype Typography, Inc.
Manufacturing Buyer: Andrew Turso
Composition and Prepress Buyer: Linda Cox
Cover Administrator: Linda Knowles
Interior Designer: Denise Hoffman
Electronic Composition: Omegatype Typography, Inc.

For related titles and support materials, visit our online catalog at www.ablongman.com.

Between the time Website information is gathered and then published, it is not unusual for some sites to have closed. Also, the transcription of URLs can result in typographical errors. The publisher would appreciate notification where these errors occur so that they may be corrected in subsequent editions.

Library of Congress Cataloging-in-Publication Data

Herrera, Socorro Guadalupe.
   Mastering ESL and bilingual methods : differentiated instruction for culturally and lingustically diverse students / Socorro Guadalupe Herrera, Kevin G. Murry.
      p. cm.
   Includes bibliographical references and index.
   ISBN 0-205-41060-X
      1. English language—Study and teaching—Foreign speakers. 2. English language—Study and teaching—United Staes. 3. Multicultural education—United States.
4. Language and culture—United States. 5. Bilingualism—United States. I. Murry.
Kevin G. II. Title.

PE1128.A2H4675 2005
428'.0071—dc22

                                                                                      2004050573

Printed in the United States of America

10   9   8   7   6   09   08

Credits: pp. 1, 2, 30, 58, 93, 94, 124, 165, 166, 206, 248, 296, 330, Photos by the authors; Voices from the Field, pp. 18, 19, 50, 80, 117, 156, 189, 234, 256, 312, reprinted by permission; p. 330, from *Knots* by R. D. Laing, reprinted by permission of Routledge.

*Este libro está dedicado a la memoria de nuestras madres,
quienes sacrificios y dedicación han abierto tantas puertas
que sin ellas se hubieran quedado cerredas, sueños que
hubieran sido sólo posibilidades.*

*To the memory of our mothers, without whose sacrifice
and perseverance so many doors might have remained
closed, so many dreams remained just possibilities.*

Esther Jaquez de Herrera

Sammie Arlene Ellis Murry

■ contents

■ **c h a p t e r 3**

Linguistic Dimension of Methods for CLD Students   58

■ **p a r t t w o**

Accommodation Readiness   93

■ **c h a p t e r 4**

Changing Perspectives in Platform Development for Instructional Methods   94

chapter 5

A Framework of Accommodation Readiness   124

■ part three

Professionalism in Practice   165

■ chapter 6

Planning and Grounding
Instructional Methodology   166

■ chapter 7

The Integrated Content-Based
Method of Instruction   206

chapter 8

The Sheltered Method of Instruction   248

chapter 9

The CALLA Method of Instruction   296

chapter 10

Achieving Standards-Driven Professional Practice   330

When David Livingstone's work in Africa became known, a missionary society wrote to him and asked, "Have you found a good road where you are?" If he had, the letter indicated that the society was prepared to send some men to help with his work. Livingstone's answer was clear and to the point: "If you have men who will come only over a good road, I don't need your help. I want men who will come if there is no road." In the early years of the twenty-first century, increasing cultural and linguistic diversity in the grade-level classroom is, for many educators, as unfamiliar and intimidating as the wilds of Africa were to Livingstone's contemporaries over 130 years ago. As a consequence of this trepidation, many educators are searching for the *good road,* the recipe, for successful teaching amidst diversity. Yet, as Livingstone understood, changing times, a changing world, and changing awareness of the peoples of the world each demands a different sort of pioneer, a new brand of missionary vigilance and empathy, a willingness among those who seek to educate to pursue the road less traveled.

Somewhat paradoxically, although increasing cultural and linguistic diversity in the classroom is novel to many educators across the United States, diversity has been an ever-present reality in America since the days of British rule. Indeed, when the settlement of New Netherland was ceded to British control in 1664, at least eighteen languages, not including the languages of Native Americans, were spoken on Manhattan Island (Crawford, 1999). By 1840, bilingual public and parochial schools in the United States were fully operational in cities from Baltimore to Cleveland, from Milwaukee to St. Louis. Diversity fosters a variety of perspectives in a democracy at the same time that it bolsters creativity in the workplace; these are just two reasons why this nation, its peoples, and its economy have endured for over two hundred years.

■ Purpose

This text offers in-service teachers, district or building administrators, school specialists, preservice teachers, and paraprofessionals the opportunity to rediscover the value, the potential, the richness, and the adventure of diversity as they develop the capacity to professionally address the differential learning and transition needs of culturally and linguistically diverse (CLD) students. Although we recognize each student as a unique individual, throughout this text we use the term *CLD* to refer to those students whose cultures or languages are different from that of a dominant culture or language in U.S. society. Our journey pursues the road less traveled, and along the way we gain new insights into and reflective perspectives on ourselves and the rich cultural and linguistic assets our CLD students bring to the classroom. Among the highlights of the adventure are new approaches, the latest tools, new procedures, exceptional strategies, and new ways of knowing, all of which enhance our effectiveness with the CLD student, irrespective of her or his native language. By taking a few turns that others may have missed, our route explores new ways to reach and maximize relationships with the parents, caregivers, and extended family members of these students, as partners in appropriate pedagogical practices. By traveling the extra mile to achieve effectiveness amidst diversity, we stretch ourselves to develop new capacities for cross-cultural sensitivity, critical thinking, reflective student accommodation, and best practice with CLD students. Ultimately, we each reach our destination, our goal, having rediscovered our own abilities, our own sensitivities, and our own professionalism, as well as having discovered our own potential, which we have perhaps never explored.

As the title, *Mastering ESL and Bilingual Methods: Differentiated Instruction for Culturally and Linguistically Diverse (CLD) Students,* implies, this text is about methods. Yet it is also about differentiating instruction and professional practice to accommodate the differential learning and transition needs of the CLD student. Yes, the world of the classroom is changing. Nevertheless, each of us is capable of effecting the changes necessary to accommodate that shift and demonstrate our effectiveness amidst diversity. We begin our journey by discussing the changes occurring in the classroom and by developing a better understanding of the CLD students and family members who are significant parts of those changes. Other facets of our expedition examine the work of practitioners and researchers and the contributions they offer us in differentiating our own practices for cultural and, especially, linguistic diversity. At about the midpoint of our journey, we begin to investigate our readiness for the destination. That is, we assess our emergent capacities to provide appropriate classroom accommodations for the CLD student.

During the last leg of our quest for effectiveness amidst diversity, we acquire the tools for success, understand their historical foundations, practice their use, listen to the voices of other teachers who have used them successfully, and apply them to various dilemmas of practice. Benchmarks along the way designate where and when various tools are appropriate and when they are not. Other hallmarks of the adventure differentiate between tools and perspectives and critically assess their utility in particular situations by examining differences among an *approach,* a *method,* a *strategy,* and a *technique.* This is first accomplished by revisiting the nature, history, and applications of three major approaches to instruction for CLD students: the grammatical, the communicative, and the cognitive. Subsequently, we consider which instructional methods are products of each approach and which offers the best history of success with these students. Later, our discussions detail the contemporary and effective methods of instruction for CLD students, including the integrated content-based method, the sheltered instruction method, and the CALLA method. Among the details considered in these discussions are the components, sequences, strategies, and techniques associated with each method and their applications in professional practice.

Ultimately, we arrive at our destination having reached the goal of *instructional preparedness for cultural and linguistic diversity in the classroom.* Our adventure closes with key facets of a platform for best practice with CLD students. With these key facets, we can self-assess our ongoing effectiveness with CLD students and refine our capacities and skills so that we are increasingly successful in our professional and reflective practice amidst diversity.

Content Coverage

This first edition of *Mastering ESL and Bilingual Methods: Differentiated Instruction for Culturally and Linguistically Diverse (CLD) Students* is contemporary, comprehensive, theory and research based, and aligned with the Teachers of English to Speakers of Other Languages (TESOL)/National Council for the Accreditation of Teacher Education (NCATE) standards (TESOL, 2001) and the Guiding Principles for best practice with CLD students (Center for Equity and Excellence in Education, 1996). Each chapter in this text represents a concerted effort to enhance the professional development and preparation that educators need to build capacities for cross-culturally sensitive and empathetic perspectives, reflective practice, accommodative methodologies, instructional effectiveness with diverse populations, purposive collaboration with colleagues and staff, communication with and maximization of parents and extended family members, and self-assessment against standards of best practice with CLD students.

Organization

Part I of this text, "Hallmarks of Accommodative Instruction," examines the hallmarks of mutually accommodative instructional methods for CLD students. This accommodative instruction intentionally accounts for and incorporates findings from the sociocultural, cognitive, academic, and linguistic dimensions of the CLD student biography and schooling experience. Chapters 1 through 3 specify and discuss the sociocultural realities, cognitive growth potentials, academic challenges and processes, and linguistic development of CLD students.

Part II, "Accommodation Readiness," encourages school educators, based on their understanding of the four dimensions of the CLD student biography, to preassess their readiness for the accommodative instruction of the CLD student. Chapter 4 first describes the ways in which programming decisions (at the district or school level) can frame or restrict a teacher's instructional options for accommodation. On the other hand, in those districts and schools where CLD student programming is not already proscribed, programming decisions provide new opportunities for the appropriate instructional accommodation of CLD students. In either case, research on program models is summarized as a basis for teacher advocacy. Chapter 5 introduces the accommodation readiness spiral as a framework for teachers' preassessments of their readiness to deliver mutually accommodative instruction given a specified programming decision. The spiral serves as a preassessment tool for readiness in the following areas: critical reflection, CLD students and families, environment, curriculum, programming, instruction, application, and advocacy.

Part III, "Professionalism in Practice," recommends a professional approach to the instructional accommodation of the CLD student. This professionalism is conceptualized as involving three sequential components: planning, implementation, and evaluation. Chapter 6 provides and rationalizes recommendations for planning appropriate practices for CLD students. Chapters 7 through 9 discuss and detail three contemporary and robust methods of effective implementation. Finally, Chapter 10 discusses ways to appropriately engage in the evaluation of prior instructional planning and implementation. These processes of evaluation use nationally recognized standards of best practice with CLD students as touchstones of comparison.

More specifically, the text is divided into ten chapters. Chapters 1 through 3 detail not only the assets that CLD students bring to the school but also the singular sociocultural, cognitive, academic, and linguistic challenges they face and processes they must accomplish in the classroom. Chapter 1 is particularly concerned with those sociocultural factors that may influence the academic and transitional success of CLD students, including impacts on the affective filter, the influences exerted by the culture of the school, and the dynamics of the acculturation process. Chapter 2 explores both the cognitive and academic dimensions of the CLD student biography and details factors in each dimension that may prove especially challenging for these students. Also described are the characteristics of instruction designed to promote cognitive development and academic success, especially classroom practice that is contextualized, relevant, cognitively demanding, content-based, elaborative, differentiated for multiple learning styles and strategies, constructivist, and metacognitive. Chapter 3 examines the challenges and processes of the linguistic dimension of learning for CLD students. Of particular interest to teachers and other educators are the processes of first and second language acquisition, each of which is detailed, compared, contrasted, and discussed. Also described are the characteristics that CLD students tend to exhibit at each of the various stages of second language acquisition—from the silent period (preproduction stage) to the stage of advanced fluency.

Chapter 4 offers guidance regarding the range of programming models available for CLD students. Included is a discussion of the foundations, characteristics, and concerns associated with each program model. Research on the effectiveness of dominant models with varying populations of CLD students is highlighted. The chapter closes with a brief overview of judicial and legislative foundations of programming, including the results of groundbreaking court precedents that have influenced programming and decision making in schools.

Chapter 5 encourages the reader to self-assess both understanding of the foundations offered in Chapters 1 through 4 and his or her readiness for the appropriate accommodation of CLD students. This accommodation readiness spiral offers a rubric for self-assessment in the following progressive domains of readiness: critical reflection on practice, students and families, internal and external environment, curriculum, programming, instruction, application, and advocacy.

Chapters 6 through 9 detail appropriate instructional practices for CLD students, with particular emphases on contemporary, theory and research-driven, culturally sensitive, developmentally appropriate, and content-based instructional methods. Chapter 6 first differentiates among approach, method, strategy, and technique as a basis for communication, collaboration, and effectiveness. Subsequently, one historical (the grammatical) and two contemporary (the communicative and the cognitive) approaches to instruction for CLD students are described, explained, and discussed. Each chapter that follows is devoted to contemporary and effective methods of instruction. Chapter 7 focuses on the integrated content-based method, Chapter 8 explores the sheltered instruction method, and Chapter 9 discusses the CALLA method. Each of these chapters also illustrates the implementation of these methods in classroom practice.

Chapter 10 brings closure by highlighting recent efforts in the development of standards of best practice for the instruction of CLD students. Following an exploration of the key facets of a platform for best practice with CLD students, self-assessment rubrics are provided to facilitate (a) self-assessment comparisons of practice with national standards and benchmarks, (b) critical reflection on practice, and (c) suggestions for the refinement of professional practice with CLD students.

■ Special Features

In order to motivate reader interest, accommodate different learning styles, and offer additional insights on topics covered, this text offers the following special features:

Chapter Outlines: Each chapter begins with a chapter outline, which provides readers with both an advance organizer and a fundamental understanding of the content of each chapter.

Objectives: It is our belief that each and every educator should have access to the purpose and the ideas behind a particular lesson or chapter. Therefore, each chapter begins with an inventory of objectives to be achieved as reader outcomes for that chapter.

Standards of Best Practice: As a model for professionalism in practice with diversity, this special feature of each chapter aligns the content of all lessons and chapters with the nationally recognized TESOL/NCATE standards and the Guiding Principles for best practice with CLD students. The TESOL/NCATE teacher standards reflect professional consensus on standards for the quality teaching of pre-K–12 CLD students. Additionally, the CEEE Guiding Principles and their accompanying indicators serve as a framework to assist practitioners, policymakers, and clients as they collaborate to enhance academic enrichment and language acquisition among CLD students. (For a more in-depth rationale of our decision to use these particular sets of standards, see Chapter 10.)

Figures and Tables: Every chapter offers explanatory or illustrative figures and tables that have been specifically designed to enhance or bolster the content of the chapter. Educators can capitalize on these features to understand the scope and breadth of various research-based practices identified in this book.

Text Boxes: Content enhancements in the form of text boxes are included in each chapter. Some of these features provide explanatory or illustrative information on topics covered in that chapter. Others introduce new but related information. Three types of text boxes are used throughout the text to illustrate (Differentiated Praxis), explain (Fallacies and Facts), and offer additional perspectives (Voices from the Field). Three additional types of text boxes recur in all chapters:

- *Are You Aware?:* These content enhancements provide additional information, alternative perspectives, or illustrative examples. Some also prompt thought and reflection on the content of the text box through guiding questions.
- *Theory into Practice:* These text boxes briefly summarize a theory or theoretical concept before encouraging the reader to consider the implications of the theory or applications of it in professional practice with CLD students. Some also prompt thought and reflection on the content of the text box through guiding questions.
- *Dilemmas of Practice:* These content enrichments (some of which are framed in the form of a critical incident) first pose a dilemma of practice with CLD students. Each then offers information and suggestions regarding an appropriate resolution of such a dilemma in practice. The resolutions typically use theories, methods, strategies, and information discussed in the various chapters.

Key Theories and Concepts: In each chapter, a list of key theories and concepts is provided to remind the reader of the critical content discussed in that particular chapter.

Professional Conversations on Practice: This unique feature, which appears in every chapter, suggests topics or foci for debate about critical issues that surface in that chapter. The feature is designed to encourage critical thinking, reflection, discussion, articulation of knowledge gained, debate, metacognition, and theory-into-practice applications.

Questions for Review and Reflection: In each chapter, we pose questions that provide opportunities for self-assessment of content comprehension, concept understanding, and readiness for application to practice. The questions are applicable to educators at all levels, including preservice teachers, paraprofessionals, in-service teachers, staff specialists, and administrators.

Tips for Practice: This is a differentiating feature that provides both elementary and secondary educators with highly specific extensions of chapter content. Chapters 1 through 7 offer elementary tips, secondary tips, and sometimes general tips for educators. The Tips for Practice section of Chapter 8 is organized according to the eight components of the sheltered instruction observation protocol, the primary subject of that chapter. The tips included for Chapter 9 have been structured according to three main categories of learning strategies emphasized in the CALLA instructional sequence, which is detailed in that chapter. Finally, the tips for Chapter 10 have been organized according to the four key facets of a platform for best practice with CLD students.

Suggested Activities: This feature appears in each chapter and offers educators activities, based on chapter content, that are designed to promote the articulation of learned content, collaboration with others, applications to practice, critical thinking, critical reflection, and advocacy for CLD students and families. These activities are divided according to those applicable to preservice educators and those most useful to in-service educators.

Assessment Tips and Strategies: This feature appears at the end of Chapter 3 and summarizes the preassessment issues addressed in Chapters 1 through 3 and at the end of Chapter 6 to summarize the assessment issues discussed in Chapters 4 through 6. Because Chapters 7, 8, and 9 address specific instructional methods, this feature also appears at the end of each of these chapters.

Glossary: This feature is an auxiliary resource for current readers and for future applications of content in practice. Attention has been given to those terms that are likely to be unfamiliar to practicing educators and future educators who have had few educational experiences with CLD students.

Appendix: Because the overwhelming majority of CLD students are Spanish language dominant and because many of these are Mexican American students, this distinctive section provides examples of classroom activities specific to the background experiences and growth needs of these students. These activities are organized according to those applicable to elementary, middle, and high school. Within each of these categories, the activities are further subdivided according to those that apply to language arts, mathematics, and social studies.

Reference List: Assembled in American Psychological Association (APA) style, this feature documents the theory, research, and analyses that support our discussions, content, conclusions, recommendations, and advocacy. Additionally, the feature is a resource for preservice and in-service educators of CLD students.

■ Acknowledgments

Many friends, colleagues, and reviewers have contributed to the preparation of this text. In particular, we wish to acknowledge the many contributions of Katie Brooks, especially her spirit, creativity, sagacity, and conviviality.

Likewise, we extend a very special acknowledgment to Melissa Holmes for her conscientiousness, perspicacity, and persistence. Melissa brought many valuable qualities to this effort, not the least of which were editorial expertise, organizational acuity, attention to readability, and steadfast determination.

Special thanks are also in order to Shabina Kavimandan, who, despite many other pressing obligations, took time to provide insightful perspectives, thoughts, refinements, and reviews. Shabina's willingness to brainstorm, discuss, deliberate, and review was extremely valuable.

At the same time, we fully recognize that this text would not have been possible without the tactical and technical expertise of others, especially Sheri Meredith and Nick Austin. Sheri's contributions as master organizer were inestimable. Among these have been file management, text formatting, graphical refinement, syntax reviews, archive management, motivation, and encouragement. Her collaboration and agenda setting were each greatly appreciated. Nick Austin, who served as our technical resource for the project, contributed valuable expertise to issues of platform conversion, software maximization, text management, formatting, graphical design, and reproduction.

For their many and varied contributions from prior experience with CLD students and diverse school practice across the United States, we wish to acknowledge Katya Karathanos and Susan Ross. We have also appreciated and valued the support and contributions of Della Perez and Yolanda Gallardo, especially their insights regarding balanced literacy development for CLD students, the writing process, and the promotion of family and community involvement.

We would also like to thank the reviewers: Irma Guadarrama, University of Houston; Maria Medrano, National University; Judith O'Loughlin, New Jersey City University; Laura Sujo de Montes, Northern Arizona University; and Kip Tellez, University of California, Santa Cruz.

Finally, a number of classroom teachers who serve the differential learning and transition needs of CLD students have provided insights from their professional practice. These are appreciated and have been included primarily in the Voices from the Field feature of the text. Their experiences and adaptations illustrate the ways in which instructional methods and other aspects of professional practice can effectively and mutually accommodate the needs and assets of CLD students.

Dr. Socorro G. Herrera currently serves as associate professor of elementary education at Kansas State University and is codirector of the CLASSIC© ESL/Dual Language Program. Certified in elementary education, bilingual education, and school counseling, Dr. Herrera's recent publications have appeared in the *Bilingual Research Journal* and the *Journal of Research in Rural Education.* Her recent research and teaching in education have emphasized emergent literacy, reading strategies, the differential learning needs of second language learners, teacher preparation for diversity in the classroom, and mutual accommodation for CLD students. Dr. Herrera is an invited member of the Multicultural Education Committee of the American Association of Colleges for Teacher Education (AACTE).

Dr. Kevin G. Murry, codirector of CLASSIC© ESL/Dual Language Education at Kansas State University, is currently associate professor of curriculum and instruction (C&I). His work in C&I has focused on teacher and administrator preparation for the differential learning and transition needs of CLD students. Dr. Murry's recent research has emphasized advocacy frameworks for culturally and linguistically diverse students, the linguistic and cross-cultural dynamics of ESL instruction, portfolio-based practicum experiences, and school restructuring for linguistic diversity. His recent publications have appeared in the *Journal of Continuing Higher Education, Educational Considerations, AACTE Policy Briefs,* and the *Bilingual Research Journal.*

Mastering ESL and Bilingual Methods

Hallmarks of
Accommodative Instruction

In Part I of this text, we examine the hallmarks of mutually accommodative instructional methods for culturally and linguistically diverse (CLD) students. This accommodative instruction accounts for, and incorporates findings from, the sociocultural, cognitive, academic, and linguistic dimensions of the CLD student biography and schooling experience. In Chapters 1 through 3, we specify and discuss the sociocultural realities, cognitive growth potentials, academic challenges and processes, and linguistic development of CLD students.

objectives

The information provided in this chapter will help the educator to:

- Describe national trends toward increasing diversity in the classroom.
- Explain key terms and acronyms used in the fields of bilingual and ESL education.
- Describe assets that CLD students bring to the classroom.
- List the four critical dimensions of the CLD student biography.
- Describe key sociocultural challenges and processes for CLD students.
- Describe key implications of the sociocultural dimension for teaching and learning.

Multidimensional Foundations of Methods for CLD Students

There can be no significant innovation in education that does not have at its center the attitudes of the teachers. The beliefs, assumptions, feelings of teachers are the air of the learning environment; they determine the quality of life within it.

—Niel Postman & Charles Weingartner, *Teaching as a Subversive Activity*

chapter outline

Demographic Patterns and Student Diversity
Teacher Preparation for Cultural and Linguistic
Diversity in the Classroom

Describing Cultural and Linguistic Diversity in the Classroom
Key Terms and Acronyms
The CLD Student: Asset or Liability?

Understanding the Realities of Cultural and Linguistic Diversity in the Classroom
Expanding on the Prism Model
The Sociocultural Dimension of the CLD Student
Biography

critical standards *Guiding Chapter Content*

TESOL/NCATE teacher standards reflect professional consensus on standards for the quality teaching of pre-K–12 CLD students. Additionally, the CEEE Guiding Principles and their accompanying indicators serve as a framework to assist practitioners, policymakers, and clients as they collaborate to enhance academic enrichment and language acquisition among CLD students. Therefore, in order to help educators understand how they might appropriately target and address national professional teaching standards in practice, we have designed the content of this chapter to reflect the following standards.

TESOL ESL Standards for P–12 Teacher Education Programs

TESOL ESL—Domain 1: Language. Candidates know, understand, and use the major concepts, theories, and research related to the nature and acquisition of language to construct learning environments that support ESOL [CLD] students' language and literacy development and content-area achievement. (p. 1)

- **Standard 1.b. Language acquisition and development.** Candidates understand and apply concepts, theories, research, and practice to facilitate the acquisition of a primary and a new language in and out of classroom settings. (p. 6)

    1.b.4. Create a secure, positive, and motivating learning environment. (p. 9)

    1.b.9. Understand and apply knowledge of the role of individual learner variables in the process of learning English. (p. 11)

TESOL ESL—Domain 2: Culture. Candidates know, understand, and use the major concepts, theories, and research related to the nature and structure of culture to construct learning environments that support ESOL students' language and literacy development and content-area achievement. (p. 15)

- **Standard 2.a. Nature and role of culture.** Candidates know, understand, and use the major concepts, principles, theories, and research related to the nature and role of culture

Note: All TESOL/NCATE standards are cited from TESOL (2001). All guiding principles are cited from Center for Equity and Excellence in Education (1996).

in language development and academic achievement that support individual students' learning. (p. 15)

2.a.4. Understand and apply concepts about the interrelationship between language and culture. (p. 17)

CEEE Guiding Principles

Guiding Principle #1: Limited English proficient students are held to the same high expectations of learning established for all students.

1.1 Communities, schools, and teachers believe that limited English proficient students can achieve high standards, and they consistently help all children to succeed academically.

1.2 Communities, schools, and teachers welcome English language learners to their schools and accept and value the cultural perspectives and languages these students and their families bring to school.

1.8 Schools include limited English proficient students in all curricular and extracurricular activities, incorporating and building on the cultural perspectives and languages that these students and their families bring to school.

1.9 Teachers create classroom environments in which the efforts and contributions of every student are respected and encouraged. (p. 5)

Guiding Principle #4: Limited English proficient students receive instruction that builds on their previous education and cognitive abilities and that reflects their language proficiency levels.

4.1 School districts take into consideration the whole profile of a student, including language/cultural background, native language literacy, and appropriate and valid student assessment data when making decisions about the placement and provision of services to limited English proficient students. (p. 8)

Two major trends have characterized the field of education in the last two decades: a dramatic increase in the number of culturally and linguistically diverse (CLD) students and a shortage of teachers trained to work with this student population. According to the U.S. Department of Education (USDE), the enrollment of CLD students across the nation has grown from 2.1 million to 4.4 million over the last decade (2002). As illustrated in Figure 1.1, this increase is five times that of the total enrollment in public schools. In fact, since 1989, the CLD student population in the United States has increased by a phenomenal 104.97 percent (NCES, 2002b). Those students whose cultures or languages are different from that of the dominant culture or language in U.S. society are variously described with the terms English language learner (ELL), English as a second or other language (ESOL), limited English proficient (LEP), and more. Although we recognize each student as a unique individual, throughout the text, for reasons explained in this chapter, we use the cross-culturally respectful term *culturally and linguistically diverse* (CLD).

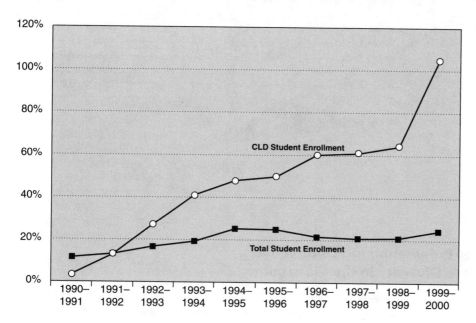

■ **figure 1.1**
K–12 CLD Student
Population and Total
Student Population
Growth in the
United States,
1990/1991–1999/
2000

Source: Data from
NCES, 2002b.

■ Demographic Patterns and Student Diversity

Not only is the number of CLD students in U.S. public schools increasing, but also the patterns of migration within the United States are changing. Traditionally, the largest, fastest growing CLD student populations have been concentrated within coastal states such as Florida, California, Texas, and New York. Although these states continue to have large numbers of CLD students, midwestern states such as Kansas, Indiana, Missouri, Nebraska, and Kentucky have experienced a dramatic increase in CLD student numbers over the past two decades. This increase has exceeded 200 percent annually in many midwestern states (NCES, 2002b).

Census Bureau projections indicate that the trend in CLD student population growth will continue. School-age children whose first language is not English will constitute an estimated 40 percent of the K–12 population in the United States by the year 2030 (U.S. Census Bureau, 2000).

Currently, out of the more than four hundred languages represented in U.S. schools, Spanish-speaking students make up 77 percent of the total CLD K–12 population. As illustrated in Figure 1.2, Spanish is by far the most common language, other than English, spoken across the nation. Other languages represent the remaining 23 percent. For example, Vietnamese, Hmong, Haitian Creole, and Korean, which round out the top five languages spoken by K–12 CLD students in the United States, each constitute 1 to 3 percent of this remainder (USDE, 2002).

■ **figure 1.2**
Languages Most
Commonly Spoken by
CLD Students in the
United States,
1999–2000

Source: Data from USDE, 2002.

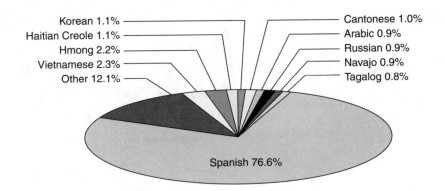

Korean 1.1%
Haitian Creole 1.1%
Hmong 2.2%
Vietnamese 2.3%
Other 12.1%

Cantonese 1.0%
Arabic 0.9%
Russian 0.9%
Navajo 0.9%
Tagalog 0.8%

Spanish 76.6%

Teacher Preparation for Cultural and Linguistic Diversity in the Classroom

This statistically significant increase in the number of CLD students in U.S. schools is placing new demands on teacher preparation and in-service professional development programs. Educators need support in developing the capacity to provide appropriate and effective instruction for CLD students. According to the National Center of Education Statistics (NCES) (1997), only 2.5 percent of teachers who teach CLD students hold a degree in either bilingual or English as a second language (ESL) education. Unfortunately, the states that have the least experience with CLD student populations face the greatest shortage of certified bilingual and ESL teachers (AAEE, 2001). Also problematic is the fact that although most CLD students spend the majority of their school day in grade-level classrooms, most teachers in these classrooms have little or no training in the differential learning and development needs of this group. Of the total number of public school teachers across the nation, only 12.5 percent of those who have CLD students in their classrooms have had eight or more hours of professional development specific to the needs of this student population (NCES, 2002a). Consequently, few teachers are prepared to provide instruction specifically designed to meet the linguistic, cognitive, academic, and affective development needs of these students.

Achievement gap getting wider

■ Describing Cultural and Linguistic Diversity in the Classroom

The preceding discussion of changing demographics and demands in public school classrooms used a vast array of acronyms. Because acronyms are commonly used in discussions of trends, issues, and practices that involve the CLD student, we now explore the definitions and connotations of some of the most frequently used acronyms and terms. Where the issue is salient, we discuss our rationale for preferred choices among acronyms and other terms that are used to describe both students and programs. Some are more exacting, more descriptive, and more cross-culturally sensitive than others. The following memorandum regarding an Office for Civil Rights (OCR) site visit more explicitly demonstrates common acronym use in practice:

MEMO

To: All teachers of CLD students

From: The District BE/ESL Office

Re: Information for OCR visit

The OCR will be visiting us next week. Before they come, we need to compile information on our CLD student population. First, create a list of all your CLD students. Then we need to know if they are FEP, LEP, or NEP. Make sure you include their LAS-O and LAS R/W scores. On the LAS tests, use forms 2C and 3A. Then write a brief description of each student's proficiency in terms of BICS and CALP. If the students are NEP or LEP, designate whether they are in a BE or ESL program, and indicate their productive and receptive proficiency in both L1 and L2. For the students participating in the ESL program, indicate the type of instruction they receive: SDAIE, CALLA, or SIOP. The BE/ESL Office needs this information ASAP. Thanks for your help.

Key Terms and Acronyms

As the preceding memorandum illustrates, a student-centered focus on instructional programming amidst diversity requires that teachers be familiar with numerous terms and acronyms. Educators and researchers use many terms to describe students whose languages and cultures are different from the average grade-level student. The term *limited English proficient (LEP)*, popularized by the federal government in the 1960s and 1970s, is typical. However, it is especially problematic. LEP does not emphasize the *asset* of multilingualism that the student may demonstrate in school. Rather, the term implies an assumed level of *deficit* in English proficiency that may not necessarily be accurate.

The long-standing use of the term *language minority student (LM or LMS)* is equally troublesome. This term, often derived from what are assumed to be typical classroom or school demographics, characteristically presupposes that students who speak a language other than English are in the demographic minority for a given school district. Any recent examination of changing public school demographics will quickly invalidate this assumption, even in some schools in midwestern states where cultural and linguistic diversity have not been a reality in the past (NCES, 2002b; USDE, 2002).

Last, but certainly not least important, is the frequent use of the term *mainstream* when referring to students in the classroom whose languages or cultures are not different from those that have previously dominated U.S. classrooms. The use of this term implies that any other students, especially students whose culture, language, or learning abilities are different, are somehow *less than,* or not a part of, the mainstream of students for whom our school systems were supposedly designed. However, diversity in the classroom is increasingly the reality of U.S. schools in the twenty-first century (U.S. Census Bureau, 2000). It has been argued that such diversity is now the fabric, the mainstream, of today's classroom (Delpit, 1995; Ovando, Collier, & Combs, 2003). Instead, we favor the use of the term *grade-level students* (Chamot & O'Malley, 1994) when referring to this segment of the student population.

In a more exacting and cross-culturally respectful vein, we advocate the use of the following term when referring to students whose culture or language are different from other grade-level students: The term *culturally and linguistically diverse (CLD) student* is the most inclusive and, in our view, is most holistically descriptive of a student whose culture or language is different from that of the dominant culture or language in U.S. society. The use of this term and its associated acronym are increasingly prevalent in educational literature (Buxton, 1999; Chamot & O'Malley, 1996; Escamilla, 1999; New York State Department of Education, 2002; Rodriguez, Parmar, & Signer, 2001). CLD students are those who speak a language other than English and who bring diverse cultural heritages and assets to the school (Baca & Cervantes, 1998; Escamilla, 1999; Murry, 1996). However, because diversity does not imply a level playing field, CLD is also most appropriately and affirmatively descriptive of the student who will need accommodative programming and instruction to facilitate his or her cultural and linguistic transitions within a content-area context.

These terms and acronyms from the field demonstrate the importance of using appropriately descriptive, cross-culturally respectful nomenclature when referring to the complex environment of and instructional programming for CLD students. Table 1.1 details other acronyms that are commonly used in language education, each of which has been reviewed for descriptive accuracy, professional utility, and cross-cultural implications. The preferred terms are those used throughout this text.

The CLD Student: Asset or Liability?

As is evident in the use of terms such as *limited English proficient* and *mainstream* in today's world of public school education, questions regarding the most appropriate ways of serving the differential learning and affective needs of this rapidly growing population of CLD students often stem from questions of assets and liabilities. You might well ask, why assets and liabilities? The sad fact is that some of our schools continue to perceive the CLD student as a liability—a student who is liable to fail because he or she cannot understand or speak the language of instruction, a student who is more likely to migrate and move away than to benefit from teacher instruction, a student who is likely to experience academic failure because of inadequate schooling or time on task, a student who is likely to bring down a school's test scores because he or she cannot keep up with other students, and more. Throughout the educational literature, this view of the CLD student appears as the deficit orientation to the linguistically or culturally different student

■ **table 1.1**   Common Acronyms from Bilingual and ESL Education

Acronym/Explanation	Definition
BICS—basic interpersonal communication skills	The language ability needed for casual conversation. This usually applies to the interpersonal conversation skills of CLD students (i.e., playground language).
CALLA—cognitive academic language learning approach	A method of instruction that is grounded in the cognitive approach and focuses on the explicit instruction of learning strategies and the development of critical thinking as a means of acquiring deep levels of language proficiency.
CALP—cognitive academic language proficiency	The language ability needed for learning academic skills and concepts in situations in which contextual clues are not present and an abstract use of language is required.
CLD—culturally and linguistically diverse	This preferred term applies to an individual or group of individuals whose culture or language differs from that of the dominant group.
CUP—common underlying proficiency	This term refers to the conceptual knowledge that acts as the foundation on which new skills are built. Both languages, L1 and L2, facilitate the development of such fundamental cognitive patterns within individuals. The language biographies serve as a bridge, connecting new information with previously acquired knowledge.
ELD—English language development	This term is used in some states for the programming model most commonly referred to as English as a second language (ESL).
ELL—English language learner	Individuals who are in the process of transitioning from a home or native language to English. However, *CLD* is the preferred term because CLD emphasizes both the cultural and linguistic assets that a student brings to the classroom.
ESL—English as a second language	A programming model in which linguistically diverse students are instructed in the use of English as a means of communication and learning. This model is often used when native speakers of multiple first languages are present within the same classroom.
ESOL—English for speakers of other languages	Instruction that focuses primarily on the development of vocabulary and grammar as a means of learning English.
FEP—fluent English proficient	A CLD student who is proficient in English.
$i + 1$—comprehensible input	New information that an individual receives that is one step beyond his or her current stage of competence. Accordingly, if the learner is competent at stage i, then input at $i + 1$ is most comprehensible and useful for producing new understandings.
ICB—integrated content-based	A communicative method that involves the concurrent teaching of academic subject matter and second language acquisition skills. This method often employs thematic units as well as content and language objectives across subject areas.
L1—first language	The first or native language acquired by an individual.
L2—second language	The second language acquired by an individual.

(continued)

■ **t a b l e 1 . 1**   Continued

Acronym/Explanation	Definition
LEP—limited English proficient	An individual who is in the process of acquiring English as his or her second language. This term is often found in government documents. However, as LEP emphasizes inadequacies rather than abilities, *CLD* is the preferred term.
NCLB—No Child Left Behind	The No Child Left Behind Act of 2001 was signed into law by President George W. Bush on January 8, 2002. Designed to close the achievement gap between disadvantaged students and their peers, this education reform calls for greater accountability for assessment results in K–12 education.
NEP—non-English proficient	An individual who is in the beginning stages of acquiring English and therefore relies heavily on nonverbal cues. The preferred term is *CLD* because the *N* in NEP highlights a deficit rather than an asset.
OCR—Office of Civil Rights	The entity of the U.S. Department of Justice responsible for exacting compliance with Title VI of the Civil Rights Act of 1964.
SDAIE—specially designed academic instruction in English	A variation of sheltered instruction that emphasizes cognitively demanding, grade-level appropriate core curriculum for CLD students. This variation primarily applies to students who have attained an intermediate or advanced level of proficiency in L2 (English).
SIOP—sheltered instruction observation protocol	A vehicle for delivering scaffolded instruction of the existing curriculum so that instruction is more comprehensible for individuals who are acquiring English.
SUP—separate underlying proficiency	This term refers to the separate conceptual knowledge bases in L1 and L2, assuming that the two languages operate independently. According to this perspective, no transfer of skills occurs between the two languages.

(Delpit, 1995; Dilworth & Brown, 2001; Flores, Cousin, & Díaz, 1991; Reyes, de la Luz, & Halcón, 2001; Sautter, 1994). Basically, this perspective stresses not the assets that the CLD student brings to the school or the classroom but the liabilities or deficits that, according to this view, characterize the hopelessness of appropriate educational accommodations for these students.

This perspective holds that CLD students are language (presumably English) deficient and culture and home deficient and, as a result, at risk of academic failure. In one sense, the prevalence of this liability or deficit perspective is not surprising given the fact that the United States is one of the few countries in the world that does not value either bilingualism or multilingualism (Crawford, 2000). This deficit point of view is evident in common statements such as, "If they would only learn English . . . " and "They can't learn science until they speak English." As we explore in this chapter, these students bring complex differences to the classroom, but linguistic differences are only a part of the picture. CLD students bring other differences that teachers need not view as liabilities.

For example, an alternative perspective on the CLD student more affirmatively recognizes and celebrates the assets this student may bring to the classroom and the school. Assets that this perspective acknowledges include:

- Multilingualism
- Experiences and schooling in another country
- Familiarity with multiple cultures and ethnicities

Just as management specialists recognize and use diversity in the workforce as one of the most powerful influences on an organization's capacity for creativity in the world of business (Florida, Cushing, & Gates, 2002; Senge, 1997; Terrisse, 2001), educators should recognize and use cultural and linguistic diversity as a powerful enrichment of a school's learning community. In fact, when CLD student differences are appropriately accommodated and classroom instruction is purposefully differentiated for diversity, these students not only match the academic performance of their native-English-speaking peers, but also their academic gains may actually exceed those of their grade-level contemporaries (Thomas & Collier, 1997).

■ Understanding the Realities of Cultural and Linguistic Diversity in the Classroom

As previously discussed, the demographic realities of today's schools demonstrate that the composition of the average classroom in the United States is rapidly changing and will continue to do so in the foreseeable future. Because educators are responsible for educating *all* students, we seek to understand what increasing cultural and linguistic diversity will mean for curriculum, instruction, pedagogy, and the teaching profession. This section of the chapter explores these realities as a foundation for discussion of the appropriate instructional methods that will accommodate cultural and linguistic diversity in a professional, responsible, empathetic, and purposeful manner. We first explore a framework from which we can begin to examine the many factors that must be accounted for in designing appropriate instructional methods for CLD students.

Expanding on the Prism Model

The prism model (see Figure 1.3) is the product of long-term, multiage, and multisite research (Collier, 1987, 1989a, 1992; Collier & Thomas, 1989; Thomas & Collier, 1997) in public school districts across the United States. This model represents a uniquely holistic way to frame the differential learning and transition needs and diverse assets that CLD students bring to the school.

Many school educators who are first confronted by the complexities of accommodating CLD students naturally assume that the students' greatest needs and most formidable challenges are linguistic. In fact, a common phrase heard in

■ **figure 1.3** Language
Acquisition for School: The Prism Model

Source: C. Ovando and V. Collier (1998),
*Bilingual and ESL Classrooms: Teaching in
Multicultural Contexts,* 2nd ed. (Boston:
McGraw-Hill). Page 89. Reprinted by
permission of the McGraw-Hill Companies.

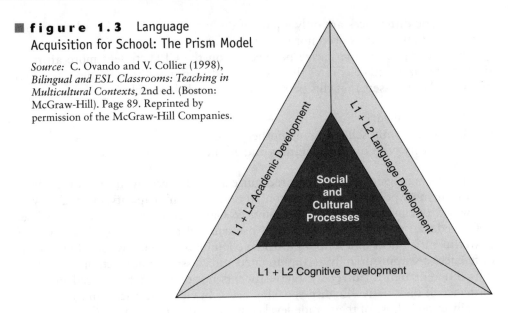

schools across the country is, "If they [CLD students] would just learn English, everything else [in their school performance] would just fall right into place." However, the research behind the prism model demonstrates that not one but four different dimensions of the CLD student biography must be addressed if these students are to be successful. Figure 1.3 illustrates each of these four dimensions of the model: linguistic, academic, cognitive, and sociocultural. Consistent with the findings of Thomas and Collier (1997), no single dimension of CLD student success should be addressed in isolation. Instead, each of the four dimensions of the prism model is interrelated and involves developmental processes that occur simultaneously for the CLD student.

In this and subsequent chapters, we go beyond the defining characteristics of the prism dimensions. We examine and discuss the challenges and processes of each dimension that we have witnessed in our work with CLD students and their teachers (in the states of Arkansas, Florida, Iowa, Kansas, Missouri, New Mexico, Nebraska, Nevada, Texas, Utah, and Wyoming), as well as in the work of others in the fields of bilingual and ESL education. These analyses begin with the essential sociocultural dimension of the CLD student biography.

The Sociocultural Dimension of the CLD Student Biography

At the heart of the CLD student biography is the sociocultural dimension. This dimension encompasses the complex sociocultural factors and variables that are critical to the transitional adjustments and the academic success of CLD students.

Insightful teachers realize the significance of this dimension in the lives of CLD students and families and are careful to account for it as they plan differentiated instruction for these students. A significant number of CLD students have either recently immigrated to the United States or recently migrated to the school. These students face a surprising number of sociocultural (especially acculturational) challenges, many of which are anxiety provoking and some of which may promote culture shock.

Sociocultural Challenges

Among such sociocultural challenges are those highlighted in Table 1.2. From a cultural standpoint, such challenges include but are not limited to the following:

- *The CLD student must adjust to a new country, city, or neighborhood.*

  Implications: The student faces difficult, survival-based challenges outside of the school, many of which may influence her or his punctuality, alertness, attentiveness, ability to concentrate, and more.

- *The CLD student must adapt to a new education system.*

  Implications: Significant differences may exist between the current and former educational systems. Such differences include public versus private, hours of school day, length of school day, type of instruction, level of interaction in the classroom, rule systems, culture of the school, and so forth. Such differences may confuse the student, puzzle the parents or caregivers, prompt the student to act inappropriately, slow the learner's progress, and more.

- *The student must cope with the nuances of the school's culture.*

  Implications: Regrettably, the culture of the school does not always welcome diversity, tolerate languages other than English, accommodate differential learning needs, or seek out parents as partners. Moreover, the messages it conveys are often subtle and incomprehensible. As a result, CLD students cope with ambiguity, anxiety, and frustration, each of which interferes with their capacity to learn effectively. Additionally, their parents or caregivers cope with misgivings, uncertainty, and alienation from the educational process.

Equally formidable for the CLD student are psychosocial challenges of the sociocultural dimension including (a) ambiguity, (b) anxiety, (c) prejudice, and (d) discrimination on the basis of skin color, nationality, language, and more. As we will discuss, any one of these multifaceted challenges can significantly inhibit the performance of a CLD student in the classroom.

Cultural Challenges of the Sociocultural Dimension As illustrated in Table 1.2, the sociocultural dimension encompasses various cultural challenges to the success of CLD students. For example, a review of educational research strongly supports the argument that the culture of the school demonstrably influences student outcomes at both the elementary and secondary levels, particularly for CLD students

■ **table 1.2**   Sociocultural Dimension of the CLD Student Biography

Challenges	Processes
Cultural Adjustment to new country, town, city, or school Recency of immigration Adaptation to a new education system Culture of the school • Disrespect for L1 and/or diversity • Minority/majority cultures • Emphasis on equality and meritocracy versus equity • School/class environment • Distance/space perspectives • Time/punctuality perspectives	**Cultural** Acculturation Developing conflict resolution skills Learning to view situations from multiple points of view
Psychosocial Affective • Ambiguity/anxiety • Homesickness • Anger and/or depression • Instructional input and environmental demands on the affective filter Intragroup Challenges • Language brokering • Separation from support network/family Intergroup • Prejudices and discrimination Socioeconomic • SES/income stability • Family employment • Access to health care • Residency status demands Sociopolitical Environment • Community and/or school • National debate over bilingual education and immigration policy • Increased terrorism and subsequent rise in xenophobia	**Psychosocial** Self-esteem development Cultural identity formation Motivation building Social identity formation Establishing positive interpersonal relationships Creating a support psychosocial network

(Patterson, Purkey, & Parker, 1986; Gault & Murphy, 1987; Golden and Gallimore, 1991; Meyer, 2000). The culture of the school can profoundly influence a CLD student's educational experience, including the student's perspective on schooling, attitude toward learning, behavior in the school, and performance in the classroom. In this sense, a school's culture encompasses at least three salient elements:

- The attitudes and beliefs of members (in this case teachers, administrators, and staff)
- The norms and rules to which members adhere
- The relationships that exist among its members

School culture affects not only students but also educators. Specifically, school culture is often pivotal in shaping teachers' attitudes toward and beliefs about change, including (a) their perspectives on increasing cultural and linguistic diversity in the school and (b) the necessity of adapting curricula and student services that accommodate such diversity (Goldman & O'Shea, 1990; Fine, 1991; Cushner, McClelland, & Safford, 2000). According to Fine (1991), entrenched educator beliefs include:

- Real change in schools is not feasible.
- Discipline problems are an overwhelming barrier to school success.
- The educational bureaucracy precludes progressive educational practices (i.e., purposive accommodations in school and classroom practices for a changing student population).

Findings by Murry (1996) suggest that such beliefs are often the product of at least four counterproductive influences associated with rigid, entrenched school cultures:

- A strict focus on norms and rule systems
- A strong emphasis on conformity
- A distinct self-consciousness about the image of the school (among staff members of the dominant culture)
- Pervasive scapegoating

According to Murry, these influences can create a school culture characterized by negativity, barriers to collegiality, competition, resistance to change, and the subversion of individual efforts to accommodate change, especially changing student populations.

Ultimately, these characteristics associated with rigid and entrenched school cultures tend to foment a variety of myths and misconceptions regarding cultural and linguistic diversity. The persistence of many of the myths has been demonstrated in recent research, as have the findings that these myths tend to pose formidable, sociocultural challenges for the CLD student (Goldenberg & Gallimore, 1991; Herrera, 1996; MIT, 1990; Murry, 1996). For example, one such myth holds that learning is due to innate abilities. Presumably, CLD students, regardless of their culture or language, are less capable of educational excellence than grade-level students of the dominant culture. Accordingly, because the school culture considers both the cultures and native languages of CLD students to be inferior, neither the educators nor the curricula place value on the celebration or affirmation of other cultures or native language support. Such myth-based cultural norms can deny many CLD students any sense of motivational pride in and affirmation of their heritage or any benefit from ongoing native language support as a means to second language acquisition.

This myth of learning abilities is but one among many that can arise from a rigid and entrenched school culture. When such myths are shared among school educators, the consequences for CLD students are both numerous and worrisome. Many of these consequences relate to schooling, others to behavior, and still others to learning and performance. To illustrate, the following are often instilled in CLD students:

Schooling
- A distrust of the long-standing message that attending school is the first step along the pathway to virtue and success in life
- A growing conviction that schools are not places that respect or value the presence and contribution of CLD students or their families

Learning
- A conception that CLD students are intellectually inferior to Whites
- A perceived sense of hopelessness about new learning in an unaffirming culture and unfamiliar language

Performance
- A belief that individual efforts in school will not be rewarded
- An increasing reluctance to participate or produce in class for fear of ridicule

Behavior
- A generalized disengagement from learning and withdrawal from active participation in the learning process
- A growing resentment toward the educational system that often results in resistant, if not rebellious, behavior

Another myth often supported by rigid school cultures holds that equity and education are in conflict. Often this myth arises from parallels between the culture of the school and the dominant, White culture (Gault & Murphy, 1987; Murry, 1996). Such parallels emphasize individualism, equality, competition, and an educational system grounded in the idea that the success of academically outstanding students is based solely on the merits of their effort and dedication (that is, a meritocracy). Yet these same parallels remain as oblivious to the changing fabric of the U.S. classroom as they do to the fact that CLD students do not compete on a level playing field. In rigid and entrenched schools, the curriculum (and not infrequently the instruction that CLD students receive) does not recognize, build on, or value the student's cultural heritage or his or her prior socialization in a different culture. School programming neither affirms nor supports the student's native language as a means to second language acquisition. Classroom instruction does not account for the acculturational, language, academic, or cognitive transitions through which the CLD student must pass in order to compete with his or her grade-level peers.

Instead, the dominant school culture tends to argue that it treats all kids the same and that each student, regardless of cultural or linguistic background, should be able to perform at grade level and compete based on merit. The consequences of this myth for CLD students, as fostered and supported by a rigid and entrenched school culture, include the following:

- Few instructional accommodations for CLD students (a situation that arises from the belief that such accommodations would be unfair to other students)
- A conviction that CLD students, not educators, are solely responsible for addressing the linguistic challenges that students confront
- A pervasive certainty that CLD students choose to fail in school because neither they nor their parents value education
- A distrust of the native language when used for instructional purposes
- A view of second language acquisition or ESL teachers and paraprofessional support personnel as unfair, special treatment
- The placement of CLD students in remedial or lower-track classes

Although the sentiment that "we treat all students the same" does not, on the surface, appear to suggest prejudice, this viewpoint in effect denies the accommodations that would provide CLD students with meaningful instruction. As a consequence, these students do not have the same educational opportunities that would allow them to be as academically successful as their native-English-speaking peers. Thus, the affirmation, "We recognize and value the different experiences, cultures, and languages that all our students bring to the classroom" can serve as a more inclusive alternative to "We treat all students the same." Reflective school educators who target schoolwide success use their CLD students' sociocultural backgrounds as the point of active student engagement for developing cognitive, academic, and linguistic abilities. Furthermore, professional educators counter the unproductive influences of a rigid and negative school culture by doing the following:

- Affirming and celebrating CLD students as school assets
- Modeling appropriate accommodations for CLD students in the classroom
- Dispelling culture-bound myths about CLD students through research, experience, collaboration, and professional practice

Psychosocial Challenges of the Sociocultural Dimension   The notion of the *affective filter* helps us understand how certain psychosocial challenges of the sociocultural dimension (especially anxiety) might inhibit (or occasionally bolster) the classroom performance of the CLD student. The concept of the affective filter is most notably associated with the work of Krashen (1981, 1982) and his attempts to explain certain processes, especially second language acquisition, through which CLD students progress. The outcomes of this work include five hypotheses, at least two of which are relevant to this discussion.

■ Voices from the Field

"I would make sure that all teachers understand how important it is for them to create a classroom environment that promotes social and language interaction. These classrooms would reflect a lot of second language interaction orally, visually, audibly and hands-on. It is very important that the teachers not only promote a lot of classroom participation but that there is a lot of peer interaction through group work. It is then and there where students are willing to take risks with their second language development. Daily writing activities are very important for student exercise and assessment of development.

It is also very important that ELL [CLD] learners feel welcome and comfortable enough to express themselves in the second language. In order for this to take place, the students must feel that their first language is important and an asset to them and their classroom. Teachers must welcome their culture and not only celebrate their heroes and holidays but try to align the student's culture to as much curriculum as possible. It is then that ELL students will feel comfortable enough to extend to the second language.

It is the responsibility of the school principal to model these practices. When the leader interacts with these students, it is important that they too appreciate and acknowledge the student's culture as an asset. They do this by learning about specific cultures and displaying it throughout the school."

■ *Wriel Chavira, educational leadership candidate, Project SILTS, Las Cruces, NM; Manhattan, KS; Portales, NM*

In order to understand Krashen's concept of the affective filter, we must first explore his *input hypothesis*. According to this hypothesis, the CLD student is able to best incorporate new information (that is, progress in language acquisition) when the input the student receives is *one step beyond* his or her current stage of competence. Krashen refers to this ideal input as *comprehensible input* and labels it with the designation $i + 1$. Accordingly, if the learner is competent at stage i, then input at $i + 1$ is most comprehensible and useful for producing new understandings.

Krashen (1982) also developed the *affective filter hypothesis,* which incorporates the work of Dulay and Burt (1977) and argues that the amount of input reaching the CLD student is influenced by a number of affective variables, including anxiety, self-confidence, and motivation. For Krashen, second language learners with a low level of anxiety, high motivation, strong self-confidence, and a good self-image are better equipped for classroom performance and second language acquisition. On the other hand, high levels of anxiety, low motivation, low self-esteem, and other affective factors can combine to raise the affective filter, reduce academic achievement, and slow language acquisition. The hypothesis argues that once the affective filter is raised, the teacher's instructional input, no matter how comprehensible, is unlikely to aid language acquisition or improve academic performance in the classroom.

As we have illustrated, the culture of the school and several associated myths concerning diversity constitute a significant challenge to the success of CLD stu-

■ Voices from the Field

Targeting Linguistic and Academic Development: Social Studies Simulation

"When I teach how Africans came to America, I list out words like Africa, uncomfortable, pain, hurt, Middle Passage, slave, slave trade, ship, boat, American colony, economy, income, and money. I make sure that I use these terms, demonstrate the relationship of the synonyms, and use the support vocabulary to build ELL [CLD] students' content vocabulary. Visual depictions of the Middle Passage help to convey the text material. I also bring in a refrigerator box and have students take turns getting in the box to demonstrate the limited amount of space that slaves had during the Middle Passage. In collaborative groups, students discuss how they personally and/or their families came to the United States. The adolescents begin to make connections in both the historic and current forms of immigration, which usually are precipitated by economic progress."

■ *Roger Syng, middle school social studies teacher, Garden City, KS*

dents in public school. However, the sociocultural dimension also encompasses psychosocial challenges through which the school climate or culture ought to support CLD students if they are to succeed in the classroom. As CLD students confront this variety of cultural and psychosocial challenges, they will also develop through a series of sociocultural processes. The outcomes of these processes will profoundly influence the student levels of performance in the classroom, collaboration with peers, and success in school.

Sociocultural Processes

Table 1.2 summarizes many of the sociocultural processes that influence the performance, behaviors, and resiliency of CLD students inside and outside the classroom. Cultural processes are as central to the dynamics of the sociocultural dimension as this dimension is to the CLD student biography and our understanding of the complex and differential needs of CLD students. Unfortunately, many educators discount the importance of understanding the intercultural dynamics that occur within schools and between the school and its community (Goodlad, 1990; Education Watch, 1996; Phelan, Davidson, & Yu, 1993). As a result, educators often fail to take students' sociocultural processes into consideration when developing curricula and delivering instruction.

As illustrated in Table 1.2, probably the most salient of sociocultural processes, especially for the newly or recently arrived CLD student, is the process of acculturation. Although each us of tends to progress through a more or less lifelong process of enculturation, not all will necessarily brave the trials and tribulations of an additional acculturation process. Through enculturation, we are initiated into our home or native culture. Through this subtle process of enculturation, we gradually

dilemmas *of Practice*

Ms. James is a recent graduate of her teacher education program and is about three months into her first year of teaching. Based on her preservice education, she is seeking to adapt and modify her instruction to accommodate the differential learning needs of her predominantly Vietnamese students. On this day she has asked the advice of a fellow teacher, Mrs. Davis, about appropriate instructional accommodations. Mrs. Davis responds as follows:

> Are we supposed to bend the rules to accommodate each and every student? Each student has his problem. Every student wants the rules bent for him. I just can't see this! No one bent the rules for me. Around here, most of us in this school don't expect the rules to be bent for anyone else, either. Ultimately, we all have to follow the rules if we plan to succeed in society.

Ms. James has just experienced her first encounter with the *culture of the school*. Regrettably, the culture of the school does not always welcome diversity, tolerate languages other than English, accommodate differential learning needs, or seek out parents as partners. Moreover, the messages it conveys are often subtle and incomprehensible. As a result, CLD students cope with ambiguity, anxiety, and frustration, each of which interferes with their capacity to learn effectively. Their parents or caregivers cope with misgivings, uncertainty, and alienation from the educational process.

■ *What advice would you offer Ms. James as she responds to the comments of Mrs. Davis? In what ways can a teacher appropriately accommodate CLD students in such an environment? How would you go about influencing the culture of the school in more positive ways?*

and almost imperceptibly develop a sense of group identity that forms our set of values, guides our beliefs, patterns our actions, channels our expectations, and gives us an ethnocentric view of the validity of our ways. Unless we geographically relocate or experience significant and frequent cross-cultural encounters in our lives, we have little occasion to question the validity of our ethnocentric worldview or our need to adapt to the perspectives and cultural ways of life that differ from those of our own enculturation.

CLD students, on the other hand, must not only come to understand the powerful yet subtle influences of their own enculturation, but they must also excel in a distinctly difficult and complex additional process of adjustment to another culture (and its dominant language). This additional process of acculturation has been variously described as a series of stages, combinations and recombinations, and periods that at least one participant author has characterized as often impossible "without severe psychological costs" (García-Castañón, 1994, p. 200). Whether these costs are debilitating and without purpose or developmental and transforming tends to be a function of the acculturation environment.

- The environment should account for the stages of acculturation through which the student will progress.
  - —*Teacher Implications:* Teachers who are aware of these stages or phases of acculturation better understand not only the painful adjustments their students must endure but also the process through which they, as teachers, will

progress in accommodating cultural and linguistic diversity as a classroom reality.

- The environment should support the individual's long-standing ethnic identity.
  - —*Teacher Implications:* Ethnocentrism is an inevitable outcome of long-standing enculturation in a particular culture. It is a product of pride, buy-in, and investment. Effective teachers know that students are best motivated in ways that support (rather than demean) their ethnic or cultural heritage. For such teachers, the affirmation of the student's home culture is a daily goal, not a once a year celebration.
- The environment should reflect and respond to the ways in which the acculturation process can affect students' academic, linguistic, and cognitive growth.
  - —*Teacher Implications:* The influences that the acculturation process can exert on the students' development are a product of the challenges that CLD students endure at each phase of acculturation. Reflective teachers empathize with students at each phase of the acculturation process in order to better understand the influences it may have on the students' language development, cognitive growth, and academic achievement. These teachers understand the students' struggles, even in cases of misbehavior arising from the hostility phase of the U-curve hypothesis (see the following paragraph).

C. Collier (1987) found that teachers' lack of understanding regarding the influences of the acculturation process was often responsible for the overreferral of CLD students to special education. In order to better understand these acculturation dynamics, let us first examine the nature of the acculturation process.

Acculturation, the process of adjusting to a new or non-native culture, is perhaps best illustrated by the four phases of the U-curve hypothesis (Cushner, McClelland, & Safford, 2000; Trifonovitch, 1977). The U-curve hypothesis, shown in Figure 1.4, specifies that the process of acculturation may be best understood as a sequential series of four phases, which occur over time. During the first, or *honeymoon*, phase of the acculturation process, the individual often experiences a certain sense of exhilaration or euphoria as he or she enjoys the novelty of life in a new culture. For instance, among CLD students and families, coming to the United States may represent a lifelong dream, a new opportunity, or a chance to reunite with family. Each of these situations tends to foster a sense of exhilaration.

However, as time passes in the new culture, the many subtle and hidden differences that exist across cultures begin to surface. Often the actions of others in the new culture seem difficult to understand, if not incomprehensible. At other times, one's own actions do not yield expected results. Ultimately, long-standing, culture-bound responses and solutions to typical questions and problems do not produce the same results. As an outcome of this cultural mismatch, CLD students commonly experience impatience, anxiety, frustration, and even anger. During this so-called *hostility* phase of the acculturation process, CLD students may begin to disengage from school. They may frequently complain of being tired or sick. They

■ **figure 1.4** U-Curve
Hypothesis

Source: K. Cushner, A. McClelland, and P. Safford (2000), *Human Diversity in Education: An integrative Approach*, 3rd ed. (Boston: McGraw-Hill). Page 97. Reprinted by permission of the McGraw-Hill Companies.

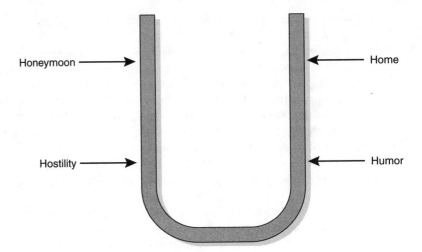

may feel so overwhelmed that they start to daydream in class, and some students may exhibit signs of rebellion against the new culture or new school setting.

This rebellion is often a sign of culture shock, a worst-case scenario of the acculturation process that occurs as more and more cultural differences surface in increasingly intense, cross-cultural encounters. As CLD students experience the increasing conflict between the cultures they know and the cultures they are learning, they may feel threatened. These students sometimes rebel against the new culture as a way of negotiating personal identity and meaning. Among the reactions that CLD students typically experience during this period are:

- A sense of alienation
- Actions that are interpreted as hostile
- Patterns of indecision
- Feelings of frustration and sadness
- An intense desire to withdraw from situations
- Symptoms of physical illness
- Exhibitions of anger grounded in resentment

Some students, especially secondary-level CLD students, never quite recover from this phase of the acculturation process (Brown, 1992; Olsen, 1988). The frustration that CLD students encounter during the hostility phase can lead to an increased rate of school absenteeism, maladaptive behavior, suspensions from class and school, or dropping out. School educators can significantly reduce the possibility of these negative results by providing a supportive, respectful, and caring school environment. CLD students who are experiencing the hostility phase of the curve also benefit from discussions with their teachers that help them better understand their own acculturation processes.

Nonetheless, if CLD students transcend the hostility phase and the depths of the U-curve, a newfound awareness of cross-cultural differences and their significance in a diverse world typically emerges from the acculturation process. CLD students learn to confront the new cultural environment in more reflective and proactive ways. In the process, they manage feelings of embarrassment, disappointment, and frustration as they begin to reshape their cultural identity in this *humor* phase of the U-curve hypothesis. Although this phase of the U-curve remains stressful, the trials of this step in the acculturation process produce an enhanced cross-cultural understanding of differences, norms, values, beliefs, and behaviors. Some CLD students learn to cope through a higher level of engagement with either the language learning community or their own academic achievement. In fact, Brown (1986, 1992) has characterized this aspect of the acculturation process as a period during which the individual must learn to synchronize his or her linguistic and cultural development.

Having reached the final leg of the acculturation journey, the CLD student enters the decisive pinnacle of the U-curve, appropriately characterized as the phase called *home*. Cross-culturally sensitive perspectives that enable culturally adept performance and productive social interactions in a second culture characterize the student's thinking and actions in this phase of the acculturation process. CLD students at this stage not only respect but also affirm cross-cultural differences. They value and celebrate their own bicultural and bilingual identity. During this phase, the CLD student delves into and understands those nuances of culture and language that allow her or him access to the full repertoire of connotative meanings of social interaction and language. Most CLD students who reach this acculturation threshold (Acton & de Félix, 1986) have attained near native literacy development and second culture understanding. Unfortunately, such individuals tend to be the exception rather than the norm.

In like manner, the CLD student's sense of self and self in relation to social groups is often shaped by the psychosocial processes of the sociocultural dimension. These psychosocial processes include the following:

- Self-esteem development
- Self-concept formation
- Social identity development
- Ethnic identity formation

In particular, the dynamics of ethnic identity formation illustrate one reason why sociocultural processes can so powerfully influence CLD students' perceptions of the school or community environment, as well as their appraisals of success probabilities in those environments.

For example, a study of ethnic identity dynamics (Félix-Ortiz, Newcomb, & Myers, 1994) found that perceptions of discrimination were proportional to the degree of ethnic identification and inversely proportional to levels of acculturation. Because perceptions of discrimination are often pivotal in the self-concept development and motivation levels of CLD students (Roberts, Phinney, Romero, &

Chen, 1996; Williams-Morris, 1996), these findings indicate that the sociocultural process of ethnic identity formation is sometimes central to the students' sense of self-worth and their motivation to succeed in life and in school.

One way for teachers to assess the degree of both a student's identification with his or her own culture and his or her level of acculturation is to preassess each prior to instructional planning through teacher–student conversations. Although these subjects are more extensively explored in a subsequent chapter, teachers who purposefully converse with their CLD students prior to instructional planning (through an interpreter, if necessary) often find that teaching effectiveness is improved, reteaching is reduced, and students are more motivated.

Sociocultural Dimension: Implications for Classroom and School Practice

CLD student success in any classroom depends on educators' understandings of and responses to the teaching and learning implications of the four interrelated dimensions of the prism model. Because the sociocultural dimension lies at the core of CLD student success or failure in school, the implications of this dimension should form the foundation of any discussion of appropriate teaching practices for CLD students. Therefore, as increasing cultural and linguistic diversity transforms the average classroom, the implications of this dimension for teaching practice become increasingly relevant.

The following bullets summarize a few of these sociocultural implications:

- Reflective teachers understand that increasing diversity in the school need not be perceived as a liability. Frustration and negativity toward increasing school diversity are not uncommon responses among teachers, staff, and school administrators. Yet changing student and community demographics are not a trend but an emergent reality of schools in the twenty-first century. At the same time, the support of CLD family members is often critical to the accommodations and

---

Are You Aware?

The low point of the U-curve hypothesis (Cushner, McClelland, & Safford, 2000; Trifonovitch, 1977), between the hostility and humor phases of this acculturation model, is the juncture at which many CLD students fall through the cracks in the system. CLD students who have difficulties at this point in their acculturation sometimes withdraw from production and academic performance, exhibit behaviors that interrupt their education, or drop out of school. In fact, many who immigrated during the primary years of their education will drop out by eighth grade.

■ *What do teachers and other school educators need to understand about this sociocultural process in order to avoid student withdrawal, preclude poor academic performance arising from acculturation issues, and prevent students from dropping out? What type of positive acculturation environment can you create?*

t h e o r y *into Practice*

The affective filter hypothesis (Krashen, 1982) asserts that the amount of language or instructional input that reaches the CLD student is influenced by a number of affective variables, including anxiety, self-confidence, and motivation. Thus, CLD students with a low level of anxiety, high motivation, self-confidence, and a good self-image are better equipped for classroom performance and second language acquisition. On the other hand, high anxiety, low self-esteem, low motivation, and other affective factors can combine to raise the affective filter, reduce academic achievement, and slow language acquisition. The hypothesis argues that once the filter is raised, the teacher's instructional input, no matter how comprehensible, is unlikely to aid language acquisition or improve academic performance in the classroom.

■ *What are the implications of this hypothesis for your professional practice (or your future practice) as an educator? In what ways will you adapt or modify instruction to reduce the likelihood that your instruction will raise the affective filter?*

modifications that school systems must make to this changing reality. Their families are a source of cultural identity, self-esteem, and social grounding for students. Family members are also a sociolinguistic resource for ongoing literacy development in the student's first language. To allow frustration and negativity within the school culture to alienate and isolate these students and their families is to further complicate the sociocultural challenges of reaching these new students, adapting and modifying for their needs, and ensuring their grade-level academic performance from the time they begin school until high school graduation. If the numbers of these new and different students are increasing in the schools, and if we continue to alienate and push them out, what then is the purpose and productivity of our school? What has been achieved? What has the school accomplished in our society? The heritage of U.S. education has developed from the preparation of the common student for the uncommon challenges of each new age, of each new frontier. In a rarely cited ruling of the United States Supreme Court, the case of *Lau v. Nichols* (1974), Justice Douglas affirms this underlying belief in the following majority opinion:

> There is no equality of treatment merely by providing students with the same facilities, textbooks, teachers, and curriculum; for students who do not understand English are effectively foreclosed from any meaningful education. Basic English skills are at the very core of what these public schools teach. Imposition of a requirement that, before a child can effectively participate in the educational program, he must already have acquired those basic skills is to make a mockery of public education. We know that those who do not understand English are certain to find their classroom experiences wholly incomprehensible and in no way meaningful. (414 U.S. 56)

Reflective teachers value the cultural and linguistic diversity that their students bring to the classroom, and they use this diversity to enrich the learning of all students.

- Effective teachers know that intuitive, instructional decision making should include time for the preassessment of CLD students in order to determine the potential impact of the affective filter on the comprehensibility of that instruction. As this chapter explores, Krashen's (1982) affective filter hypothesis tells us that instruction for CLD students, no matter how well planned or well delivered, will not affect the student if it or the surrounding circumstances of instruction raise the affective filter. Therefore, insightful teachers preassess. The professional practice of preassessment helps educators avoid instructional decisions that may prove counterproductive. Among the variables to preassess are the CLD student's recency of immigration, cultural background, prior schooling in the home country, first language (L1) and second language (L2) proficiency, family dynamics, and prior knowledge in the content areas. Because guardians, parents, family, and extended family members critically influence instructional success, home visits are an extremely effective strategy for preassessing students' sociocultural realities.

tips for practice

Elementary Education

1. You can help CLD students find an appreciation and validation of their own heritage within the lessons by:
   - Using storytelling themes with the cultures of your CLD students threaded throughout.
   - Incorporating songs, rhymes, or poems from the cultures of your CLD students.
   - Having bilingual parents or guardians of CLD students come to read with the class.
   - Providing a buddy system between CLD students who share the same cultural background.

2. You can show students that their cultures are valuable by incorporating songs within lessons that support and demonstrate an appreciation of diversity (e.g., Red Grammer's "Teaching Peace").

3. As a mode of informal assessment, observe the progress that your CLD students have made in their development of first and second language literacy skills. Have them draw or write about activities they have engaged in with their families. Make anecdotal notes as they subsequently share their drawings or read their writing projects with classroom partners.

4. Together with your CLD students, set challenging yet attainable goals regarding literacy or academic development. Individually meet with them on a frequent basis to discuss their progress in reaching these goals.

5. Many assumptions and stereotypes regarding diverse groups arise from a simple lack of knowledge. You can work to increase the understanding and respect that your students have for one another by asking CLD students to share their insightful perspectives on lessons as related to their own cultural heritage.

6. Observe your students to see how well they appear to be adjusting to their new classroom environment and how they are interacting with their peers. Listen closely to the comments and concerns of your students.

Secondary Education

1. Prevent misunderstandings and misinterpretations of behavior such as eye contact, space issues, or physical contact by learning as much as possible about the cultures of your CLD students. You can do this by using the Internet, books and magazines, and community members of the respective cultures as resources.

2. Organize a mentoring program (with an organization, an institute of higher education, or a business) for CLD students in order to provide professional role models from the community.

3. Observe the progress that your CLD students have made in their development of first and second language literacy skills. Have them write a paragraph in which they describe activities engaged in with their families, such as swimming, camping, cooking, or shopping.

4. Help CLD students make connections to new content vocabulary and concepts by previewing in their first languages before presenting the lesson in English.

5. To enhance the self-esteem of your CLD students:
   • Constantly reinforce their potential to succeed.
   • Make it a point to praise their efforts rather than overcorrecting their errors.

6. In order to help newcomer CLD students feel welcome and comfortable in their new classroom environment, pair them with mentors who have been through the acculturation process and can provide support and encouragement.

7. Use interactive journals between CLD students and yourself in order to encourage:
   • The development of literacy skills.
   • A positive student–teacher relationship.
   • Meaningful communication through writing.

General Education

1. Reinforce the value of the languages and cultures of your CLD students by doing the following:
   • Familiarize yourself with the original or native names of your students and how to correctly pronounce them (e.g., call Jorge *"Hor-hay"* rather than Americanizing his name by calling him "George").
   • Have your CLD students teach you basic greetings and commonly used phrases in their native languages.
   • Encourage CLD students to wear or bring their native clothing to school as living symbols of their heritages.
   • Select curriculum materials in which the cultures of your CLD students are reflected and

circumstances specific to second language learners are addressed.
   • Request that books representing the native languages and cultures of your CLD students be ordered and made available to the students in the library and for classroom use.

2. Provide a welcoming and safe classroom environment by taking the time to do the following:
   • Praise students genuinely with positive remarks for participation and involvement in classroom activities.
   • Make it a point to have daily contact and show interest in the personal lives of your CLD students (e.g., ask about family).
   • Encourage CLD students to speak when they are comfortable with doing so instead of forcing them to speak before they are ready.
   • Implement consistent and predictable daily routines to clarify classroom expectations.

3. Create positive, productive relationships between home and school by making the following efforts:
   • Visit the homes of your CLD students.
   • Share the child's successful school experiences with the parents or guardians (take an interpreter if needed).
   • Visit, phone, or e-mail parents or guardians of CLD students on a consistent basis to involve them in the learning and language acquisition processes of their children.

4. Challenge your CLD students academically and cognitively by grouping or pairing CLD students of various proficiency levels. By doing this, students at lower levels of language proficiency can gain a better understanding of complex concepts through the help of their peers.

5. By collaborating with other teachers, you can share observations and information regarding the strengths and skills your CLD students bring to the classroom. Capitalize on this knowledge within your own classroom practice. SMILE ☺. It's a universal language!

◾ key theories and concepts

academic dimension	cultural processes	enculturation
acculturation	culture of the school	equity v. equality
cognitive dimension	deficit perspective	Krashen's affective filter hypothesis

Krashen's input hypothesis   prism model   sociocultural dimension
linguistic dimension   psychosocial processes   U-curve hypothesis

professional conversations on practice

1. Given the ways in which one's enculturation takes place, discuss what aspects of their socialization might prompt teachers to hold a deficit perspective of CLD students.

2. This chapter explores the many challenges the culture of the school can pose for CLD students. Discuss ways in which an informed teacher might counter the counterproductive influences of such a culture.

3. The differences between a perspective that emphasizes equality and one that stresses equity

were summarized in this chapter. Discuss the following questions:

a. Which of the perspectives did you identify with before you read this chapter?

b. According to which perspective were you socialized?

c. Are you now equally comfortable with the other perspective? Why or why not?

d. Which perspective is most likely to prove effective with CLD students? Why?

questions for review and reflection

1. What language group overwhelmingly represents the largest number of CLD students nationwide? What percentage of CLD students belongs to this group?

2. What are the four dimensions of the prism model? Which dimension is central to the model and why?

3. What type of input is central to Krashen's input hypothesis? Why is this type of input considered important? What are the characteristics of this type of input?

4. What is the affective filter? What sorts of conditions raise the affective filter? What are typical consequences of instruction that raise the affective filter?

5. What are the phases of the U-curve hypothesis? Which of these phases is typically most prob-

lematic for CLD students, and why? What does the U-curve hypothesis explain?

6. What sociocultural challenges for CLD students are associated with schooling in the United States? Name and explore at least three.

7. What characteristics are associated with a supportive classroom environment for acculturation among CLD students?

8. What reactions do CLD students typically experience during the hostility phase of the U-curve? Why should teachers be aware of these potential reactions? What can teachers do to support CLD students during this phase of acculturation?

suggested activities

Preservice Teachers

1. Based on information learned from this chapter, create a protocol and interview a CLD student. Based on the findings of your interview,

identify two sociocultural challenges that the student confronts in all-English classroom settings. Finally, discuss the planning implications of these challenges for classroom instruction.

2. Read the following case study of Raja, a student from Saudi Arabia. Identify student strengths and needs in terms of sociocultural processes. List activities or accommodations to maximize teaching and learning for this student.

Raja

Raja grew up in Saudi Arabia, where he attended school regularly, was a very good student, and enjoyed his childhood and preteen years. Recently, he turned thirteen and his family moved to Kansas City. Raja had studied some English in school, but like the rest of his family, he knew only a few phrases. His father was a teacher in Saudi Arabia, but with such limited English he could find only a job as a janitor at a major shopping mall. Following the events of 9/11, Raja experienced alienation from classmates who had once spoken to him. Even some of his teachers treated him differently. Consequently, Raja began conversing more in English outside of his household, even with those he used to hold conversations with in his first language. He also felt reluctant about speaking with his family members in his native language. Raja started to feel lonely, cut classes on a regular basis, and look for work outside of school to occupy his time. He did not feel that he fit in.

3. Interview a local ESL or dual language teacher to determine how he or she assesses CLD students for placement. In what ways does the teacher collect information about a CLD student's sociocultural background? Discuss recommendations that you would offer, based on what you have learned.

In-Service Teachers

1. Think about your CLD students. List two sociocultural challenges you have observed among these students and develop and explain strategies for addressing these needs.

2. Consider what you have learned from this chapter and create a student and family intake questionnaire that asks, in a nonthreatening manner, key questions about the sociocultural backgrounds of CLD students. List multiple ways to obtain this information. Try the questionnaire on students in your classroom. Discuss what you learned and the implications this new knowledge has for teaching.

3. The sociocultural adjustment challenges of CLD students differ in elementary, middle, and high school. Think about observations you have made during your teaching career and discuss ten ways to address and accommodate these sociocultural age differences. What implications do these differences have for teaching and learning?

objectives

The information provided in this chapter
will help the educator to:

- Describe the nature of the cognitive
  and academic dimensions of the CLD
  student biography.
- Discuss key cognitive challenges and
  processes for CLD students.
- Describe key implications of the
  cognitive dimension for teaching and
  learning.
- Discuss key academic challenges and
  processes for CLD students.
- Describe key implications of the
  academic dimension for teaching and
  learning.

Cognitive and Academic Dimensions of Methods for CLD Students

Success is to be measured not so much by the position that one
has reached in life as by the obstacles that one has overcome
while trying to succeed.

—Booker T. Washington, educator, *Up from Slavery*

critical standards *Guiding Chapter Content*

TESOL/NCATE teacher standards reflect professional consensus on standards for the quality teaching of pre-K–12 CLD students. Additionally, the CEEE Guiding Principles and their accompanying indicators serve as a framework to assist practitioners, policymakers, and clients as they collaborate to enhance academic enrichment and language acquisition among CLD students. Therefore, in order to help educators understand how they might appropriately target and address national professional teaching standards in practice, we have designed the content of this chapter to reflect the following standards.

TESOL ESL Standards for P–12 Teacher Education Programs

TESOL ESL–Domain 1: Language. Candidates know, understand, and use the major concepts, theories, and research related to the nature and acquisition of language to construct learning environments that support ESOL [CLD] students' language and literacy development and content-area achievement. (p. 1)

- **Standard 1.b. Language acquisition and development.** Candidates understand and apply concepts, theories, research, and practice to facilitate the acquisition of a primary and a new language in and out of classroom settings. (p. 6)

  1.b.9. Understand and apply knowledge of the role of individual learner variables in the process of learning English. (p. 11)

  1.b.12. Help ESOL students develop academic language proficiency. (p. 12)

TESOL ESL–Domain 3: Planning, Implementing, and Managing Instruction. Candidates know, understand, and are able to use standards-based practices and strategies related to planning, implementing, and management of ESL and content instruction, including classroom organization, teaching strategies for developing and integrating language skills, and choosing and adapting classroom resources. (p. 21)

- **Standard 3.a. Planning for standards-based ESL and content instruction.** Candidates know, understand, and apply concepts, research, and best practices to plan classroom instruction in a supportive learning environment for ESOL students. Candidates serve as effective

Note: All TESOL/NCATE standards are cited from TESOL (2001). All Guiding Principles are cited from Center for Equity and Excellence in Education (1996).

English language models as they plan the classroom for multilevel classrooms with learners from diverse backgrounds using standards-based ESL and content curriculum. (p. 21)

    3.a.3. Plan students' learning experiences based on assessment of language proficiency and prior knowledge. (p. 23)

- **Standard 3.c.** Candidates are familiar with a wide range of standards-based materials, resources, and technologies and choose, adapt, and use them in effective ESL and content teaching. (p. 26)

    3.c.3. Employ appropriate variety of materials for language learning, including books, visual aids, props, and realia. (p. 27)

CEEE Guiding Principles

Guiding Principle #2: Limited English proficient students develop full receptive and productive proficiencies in English in the domains of listening, speaking, reading, and writing, consistent with expectations for all students.

2.6 All teachers teach limited English proficient students the full range of language uses, including social communication as well as the advanced academic and technical uses of language in core content areas. (p. 6)

Guiding Principle #3: Limited English proficient students are taught challenging content to enable them to meet performance standards in all content areas, including reading and language arts, mathematics, social studies, science, the fine arts, health, and physical education, consistent with those for all students.

3.5 Schools assure that limited English proficient students have access to and use learning resources such as computers, calculators, libraries, and laboratories. (p. 7)

Guiding Principle #4: Limited English proficient students receive instruction that builds on their previous education and cognitive abilities and that reflects their language proficiency levels.

4.7 Teachers identify and design instruction that is adapted to varied learning styles and individual student strengths (e.g., spatial, musical, interpersonal, verbal and logical-mathematical abilities).

4.9 Teachers use instructional approaches, such as cooperative learning and experiential learning that are sensitive to the multiple experiences of learners and that address different learning and performance modes. (p. 8)

Classroom performance is significantly based on learning, and at the heart of learning is understanding. That is, to learn something new, students must necessarily derive the meaning of new information. Among conscious or subconscious questions the learner may ask are the following: Is the new information similar to or different from what I already know? Does it fit? Is it consistent with patterns or schemata of knowledge I have already developed? Does it seem to make sense? If it does not fit an existing schema, how will I resolve the difference? How can I make sense of it? Is a new perspective on this information or my schema needed? Does this change what I know or what I thought I knew? Each of these questions necessarily involves *cognition*—the act or process of coming to know or to understand something. If such questions are part of an explicit sequence or pattern of examining what one knows or seeks to understand, then these questions involve *metacognition,* or one's thinking about one's thinking processes.

Therefore, if we can describe learning in terms of understanding and cognition, then it ought to concern us a great deal when research and analysis (Burns, 1993; Shepard, 1997) suggest that the understandings that many children come to achieve as a result of instruction can be characterized as *fragile.* If the goal of instructional methodology is to achieve learning, and learning surrounds understanding, then what has been accomplished when the result is a fragile understanding? More fundamentally, what is a fragile understanding?

Basically, a fragile understanding exists when the student appears to know a concept in one context but does not appear to know that same concept in another way or in another setting (Burns, 1993). Although such a situation might arise as a result of incomplete learning processes, it is not uncommon for a student to master the learning of a concept but prove unable to transfer that learning. Shepard (1997) has argued that this inability to transfer learning—that is, a fragile understanding—often occurs because the student has mastered not the concept but certain classroom routines. For Shepard, instructional methods that emphasize robust understandings are the supports that students need to ensure the transfer of understandings. Teachers who use instructional methods that target these robust understandings do the following:

- Frequently check students' prior knowledge
- Regularly prompt students to think about existing understandings in novel ways
- Encourage students to derive new connections between existing schemata and new contexts

The notion of *transfer* is a particularly critical one for CLD students. If these students are to prove successful in the content areas, they must exhibit the ability to transfer knowledge, skills, and capacities learned in the first language to learning and understandings in content-area domains taught in a second language. Ultimately, it becomes apparent that the instructional methods necessary to prevent fragile understandings and to ensure transfer must focus on the cognitive dimension of student learning, especially the student's capacity for the metacognition necessary to achieve deep and robust understandings. The next section explores this cognitive dimension of the CLD student biography and the many implications for understanding, transfer, and learning.

■ The Cognitive Dimension of the CLD Student Biography

Chapter 1 summarizes the four dimensions of the prism model: the sociocultural, the cognitive, the academic, and the linguistic. As discussed, the prism model (Thomas & Collier, 1997) represents a uniquely holistic way to frame and better understand the differential learning needs of CLD students, as well as the many adjustment and process difficulties faced by this population.

Nonetheless, a deep understanding of the cognitive dimension requires us to transcend this dimension's defining characteristics. To this end, we specify and explore the challenges and processes of this dimension that we have witnessed in our work with CLD students and in the work of others. Such specifications and explorations of the cognitive and academic dimensions of the CLD student biography are the subjects of this chapter. These analyses begin with the many challenges and processes we have associated with the cognitive dimension. As we begin, the reader should keep in mind that the four dimensions of the CLD student biography are interrelated and not mutually exclusive.

Perhaps the most neglected challenges and processes that CLD students must transcend to be successful in school settings are those of the cognitive dimension. One reason for this neglect, especially at the level of practice, may be the complexities of this dimension and the recency of research that genuinely integrates our understanding of how this dimension interrelates with other dimensions of the prism model. In fact, August and Hakuta (1997), in conjunction with the meta-analyses of the National Research Council, have argued that serious research questions remain in at least seven major domains of the cognitive dimension, including:

- The nature of the relationship between language proficiency and literacy skills
- The consequences of acquiring nominal content knowledge in a first language and then switching languages for the learning of higher levels of content material
- The identification of which features of second language knowledge and acquisition are additive for cognition

Cognitive Challenges

Our experiences with CLD students, as well as recent research and analysis in education, have provided some insights into certain key challenges that students face within the cognitive dimension of the CLD biography (Chamot, Dale, O'Malley, & Spanos, 1992; Chi, de Leeuw, Chiu, & LaVancher, 1994; Cobb, 1994; Fitzgerald, 1995; Purcell-Gates, 1996; Rosebery, Warren, & Conant, 1992; Young & Leinhardt, 1996). Among these cognitive challenges for CLD students are those summarized in Table 2.1 on page 36.

A number of these cognitive challenges highlight the interrelationships between the cognitive and the sociocultural dimensions. For example, interrupted cognitive development in the student's first language is a frustrating challenge for CLD students, some of whom have immigrated from war-torn countries where long periods of irregular schooling are commonplace. Recent demographic evidence suggests that the number of CLD students emigrating from such environments may be increasing (NCES, 2002b).

In like manner, strong cognitive–sociocultural connections exist with respect to learning styles. Learning styles can be understood as "the preferences students have for thinking, relating to others, and for particular types of classroom envi-

Are You Aware?

Reflective secondary school educators know that it is crucial to keep the following developmental issues in mind when teaching adolescent CLD students:

- **Self-concept/self-esteem:** Cresswell (1994) argues that teachers can create a safe environment for all adolescents by being friendly, having open-door policies, and, most important, taking time to get to know their students. Adolescents will flourish when they feel appreciated and know that open communication and flexibility between themselves and the teacher is considered important. Teachers must also find opportunities to value students' native languages and cultures in order to contribute to positive self-concept. One way to validate CLD students' native languages and cultures is to discuss the advantages the bilingual student will have in the job market. Because the United States continues to become more diverse in its population, the bilingual employee may have the opportunity to earn a higher salary than the employee who speaks only one language. Therefore, the adolescent CLD may feel more confident about his or her own native language and culture.

- **Peer acceptance and socialization:** Adolescents often believe that others' thoughts are focused on them (a common form of narcissism). Consequently, they are preoccupied with their own appearance, body, and behavior. At this age, "everyone is talking and thinking about me." Adolescents have a strong desire to belong to a group for feelings of self-worth. Because of their common struggles and shared anxieties, CLD adolescents become a tight-knit group and often sit together in the cafeteria and at assemblies and other school functions.

- **Physical development:** Adolescents are becoming capable of reproducing, so their hormonal levels are surging. This is often the source of negative and inappropriate behavior displayed in classrooms. Additionally, adolescents experience growth spurts, metabolism changes, maturation of genitalia and voice, and increased body and facial hair. With this in mind, teachers should be aware that CLD students are experiencing not only these expected physical changes but also the additional stresses related to cultural and linguistic differences.

- **Development of abstract reasoning:** Adolescents often tend to view parents as less capable influences on them. Teachers have an even greater responsibility to influence intellectual development by being caring and nurturing role models. Goldstein (1999) suggests that caring relationships are a central part of intellectual growth and development. These interactions are necessary and fundamental in enabling and leading to cognitive development. Krashen (1982, 1985) argues that CLD students learn more effectively when their anxiety level is lowered (the affective filter hypothesis). In a caring and nurturing environment in which the anxiety level is minimal, CLD students' cognitive development will flourish as they take more risks in the second language.

ronments and experiences" (Grasha, 1990, p. 23). Students' preferred learning styles are the product of socialization and cognitive development in the primary or home culture. When a persistent discrepancy exists between the modes of educational interaction in the classroom (instruction, inquiry, problem solving, dialogue, etc.) and the modes of learning to which students have been primarily socialized, challenges to student learning and success are exacerbated (Bennett, 1999; Garcia, 1996; Gay, 2000). Therefore, effective teachers preassess the kind of prior teaching the CLD student has received and the types of learning environments to which she or he has been exposed.

■ **t a b l e   2 . 1**   Cognitive Dimension of the CLD Student Biography

Challenges	Processes
Interrupted cognitive development in the first language (L1).	Development of the declarative knowledge base
Interpreting and hypothesis testing of the system of rules that organizes the second language (L2).	Development of the procedural knowledge base
Curricula and programming for the culturally and linguistically diverse (CLD) students that are reductionistic, skills-based, and bereft of opportunities for higher-order thinking.	Capacity building for short-term, working, and long-term memory
Cognitively demanding, decontextualized learning tasks and environments.	Ongoing cognitive academic language proficiency (CALP) development in L1 (A process of at least three dimensions of the CLD student biography)
Instruction that fails to target a variety of preferred learning styles.	
U.S. classroom instruction often fails to tap the deep, prior knowledge structures that CLD students bring to complex problem solving.	CALP development in L2 (A process of at least three dimensions of the CLD student biography)
Alphabetic writing systems represent words at a deep level of abstraction.	
In English, vocabulary knowledge and comprehension are primary determinants of reading comprehension ability.	Learning strategy development
Successful second language learners often focus on word meaning, whereas mainstream reading instruction often emphasizes word phonetics.	• cognitive • social affective • metacognitive
The core structures or epistemologies of some subject areas (e.g., history, science) are exceptionally difficult for CLD students.	Capacity building for concept formation in L2
Some content areas (e.g., history) require a high level of declarative and procedural knowledge integration.	

Students from the Asian American, Native American, Mexican American, and African American cultural groups often employ styles of inquiry and response that differ from predominant styles in classrooms. Students from these groups who exhibit strong cultural affiliations may favor oral and communal interactions (Appiah & Gates, 1997; Nieto, 1999), divergent (exploratory) lines of inquiry (Valdes, 1996), and inductive (whole to part) lines of reasoning (Freeman & Freeman, 2001). On the other hand, teachers socialized in the dominant culture tend to emphasize convergent (prompt-answer) questions and model deductive problem solving (Bennett, 1999; Gay, 2000). These teachers tend to structure classroom interactions that focus on the particular, build from part to whole, reason from the specific to the general, and emphasize a didactic dialogue. Given these discrepancies, schools often recognize and wish to act on the differences in socialization between teachers and CLD students. Nonetheless, in attempts to defend their practice, many teachers tend to argue the impossibility of targeting the preferred learning styles of all students in the classroom. These educators fail to realize that the intent of the learning styles research was not to argue the necessity of planning instruction that targets all the preferred learning styles represented in a given classroom. Instead, this research informs us that an awareness of the major groups of learning styles present within a classroom can assist the teacher in targeted, instructional planning that anticipates differential student needs. Such awareness also facilitates teaching modifications that are:

- Cross-culturally sensitive
- Effective in reducing the need for reteaching
- Designed to reduce the slope of the learning curve for all students

Interrelationships between the cognitive and sociocultural dimensions become alarmingly evident when curriculum programming in the school or instruction in the classroom evolves from untested assumptions. This is especially the case when school educators assume what prior knowledge the CLD student does or does not bring to the learning environment. Because the CLD student, by definition, generally exhibits some level of limited English proficiency, schools often mistakenly assume that the student's prior knowledge in the content areas is limited as well. Additionally, some educators assume that because a CLD student does not speak English well, she or he cannot learn in an English-speaking environment.

Not surprisingly, then, educators who make these sociocultural attribution errors seldom set aside appropriate time or secure the services of support personnel (e.g., translators or native language collaborative groups) to assess students' prior knowledge in the content areas before planning instruction. As a consequence, many CLD students are not cognitively stretched toward new and grade-level-appropriate learning in the content areas. Regarding the cognitive dynamics of this challenge for CLD students, August and Hakuta (1997) have noted:

> The depth, interconnectedness, and accessibility of prior knowledge all dramatically influence the processing of new information. . . . Knowledge is a complex integrated network of information of various types: ideas, facts, principles, actions, and scenes. Prior knowledge is thus more than another chunk of information. It might facilitate, inhibit, or transform a new learning task. Students must connect their own prior knowledge with new information continuously, while teachers must understand how well students are making these connections. (pp. 69–70)

As this passage explains, the elaboration of a student's prior knowledge is critical to cognitive development and transformative learning. When classroom instruction does not explicitly teach and encourage CLD students to make connections between their prior knowledge and the key content concepts they are learning, these students face formidable challenges to their academic success and to their ongoing cognitive development.

Other cognitive challenges for CLD students (see Table 2.1) underscore the interrelationship between the cognitive and the linguistic dimensions of the prism model. For example, the ongoing debate over phonics versus whole language has significantly influenced classroom literacy development instruction in schools throughout the nation (Routman, 1996; Freeman & Freeman, 2001). This trend is especially problematic for CLD students because long-standing research and analysis has regularly indicated that successful second language learners benefit from literacy instruction that emphasizes word meaning rather than the phoneme structure of the word (Adams, 1990; Jimenez, García, & Pearson, 1996; Krashen, 2000). For instance, the research of Jimenez et al. (1996) indicates that CLD students benefit most from a *constructivist* literacy development environment, in which students focus on the construction of meaning as central to learning. According to these and other authors, a constructivist, cognitively demanding learning environment encourages students to make cognitive connections between their prior knowledge and current content context (Au & Carroll, 1997; Jimenez et al., 1996; Morrow, Pressley, Smith, & Smith, 1997). Because CLD students have access to two or more languages, linguistic connections such as cognates and reading strategies can facilitate meaning construction between languages and enhance their growth in the cognitive dimension.

Constructivist learning environments make possible the cognitive–linguistic and cognitive–sociocultural connections at the contextual, intracultural, and affective levels. First, the rich use of context in these environments encourages pattern recognition, especially in literature-based instruction (Au, 2000). This pattern recognition in turn fosters the derivation of meaning through integration with what the learner already knows (Freeman, 1995; García, 2000). For example, a constructivist learning environment at the elementary level might emphasize a lesson on colors in connection with a literature-based story on colors, such as *Mouse Paint* (Walsh, 1989). Students might begin with a hands-on activity involving the primary colors red, blue, and yellow. The teacher would then encourage mixed groups of students to discover what other colors they might create by mixing the primaries. As students discover new colors, they would be named in Spanish and in English, and the names would be placed on separate language word walls, along with the primary colors combined to achieve them. Then students might be prompted to discuss how each color makes them feel. Names of these feelings would be added to the word walls. Later, students would be encouraged to use prior experiences to make a list of things they know are associated with each color created, and these would be added to the word walls in Spanish and in English. Having established the context of the story, the book would then be previewed in Spanish for the CLD students. Finally, the story would be read and learned in English with an emphasis on the fact that the mice in the story mix paint to create new colors according to the same patterns the students used in their hands-on activity.

Constructivist environments also tend to emphasize the relevance of new information to the learner. Relevance arises from the learner's cultural lens, which filters incoming information according to schemata established by long-standing socialization in that culture. When teachers present information or instructional input that relates to what the CLD student already knows and understands, the student is more likely to recognize the information as relevant and worthy of integration into existing schemata. On the other hand, students will most likely treat learning input that markedly differs from prior knowledge and experiences as irrelevant. Thus, constructivist learning environments highlight the need for teachers to preassess what prior knowledge and experiences the CLD student brings to the classroom as a basis for enhancing cognitive development.

Finally, constructivist learning environments often encourage the active and *affective* involvement of the learner in the construction of meaning. Research on this emphasis indicates that a strong affective (emotional) response to what is being learned helps students remember what they learn (Cahill, Prins, Weber, & McGaugh, 1994). Therefore, effective teachers foster a learning environment that emphasizes prior knowledge, creates a context for understanding, makes new concepts relevant, and helps students connect emotionally to what they are learning. In such an environment, CLD students have the greatest potential for cognitive growth.

CLD students often encounter cognitive challenges when they need to communicate in a second language and perform in cognitively demanding academic settings. Cummins (1991) has described a theoretical framework he developed for understanding some of the situational environments and demands that CLD students encounter as they proceed through the process of developing a cognitive, academic level of second language proficiency. In his model of situational environments, Cummins considered three critical processes influencing second language acquisition:

- The development of communicative competence in the target language
- Different cognitive and contextual demands on language competence
- The correlations between first and second language development

Cummins created the framework by using two intersecting continua. One continuum considers communicative situations to the extent that they are context-embedded versus context-reduced. In a *context-embedded* situation, CLD students use readily available paralingual cues, such as the context in which the discourse occurs, body language, and prior knowledge, to actively construct meaning. A routine interpersonal conversation is an example of a context-embedded situation. If a CLD student does not understand, he or she might ask for clarification or derive the meaning of a communication from the context of the conversation. Another example of a context-embedded situation would be a conversation concerning the weather.

In a *context-reduced* situation, the participant has few if any paralinguistic cues to facilitate meaning construction. Therefore, meaning must come from the language itself. One such situation is a classroom lecture on valence theory in a high school chemistry course.

The second continuum in Cummins's model considers communicative situations to the extent that they are cognitively undemanding versus cognitively demanding. In a *cognitively undemanding* situation, CLD students process small amounts of information requiring little cognitive engagement. An academic example of such a situation in language arts would be a classroom discussion of a story that is illustrated by a Big Book, which is shared among class members. In a *cognitively demanding* situation, CLD students deal with significant amounts of complex information that they are asked to process and assimilate. Such a situation typically demands tremendous cognitive engagement. An example of such a situation might be one in which a teacher asks students to identify, analyze, and discuss at least five major themes of the novel *Moby Dick*.

In describing the development of communicative competence or proficiency, Cummins (1991) integrated the two continua in an intersecting manner in order to create four quadrants describing situational language demands (see Figure 2.1). Quadrant A distinguishes a context-embedded, cognitively undemanding communicative situation. Quadrant B defines a context-embedded, cognitively demanding communicative situation. Quadrant C characterizes a context-reduced, cognitively undemanding communicative situation. Finally, quadrant D describes a context-reduced, cognitively demanding communicative situation.

As a language learner develops greater communicative competence or proficiency, tasks that were once cognitively demanding become less demanding, and the understanding that once required heavy contextual support becomes more easily comprehensible with fewer paralinguistic cues. As a language learner acquires a second language, the before-and-after charting of the language demands of a particular situation would reveal a shift from the bottom right quadrant (quadrant D) to the top left quadrant (quadrant A). For example, when a CLD student first moves to the United States and begins to learn English, writing a paragraph that lists three factors that led to the U.S. Civil War would most likely be an extremely context-reduced, cognitively demanding situation. However, if that student is schooled in the United States for several years through various academic environments that directly or indirectly address U.S. history, writing the same paragraph could prove a less context-dependent and more cognitively undemanding situation.

The most important understanding that teachers can gain from this theoretical framework is that what may appear to a teacher as a relatively simple task may actually be quite demanding in a cognitive sense for the CLD student. This is often the case for a student who does not have the prior knowledge and the second language capacities necessary to successfully complete the task. In order to develop cognitive, academic language competence or proficiency in L2, CLD students need to participate in a highly contextualized, language-rich instructional environment generated by a curriculum that focuses on meaning construction and cognitive, academic language development. Subsequent chapters of this text provide an in-depth exploration of ways to foster such an environment for academic and language learning.

As these examples illustrate, the cognitive dimension encompasses a variety of challenges for CLD students. Many of these challenges involve not just the cognitive dimension but also that dimension interacting with the sociocultural and linguistic dimensions.

Cognitive Processes

No less important to the success of the CLD student are the key processes of the cognitive dimension. Many of these cognitive processes are summarized in Table 2.1. Re-

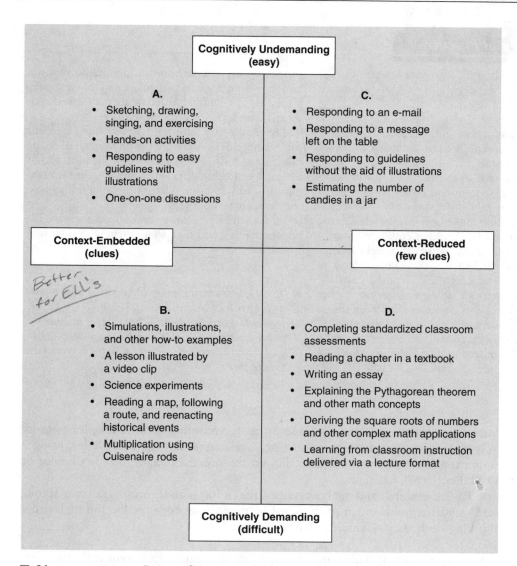

**Cognitively Undemanding
(easy)**

A.
- Sketching, drawing, singing, and exercising
- Hands-on activities
- Responding to easy guidelines with illustrations
- One-on-one discussions

C.
- Responding to an e-mail
- Responding to a message left on the table
- Responding to guidelines without the aid of illustrations
- Estimating the number of candies in a jar

**Context-Embedded
(clues)**

**Context-Reduced
(few clues)**

Better for ELL's

B.
- Simulations, illustrations, and other how-to examples
- A lesson illustrated by a video clip
- Science experiments
- Reading a map, following a route, and reenacting historical events
- Multiplication using Cuisenaire rods

D.
- Completing standardized classroom assessments
- Reading a chapter in a textbook
- Writing an essay
- Explaining the Pythagorean theorem and other math concepts
- Deriving the square roots of numbers and other complex math applications
- Learning from classroom instruction delivered via a lecture format

**Cognitively Demanding
(difficult)**

■ **f i g u r e 2.1** Range of Contextual Support and Degree of Cognitive Involvement in Communicative Activities

Source: Adapted from Cummins (1981), p. 12. Used with permission.

cent interest in cognitive processes has caused researchers to explore the potential value of learning strategy development for CLD students (Chamot & O'Malley, 1994; Chamot & El-Dinary, 1999; Cohen, 1998; Diaz-Rico & Weed, 2002; García, 1998; Jimenez, 1997; Peregoy & Boyle, 2000).

Learning strategies can be understood as the patterns of thinking or goal-driven activities that help the learner attain targeted learning outcomes. The notion of a cognitive approach to learning strategies is grounded in a constructivist perspective on

dilemmas *of Practice*

Mrs. Bailey, a tenth-grade history teacher at Carver High, frequently encourages her CLD students to watch one hour of television in English daily. She also shows movies in English to her CLD students. Are television and movies in the second language a good source of comprehensible input for second language acquisition?

Television and movies can be useful for promoting second language acquisition *if* they are connected to grade-level content. *Contextualization* is essential when using television and movies in the classroom, and these types of media should be connected to content objectives. Although some teachers feel that simply bathing students in the second language is an effective way of enhancing their linguistic capabilities, Mrs. Bailey *may* be doing a disservice to her adolescent CLD students. Snow et al. (1976) argues that without support and guidance, adolescents are neither emotionally receptive nor able to interact productively with others in order to achieve the *i + 1* level of comprehensible input that Krashen (1982)

proposes for L2 acquisition. Additionally, television and movies in a second language may cause anxiety if they are not contextualized or are not viewed at intervals with time for group discussion.

Better yet, Mrs. Bailey might use video segments for meaningful development of an integrated or thematic unit. Pally (1994) argues that the potential for learning is much higher when the medium is maximized in this fashion. Mrs. Bailey might also have the students videotape special moments from lessons, such as presentations, performances, or discussion circles, and then share them with their family members.

■ *What other strategies involving media or technology might Mrs. Bailey use to help her CLD students learn English? What does it mean to contextualize media and technology appropriately within your classroom practice or your future practice?*

learning as a proactive and dynamic process. According to this view, learning involves selecting information, organizing it, relating it to prior knowledge, using it in appropriate contexts, and reflecting on the process (Gagné, 1985; Chamot & O'Malley, 1994).

Recent research and analysis suggest that a focus on learning strategies among CLD students holds much promise for helping these students develop high-order thinking skills. Key research findings include:

- More proficient CLD students use more strategies more frequently than less proficient second language learners (Chamot & El-Dinary, 1999; Cohen, 1998; García, 1998; Jimenez, Garcia, & Pearson, 1996).
- More proficient CLD students better monitor their comprehension than less proficient students (Chamot & El Dinary, 1999; Jimenez et al., 1996).
- More proficient CLD students use more effective strategies than less proficient learners (Chamot & El-Dinary, 1999; Cohen, 1998).
- CLD students can learn to use new learning strategies through explicit instruction and modeling (Chamot & O'Malley, 1996; Gersten, 1996; Jimenez, 1997; Muñiz-Swicegood, 1994).
- Transfer of learning strategies can occur between languages (García, 1998; Jimenez, 1994; Jimenez et al., 1996; Muñiz-Swicegood, 1994).

- CLD students have greater comprehension when they make strategic use of both languages to construct meaning from text (García, 1998; Jimenez, 1997; Jimenez et al., 1996).

Chamot and O'Malley (1994) have summarized three broad categories of learning strategies. These categories illustrate the cognitive processes that CLD students use to construct meaning. *Cognitive learning strategies* are among the first described. These strategies typically involve the mental or physical manipulation of the material to be learned. For example, a CLD student might physically separate items to be learned into groups, or he or she might mentally categorize information using a graphic organizer in order to create a more relevant organization for long-term memory. Among specific cognitive strategies highlighted by Chamot and O'Malley are resourcing, grouping, note taking, and elaboration. The elaboration of prior knowledge involves the mental manipulation of new information. In this process, a CLD student compares information and draws analogies from existing background knowledge. Accordingly, the cognitive strategy of elaboration applies to all four literacy domains: listening, speaking, reading, and writing. By pre-assessing the prior experiences and knowledge that CLD students bring to the classroom, teachers are encouraging students to elaborate on that knowledge.

Social affective strategies highlight the interconnectedness of the cognitive and the sociocultural dimensions of the CLD student biography and may involve the learner as an individual or the learner in interaction with another or others. At the individual level, one such strategy is using self-talk as a means to increase self-confidence and reduce anxiety. At the interactive level, "social/affective" learning strategies include cooperation and questioning for clarification. Regarding the latter, Chamot and O'Malley (1994) have written, *"Asking questions for clarification* is particularly critical for ESL students because they will so often need to exercise this skill in their grade-level classrooms" (p. 63). This strategy enables students to obtain an additional explanation for clarification or verification of their understanding from either a peer or a teacher. Chamot and O'Malley also argue that self-talk is beneficial to CLD students because it tends to reassure students and lower their anxiety levels, thereby lowering the affective filter. Teachers are in a unique position to encourage the use of both of these social affective strategies by fostering a communicative learning environment in which CLD students are encouraged to voice their concerns and their learning strategies, irrespective of their L2 abilities.

Metacognitive learning strategies relate solely to the student and his or her own cognitive processes. Planning, monitoring, and evaluating the learning process represent further subdivisions of metacognitive strategies. As the name implies, CLD students use metacognitive strategies to understand the learning process. At the level of planning, metacognitive strategies include advance organization, organizational planning, selective attention, and self-management (Chamot & O'Malley, 1994). The selected attention strategy concentrates on cognitive development and metacognitive planning for specific words, phrases, images, or types of information that contribute to learning.

Three broad categories of learning strategies emphasized in the literature on methods for CLD students are cognitive, metacognitive, and social affective (Chamot & O'Malley, 1994). These strategies are a product of cognitive theory (Gagné, 1985; Shuell, 1986) and research on learning strategies (O'Malley & Chamot, 1990). In regard to learning strategies, Chamot and O'Malley (1994) have argued that (a) active learners are better learners, (b) academic language learning is more effective when supported by learning strategies, and (c) learning strategies transfer to new tasks. Metacognitive learning strategies primarily relate to the student and his or her own planning, monitoring, and evaluating of cognitive processes. The metacognitive learning strategy of *selective attention* encourages students to listen or read selectively, scan, and find specific information such as key words, phrases, ideas, linguistic markers, and more.

■ *What are the implications of this metacognitive learning strategy for literacy development among CLD students? In what ways might you teach CLD students to maximize this learning strategy in their literacy development? What do you anticipate would be the most difficult aspect of the strategy to teach? How might you overcome this difficulty?*

The metacognitive strategies involving literacy development include monitoring comprehension and monitoring production (Chamot & O'Malley, 1994). As CLD students monitor comprehension, their metacognition focuses on whether they are understanding what they are listening to or reading. If CLD students are not understanding, they apply corrective strategies to construct meaning. As CLD students are speaking or writing, they monitor production to ensure that the language being produced is understandable to others.

Cognitive Dimension: Implications for Classroom and School Practice

The teacher's thorough understanding of the CLD student's prior schooling or knowledge base enables informed instructional planning. Students' prior schooling experiences may vary by country of origin and type of school (e.g., private versus public school). Proactive teachers explore both the environment of prior schooling and the teaching styles used. Because preferred learning styles are greatly influenced by these prior experiences, effective teachers use this information to gauge CLD student responses to the new environment and for future planning.

Assumptions about the knowledge base that CLD students bring to the classroom are common. A student's limited English proficiency does not imply a limited knowledge base. Conversely, even though CLD students come to school with a rich knowledge and experience foundation, educators cannot assume that all students come with the same knowledge and experiential backgrounds. In a culturally rich classroom, insightful teachers pay particular attention to the extensive prior learning and experiences of each student. For example, although a student who has just arrived in the United States from Bosnia or Cambodia may know little about the U.S. Civil War, she or he may have an extensive understanding of the realities of civil war as well as its socioeconomic impact on a country. Such a student may possess a much richer understanding than students who have spent their entire lives in the United States. Similarly, a student from Costa Rica may have extensive personal knowledge of the rain forest. Teachers might capitalize on such knowledge in a lesson on climate.

Reflective teachers use informal conversations (translated as necessary) with the CLD student (or family caregiver) to avoid assumptions regarding prior learning and cognitive development. These teachers maximize such conversations to understand the extensive and rich experiences that their CLD students bring to the classroom. Such practices facilitate accommodative instructional planning and eliminate redundancy. In this way, informed instructional planning builds on students' existing knowledge or cognitive skills base. For instance, a secondary-level CLD student will not benefit from memorization of the alphabet in English. Effective teachers plan lessons that take into consideration the cognitive-developmental level of the student.

Reflective teachers find an appropriate balance through instruction that is cognitively demanding yet comprehensible. Such a balance will enhance CLD student success in the classroom. Just as an assessment of prior knowledge or cognitive skills should guide planning for cognitively demanding instruction, teacher monitoring for L2 proficiency and stage of second language acquisition (SLA) should guide the comprehensibility of instructional input. Empathetic teachers recognize that comprehensible input should flow from the student's current language abilities, as suggested by his or her stage of SLA (these stages of SLA are detailed in the next chapter). Incomprehensible instructional input increases the need for reteaching and slows the student's progress toward language and academic growth. Instruction that targets comprehensible input involves frequent checks for understanding. Figure 2.1 provides a useful tool for assessing the balance to be targeted between cognitively demanding and comprehensible instruction.

■ The Academic Dimension of the CLD Student Biography

Necessarily, the academic dimension of the CLD student biography involves those readily apparent aspects of the curriculum and instruction that students receive in their matriculation from prekindergarten classrooms to high school graduation and beyond. Less apparent, but equally critical to this dimension, is an understanding of the differential academic challenges that CLD students encounter, especially those that relate not only to curriculum and instruction but also to academic policy. At the same time, the dimension also accounts for those processes that are crucial to successful academic performance in the public schools. CLD students must not only master a second language but also develop the academic language necessary to perform well in the subject-area domains.

Academic Challenges

The range of multifaceted academic difficulties that CLD students frequently encounter in schools is formidable and is exemplified by those challenges summarized in Table 2.2. Many of these challenges intensify with each succeeding grade level and increasingly test the academic language abilities of these students. These academic challenges (see Table 2.2) can be categorized according to those that pri-

■ **t a b l e   2 . 2**   Academic Dimension of the CLD Student Biography

Challenges	Processes
Curriculum and Instruction: Reductionistic curriculum often driven by a strict focus on high-stakes assessments Inadequate opportunities for classroom interactions involving academic, especially domain-specific, language Content-area assessments • Inordinately product v. process centered • Decontextualized, often standardized • Sometimes norm rather than criterion referenced • Frequently focused on declarative v. procedural knowledge • Typically bereft of opportunities to demonstrate critical thinking Lack of readiness among subject-area and grade-level teachers for the differential academic learning needs of CLD students Disproportionate number of CLD students placed in special education and remedial classrooms and the curricular difference between those settings and grade-level classrooms Academic presentation formats of content-area textbooks • Technical vocabulary • Domain-specific vocabulary • Unfamiliar grammatical structures • Complex discourse organization • Suppositions about prior knowledge and experiences grounded in the dominant culture **Academic Policy:** Language learning as a remedial focus v. language acquisition as a subcomponent of content-area academic learning Lack of recognition or reward structures for process gains as well as incremental gains in academic performance and product-measured improvement Criterion- and assessment-based exclusion from gifted and talented programs	Transfer of academic knowledge and skills from L1 to L2 Integration of concepts learned and to be learned across academic disciplines The resolution of knowledge gaps based on current and prior curriculum and academic experiences Academic language development in L2 (A process of at least three dimensions of the CLD student biography) • BICS/CALP distinction Domain-specific capacity building for academic performance • To address domain-specific: —Discourse organization —Grammatical forms and structures —Vocabulary —Required academic language skills in the following minimum subject domains: • Mathematics • Science • Social studies • Language arts

marily relate to issues of curriculum and instruction, or those that mostly relate to academic policies (especially those formulated at the district level). Among the academic challenges involving curriculum and instruction are product- versus process-centered assessments in the content areas, the presentation formats of content-area textbooks, and inadequate opportunities to practice domain-specific academic language. Academic policy challenges for CLD students include a compensatory focus on language learning, a lack of recognition or reward structures for process gains, and virtual exclusion from gifted and talented programs.

From the standpoint of curriculum and instruction, one of the most contemporary, harmful, and emergent academic challenges for CLD students is the trend toward increasingly reductionistic curricula driven by a strict focus on high-stakes assessments at the national, state, or local levels. Extra-educational and national reform agendas, such as the No Child Left Behind initiative, drive efforts to increase accountability, as measured by high-stakes assessments, often at the expense of low socioeconomic status (SES) and CLD students. Such efforts have been the trend for a number of years, not only at the national level but also in several states across the country.

reductionistic curricula

Several researchers have tracked, studied, and analyzed the outcomes of many such reform initiatives (Bastian, Fruchter, Gittell, Greer, & Hoskins, 1986; Berlak, 1999; Darling-Hammond, 1992; Earl & LeMahieu, 1997; Lieberman & Grolnick, 1997; McLaren, 1998; McNeil, 2000a, 2000b). In general, these outcomes indicate that school and practitioner accountability systems that are directly linked to high-stakes assessments drive a number of problematic consequences, especially for students in schools with high percentages of low SES and CLD students. First among these consequences is a predictable tendency among educational practitioners, whose performance evaluations and employment may depend on student standardized test scores, to *teach to the test* (Berlak, 1999; McNeil, 2000b). This focus on facts and decontextualized processes in turn leads to practitioner and district-initiated efforts to substitute commercial test prep materials for the regular curriculum (Earl & LeMahieu, 1997; McNeil, 2000b). Such substitutes for the regular curriculum prevent many educators from providing cognitively, academically, and linguistically rich instruction that speaks to the sociocultural realities of our society. According to McNeil (2000b):

> Teachers, even those who know their subjects and their students well, have much less latitude when their principals purchase test-prep materials to be used in lieu of the regular curriculum. The decision to use such materials forces teachers to set aside their own best knowledge of their subject in order to drill their students on information whose [*sic*] primary (and often sole) usefulness is its likely inclusion on the test. Examples of this splitting of personal and professional knowledge, and the requirement to do so, abound. (p. 2)

Indeed, this setting aside of teachers' professional knowledge and capacities yields a reductionistic curriculum that is inordinately focused on basic skills, redundant workbooks, drill-and-practice approaches to instruction, rote memorization of decontextualized facts and declarative knowledge, isolated practice of computations, and repetitive routines that target the retention of basic test-taking strategies.

In turn, this dumbing down of the curriculum yields notable consequences for students, especially low SES students and CLD students, whose likelihood of academic success is profoundly threatened and challenged (Berlak, 1999; Earl & LeMahieu, 1997; McNeil, 2000a, 2000b). According to McNeil (2000b), who researched the outcomes of high-stakes testing and reductionistic curricula, the major content areas (especially reading, writing, and mathematics) show evidence of such consequences. In the area of reading, the teachers she studied reported that curriculum reductionism and test prep concentration actually hampered students' ability to "read for meaning outside the test setting" (McNeil, 2000b, p. 3). Teachers who participated in her research reported that students:

- Were undermined in their ability to read sustained passages.
- Exhibited a reduced capacity to read longer works.
- Had so internalized the format for reading test skills to such a degree that many had not formed the habits necessary to read for meaning and comprehension.

In the area of writing, the teachers whom McNeil studied reported that students, especially low SES students, had become so programmed to basic skills of the test format for the persuasive essay that what they wrote was "of virtually no importance; conforming to the form was the requirement, and the students practiced every day" (2000b, p. 4). Paradoxically, in this situation, teaching to the test so ingrained students in form and structure that the need for communication was lost in a writing exercise entitled "The Persuasive Essay."

Of perhaps greatest concern are McNeil's (2000b) findings regarding the impact of a reductionistic, test-focused curriculum on the mathematics skills and capacities of low SES and CLD students. Her findings indicate that instruction driven by this curriculum did not focus on critical capacities such as problem conceptualization, selection among possible approaches, or metacognition about the procedural knowledge used to solve the problem. Instead, teachers were prompted (consistent with the notion of teaching to the test) to emphasize reductive mathematics, computational accuracy, familiarity with basic operations, and test-taking strategies.

As these examples illustrate, a reductionistic curriculum driven by the anticipated performance of students, their teachers, and their schools in high-stakes assessments, like other challenges of the academic dimension, poses a formidable obstacle to the success of CLD students in public school. Such academic challenges, whether most directly related to curriculum and instruction issues or to policy issues, demonstrate that the success of these students in the content areas involves much more than the question of whether the student is willing to learn English.

In addition to a standardized-test-driven, reductionistic curriculum, a misunderstanding of the role of native language in a student's academic development can limit a CLD student's academic growth potential. In fact, the findings of Saville-

Troike (1984) strongly suggest that for many complex challenges and tasks in the academic areas, CLD students may actually be delayed in their development by the insistence that such challenges be addressed in the target language (i.e., English). Her findings indicate that CLD students are more successful in addressing such complex cognitive tasks in their own native language. Among such complex challenges are the context-reduced tasks of reading, writing, drawing inferences, and forming schemata. When these challenges are targeted in the native language, the skills attained and the processes learned will then transfer to a target or second language, such as English (Saville-Troike, 1984). An academic environment that maximizes social interaction among students to build both native and target language proficiency among CLD students facilitates this transfer of content, processes, and strategies from L1 to L2.

Academic Processes

No discussion of the academic dimension of methods for CLD students would be complete without an exploration of the processes involved for CLD students. The right-hand column of Table 2.2 provides an overview of these processes. Some of these processes, like others associated with dimensions of the model already explored, continue to demonstrate the interrelatedness of the four dimensions of the prism model. For example, the first two academic processes listed in Table 2.2, academic language development and the transfer of academic knowledge and skills from L1 to L2, emphasize relationships among the cognitive, linguistic, and academic dimensions. Similarly, the processes that seek to integrate concepts from prior knowledge with those to be learned in the various academic disciplines again stress both the academic and cognitive dimensions of the CLD student biography.

The process of academic language development in L2 is a particularly difficult and longitudinal test for CLD students. It is also a process that often generates confusion within the learning community. Much of this confusion arises from a lack of understanding about the distinction between basic interpersonal communication skills (BICS) and cognitive academic language proficiency (CALP). That is, the confusion is grounded in the difference between conversational and academic language use. This distinction evolved during the 1970s and 1980s when second language educators and researchers became concerned that CLD students who exhibited second language proficiency in primarily oral and interpersonal communications did not perform well when using their second language in academic contexts (Chamot & O'Malley, 1994). In response to this ambiguity, Cummins (1981) developed a theory describing second language proficiency in terms of BICS and CALP. More recently, Cummins (1994) has begun to refer to these different constructs of language proficiency simply as conversational language and academic language.

CLD students who have achieved a conversational level of language proficiency have the ability to communicate interactively in familiar situations in which the context of communication tends to support the meaning of the discourse (Cummins, 1989). Most students in a second language environment can acquire

■ **Voices from the Field**

BICS and CALP

"The ELL [CLD] adolescent who communicates effectively in casual conversation may still lack conceptual understandings in academic language. During a Linguistics course, I selected one of my favorite ELL eleventh graders to take the Language Assessment Scale [LAS] as part of a course assignment. The ELL student, a current stand out in both choir and orchestra, enthusiastically agreed. During the exam, she struggled with the objectives. After scoring it, I truly recognized the difference between BICS (conversational language) and CALP (academic language). My student was strong in verbal communication, but it was now up to me to use conversational language as the entry point to increase her understanding of academic language. I immediately began planning a variety of ways that all of my ELL high school students could collaboratively practice using content vocabulary at progressively higher levels of complexity and interrelatedness."

■ *Tom Ressler, high school ESOL instructor, Kansas City, MO*

conversational proficiency in two to four years (Thomas & Collier, 1997). These language learners *appear* to be fluent speakers of the second language. However, according to Cummins (1989), students who have acquired only a conversational and not an academic level of proficiency have difficulty when trying to understand and communicate about cognitively complex concepts in the target language, especially in academic contexts.

For CLD students, competitive performance in the content areas of the academic setting involves more than interpersonal communication skills (BICS). Because these students must typically communicate in English in the school environment, the content classes such as science, social studies, mathematics, and language arts become their communicative environment (Mohan, 1986). Moreover, based on extensive longitudinal research on second language learning processes, Collier (1995a) has argued that such academic contexts demand a deep level of academic language proficiency in L2.

Accordingly, instructional support for the development of cognitive academic language proficiency in L2 must extend well beyond the teaching of conversational skills or even basic English skills. It must encompass the development of cognitive and academic language skills in the second language (Cummins, 1989). Informed teachers plan instruction that targets academic language development using the content-area curriculum. As needed, key curriculum concepts are previewed or contextualized, but these concepts remain the focus of instruction for academic and linguistic (CALP) development. Teachers may also choose to scaffold their instruction. Such scaffolding involves the incorporation of instructional aids, student interaction, and other lesson modifications to ensure that content concepts are comprehensible to CLD students.

Academic language proficiency in L2 involves the capacity to understand and produce language that is both abstract and complex. Second language learners who have acquired academic language proficiency have reached an advanced level of language development. The advanced language competencies associated with this development include the ability to understand language in a decontextualized, unfamiliar situation with limited interaction (Cummins, 1989). CLD students who have acquired academic language in L2 do not require nonverbal cues to construct meaning from a given situation (Chamot & O'Malley, 1994). Additionally, these students are able to comprehend and participate effectively in cognitively complex linguistic and academic tasks (Cummins, 1989).

Bilingual students who have become proficient in social conversation but have not yet reached an academic level of language proficiency often appear to be fluent speakers of English. However, they cannot function in the second language at full capacity in academically and cognitively complex situations. Constructing meaning using unfamiliar academic concepts and new cognitive processes can be difficult for any student. Learning in a second language multiplies the difficulty of the task for CLD students because they must construct meaning from a less familiar language, unfamiliar academic concepts, and new cognitive processes all at the same time. In routine conversational language uses, a CLD student can focus on meaning construction alone. For academic language uses, a CLD student must negotiate meaning while juggling multiple processes.

Another set of academic processes involves capacity building that is particular to subject-area domains with the goal of enhanced academic performance. This domain-specific capacity building is particularly difficult for CLD students because it typically demands a number of adjustments, each of which varies by subject area and involves increasing academic language proficiency in the second or target language (L2). These demands require the student to excel in domain-specific adjustments to the following:

- Discourse organization of the domain
- Grammatical forms and structures particular to that domain
- Specialized vocabulary of the domain
- Particular academic language skills necessitated by the nature of the domain

Each of these difficult adjustments for CLD students depends on the content area in question. Some examples from the key content areas illustrate the complexities involved.

In mathematics, adjustments to the vocabulary of the subject domain are often difficult for CLD students for at least three reasons. First, the mathematics classroom tends to abound in assumptions concerning students' prior knowledge of specialized terms such as *denominator, subtraction, minuend, devisor, subtrahend,* and *multiplication.* Second, terms that have one meaning in one subject domain can assume an entirely different meaning in the vocabulary of mathematics; such terms include *quarter, column, product, rational, even,* and *table* (Chamot & O'Malley, 1994). Finally, the vocabulary of mathematics tends to encompass a

Differentiated Praxis

The Art of Practicing One's Craft

Huy, a sixteen-year-old adolescent, recently enrolled in a rural midwestern school district after only two weeks in the United States. After taking a language proficiency test, he scored as a non-English speaker. He has had formal and continuous schooling since the age of four. However, no formal school records have been provided to the school. Therefore, he has been placed in ninth-grade, remedial, content-area courses. Huy excels in his art, mathematics, and science classes. He is even asked to assist his peers with their math assignments. He is quiet and well-mannered with both students and staff. After several weeks, his math teacher notices that Huy has become distracted and inconsistent in completing his class work. His math teacher also notices that Huy becomes frustrated when asked to assist his peers with assignments.

Individualized Instruction

Academic Needs: Huy has had continuous and formal schooling. His teachers should preassess his level of literacy development and capacities for math, science, and social studies using his native language. It is also important to preassess what his strongest subjects have been.

Instructional Modifications: Preassess Huy's existing content-area knowledge through conversations (translated as necessary) with him, his parents or caregivers, or a paraprofessional who speaks his first language. Build on Huy's existing skills to capitalize on prior knowledge. (It may be that he does not need to be placed in remedial classes, especially if he is provided accommodative instruction.)

Linguistic Needs: Huy has scored as a non-English speaker in language proficiency. He may need time to discuss content with other native-language-speaking peers. He will need extensive instructional adaptations in the content areas and in grade-level vocabulary.

Instructional Modifications: Provide extensive wait time; use slower and enunciated speech. Review and illustrate key terms for lessons. Create opportunities for Huy to use his native language in class with other peers. Heterogeneous grouping may alleviate his problems in working with peers.

Cognitive Needs: Huy enjoys working alone. He excels in art, math, and science, especially when given the freedom to express himself. When not challenged, Huy becomes bored, even angry.

Instructional Modifications: Give him the choice to work alone. Do not impose the task of tutoring other students unless he has offered to do so. Find ways for Huy to extend his learning by asking him to do his own research on topics of interest related to your class; such modifications are more likely to keep him challenged.

Sociocultural Needs: Huy is concerned with pleasing his teachers. He is the youngest of five sisters and brothers. His siblings often supervise him.

Instructional Modifications: Find out about Huy's interests and hobbies. Integrate his interests into your daily instruction. Teach the class about Huy's native country and make connections to your grade-level content. Such accommodations will prove to be a validating experience for Huy and will provide an opportunity for other students to learn about other cultures.

variety of homophones (words that sound like other common words) and can be especially troublesome for CLD students who are unaccustomed to the new language. Examples of such domain-specific homophonic pairs include *angle* and *ankle, addition* and *audition,* and *factor* and *factory* (Garbe, 1985). Accordingly, reflective teachers review the academic curriculum for vocabulary that may be problematic for CLD students. These teachers are then in a proactive instructional position to preview, scaffold, or contextualize this vocabulary as needed to enhance the academic development of CLD students.

The domain of science is exceptionally demanding on the academic language skills and capacities of CLD students. Scientific inquiry requires students to propose and defend hypotheses, or arguments, and to use complex linguistic structures and advanced reasoning. These linguistic structures often prove exceedingly complex for second language learners (Anstrom, 1998b; Chamot & O'Malley, 1994; Rosebery, Warren, & Conant, 1992). Teachers can assist CLD learners in this domain by teaching them metacognitive strategies that focus the students' attention not only on the products of academic thinking but also on the processes.

In the language arts domain, the variety of texts and materials used often demands extraordinary capacity building for academic performance among CLD students. Earlier discussion in this chapter highlights the many ways in which students can maximize past experiences and prior knowledge to make sense out of texts and draw meaning from learning materials. Yet the CLD student in the language arts classroom is often asked to read and comprehend (at a high level of complexity) texts and materials that are culturally unfamiliar, use complex vocabulary, involve convoluted themes and propositions, rely on antiquated syntax, or are grounded in culturally different writing genres (Anstrom, 1998b; August and Hakuta, 1997; Escamilla, 2000; Kameenui & Carnine, 1998; Sasser, 1992). Effective teachers help CLD students with these difficulties by using differentiated instructional strategies such as:

- Preteaching culturally different concepts
- Previewing key vocabulary
- Webbing or otherwise illustrating major themes
- Discussing the ways in which writing genres can differ

As these examples demonstrate, there are a number of content areas in which domain-specific capacity building for academic performance involves difficult processes for the CLD student. Such processes dramatically illustrate the interconnectedness of the four dimensions of the CLD student biography: the academic, the cognitive, the linguistic, and the sociocultural.

Academic Dimension: Implications for Classroom and School Practice

Reflective teachers avoid a reductionistic approach to lesson planning. Often educators associate a limited ability to speak the language of instruction with an inability to perform academic tasks at grade level. Educators sometimes use materials that are reductionistic and unmotivating, such as drill-and-practice methods for content-area teaching. However, CLD students are often able to learn grade-level academic concepts when the curriculum (or instruction) is appropriately adapted to accommodate CLD learners. Effective teachers provide all learners with culturally, academically, cognitively, and linguistically rich instruction. Additionally, high expectations for academic performance are realistic when this instruction is appropriately adapted and modified for CLD students.

Insightful teachers know that the BICS/CALP distinction is crucial to the academic success of CLD students in the content areas. If second language development for CLD students is to build academic language proficiency, then the academic curriculum must serve as the content for language instruction. Effective teachers of these students maximize accommodative strategies to adapt the content-area curriculum and classroom instruction for CALP development in L2. For example, teachers can examine the curriculum to identify the key academic vocabulary to teach in lessons. This vocabulary can then be previewed before each lesson. Teachers should isolate critical lesson concepts to teach from the content-area curricula. They can then modify and scaffold instruction to teach these concepts in a comprehensible manner. Such modifications might include photo illustrations of concepts, hands-on activities with manipulatives, heterogeneous peer group learning, and more.

tips for practice

Elementary Education

1. Prompt CLD students to think of different ways to solve problems by asking such questions as, "In what other ways could Katya have figured that out? Are there any other possible solutions? How did you arrive at that answer?"
2. Provide opportunities for students to practice content-area vocabulary through choral reading or paired writing activities.
3. Identify the prior knowledge your students bring to the classroom in order to make connections to the ideas and concepts that you are teaching. This can be accomplished in the following ways:
   - Use KWL charts. These charts use three columns that are filled in by the teacher with the help and suggestions of the class. The headings for the columns read as follows: What I KNOW, What I WANT to know, and What I have LEARNED.
   - Incorporate a variety of preassessments such as freewriting, observation, journals, and more. Preassess in the native language

as needed and have materials translated as necessary.
   - Ask questions and dialogue with students about the topic. Use paraprofessionals or volunteers as necessary to translate.
4. Establish learning centers so that your CLD students can explicitly practice the learning strategies on which you are focusing.
5. (Social Studies) Use visuals such as time lines, maps, and diagrams to clarify complex concepts as much as possible. For example, to better illustrate the Industrial Revolution and its influence on U.S. history, CLD students might choose an invention of that time and use a time line to highlight its causes and effects in history.

Secondary Education

1. (Science) Rather than writing or dictating instructions to CLD students, model or demonstrate the steps of an experiment as CLD students observe. In cooperative groups, students can then discuss and create an outline that includes the main steps that you modeled.

2. (Science) Instead of emphasizing isolated concepts, implement theme-based units to help CLD students see the relationships and connections between science principles and processes. For example, a unit on the environment can include concepts related to the processes of the environment such as the growth of living things and cycles (e.g., weather cycles, life cycles, and the water cycle).

3. (Social Studies) Identify where the students in your classroom are from. Use graphic organizers (e.g., Venn diagrams or T-charts) to compare and contrast the languages and cultures of the native countries or regions of origin for your students.

4. (Math) Model successful problem-solving strategies by thinking out loud for your students while you work through and solve word problems.

5. (Math) In cooperative groups, have CLD students create a story problem that applies to the new concepts learned. Ask them to trade with another group, which will then work to solve the problem.

6. (Language Arts) Provide closure to your content-area lesson with learning logs. Learning logs consist of journal entries written by the students. These logs provide students with an opportunity to reflect on the concepts and processes they have learned and to practice solidifying their thoughts through writing.

General Education

1. Provide CLD students with opportunities to meaningfully and consistently use their native language as a means to cognitive academic language development. The following are some suggestions:
   - Provide support or scaffolding materials, especially those that complement the content being taught, in the native languages of the CLD students.
   - Teach concepts and key vocabulary in the native language through the assistance of a community volunteer or a bilingual peer who is proficient in the CLD student's native language.
   - Incorporate content cues in the native language by providing your CLD students with

translated key concepts to preview at home prior to the lesson in English.
   - Pair or heterogeneously group CLD students of varying levels of language proficiency.

2. To enhance academic and cognitive growth, explicitly teach your CLD students metacognitive learning strategies by doing the following:
   - Ask students to describe their thought processes in solving a particular problem or in addressing a particular academic challenge.
   - Guide students to predict the content of a lesson by focusing on pictures and illustrations in the chapter.
   - Emphasize the fact that after mastering learning strategies, the students can continue to apply the strategies to other subject areas as well.

3. Through social interactions and the help of more capable peers, CLD students can be challenged academically and cognitively. You can help foster collaborative achievement by forming heterogeneous cooperative groups that guide students to do the following:
   - Collectively discuss and practice new concepts and skills.
   - Share with one another how new concepts relate to their cultures, home environments, or past experiences.
   - Write sentences summarizing the main concepts of a reading selection and then share and compare with their peers.

4. Make instruction more meaningful through the incorporation of manipulatives and games. The Internet and a variety of computer software can be used as resources. These activities involve students in the learning process in relevant and authentic ways.

5. In order to target the differential needs and diverse learning styles of students, use a variety of strategies such as visuals, graphic organizers, hands-on activities, and guarded vocabulary (i.e., adjusting the pace and complexity of vocabulary used).

6. Provide grade-level instruction that is content-based and uses age-appropriate material. Note that modifications such as scaffolding may be necessary for the clarification of the content being taught.

■ key theories and concepts

academic dimension
academic knowledge transfer
academic language development
BICS/CALP
cognitive dimension
cognitive learning strategies
cognitively demanding
cognitively undemanding

constructivist learning
  environments
context-embedded
context-reduced
contextualization
elaboration
learning styles
metacognitive learning strategies

preteaching
previewing
prism model
reductionistic curricula
relevance
social affective learning strategies
teaching to the test

■ professional conversations on practice

1. Explore various learning tasks for students. Then discuss whether each task is context-embedded or context-reduced and whether each task is cognitively undemanding or cognitively demanding. Chart your findings for each task according to the quadrant described in this chapter.

2. This chapter details three types of learning strategies that CLD students can use to enhance their cognitive development and improve their academic performance. Discuss ways in which an educator might teach each of these three types of learning strategies: cognitive, metacognitive, and social affective.

3. Among the four dimensions of the CLD student biography, one dimension is frequently neglected. Discuss some of the challenges and processes of this dimension that CLD students must transcend in order to be successful in school. Discuss why the dimension is often overlooked.

■ questions for review & reflection

1. What does it mean to *contextualize* a learning environment and what does it involve? Reflect on and discuss the ways in which your socialization has or has not prepared you to contextualize learning.

2. What is the primary origin of students' preferred learning styles? Should all instruction target the preferred learning style of the CLD student? Why or why not?

3. What are some characteristics of a constructivist learning environment (list at least three)? In what ways is such an environment beneficial for CLD students?

4. Explain the concept of *elaboration*. What are the connections that teachers should be aware of between elaboration and the prior knowledge, skills, and capacities that a CLD student brings to the classroom?

5. What sorts of factors external to the school, especially sociopolitical factors, often lead to reductionistic curricula in schools? Reflect on and discuss the teacher's potential role in countering such influences.

6. What teaching strategies help CLD students cope with the complex vocabulary of mathematics and science lessons or classes? How does a teacher implement these strategies?

7. Describe the importance of the relevance of new information to the CLD learner. In what ways do constructivist learning environments emphasize or enhance instructional relevance?

8. In what ways might a teacher encourage CLD students to maximize the social affective learning strategy of asking questions for clarification? Reflect on and explain why the CLD student might not already be comfortable with the use of such a strategy.

suggested activities

Preservice Teachers

1. Observe a grade-level class in which CLD students are instructed. What modifications or accommodations is the teacher making to deliver more comprehensible classroom instruction?

2. By observing her or his instructional methods, identify the specific strategies the teacher incorporates to make the content more cognitively challenging for CLD students.

3. Interview a CLD student regarding the learning strategies the teacher uses that seem to help the student acquire the language and content more easily.

In-Service Teachers

1. Imagine that you are a middle school science teacher who instructs a grade-level class that is composed of native-English-speaking and CLD students who are at varying levels of English proficiency. You are about to begin a unit on volcanoes. What instructional accommodations can you add that will help *all* students in your class meet the academic standards embedded in the topic?

2. Keeping in mind the various backgrounds of your students, list some of the varied types of learning styles your students might bring to the classroom and how you could capitalize on each one with instructional accommodations.

3. Give students a list of challenging or new vocabulary words they will be encountering in a lesson. Once they are in heterogeneous cooperative groups, instruct them to group related words and then create their own categories under which to place these grouped words. They may need to use a thesaurus or dictionary to get some sense of the meaning of the words during this process. Before beginning the lesson, have groups discuss and compare their categories and their rationale for placing specific words in these categories. The purpose of this activity is to activate prior knowledge and stimulate students' thought processes as they manipulate these words in the context of their own experiences and prior knowledge. This strategy makes such words more personally relevant and provides a foundation for encountering them in the lesson, which may present a less familiar context.

The information provided in this chapter will help the educator to:

- Discuss the nature of the linguistic dimension of the prism model.
- Compare and contrast first language acquisition (FLA) and second language acquisition (SLA).
- Describe the ways in which the presence or lack of L1 support influences time to SLA.
- Discuss Krashen's natural order hypothesis and implications for SLA.
- Identify the stage of second language acquisition exhibited by a CLD student.
- Discuss the ways in which CALP development in L1 supports SLA.
- Describe the array of CLD student biographies that may be represented in a grade-level classroom.
- Discuss the linguistic challenges that CLD students may face in public school classrooms.
- Describe the linguistic processes that may prove difficult for CLD students as they acquire a second language.

Linguistic Dimension of Methods for CLD Students

You think in words; for you, language is an inexhaustible thread you weave as if life were created as you tell it. I think in the frozen images of a photograph. Not an image on a plate, but one traced by a fine pen, a small and perfect memory with the soft volumes and warm colors of a Renaissance painting, like an intention captured on grainy paper or cloth. It is a prophetic moment; it is our entire existence, all we have lived and have yet to live, all times in one time, without beginning or end.

—Isabel Allende, *The Stories of Eva Luna*

critical standards *Guiding Chapter Content*

TESOL/NCATE teacher standards reflect professional consensus on standards for the quality teaching of pre-K–12 CLD students. Additionally, the CEEE Guiding Principles and their accompanying indicators serve as a framework to assist practitioners, policymakers, and clients as they collaborate to enhance academic enrichment and language acquisition among CLD students. Therefore, in order to help educators understand how they might appropriately target and address national professional teaching standards in practice, we have designed the content of this chapter to reflect the following standards.

TESOL ESL Standards for P–12 Teacher Education Programs

TESOL ESL—Domain 1: Language. Candidates know, understand, and use the major concepts, theories, and research related to the nature and acquisition of language to construct learning environments that support ESOL [CLD] students' language and literacy development and content-area achievement. (p. 1)

- **Standard 1.a. Describing language.** Candidates demonstrate understanding of language as a system and demonstrate a high level of competence in helping ESOL students acquire and use English in listening, speaking, reading, and writing for social and academic purposes. (p. 2)

  1.a.1. Apply knowledge of phonology (the sound system) to help ESOL students develop oral, reading, and writing (including spelling) skills in English. (p. 3)

Note: All TESOL/NCATE standards are cited from TESOL (2001). All Guiding Principles are cited from Center for Equity and Excellence in Education (1996).

1.a.3. Apply knowledge of syntax (phrase and sentence structure) to assist ESOL students' development of written and spoken English. (pp. 3–4)

1.a.9. Locate and use linguistic resources to learn about the structure of English and of students' home languages. (p. 6)

- **Standard 1.b. Language acquisition and development.** Candidates understand and apply concepts, theories, research, and practice to facilitate the acquisition of a primary and a new language in and out of classroom settings. (p. 6)

   1.b.5. Understand and apply current theories and research in language and literacy development. (p. 9)

   1.b.6. Recognize and build on the processes and stages of English language and literacy development. (p. 10)

   1.b.7. Recognize the importance of ESOL students' home languages and language varieties and build on these skills as a foundation for learning English. (p. 10)

   1.b.13. Help ESOL students develop effective language learning strategies. (p. 13)

CEEE Guiding Principles

Guiding Principle #2: Limited English proficient students develop full receptive and productive proficiencies in English in the domains of listening, speaking, reading, and writing, consistent with expectations for all students.

2.3   Schools recognize that the development of second language literacy is highly correlated with and accelerated by literacy development in the native language and, therefore, facilitate the continued development of literacy in the native language.

2.4   Schools articulate and implement a sequence of language support services that reflect their students' stages of English language acquisition (e.g., from new arrival centers to mainstream classrooms with language support).

2.5   All teachers understand the holistic nature of language and integrate their teaching and assessment of listening, speaking, reading, and writing.

2.6   All teachers teach limited English proficient students the full range of language uses, including social communication as well as the advanced academic and technical uses of language in core content areas.

2.11 Limited English proficient students recognize that the development of second language literacy is accelerated by literacy development in their native language and utilize opportunities to continue their development of literacy in the native language. (p. 6)

Inevitably, discussions about education for the English language learner tend to focus on issues that pertain to the linguistic dimension of the CLD student biography. Chapter 1 summarizes the four dimensions of this biography, the sociocultural, the cognitive, the academic, and the linguistic. As discussed, this more inclusive perspective of a CLD student biography represents a more holistic way to frame the differential learning needs and transition adjustments of CLD students. In this chapter, we focus our attention on the challenges and processes of the linguistic dimension of the CLD student biography; we discuss relevant issues that have surfaced during our work with CLD students and their teachers and in the work of others in the fields of bilingual and ESL education.

■ The Linguistic Dimension of the CLD Student Biography

Not only is a focus on the linguistic dimension predictable in discussions of the CLD student, but it is also a dimension about which a great deal of confusion frequently exists. The following are examples of questions that tend to arise:

- "He's only a second grader; shouldn't he learn to read and write in English from the beginning?"
- "She's been in my class for three weeks and has scarcely said one word in English; do you think we ought to refer her for special education testing?"
- "I've heard her. She speaks English just fine when she's in a game on the playground. Why can't she understand in the classroom?"

Dynamics of First Language Acquisition (FLA)

Indeed, language and literacy development, whether in the first or the second language, involve difficult challenges and complex processes. For those of us who are native English speakers, it is easy to forget the difficulties and transitions that we progressed through in learning our own first language. None of us was born fluent in our native language. However, we sometimes expect newly arrived CLD students to respond as if they simply acquired a new language by crossing a border. Each of us, in acquiring our own first language, completed a complex series of processes and transitions, beginning with the development of our oral language capabilities. Fortunately, many of us experienced nurturing environments for this oral language acquisition. We were bathed in the language through so-called *motherese,* and our language acquisition trials were praised, scaffolded, supported, and reinforced by family, extended family, friends, and caregivers. By age five, most of us had subconsciously developed rudimentary understandings of our first language phonology (sound patterns), vocabulary, syntax (sentence structure), semantics (word meanings), and pragmatics (understandings of language use in context). Yet our first language development saga was not yet half accomplished.

A significant number of us experienced our introduction to written language through our transition to formal schooling. Our progression through the various grade levels of this formal education in our first language enhanced our mastery of the language domains (phonology, morphology, syntax, semantics, and pragmatics). As we developed and reached puberty, more complex aspects of oral language acquisition were occurring, including enhanced understandings of the following: the structure of language, discrete distinctions among phonemes (the basic sound units of the language), and differences in meaning, vocabulary, and uses and interchanges of the language (Lightbrown & Spada, 1993; Ninio & Bruner, 1978; Ochs & Schieffelin, 1984). Indeed, by the time we reached adolescence, successive, incremental exposure to the core subject areas (including the sciences, mathematics, and the language arts) had progressively increased our capacity to comprehend the cognitively complex language of instruction, textbooks, and media. Nonetheless,

Are You Aware?

CLD students who are newcomers often have no prior experience with the target language (i.e., English). These students must build both social and academic language proficiency in the target language in order to compete in the content areas with native English speakers. When the CLD student is schooled only in the second language (i.e., English), multifaceted and longitudinal research has consistently demonstrated that the attainment of grade-level norms will require a minimum of five to ten years and will require even more time when the student does not already have an established literacy base in his or her first language (e.g., Collier, 1987, 1989a, 1992; Collier & Thomas, 1989). On the other hand, when the CLD student has been schooled in both the first and second language, at least through the fifth or sixth grade, she or he is often able to maintain grade-level norms in L1 and attain grade-level norms in L2 in four to seven years (Collier, 1992; Genesee, 1987; Ramírez, 1992).

our process of first language development was not yet complete. In fact, many researchers argue that only 50 percent of our first language acquisition processes are complete by age six, and most individuals require the remainder of their lifetime to complete these processes (Akmajian, Demers, Farmer, & Harnish, 1995; Schieffelin & Eisenberg, 1984).

Differences between First and Second Language Acquisition

No less complex, and in many ways much more intimidating, is the task of second language acquisition for the CLD student. Table 3.1 explores the similarities and differences between first and second language acquisition. As the CLD student is proceeding through second language acquisition, the student is seldom afforded the luxury of an extended period of oral language development as a foundation for other aspects of literacy development. Additionally, the CLD student is rarely able to rely on a home environment that bathes her or him in the second language and scaffolds the trials of second language acquisition. Many parents or caregivers of CLD students are also learning a second language themselves. This is not to say that their capacity to continue the CLD student's development in L1 at home is not also valuable. On the contrary, ongoing development in the native language is indispensable to the student's continuing CALP development in L1. Nonetheless, these parents are not always able to bathe the student in the language that the school culture tends to expect.

Seldom is the CLD student able to maximize an incrementally successive transition to the cognitively complex forms of the second language used in such subject areas as the sciences and mathematics. Instead, most CLD students, especially secondary-level students, must spend their school days catching up with their peers not only in the language of instruction but also in the prior linguistic knowledge expectations of their subject-area instructors. Elementary-school-age, native-English-speaking children begin kindergarten or first grade with at least five years of conversational English development. Older native-English-speaking children begin

■ **t a b l e   3 . 1**   Ways in Which First and Second Language Acquisition Compare and Contrast

L1 Acquisition	L1 and L2 Acquisition	L2 Acquisition
Parents or care-takers are the primary language models for first language learners. First language learners have innumerable opportunities to interact with language models. Most first language learners acquire a high level of first language proficiency. First language acquisition is arguably internally motivated by an innate cognitive process, although environmental factors shape development. Most people develop a first language.	Through a process called overgeneralization, a language learner may indiscriminately apply a language rule to many different situations. (e.g., *He goed to the store yesterday.*) Learners acquire language by interacting with others. Learners go through a silent period. Learners need comprehensible input. A highly contextualized, language-rich environment will facilitate language acquisition. Language acquisition is cognitively demanding. Language acquisition involves conceptualizing information in new ways and developing new ways of processing information. Language acquisition occurs in predictable stages. Language acquisition is a dynamic process during which learners actively construct meaning using prior knowledge, experience, and context.	Second language learners already have a language for communication and thought. Second language learners can transfer knowledge about language (metalinguistic awareness) and thought processes from the first to the second language. Peers and teachers are the primary language models for second language learners. Second language learners have a greater repertoire of language learning strategies. The second language learner may make language mistakes in the second language because he or she is applying rules from the first language to the second language. Second language learners can code switch, which involves using both languages to create greater meaning than could be achieved by relying on only one language. Second language learners can use cognates to comprehend new words in the second language. Second language learners often need more time to process information. Second language learners have greater prior knowledge and experience to rely on as they acquire the second language. Second language learners often have fewer opportunities to interact with second language models. Second language acquisition is arguably externally motivated by sociocultural factors, although innate cognitive processes facilitate the acquisition process. Not all people develop a second language. Second language learners can lose a first or second language if they do not use the language. Many people do not acquire a high level of second language proficiency. Second language learners who reach high levels of bilingual proficiency tend to have greater cognitive abilities than monolingual language learners.

middle or high school with several years of both conversational and academic English development. CLD students often begin schooling in English with little or no conversational or academic development in English. Yet some schooling systems expect such students to understand and function *without accommodations* at grade level, even while their native-English-speaking peers have spent several years developing the necessary English language skills for grade-level academic achievement.

Of particular concern, schools rarely afford the CLD student the sort of pedagogic environment that research has suggested is critical to second language acquisition. Specifically, Wong Fillmore (1991) found that at least three environmental components are crucial to second language learning. The first component involves learners who recognize the need to learn the second or target language and who are motivated to do so. Second, the processes involved require speakers of the target language. These speakers must be fluent enough in the target language to provide learners with access to the language and assistance in language transitions. Third, a social setting is necessary to second language learning. This setting must bring together the learners and the fluent speakers of the target language in contact that is frequent enough to enable language learning. Furthermore, the findings of Wong Fillmore indicate that all three environmental components are necessary to successfully target language learning. Wong Fillmore argues that an environment that is missing any one of these components will render language learning difficult, if not impossible.

Demands of Second Language Acquisition (SLA)

Additional research and analysis has also indicated that the complex processes involved in second language acquisition not only demand certain crucial environmental conditions, but they also require the targeting of a certain type of language competence. Since Hymes (1972) introduced the term *communicative competence,* our understanding of the complexities involved in knowing a language has greatly expanded. Communicative competence is that level of language expertise that enables users to "convey and interpret messages and to negotiate meanings interpersonally within specific contexts" (Brown, 1987, p. 43). This notion of language knowledge suggests that knowledge of grammatical structures is insufficient as a goal for second language acquisition. Rather, the curriculum and instruction required for communicative competence in a second language must target at least four areas of language knowledge: grammatical competence, sociolinguistic competence, discourse competence, and strategic competence (Canale, 1983). As each of these is discussed, teachers might think about ways in which they can target these four areas of language knowledge as they plan their curriculum and instruction for CLD students.

Grammatical competence calls for curriculum and instruction that prepares the CLD student to incorporate and apply the language code. This competence requires at least some knowledge of pronunciation, vocabulary, word formation and meaning, sentence formulation, and spelling. Grammatical competence gains in importance as the student advances through the various stages of language proficiency.

Sociolinguistic competence is a goal of curriculum planning and language instruction that is intentionally focused on appropriate use of the target language in sociolinguistic contexts. Educators must consider several factors related to this competence, including the norms of interaction, the status of communicators, and the purposes of interaction. Language programming that emphasizes the rules and basic skills of the target language seldom addresses this competence.

Discourse competence requires reflective curriculum planning and interactive language instruction. Such competence reflects the CLD student's capacity to combine, recombine, and connect language utterances into a meaningful product. The notion of discourse competence accounts for the fact that a grammatically correct language utterance may, nonetheless, prove incomprehensible to the recipient of that language message.

Strategic competence often necessitates a curriculum that emphasizes paralinguistic clues such as language registers (one such register is the use of formal versus informal language). This competence also demands instruction that stresses the pragmatics of the second or target language (i.e., the appropriate use of the language in various contexts). According to Canale (1983), speakers of the target language may employ strategic competence to:

- Compensate for breakdowns in communication (as when a speaker does not know the precise term he or she wishes to use and is forced to use an imprecise, sometimes confusing one as a substitute).
- Enhance the efficacy of the message communicated (as is the case when a communicator adds body language to her or his message to reinforce communication).

The process of second language acquisition, therefore, requires a variety of skills and understandings necessary for the effective use of the second language. The linguistic dimension of the CLD student biography involves a number of complex challenges, some of which directly relate to this and other linguistic processes.

■ Challenges of the Linguistic Dimension

Although the range of linguistic challenges described is by no means exhaustive, Table 3.2 summarizes those challenges that directly or indirectly relate to issues of language transition as well as curriculum and instruction. Among the challenges associated with language transition are the following:

- A lack of authentic, constructivist, and interactive environments for language transition in schools and classrooms
- A lack of understanding about the time required for language development and language transition
- A shortage of educators trained to teach bilingual education or to provide native language support to CLD students

These challenges suggest that a number of variables including environment, teacher expectations, and staffing may contribute to the language transition challenges of

■ **t a b l e 3 . 2**   Linguistic Dimension of the CLD Student Biography

Challenges	Processes

Language Transition
• Lack of authentic, constructivist, and interactive environments for language transition in schools and classrooms
• Lack of understanding about the time required for language development and language transition
• Inappropriate levels of educators trained to teach bilingual education or provide native language support to CLD students
 	
Curriculum and Instruction
• Limited efforts toward either curricular or instructional accommodations and modifications for the CLD student
• Widespread reliance on ineffective program models for language transition
• Shortage of supplementary materials with which to provide instructional native language support
• Limited exposure to authentic literacy activities
• An instructional focus on isolated basic skills of the target language
• Fragmented literacy instruction and postponed exposure to writing in L2
• A phonics focus in language arts instruction
• An inordinate focus on decoding skills in reading classes
• Lack of understanding about the invalidity of the interference hypothesis
	Ongoing CALP development in L1
	Second language acquisition
	CALP development in L2
	Literacy development processes
	• Vital literacy processes
	  —Comprehension
	  —Composition
	• Necessary but not sufficient literacy processes
	  —Word recognition
	    • Contextual clues
	    • Word families
	    • High-frequency words
	    • Alphabetic principle
	  —Spelling
	    • Provincial
	    • Invented
	• Intermediate literacy processes
	  —Concepts about print
	  —Phonemic awareness
	  —Letter identification

the linguistic dimension that CLD students must transcend to be successful in school. Among the difficulties for CLD students associated with curriculum and instruction are the following challenges:

- Weaknesses in curricular accommodations for the CLD student
- Widespread reliance on ineffective programming models for language transition and acquisition
- A shortage of resource materials that enable native language support
- Limited exposure to authentic literacy development activities
- An instructional focus limited to the basic skills of the target language
- Postponed exposure to the literacy domain of writing
- A phonics focus in language arts instruction
- An inordinate focus on decoding skills in reading instruction

Time Required for Second Language Acquisition

If one closely examines the language transition challenges of the linguistic dimension, perhaps the most pervasive is a general lack of understanding about the time required for a CLD student to acquire CALP skills in the second or target language. As prior discussion has detailed, the CLD student must attain CALP proficiency in the target language if he or she is to be successful in content-area learning and achievement throughout schooling and to reach high school graduation. Newly arrived CLD students, many of whom have no prior experience with the target language (i.e., English), must build both social and academic language proficiency in the target language in order to compete in the content areas with their native-English-speaking peers. Multifaceted and longitudinal research has consistently demonstrated that when the CLD student is schooled only in L2, meeting this linguistic challenge of attaining grade-level norms will require a minimum of five to ten years and will require even more time when the student does not already have an established literacy base in L1 (Collier, 1987, 1989b, 1992; Collier & Thomas, 1989; Cummins, 1981, 1991, 1992; Cummins & Swain, 1986; Dolson & Mayer, 1992; Genesee, 1987; Ramírez, 1992). On the other hand, when the CLD student has been schooled in L1 and L2 at least through the fifth or sixth grade, she or he is often able to maintain grade-level norms in L1 and attain grade-level norms in L2 in four to seven years (Collier, 1992; Genesee, 1987; Ramírez, 1992).

   To effectively address curricular and instructional challenges, it is especially important for educators to understand the ways in which these findings of field research with CLD students stand in direct contrast to:

- A history of transitional bilingual programs that fund simultaneous L1 and L2 education only through third grade
- A long-standing history in some school districts of ESL pull-out programs that provide no support in L1 and transition CLD students to all-English classrooms as early as the second or third grade
- A recent national trend toward so-called newcomer programs that purport to transition CLD students to all-English instruction in periods as short as *45 days*

Just as first language acquisition is a complex, long-term endeavor, so too is the challenge of acquiring grade-level academic language proficiency in a second language. Therefore, effective educators consider the complex relationships among the linguistic, sociocultural, cognitive, and academic dimensions of the CLD student biography as their CLD students work to overcome the multifaceted challenges that the linguistic processes present.

Exposure to Authentic Literacy Instruction and Activities

As illustrated in Table 3.2, a complex set of curricular and instructional challenges are associated with the linguistic dimension of the CLD student biography. Many CLD students demonstrate limited English proficiency. Therefore, instruction and

t h e o r y *into Practice*

Canale (1983) found that successful second language development must target at least four critical forms of language knowledge in order for the language learner to acquire communicative competence. These forms of knowledge are discourse competence, grammatical competence, sociolinguistic competence, and strategic competence. *Strategic competence* often necessitates a curriculum that emphasizes paralinguistic clues such as language registers (one such register is the use of formal versus informal language). This competence also demands instruction that stresses the pragmatics of the second or target language (i.e., the appropriate use of the language in various contexts). Speakers of the target language may employ strategic competence to

(a) compensate for breakdowns in communication (as when a speaker does not know the precise terms he or she wishes to use and is forced to use an imprecise, sometimes confusing one as a substitute) and (b) enhance the efficacy of the message communicated (as is the case when a communicator adds paralinguistic clues such as body language to her or his message to reinforce communication).

■ *What types of paralinguistic clues do you typically use when someone does not understand your message? What are the implications of strategic competence for teaching methods used with CLD students?*

classroom activities that provide only limited exposure to authentic literacy pose considerable difficulties for these students. Nonetheless, it is not uncommon among grade-level teachers to approach literacy development for these students as a series of sequential hurdles through which the student must progress, beginning with oral literacy activities focused on basic concepts and skills. At the heart of these practices is often the belief that CLD students need to have specific (especially basic) skills in place before engaging in authentic literacy experiences.

However, research on literacy development indicates that CLD students should be bathed in rich and authentic literacy activities from the early stages of literacy development (Anderson, 1999; Clay, 1991; Kole (in press); National Reading Panel, 2000; Perez, 2002). This research stresses the value of allowing CLD students to maximize their own prior experiences, culture, background knowledge, and reasoning to actively and interactively contribute to instruction and activities designed to promote literacy development.

Accordingly, it is important to recall that before entering school, CLD students have often been exposed to a variety of activities that have contributed to their own literacy development. For example, many CLD students have prior experiences with reading and writing in their native language. The notion of *common underlying proficiency (CUP)* (Cummins, 1981) informs us that most reading and writing skills learned in the native language will transfer to a second language and therefore need not be redeveloped in English (the concept of CUP is detailed in Chapter 4). Likewise, many CLD students have experiences with environmental print in both the native language and English. Each of these experiences creates a knowledge base for the CLD student in regard to literacy. Effective teachers of CLD students preassess these prior experiences and skill bases before they assume that classroom instruction and literacy activities should begin with basic skills and concepts.

Authentic literacy instruction maximizes not only the prior literacy experiences of the CLD student but also his or her background knowledge, literacy skills base, and cultural heritage. This brand of literacy development emphasizes relevancy, elaboration on prior socialization and experiences, the actual daily instruction and activities of the classroom, and the daily out-of-school experiences of learners. To ensure that literacy instruction is authentic, Kameenui and Carnine (1998) suggest that school educators (a) focus on the most critical concepts within the content areas, (b) emphasize explicit strategies for learning words and concepts from context, (c) scaffold student instruction through the gradual deepening of vocabulary knowledge, (d) build a connection between new knowledge and existing knowledge, and (e) review the most important conceptual knowledge in a way that deepens the CLD learner's understanding as efficiently as possible. These recommendations have a number of implications for literacy development among CLD students. First, a focus on the most critical concepts within the content areas suggests that authentic literacy instruction and activities should be content-based rather than grounded in basic concepts such as colors, seasons, or months of the year.

Second, instructional scaffolding enables the CLD student, with support, to engage in literacy activities that build on a prior skill or knowledge base while stretching toward the development of new literacy skills. Scaffolding involves extensive instructional and contextual support in the early stages of learning, followed by a gradual withdrawal of such support as the student's performance suggests independence.

Third, scaffolding can also be used to deepen the meaning of literacy activities. For example, instead of asking CLD students to learn about the seasons of the year by memorizing their names from stereotypical illustrations, these students might be engaged in a series of authentic activities designed to teach various weather phenomena associated with a season change. Accordingly, to learn about the rains often associated with the change from winter to spring, students might be scaffolded in authentic activities such as (a) observing clouds and noting their types, (b) placing a rain gauge and collecting data on rainfall over time, (c) observing the impact of rain on the environment, and (d) comparing spring rainfall in the United States to rainfall typical in the students' home countries. Scaffolded literacy development might involve listening to thunder, reading about the cloud types that were observed, discussing and comparing data on rainfall, and writing about the impact of rainfall on the environment, or writing about comparisons of spring rainfall across countries. Because these activities involve phenomena that are a part of students' seasonal experiences, they are *relevant* to the learners. And because these authentic experiences prompt comparisons with prior knowledge, they are elaborative.

Finally, because these literacy development activities encourage comparisons across countries, they can be designed so as to emphasize multiculturalism or the affirmation of a CLD student's prior socialization in a particular culture. Activities designed in this manner tend to prompt a sense of pride in one's heritage as well as the motivation to learn about other cultures and languages.

■ Processes of the Linguistic Dimension

Table 3.2 also summarizes many of the processes that are most associated with the linguistic dimension of the CLD student biography. Many of these processes are interrelated. For instance, the linguistic process of ongoing CALP development in the first language is essential to the process of second language acquisition. The literacy development processes, also summarized in Table 3.2, illustrate the complexities of attaining literacy in either one's first language or a second language.

Linguistic Process of Second Language Acquisition

The linguistic process of second language acquisition is perhaps most relevant to the appropriate education of CLD students. Although competing theories abound as to the nature of this process (Bialystok, 1990b; Krashen, 1982; McLaughlin, 1990), the literature exhibits a generalizable consistency as to the fundamental stages of the second language acquisition process.

Krashen's Natural Order Hypothesis

The notion of stages of second language acquisition is consistent with what Krashen (1982) has referred to as the *natural order hypothesis*. This hypothesis asserts that language is acquired in a more or less natural order—a predictable sequence of progression. Although individual variations will exist among students, certain grammatical features of the language tend to be acquired early, whereas others are acquired later in development. For example, morphemes that serve as verb endings (as in the bound morpheme *-ing*, found in the word *studying*) tend to be acquired early. Conversely, morphemes that enable possession (as in the possessive *-s* in the sentence *We rode Irma's horse.*) tend to be acquired late in the developmental process. In a larger sense, this natural order accounts for the fact that language learners tend to progress from listening to speaking and then develop capacities for reading and writing.

Stages of Second Language Acquisition

From the perspective of secondary education, Table 3.3 describes the various stages of the linguistic process of second language acquisition, beginning with the stage of preproduction and culminating in the stage of advanced fluency. Although the stages are discussed from the perspective of secondary education, they are applicable to CLD students of every age. The first stage of the process of second language acquisition, the preproduction stage, is often called the *silent period* because the CLD student may not communicate during this period except in nonverbal ways. During this period, the CLD student is primarily listening to the new or target language and trying to understand its patterns and rules before attempting production in that language. CLD students who are nonverbal during this stage of acquisition, which may last for several months (Ovando, Collier, & Combs, 2003), nonetheless have been found to progress in L2 acquisition as well as, or better than, their more verbal peers (Saville-Troike, 1984; Wong Fillmore & Valadez, 1986). Generally, the

■ **table 3.3**   Stages of Second Language Acquisition, with Emphasis on the Adolescent CLD Student

Please note: This chart represents the stages of second language acquisition. Many students may fall between stages and/or remain in one stage for a temporary period of time.

Stage of SLA	Student Descriptors	Student Performance Outcomes	Tips for Teachers
Preproduction	Students tend to be in a nonverbal (silent) period in which the second language may be mostly if not completely incomprehensible. Adolescent CLD students may exhibit high levels of anxiety, frustration, and withdrawal due to a variety of stressors such as cultural differences, self-concept, peer acceptance, and developmental, physical changes. Adolescent CLD students often demonstrate faster academic language growth than younger students based on superior L1 in reading, writing, speaking, and listening, as well as superior cognitive development in L1. Adolescent CLD students may demonstrate non-verbal communication for	The adolescent CLD student will typically be able to: • Readily gain familiarity with sounds, rhythms, and patterns of English based on his or her prior foundational knowledge and experiences with the first language. • Depend more heavily on visuals related to academic content such as labeled pictures, diagrams, charts, graphic organizers, maps, and word walls for understanding. • Focus on listening to and internalizing the language. He or she may not participate orally but may demonstrate understanding nonverbally through pointing, gesturing, and drawing. • Use reference points for guidance, clarification, and	Provide adolescent CLD students with comprehensible classroom experiences by using more English proficient peers as models. Pair CLD students who are less proficient in English with more English proficient bilingual students who can preview the lesson in the native language. Use a variety of visuals, physical movements, gestures, and verbal cues to support and expand the non-English proficient (NEP) student's language acquisition process. Avoid forcing any CLD student to speak prematurely by appropriately allowing for the silent period. Allow him or her to speak when he or she is ready and comfortable to take risks in English. Tap into the NEP adolescent's prior knowledge by having a bilingual peer assist the NEP student in filling out KWL charts. Tie students' personal experiences into lessons as much as possible. Using students' experiences validates the knowledge and culture the CLD student brings to the classroom. Provide models for the students to use as a guide with assignment checklists on the chalkboard. Look for NEP student understanding through observation of student demonstrations, nodding, pointing, and answering yes/no questions. Recognizing and accepting NEP students' nonverbal communication will lower the affective filter so that he or she may feel more comfortable taking risks in English.

(continued)

■ **table 3.3**   Continued

Stage of SLA	Student Descriptors	Student Performance Outcomes	Tips for Teachers
Preproduction *(continued)*	understanding such as pointing, nodding, and smiling. Students may display periods of inattentiveness. Learning in a second language can be exhausting because students must construct meaning in a new culture for cognitive and academic purposes.	clues as to what is being taught and addressed (such as procedures posted; written directions; posted homework assignments, dictionaries, or word walls in the room). The CLD adolescent may also need clarification of directions and content in the first language with the help of a bilingual peer. • Speak and understand high-frequency, contextualized words and simple phrases.	Provide a print-rich classroom with labels and word walls for students to use as a reference throughout units on which you may be working. Provide additional wait time to students. Guard vocabulary through slowed rate of speech, clear enunciation, idiom avoidance, repetition, and key vocabulary emphasis. Write language and content objectives on the board for CLD students and refer to them throughout the lesson. Try to include a variety of listening, speaking, reading, and writing activities to achieve your language objectives. Provide an outline of notes (in the student's first language, if possible) to CLD students during a lecture presentation. Provide a predictable daily routine so that the adolescent CLD student understands teacher expectations. Frequently, an apparent problematic behavior is a symptom of the NEP student's inability to understand. Provide choral reading experiences and chants to lessen the anxiety level (lower the affective filter) for taking risks in English.
Early Production	The adolescent CLD student tends to read phonetically according to his or her native language pronunciation and literacy skills. The adolescent CLD student listens with greater	The adolescent CLD student may be able to: • Speak using isolated words and phrases. • Verbally identify people, places, and objects. • Manipulate objects and ideas	Provide a classroom library of scaffolded reading material that has age-appropriate content for the adolescent at this stage. Inappropriate age-level reading material may be insulting or embarrassing to adolescents who are accustomed to a much higher level of literature in the first language. Use age-appropriate, relevant, and rich literature in classroom instruction.

■ **table 3.3** Continued

Stage of SLA	Student Descriptors	Student Performance Outcomes	Tips for Teachers
Early Production *(continued)*	understanding to contextualized, basic information and social conversation. The adolescent CLD student repeats memorable language commonly used in social conversation with peers. Students recognize connections between the native language and second language and use these connections as tools in acquiring the second language. The adolescent CLD student will use contextual cues such as pictures, graphs, and prior knowledge to facilitate reading comprehension.	mentally using foundational knowledge from his or her L1. • Use routine expressions independently. • Participate in guided, highly contextualized discussions.	Preteach key vocabulary and concepts in order to increase student comprehension. Have students label or manipulate pictures and real objects to promote comprehension. Provide students with learning strategies to discover connections between the native language and English. For example, teach Spanish speakers to look for cognates, e.g., *animales = animals*. Provide cooperative learning experiences to encourage student discussion. Support the use of the first language for clarification of content-area concepts. Provide students with opportunities for problem solving to promote higher-order thinking skills. A common misconception is that CLD students' limited English language proficiency also limits their reasoning skills. Students should be challenged regardless of their language proficiency levels. Provide as many visual aids as possible to support meaning construction.
Speech Emergence	The adolescent CLD student may exhibit increased proficiency in decoding and comprehending English text. As the student becomes more comfortable with the school culture, he or she may take more risks with oral language and speak in short sentences with syntax errors.	The adolescent CLD student may be able to: • Understand grade-level concepts more clearly and be able to increase the transfer from prior knowledge concepts learned in his or her native language.	Guard vocabulary and introduce concepts through the use of KWL charts, webs, story maps, and picture prompts. Model responses to literature for students by explaining, describing, comparing, and retelling. Provide a variety of content-area texts, trade books, and newspapers related to subject or topic. Focus on communication in meaningful contexts in which students express themselves in speech and print.

(continued)

■ **t a b l e   3 . 3**   Continued

Stage of SLA	Student Descriptors	Student Performance Outcomes	Tips for Teachers
Speech Emergence *(continued)*	He or she may demonstrate increased understanding of extended conversation and dialogue, simple stories with some details, and simple idiomatic expressions.	• Engage in much more independent reading as a result of increased oral language proficiency. • Write using a more extensive vocabulary and varied writing style. • Begin self-evaluation of writing through editing.	Respond genuinely to student writing, hold conferences that highlight student strengths and progress, and have students set their own realistic language goals. Provide students with opportunities to read, write, listen, and speak in their native languages. Provide literature relevant to adolescent life in order to increase student interest and motivation to read. Post tips for writing and editing as an easy reference and reminder to students. Model reading comprehension strategies.
Intermediate Fluency	The adolescent CLD student has increased understanding and application of word-attack and comprehension skills. He or she exhibits growth in accuracy and correctness regarding listening, speaking, reading, and writing. The adolescent CLD student uses his or her native language as a resource and may also be eager to help peers and teachers with translations and brokering. The adolescent CLD student uses richer and fuller sentences with a varied vocabulary.	The adolescent CLD student may be able to: • Explore and use extensive vocabulary and concepts in the content areas and make more language connections to L1. • Read a wider range of narrative genre and content texts with increased comprehension. • Summarize and make inferences in reading more readily. • Use language to express and defend opinions.	Structure and guide group discussions to facilitate more advanced literature studies. Provide for a variety of realistic writing experiences that are relevant to students. Encourage creativity and an increased sense of aesthetics by initiating drama, art, music, and other forms of creative expressions. Publish student-authored stories, newsletters, poems, and more. Continue to shelter instruction and check for CLD adolescent understanding. Encourage students to continue growth in the native language by providing them materials to read in the native language, allowing them to assist less proficient peers, and encouraging them to help new CLD students with their transitions to a new school and culture. Be aware of the common misconception regarding the CLD student's level of social language (BICS) with his or her level of understanding of the academic content language (CALP). Continue to provide

■ **table 3.3**   Continued

Stage of SLA	Student Descriptors	Student Performance Outcomes	Tips for Teachers
Intermediate Fluency *(continued)*	In reading comprehension, the adolescent CLD student can extract more meaning from the actual text and relies less on contextual cues.	• Experiment with more sophisticated vocabulary and complex sentence structure.	scaffolding in instruction such as cooperative learning, visuals relating to the content area, experiences using manipulatives, previewing of key terms and concepts, etc.
Advanced Fluency	This adolescent CLD student is characterized as an abstract thinker. His or her reading interests become individualized and more varied. The adolescent CLD student develops highly accurate language and grammatical structures that approximate those of native-English-speaking peers. This student may (and ideally should) view his or her native language as an asset on which to draw for the enhancement of his or her acquisition of English. At this level, the adolescent CLD student uses multiple strategies to facilitate reading comprehension.	The adolescent CLD student may be able to: • Produce language with varied grammatical structures and more complex vocabulary, including idiomatic expressions. • Capitalize on the native language as a constant resource for understanding the second language. • Demonstrate writing skills that approximate that of a native-English-speaking peer. • Read frequently for information and pleasure.	Promote ongoing development through integrated language arts and content-area activities. Encourage adolescents to continue growth in native language at home, at school, and in the community. For lesson closure, have students review daily content and language objectives to assess their progress. Encourage students to interact and support other English language learners who are transitioning into a new school and culture. Provide opportunities for more proficient students to work as peer tutors, not only to reinforce their own learning, but also to assist others with comprehension. Arrange collaborative groups so that highly English proficient CLD adolescents are partnered with less English proficient CLD students. Encourage students to engage in metacognitive regulation concerning their own learning processes and strategies.

silent period is a nonproblematic stage of the second language acquisition process, except in those cases in which educators or staff erroneously conclude that the student's silence is somehow indicative of other, nonlinguistic problems such as a learning disability. After the preproduction stage, language learners generally proceed through the stages of early production, speech emergence, intermediate fluency, and advanced fluency (see Table 3.3). In this way, the capabilities of CLD students advance from the early production stage of phonetic reading in the new language to the advanced fluency stage of abstract thinking in the new or target language.

Like other linguistic processes, second language acquisition necessarily involves certain challenges that are also part of the linguistic dimension of the CLD student biography, including challenges such as the many misunderstandings that surround the silent period of the process. Therefore, effective teachers not only understand the dynamics of each stage of SLA, but they also realize the implications of each stage for curriculum and instruction. Additionally, such educators know what to expect in the learning progress of CLD students.

Linguistic Process of Understanding Concepts about Print

Concepts about print constitute an intermediate literacy process that focuses on the various aspects of how the written word is structured. According to Herrera (2001), critical concepts about print that CLD students should acquire include

dilemmas *of Practice*

Mr. Hauschild, third-grade teacher at Stover Elementary in Sunshine, California, teaches a CLD student, Emilio Vasquez, who arrived from Monterrey, Mexico, in January. Six weeks after arriving, Emilio rarely speaks in class and is generally unresponsive to questions. Mr. Hauschild has concluded that Emilio may have a learning disability and should be tested for special education. He has made a referral for testing next week.

The first stage of the process of second language acquisition, the preproduction stage, is often called the *silent period* because the CLD student may not communicate during this period except in nonverbal ways. During this period, the CLD student is primarily listening to the new or target language and trying to understand its patterns and rules before attempting production in that language. CLD students who are nonverbal during this stage of acquisition, which may last for several months (Ovando,

Collier, & Combs, 2003), nonetheless have been found to progress in L2 acquisition as well as, or better than, their more verbal peers (Saville-Troike, 1984; Wong Fillmore & Valadez, 1986). Generally, the silent period is a nonproblematic and temporary stage of the second language acquisition process, except in those cases in which educators or staff erroneously conclude that the student's silence is somehow indicative of other nonlinguistic problems such as a learning disability. Although teachers should always check to ensure that instruction is not raising the student's affective filter, a period during which the CLD student does not produce significant language is often a natural stage of second language acquisitions.

■ *Should Mr. Hauschild refer Emilio? If not, what teaching actions should Mr. Hauschild take? In what ways might he involve Emilio's parents?*

(a) understanding that print carries a message, (b) realizing that print corresponds to speech, word for word, (c) perceiving the directionality of print, and (d) recognizing the parts of texts. Therefore, when instructing CLD students, it is important for teachers to consider each of these aspects of concepts about print and the implications they may have on the literacy development of CLD students.

Print Carries a Message

Of pivotal importance to literacy development is the critical concept that print carries a message. Messages are incorporated into various forms of text through the written word. For example, storybooks, magazines, letters, e-mail, and notes are all vehicles of communication. Grade-level students are typically engaged in a variety of daily literacy activities that incorporate these venues of communication. From such activities, they gradually develop the understanding that all print carries meaning. In the classroom setting, some of the ways that teachers demonstrate the communicative power of print are by reading aloud, posting daily calendars, and engaging students in rich literacy activities throughout the day. In this manner, teachers build on students' communicative abilities and constructs to provide contextual foundations for literacy development.

CLD students sometimes have difficulty with associations between print and meaning. This is especially the case when classroom instruction does not recognize the communicative capacities and constructs that CLD students already bring to the literacy process. Although CLD students may not yet be able to convey this capacity in L2 (English), some CLD students have already developed an emergent understanding that print carries meaning, because they have been exposed to the various uses of print for multiple purposes in L1. Unfortunately, classroom instruction that does not build and elaborate on these emergent understandings is not only redundant, but it also tends to negate the potential value of the CLD student's assets in ongoing literacy development.

Perceptive teachers, therefore, preassess and maximize what the CLD student already knows about connections between print and meaning. Among the strategies that can be used to elaborate on students' emergent understandings of print concepts are hands-on activities. For example, CLD students might gain hands-on experience with bouncing balls as a way to associate meaning with the text of a story about basketball.

Print Corresponds to Speech

The recognition that print corresponds to speech word for word is also crucial to literacy development. This concept about print first draws attention to the organization of the individual letters that are used to make up words and ultimately the body of a text. Later, individuals become familiar with the sounds that correlate to these symbols. Then students learn to manipulate and join smaller isolated sounds to form syllables that compose words, which ultimately extend into phrases and sentences. These processes of increasing familiarity with sound–symbol correspondences later facilitate the capacity to decode words. This capacity serves as the precursor to an understanding that print corresponds to speech.

Regrettably, instruction for CLD students too often emphasizes the organization of the individual letters used to make up words and the sounds that are associated with each letter. Such phonics-based instruction tends to overengage CLD students in drill and practice focused on individual letters and sounds taught in isolation. Although phonics instruction has its place in teaching CLD students about sound–symbol correlations, its strict emphasis on letters and sound patterns does little to encourage balanced literacy development or reading comprehension. As demonstrated by Table 3.2 and research on literacy development (Anderson, 1999; Clay, 1991; Delgado-Gaitán, 1989; Hudelson & Serna, 1994; National Reading Panel, 2000; Perez, 2002), reading comprehension and balanced literacy development involve much more than proficiency in decoding skills.

Many CLD students have already developed extensive decoding skills in their first language. They use their native language to make sound–symbol correspondences to the written word. This capacity need not be learned twice. Instead, given an appropriate instructional environment and elaborative planning, this capacity will transfer to the second language.

Furthermore, effective teachers plan instruction for literacy development by emphasizing cognates. A cognate is a word in a particular language, the form and definition of which resemble a word in a different language (e.g., *animals* [English] and *animales* [Spanish]). An emphasis on cognates is especially effective with students whose first language is Spanish, because a significant number of cognates exist between English and Spanish. Such cognates can facilitate the rapid transfer of capacities in L1 to L2 with regard to the recognition of sound–symbol correspondences.

Directionality

The recognition of the directionality of print is equally crucial to literacy development. For instance, a child learning to read in English may not understand immediately that text is to be read from the top of the page to the bottom, or that each line of a text is to be read from left to right. Students who are unfamiliar with directionality might begin reading on the right side of the page instead of the left as they use visual cues to decipher meaning.

Issues of directionality may be of particular concern with certain CLD students, depending on the script typically used in their native language. Those students whose languages do not follow the written directionality patterns of the English language may struggle with this concept about print. Prime examples of directionality differences can be found in script languages such as Hebrew, Chinese, and Hmong.

Insightful teachers are aware of these crosslinguistic differences and provide additional instructional scaffolding designed to ease students through transitions to unfamiliar patterns of directionality. These teachers typically begin with comparisons across languages to establish context. Subsequent instruction often stresses short segments of text and progresses to longer segments as students build the capacity to accept changes in directionality. Special attention is given throughout to the pace of instruction; a rapid pace used at any juncture in the learning process has a tendency to raise the student's affective filter.

Parts of Texts

Of crucial importance to reading comprehension is the recognition of the various parts of a text (front cover, back cover, title page, table of contents, etc.). CLD students, however, may arrive in the classroom having little experience with texts or the organization of texts. For CLD students who arrive from war-torn countries, their prior experiences with schooling and literacy development were often interrupted and inconsistent. Other CLD students may be children of poverty who have only limited familiarity with the written word. Still others have been socialized to cultural traditions emphasizing stories passed down orally from generation to generation. The early literacy experiences of such students typically do not stress texts or the organization of texts. Therefore, the potential for instructional assumptions about this aspect of concepts about print is high.

When providing literacy instruction, teachers typically build on this basic understanding by engaging students in rich explorations of text. Development activities typically associated with such explorations include (a) surveying texts, (b) explicitly teaching students how to identify the title page, (c) demonstrating the use of the table of contents, and (d) manipulating back matter sections, such as the index and appendixes. Reflective teachers of CLD students provide additional and explicit strategy instruction that stresses both the manner in which texts may be organized and the ways in which that organization can be maximized to improve comprehension. For example, once the CLD student recognizes that the illustrations of a text can depict certain key events or messages, she or he may occasionally refer to these to establish the context of a story. Similarly, once the CLD student recognizes that the chapters of certain texts might close with a summary of events or concepts discussed, she or he may use those summaries to better comprehend the text.

■ Linguistic Dimension: Implications for Classroom and School Practice

This chapter summarizes many of the challenges and processes associated with the linguistic dimension of the CLD student biography and schooling experience. As we proceed through the remaining chapters of the text, many of these processes and challenges are further elaborated, analyzed, and discussed in relation to instructional approaches, methods, and strategies. Nevertheless, at this juncture it is useful to briefly explore some of the immediate implications of these linguistic challenges and processes for classroom practice with CLD students.

Instructional Planning for CALP Development in L1 and L2

Reflective teachers know that effective practice for CLD students requires an understanding of the dynamics involved in first and second language acquisition.

■ Voices from the Field

"In my 2nd grade class, I have a student from India. He has been in Iowa for four years. His English is quite good, but he is still developing some sounds such as the 'th' and 'sh' sounds. This student is very bright and social. However, I was noticing that his reading scores on tests and probes were very low, below the passing level. These scores were not indicative of this student's demonstrated ability in class. I decided that his BICS is well developed, however his CALP is still in the developing stages (which is normal for an ELL [CLD] student). Because his CALP is still developing, his comprehension of a story from his brain to pencil and paper is a weak area. This student does much better when retelling a story or when he is allowed to read tests out loud with assistance with words he does not know.

As I thought about these language issues, I wondered how the teachers who had him in class the previous two years did not see this problem. I was told that he is a little above average in reading, and he will "do just fine" in the English language-based classroom. I was completely under the impression that he would be like any other student in my class; he had a very solid English base and would progress as all my other students would. I also found out that his parents speak little or no English at home, so he speaks a different language at home (which is good, as this enables him to develop L1).

I am also wondering how and why he has been passed on from grade to grade with little ESL support. To my knowledge, the first time that this boy was assessed using an ELL test (our district uses the IDEA) was this year. I fully realize that we have only two ELL [CLD] students in our district, but do those two children not matter enough to our administration to try to make some changes? I am glad I have taken ESL/Dual Language Methods and am currently in ESL Assessment. I hope that the information that I learn will only help me teach ALL of my students better.

At the same time, I feel challenged to learn more and to do better for this student. I have realized that he is still acquiring his CALP, and I need to be supportive as a teacher to enable him to learn the best that he can. But how can I continue to assess him properly when the support of our district isn't necessarily there? I want to be able to serve as a resource for this child's teacher next year, who probably has had little or no training in educating ELL students, but am I really that much more educated?

I am constantly thinking, 'How can I be a resource for other teachers and our administration, when I really have so little knowledge of ESL instruction AND assessment myself?' I also wonder if my district should be justified in hiring a trained ESL teacher, even though we have only two ELL students. At what point do they hire an outside professional?

As I completed the first class, I understood that I had made some invalid assumptions concerning my ELL student. First, I had assumed that since he has been in a full-English educational program since preschool, his language would be

Table 3.4 illustrates the ways in which first and second language acquisition are similar and different. Because ongoing CALP development in L1 accelerates L2 acquisition, educators should give special consideration to learning environments and forms of classroom instruction that provide whatever levels of ongoing nawell-developed and I would treat him as I would any other student in my class when it came to language skills. I also had assumed that since his oral comprehension was good, he could automatically transfer that knowledge to paper. Neither of my assumptions held any validity. Based on what he has shown me academically in this area, I now know that he is still learning language skills and vocabulary. He continues to struggle with unfamiliar words, therefore impeding his comprehension. I also realized during this "revelation" that I need to continue to learn about ELL students because my ELL student this year will NOT be my last.

I have completed my first course in ESL. I have learned so much practical knowledge to take with me to my classroom it is overwhelming. I will start implementing teaching strategies to help my students learn better one by one. I need to teach explicitly, start with one strategy, help my students to learn it well, apply it to real-life, and then move on to another. I understand that times in this process will most definitely be frustrating and discouraging. But, I must keep working ahead through these rough times for the good of all my students. I also need to think of alternate assessment and testing tools to check the progress of my ELL students.

Professionally, I need to continue taking classes that will help me better understand the ELL learner. I am so invigorated with the knowledge I have gained and been able to use in my class. It is hard enough for a child to work through a day of school, let alone work through that day of school AND try to learn the language that the teacher is speaking at the same time. I recently had parent-teacher conferences; when I was talking with my ELL student's mother, I told her I was taking this class and described some of the things that she can do as a parent to help her child continue to learn English. One of the things that I stressed to her was The Balloon Theory of Language Proficiency that was discussed in ESL/Dual Language Methods. It is very important for her child to continue to learn his first language (Punjabi), so that the concepts he learns in his L1 will carry over to his English. She really seemed to appreciate my attempt to learn how to better educate her child. I hope I better facilitate his learning by using CALLA strategies and other instructional methods that will help him to gain a more concrete grasp on the English language. I will continue to have him answer story comprehension questions orally, and have his reading tests read aloud to him. I know that he is a good reader, but the frequent unfamiliar words that pop up in new stories hinder his comprehension. Right now, I want to focus on what he CAN do, not what he cannot do. Having a positive educational experience is my optimal goal."

- *Sara Van Manen, elementary teacher, Bondurant, IA*

Note: Relationships between first and second language proficiency (Cummins, 1981), which this teacher refers to as "the balloon theory," are detailed in Chapter 4.

tive language support are feasible. Insightful teachers also recognize that errors are inevitable as one learns a second language. What the student understands and knows, he or she may not always be able to successfully articulate. However, through such errors, students build their cognitive and academic levels of

■ **t a b l e   3 . 4**   Similarities and Differences between a Student Engaged in First Language (L1) Acquisition and a Student Engaged in Second Language (L2) Acquisition

	L1	L2
Reads more slowly		X
Needs more processing time		X
Silent period	X	X
More likely to need to monitor comprehension		X
Has more than one language to draw on to construct meaning (cognates, root words, and more)		X
Tends to have more metalinguistic awareness		X
More likely to experience anxiety over language production		X
Needs comprehensible input	X	X
Uses prior knowledge to construct meaning	X	X
More likely to have 5 years of exposure to dominant language of school before beginning school	X	
Tends to overestimate L1 language ability	X	
Tends to underestimate the potential role of L1 proficiency in L2 acquisition		X
Usually has experience with multiple cultures		X
Goes through stages of language acquisition	X	X

proficiency in L2 as they explore the nuances of the target language. Reflective teachers provide opportunities for CLD students to demonstrate what they understand in a variety of ways and through different media of discourse.

Anticipating and Preassessing for the Array of Student Biographies

Effective teachers anticipate that CLD students may bring to the classroom a vast array of student biographies. Therefore, as professionals they preassess these student biographies as a basis for instructional planning. At *minimum,* such educators preassess the following for each CLD student:

- Sociocultural/acculturation biography
- First language biography
- Second language biography
- Schooling/academic knowledge biography

Table 3.5 provides a summary of the biography characteristics typically associated with CLD students who (a) have newly arrived in the United States and are below grade level, (b) have newly arrived in the United States and are at grade level, (c) have had some education in the United States but are two or more years below grade level, and (d) have had variable levels of education in the United States and are at grade level. Patterns of classroom and school behaviors and actions that are characteristic of CLD students within each of the previously mentioned groups are also explored in Table 3.5.

After preassessing the biographies of their CLD students, effective teachers reflect on the ways in which they can modify their instruction to better accommodate the needs and assets these students bring to the classroom. Though by no means exhaustive, Table 3.5 provides ideas for teacher actions that would be professionally appropriate given the individual backgrounds of the CLD students present in the classroom. For example, to best accommodate a CLD student who has newly arrived and is below grade level, a reflective teacher would recognize that the child may not be speaking much because he or she is still in the preproduction stage (silent period). Therefore, the teacher emphasizes language comprehension rather than speech production. The teacher also scaffolds instruction and support. In contrast, if a CLD student has been in the United States for four years and is at grade level, a teacher might best accommodate the student by emphasizing literacy development, especially reading and writing. Furthermore, the teacher provides (a) content-based sheltered instruction, (b) learning strategy instruction, and (c) scaffolded auxiliary support from paraprofessionals, peers, or parents.

Fostering Communicative, Constructivist Language Acquisition Environments

Insightful teachers understand that second language acquisition takes place in highly communicative, constructivist environments that provide multiple opportunities for social language interaction. Successful teachers provide language-learning environments that foster the construction of meaning from context and from communication. For example, thematic units grounded in interactive learning encourage hands-on applications that contextualize language. These units also encourage language interactions that are cognitively demanding and academically relevant. Similarly, heterogeneous peer groupings for thematic activities provide the assistance of the more language-capable peer in academic and social interactions focused on learning.

■ t a b l e 3.5 Array of CLD Student Biographies

CLD Student Description	Typical Characteristics of Sociocultural/ Acculturation Biography	Typical Characteristics of First Language Biography	Typical Characteristics of Second Language Biography	Typical Characteristics of Schooling/ Academic Knowledge Biography	Typical Characteristics of Classroom/School Behaviors/Actions	Professionally Appropriate Teacher Actions
(NABG) Newly arrived and below grade level	In U.S. 2 yrs or less Ltd. socialization outside home or work Env. May have lived in a war-torn country LA may range from culture shock to a transition stage Score of 8–16 on AQS	Strong BICS, but Ltd. CALP Dev. in L1 Sometimes illiterate in L1 Will require high levels of ongoing NLS	Ltd. BICS or CALP Dev. in L2 Is quite likely to be in silent period of SLA Will require considerable time to acquire L2 literacy Is likely to experience difficulty in acquiring CALP skills in L2	Ltd., interrupted, or inconsistent schooling in HC Will require in-depth, translated preassessment of prior academic knowledge and high-level Aux. instructional support Unlikely to use learning strategies	May exhibit: • Fear of or confusion in the school/classroom Env. • Lack of eye contact with the teacher &/or understanding of classroom protocol • Anxiety, withdrawal, hyperactivity; Ltd. interaction with peers or unexpected levels of touch	Home visit–based welcome, preassessment, and planning Heavy emphasis on acclimatization to school/class Ongoing CALP Dev. in L1 via paras, parents, resources, media SLA emphasis on comprehension v. production Scaffolded instruction/support
(NAGL) Newly arrived and at grade level	In U.S. 2 yrs or less Some socialization outside home or work Env. LA may range from culture shock to more acculturated	Strong BICS, and moderate-high level of CALP Dev. in L1 Will require moderate-high levels of ongoing NLS	Ltd. BICS or CALP Dev. in L2 May be in the preproduction or early production stage of SLA Will require considerable	Expected levels of schooling in HC Will require appropriate levels of translated preassessment of prior	May exhibit: • Frustration with inability to perform at expected levels in school • Desire to seek ways to demonstrate to teacher what he/she knows	Home visit–based welcome, preassessment, and monitoring Heavy emphasis on acclimatization to school/class Ongoing CALP Dev. in L1 via

Score of 16–20 on AQS		time to acquire L2 literacy May be likely to experience difficulty in acquiring CALP skills in L2	academic knowledge and moderate levels of Aux. instructional support May use learning strategies	• Rapid drop in level of self-esteem, frustration, acting out, boredom, attention-getting actions	paras, parents, resources, media SLA emphasizes L2 literacy Dev. Content-based & scaffolded instruction, Aux. support
(USBG) Some education in the U.S., but 2 years or more below grade level In U.S. 3 or more years At least moderate socialization outside the home LA may range from transitional to more acculturated Score of 20–24 on AQS	Strong BICS, and medium-moderate level of CALP Dev. in L1 Will require moderate levels of ongoing NLS	High-level BICS, and moderate CALP Dev. in L2 May be in the early production or speech emergence stages of SLA	Low-variable levels of Ed. in HC May have experienced inconsistent Ed. in U.S. Appropriate levels of pre-assessment and instructional support essential Ltd. learning strategy use	May exhibit: • Increasing understanding of school/classroom protocol • Responsiveness to teacher, but Ltd. class participation, Ltd. response to homework/other assignments • Lack of confidence in academic tasks, reliance on oral responses & participation, Ltd. independence	Stress homogeneous & heterogeneous, cooperative learning groups Ongoing CALP Dev. in L1 via paras, parents, resources, media SLA emphasizes L2 literacy Dev. Content-based, sheltered instruction with scaffolded Aux. support from teacher, paras, peers, parents

(continued)

■ **t a b l e   3 . 5**   Continued

CLD Student Description	Typical Characteristics of Sociocultural/ Acculturation Biography	Typical Characteristics of First Language Biography	Typical Characteristics of Second Language Biography	Typical Characteristics of Schooling/ Academic Knowledge Biography	Typical Characteristics of Classroom/School Behaviors/Actions	Professionally Appropriate Teacher Actions
(USGL) Variable levels of education in the U.S. and at grade level	In U.S. 3 or more years

Significant socialization outside the home

LA may range from transitional to more acculturated

Score of 24+ on AQS is not uncommon | Strong BICS and CALP Dev. in L1 are typical

Will require maintenance levels of ongoing NLS | High-level BICS, and variable-high levels of CALP Dev. in L2

Is often in the speech emergence or intermediate fluency stages of SLA | Expected levels of Ed. in HC

Typically consistent patterns of Ed. in U.S.

Appropriate levels of pre-assessment and instructional support needed

Learning strategy use is likely | May exhibit:
• Participation & some volunteerism in school protocol and activities
• Increasingly appropriate understanding and interaction with teacher/peers
• Moderate to medium levels of self-esteem and confidence | Stress independent & cooperative learning

Ongoing CALP Dev. in L1 via paras, parents, resources, media

SLA emphasizes production, reading, and writing

Content-based, sheltered and learning strategy instruction with scaffolded Aux. support |

Legend
AQS—acculturation quick screen
Aux.—auxiliary
BICS—basic interpersonal communication skills
CALP—cognitive academic language proficiency
Dev.—development
Ed.—formal education
Env.—environment
HC—home country
LA—level of acculturation
Ltd.—limited

Literacy—listening, speaking, reading, and writing
NLS—native language support
SLA—second language acquisition

tips for practice

Elementary Education

1. Tap into the prior knowledge and experiences of CLD students and the varying levels of language proficiencies they have in order to make connections between content and students' previous experiences and to engage them all in a discussion. This will motivate students and create meaningful connections and contexts for lessons or activities to be implemented while providing a way for them to practice oral skills successfully. For example, during a unit on the topic of physical fitness, simply ask students to raise their hands if they exercise. Those not quite proficient in English would be able to answer and participate; those more proficient in English could then discuss what they do daily and provide translation if needed for those not feeling comfortable responding in English.

2. Provide CLD students with authentic and rich grade-level reading material. This needs to be linguistically simplified for varying proficiency levels, relevant to students' lives, and able to support content taught within the classroom. Such material should also include reading in the CLD students' native language and might include trade books, magazines such as *Ranger Rick* or *Weekly Reader,* local or national newspapers, novels for literature groups, pamphlets on specific topics, brochures from a local travel agency, cookbooks, and more. These materials help CLD students make connections with content, promote literacy, and encourage the love of reading in a meaningful manner.

3. To overcome CLD student frustration when beginning to write in English:
   • Write interactively with your students. For example, ask CLD students to write a letter to you on a topic of choice using their journals (students may write in the native language as necessary). Write responses to your students in a letter format. Not only will they begin to write more, but also you will learn much more about your students through interactive journals.
   • Beginning with two-minute sessions and progressing to longer periods, ask students to freewrite in English or the native language about a topic connected to their current realm of learning. If they reach an impasse in their writing, have them continue to write interconnected loops. The design is to keep the writing utensil moving so that students remain focused on the writing objective until a writing idea comes to mind. Increase the number of minutes as you perceive that students are becoming more comfortable with writing.
   • Write a language experience story together about a field trip or other eventful topic, such as a school assembly involving a motivational speaker or an interesting event that all students have experienced. CLD students can then rewrite the original class story individually, adding or deleting any portion in order to make the story more personal.

4. To increase student comprehension and help support the language acquisition process, the following are suggested:
   • Teach key content vocabulary and concepts using visual cues to help CLD students learn to integrate phonics into the context of what they are reading. Use books or magazines with pictures to represent the content that CLD students have read. Also use simple language to describe what is occurring in the lesson.
   • Focus on communication in meaningful contexts that allow students to express themselves in speech and print, such as developing a class newsletter or poetry corner.

5. Keep the affective filter low for CLD students by encouraging them to use the second language in various ways, such as:
   • Labeling pictorial charts with key vocabulary and concepts
   • Accepting inventive or creative spelling
   • Modeling correct speech instead of correcting errors directly ("Yes, Laura, you do have two *feet.*")

- Providing opportunities for students to collaborate on projects
- Assigning a study buddy
- Providing a word bank for oral, writing, and reading assignments
- Continuing ongoing development of content material through integrated language arts and content-area activities.

Secondary Education

1. Provide opportunities for the CLD students who are at the initial stage of second language proficiency (i.e., the preproduction stage of SLA) to demonstrate what they understand in different ways and through different media by engaging in the following:
   - Have the CLD student draw a picture collage or use pictures from a magazine to make a collage connected to the theme or content topic of focus.
   - Encourage CLD students to point to an appropriate response using pictures, graphs, or charts.
   - Allow CLD students to respond to assignments or activities in writing or orally in the native language.
   - Have students use thumbs up/thumbs down or pencils up/pencils down for visual cues as a comprehension indicator. In this way, the CLD student can let the teacher know privately whether he or she has understood the lesson.
2. Post a guide with a structured checklist for the activities each student needs to complete. Keep these on display for everyone to refer to throughout the lesson so that CLD students can check their progress as each activity goes along.
3. Provide an outline of lessons (in the native language, if possible) for CLD students. Students can use these outlines for note taking and for following along during presentations.
4. Keep a supply of age-appropriate easy reading materials in your classroom. Lower- or primary-level reading material may be insulting to adolescents and raise the affective filter while lowering self-esteem.

5. Promote higher-order thinking for CLD students of all language proficiency levels through opportunities to problem-solve. *Be aware that CLD students' limited English proficiency does not limit cognitive skills.*
6. Scaffold a lesson for student understanding by asking CLD students to write down one question on a strip of paper about the content or topic. Then ask them to share that question with a partner and discuss their answers. Finally, have pairs share their discussions with the class, on a voluntary basis.
7. Provide literature or reading materials that reinforce content concepts in the native language. Concepts learned and clarified in L1 aid in the transition to L2 by providing ongoing CALP development in L1.
8. To encourage writing for a purpose and create meaningful connections between content and writing, provide CLD students the opportunity to write for different purposes. For example, have CLD students write narrative, comparative, or informative papers in meaningful ways, such as a narrative or informative article for a class magazine, a paper that compares and contrasts arthropods learned in biology, and so forth.
9. Provide a low-risk way to orally practice the second language, review content, and promote oral skills by allowing students to open and close lessons by orally reviewing or reading the day's posted language and content objectives.

General Education

1. Encourage student creativity and participation by initiating drama, art, music, and other forms of creative expression.
2. Provide language-learning environments that foster the construction of meaning from context and from communication. Focus learning objectives on areas in which CLD students are able to use hands-on applications to contextualize language. For example, use pictures or real-life examples of plants and animals to relate the concept of classification in biology.

3. Provide cooperative learning experiences to encourage student discussion. This will also support the use of the first language for clarification by allowing CLD students to interact with a more capable peer.
4. Support and elaborate the language acquisition processes of CLD students by:
   • Teaching key vocabulary and concepts using pictures and real objects that the students label and manipulate.

• Using visuals, physical movements, gestures, and verbal cues.
• Providing reading materials with a pattern. For elementary levels, this can include word family patterns; for secondary levels, this can include sentence or even paragraph patterns in text.

■ key theories and concepts

communicative competence

communicative language learning environment

discourse competence

first language acquisition

grammatical competence

Krashen's natural order hypothesis

linguistic dimension

prism model

silent period

sociolinguistic competence

stages of second language acquisition

strategic competence

time required for second language acquisition

Wong Fillmore's components crucial to SLA

■ professional conversations on practice

1. Discuss why school educators who are charged with the responsibility of educating CLD students often focus almost exclusively on the linguistic dimension of the prism model. Discuss how this dimension is interrelated with the other three dimensions of the prism model.
2. Discuss the ways in which first and second language acquisition compare and contrast. Discuss how the comparisons can be used as a foundation for teaching CLD students in grade-level classrooms.
3. Discuss which three environmental components are crucial to second language acquisition (SLA), according to Wong Fillmore (1991). Discuss in detail the implications of the third component for the teacher's organization of the classroom environment.

■ questions for review and reflection

1. Reflect on the process of first language acquisition. What percentage of first language acquisition is typically complete by age six? How long does it typically take an individual to acquire the remainder of her or his first language?
2. Define communicative competence. What is the crucial role of context in communicative competence?
3. Reflect on your own experiences in first language acquisition. At what age and in what ways did you acquire the phonology of your primary language? At what age and in what ways did you acquire the syntax of your primary language?

4. What are the stages of second language acquisition? Explain which stage you would consider the most difficult and why?

5. Reflect on the stages of SLA. Which stage(s) is associated with limited language production in L2? At what stage does the CLD student possess CALP capacities in L2 and on what basis did you arrive at that conclusion?

6. What is involved in understanding the semantics (i.e., word meaning) of a language? Why is the notion of language semantics so important to a constructivist language-learning environment?

7. When the CLD student is schooled only in L2, what period of time is typically required for the CLD student to attain grade-level norms?

8. When the CLD student has been schooled in L1 and L2, at least through the fifth or sixth grade, what period of time is typically required for the CLD student to attain grade-level norms?

suggested activities

Preservice Teachers

1. Negotiate with a teacher of CLD students in order to target three separate observations of one CLD student. Through observation, identify what level of second language acquisition the CLD student demonstrates. Based on your observations, provide a rationale as to why this student is at this specific level of second language acquisition. What characteristics were apparent? What successful modifications does the teacher provide for this specific level of second language acquisition? Discuss what further modifications you would add.

2. Sergio, a sixth grader of Cuban descent, demonstrates understanding of questions asked by the teacher but still cannot respond in English. At baseball practice, Sergio can be overheard occasionally discussing baseball figures with some of his native-English-speaking peers in the dugout. At what level of second language acquisition would you identify Sergio? What characteristics support your finding? Discuss three strategies an educator serving Sergio could use in his or her classroom to foster his English language acquisition.

3. Think ahead to your future practice as an educator of CLD students. List and describe three ways you will adapt and modify instruction or practice for CLD students at the various stages of second language acquisition represented in your classroom (choose at least three stages to highlight). How will this affect your instructional planning? What type of literacy environment will be helpful for your CLD students in order to promote literacy in the second language?

In-Service Teachers

1. Videotape a lesson that you teach to your class. Watch it at a later time and identify ways you have provided modifications for the various stages of English language acquisition represented in your classroom. Discuss the different ways you address the needs of your CLD students at the initial stages of English language acquisition and the needs of those who are more experienced or proficient with the English language. Are your current modifications successful? What challenges exist? List two ways to address the challenges and then describe at least two additional modifications you would make for students who are at varying language proficiency levels in English (L2).

2. Alba is a tenth-grade student from Bolivia who recently arrived in the United States. She has no language proficiency in English at all but has been schooled in Bolivia up to grade level in Spanish. Your colleagues are struggling with how to educate her appropriately within their own content areas. What role can native language support provide for Alba's academic success? List and explain five ways your colleagues can help lower the affective filter and meet Alba's academic language proficiency needs within their content areas.

3. Select a content area of focus. What linguistic challenges do you encounter within this content? Are language expectations unrealistic for the levels of language proficiency represented by students? Is there a real or perceived short-age of materials to enable L1 support? Collaborate with colleagues to brainstorm ways you can address these challenges for the various language proficiency levels represented in your classroom.

assessment tips and strategies

The following preassessment tips and strategies are drawn from the content of Chapters 1 through 3

PREASSESSMENT

Prior to instructional planning, educators should preassess the degree to which CLD students identify with their own cultures as well as the students' levels of acculturation. Preassessment determines the potential impact of the affective filter on the comprehensibility of instruction, and helps educators avoid instructional decisions that may be counterproductive. Moreover, constructivist learning environments highlight the need for teachers to preassess the prior knowledge and experiences CLD students bring to the classroom. Rather than assuming that classroom instruction and literacy activities should begin with basic skills and concepts, effective teachers of CLD students use the information gathered from preassessments to guide their instruction. Educators should preassess the following areas of the CLD student biography:

- Sociocultural/acculturation biography
- First language biography
- Second language biography
- Schooling/academic knowledge biography

Preassessment Tips

- Explore the student's cultural background and prior schooling experiences.
- Preassess levels of capacities and development in math, science, and social studies the student has achieved. Some of these will have been achieved mostly in L1 and in the native country. Others may have been achieved in the United States through instruction in L2.
- Identify what the CLD student's strongest subject has been.
- Preassess L1 and L2 proficiency.
- Preassess the CLD student's family dynamics and extended family resources.
- Preassess the CLD student's sociocultural realities, including recency of immigration.
- Provide opportunities for the CLD student to demonstrate what he or she understands in a variety of ways and through different media of discourse.
- Preassess the student's levels of literacy development in order to maximize what the CLD student already knows about the connections between print and meaning.

Preassessment Strategies

- Use informal conversations to improve teaching effectiveness, to reduce reteaching, to motivate students, and to avoid making assumptions regarding the learning and cognitive development of CLD students.
- Identify the prior knowledge your students bring to the classroom in order to make connections to the ideas and concepts you are teaching:
  —Use KWL charts.
  —Use freewriting and journal activities.
  —Ask questions and dialogue with the student about the topic.
  —Preassess the sociocultural realities of CLD students by conducting home visits.

Accommodation Readiness

In Part II, we encourage educators to preassess their readiness for the accommodative instruction of their CLD students based on their understanding of the four dimensions of the CLD student biography. In Chapter 4, we describe the ways in which programming decisions can serve to frame or restrict a teacher's instructional options for accommodation. On the other hand, in those districts and schools where CLD student programming is not already proscribed, programming decisions provide new opportunities for the appropriate instructional accommodation of CLD students. We also summarize research on program models as a basis for teacher advocacy. In Chapter 5, we introduce the accommodation readiness spiral as a framework for teachers' preassessments of their readiness to deliver mutually accommodative instruction given a specified programming decision. The spiral is a preassessment tool for readiness in the following areas: critical reflection, CLD students and families, environment, curriculum, instruction, application, and advocacy.

The information provided in this chapter will help the educator to:

- Discuss recent research on the effectiveness of program models for CLD students.
- Identify variables found to be strong predictors of academic success among CLD students.
- Describe the comparative effectiveness of program models for CLD students.
- Compare and contrast separate underlying proficiency (SUP) and common underlying proficiency (CUP).
- Describe the iceberg metaphor and what it illustrates.
- Contrast additive and subtractive bilingualism.
- Describe complicating variables that preclude bilingual programming in some school districts.
- Summarize the range of program models for CLD students.
- Analyze the pros and cons of various forms of the ESL program model.
- Discuss the possible applications and concerns associated with limited-use program models.

Changing Perspectives in Platform Development for Instructional Methods

Don't be afraid to take a big step. You can't cross a chasm in two small jumps. A person who follows in another's track leaves no footprints. Thus, the task is not so much to see what no one yet has seen, but to think what nobody yet has thought about that which everybody sees.

—Arthur Schopenhauer

chapter 4

chapter outline

Effective Program Models for CLD Students: Research and Analysis

Predictors of Academic Success among CLD Students

Findings of Research: The Case for Bilingual Education

Bilingual Education and the SUP–CUP Distinction

When the Ideal Is Not Ideal

Complicating Variables

Range of Program Models for CLD Students

English as a Second Language (ESL)

Transitional Bilingual Education

Developmental Bilingual Education

Two-Way Immersion

Limited-Use Program Models

Sociopolitical Foundations of Quality Programming

Lau v. Nichols (1974)

Castañeda v. Pickard (1981)

Plyler v. Doe (1982)

critical standards *Guiding Chapter Content*

TESOL/NCATE teacher standards reflect professional consensus on standards for the quality teaching of pre-K–12 CLD students. Additionally, the CEEE Guiding Principles and their accompanying indicators serve as a framework to assist practitioners, policymakers, and clients as they collaborate to enhance academic enrichment and language acquisition among CLD students. Therefore, in order to help educators understand how they might appropriately target and address national professional teaching standards in practice, we have designed the content of this chapter to reflect the following standards.

TESOL ESL Standards for P–12 Teacher Education Programs

TESOL ESL—Domain 1: Language. Candidates know, understand, and use the major concepts, theories, and research related to the nature and acquisition of language to construct learning environments that support ESOL [CLD] students' language and literacy development and content-area achievement. (p. 1)

- **Standard 1.b. Language acquisition and development.** Candidates understand and apply concepts, theories, research, and practice to facilitate the acquisition of a primary and a new language in and out of classroom settings. (p. 6)

  1.b.4. Create a secure, positive, and motivating learning environment. (p. 9)

  1.b.7. Recognize the importance of ESOL students' home languages and language varieties and build on these skills as a foundation for learning English. (p. 10)

Note: All TESOL/NCATE standards are cited from TESOL (2001). All Guiding Principles are cited from Center for Equity and Excellence in Education (1996).

CEEE Guiding Principles

Guiding Principle #1: Limited English proficient students are held to the same high expectations of learning established for all students.

1.1 School districts involve all stakeholders (e.g., English as a second language and bilingual teachers, core content teachers, parents of limited English proficient students, current or former students, community members, and others knowledgeable about instruction for English language learners) when developing policies, standards, and assessments, and when implementing staff development and instructional programs for students who are learning English as a second language.

1.2 School districts ensure representation by persons knowledgeable about instruction for English language learners (e.g., English as a second language and bilingual teachers, parents of limited English proficient students, current or former students, and community members) when developing policies, standards, and assessments, and when implementing staff development and instructional programs for the entire school population.

1.9 Teachers create classroom environments in which the efforts and contributions of every student are respected and encouraged. (p. 5)

Given that the United States is one of the few nations of the postmodern world that does not value multilingualism (Crawford, 2000), it is ironic that one of the distinguishing characteristics of the original thirteen colonies was multilingualism (Kloss, 1997). By 1800, Dutch, French, German, Russian, Spanish, and Swedish communities existed in the United States, many of which had established schools where students were either taught bilingually or exclusively in languages other than English (Brisk, 1981). In fact, not until the passage of the Nationality Act of 1906 did the United States begin to require male immigrants to pass an English proficiency test as a means of limiting immigration, primarily from China and southern Europe (Leibowitz, 1971).

The wave of bilingual education programs across the United States that occurred as a result of Supreme Court cases such as *Lau v. Nichols* (1974), as well as the passage of the Bilingual Education Act (1968), was effectively a rebirth of some appreciation for multilingualism in this country. Bilingual education is a type of educational program model for CLD students. Bilingual education programs for CLD students have emerged as a result of not only sociopolitical influences but also sociocultural influences. For example, Chicano and other Latino activists who were interested in school curricula that more actively reflected the contributions of Mexicans and Mexican Americans to U.S. society played a significant role in the reemergence of bilingual education during the 1960s and 1970s (Crawford, 1992a; Donato, 1997; Valdez & Steiner, 1972).

This chapter explores a variety of widely used program models for CLD students, including bilingual and ESL education, and it summarizes some of the recent research on the effectiveness of various program models for CLD students. This chapter also explores various sociopolitical influences on programming for CLD students. As we discuss these sociopolitical influences on programming, we emphasize the role of court precedent in shaping the range of program models available to school districts and their educators as well as the current characteristics of those models.

Effective Program Models for CLD Students: Research and Analysis

Without doubt, among the most robust and purposeful studies on program effectiveness conducted in the last quarter-century has been the multifaceted, multisite, longitudinal research of Virginia Collier and Wayne Thomas (Collier, 1987, 1988, 1989a, 1989b, 1992; Collier & Thomas, 1988, 1989; Thomas, 1992, 1994). This research primarily examined (a) the length of time needed for CLD students to reach grade-level academic proficiency in L2, (b) program and instructional variables influencing students' academic achievement, and (c) development toward cognitive academic language proficiency. From a similar study, the researchers also acquired, analyzed, and compared findings to the Ramírez data set (Ramírez, Yuen, Ramey, & Pasta, 1991). The school systems that were studied operated established, strongly supported programs with experienced staff. The sample consisted of approximately 42,000 students a year. The following are among the types of data analyzed: student background variables; program types; academic achievement, as measured by standardized tests; performance assessment measures; courses in which students were enrolled; and grade point average.

Predictors of Academic Success among CLD Students

Among all possible variables studied, the researchers found that three key predictors of academic success were more influential than any other factors analyzed. More predictive of CLD student success than poverty or socioeconomic status (SES), school location, status of the student's language group, or the student's background were these three variables:

- Cognitively complex academic instruction primarily delivered through the student's first language and maintained for as long as possible, but secondarily delivered through the second language for a portion of the school day.
- The intentional use of current approaches in the teaching of the academic curriculum through both L1 and L2, including active, discovery, and cognitively complex learning.
- Purposive changes in the sociocultural context of schooling, such as the integration of CLD students with English speakers in a context that is supporting and affirming for all; the development of an additive bilingual context, in which bilingual education is perceived and respected as a gifted and talented program for all students; and the transformation of majority and minority relations in school to a positive, safe environment for all students.

Not only were these three variables found critical to CLD student success, but it was also found that schools incorporating all three of these variables into their pedagogical structure were more likely to graduate CLD students who were academically successful in high school and in higher education.

Findings of Research: The Case for Bilingual Education

Among other analyses arising from this research were conclusions regarding program effectiveness, as summarized by Thomas and Collier (1997, 2002). In general, these conclusions are consistent with those of long-standing research on program models that target second language acquisition (SLA) and academic achievement among CLD students (General Accounting Office [GAO], 1987; Willig, 1981, 1985; Ramírez, 1992). These analyses examined the effectiveness of a number of program models for second language acquisition among CLD students, including ESL and bilingual education programs. Many of the conclusions Thomas and Collier (1997, 2002) arrived at are illustrated in the graphic summary depicted in Figure 4.1. The first of these conclusions reads as follows:

> For students who are schooled in the United States, from Kindergarten on, the elementary school program with the most success in language minority [CLD] stu-

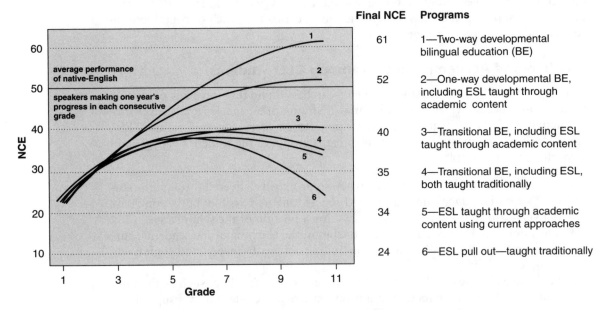

■ **figure 4.1** Patterns of K–12 English Learners' Long-Term Achievement in Normal Curve Equivalents (NCEs) on Standardized Tests in English Reading Compared across Six Program Models

(Results aggregated from a series of 4- to 8-year longitudinal studies from well-implemented, mature programs in five school districts.)

Source: Copyright Wayne P. Thomas and Virginia P. Collier (1997). Reprinted by permission.

dents' long-term academic achievement, as measured by standardized tests across all subject areas, is *two-way, developmental bilingual education* [italics added]. As a group, students in this program maintain grade-level skills in their first language at least through sixth grade and reach the 50th percentile of NCE in their second language generally after 4–5 years of schooling in both languages. They also generally sustain the gains they made when they reach the secondary level. (Thomas & Collier, 1997, p. 41)

Among characteristics also found to enhance the effectiveness of these two-way developmental bilingual education programs were the following: (a) the promotion of equal status for each language, (b) the fostering of parental involvement, and (c) the use of instructional approaches that stressed whole language, natural language acquisition in the content areas, and cooperative learning environments. These researchers also concluded that bilingual programs that remained in place at least through the sixth grade (i.e., late-exit bilingual programs) yielded substantial academic and cognitive development in L1 and L2 among CLD students. These CLD students were generally able to reach the 50th percentile of the normal curve equivalent (NCE) within four to seven years. The students also maintained their academic gains at the secondary level in content-area classes taught in English.

Finally, Thomas and Collier (1997) have summarized their findings regarding the length of time required for CLD students to reach the 50th percentile on standardized tests in the second (English) language. Briefly, their findings are as follows: When CLD students are schooled in L2 (English) in the United States and tested in L2, (a) students who have completed at least two to three years of schooling in their home country (that is, in L1) require five to seven years to reach the 50th percentile, and (b) students who completed no schooling in L1 require at least seven to ten years to reach this goal.

On the other hand, when CLD students are schooled bilingually in L1 and L2 in the United States, shorter periods of time are typically needed to reach the 50th percentile. For example, when CLD students are tested in L1, they tend to be at or above grade level. When they are tested in L2 (English), even students who would, by inference, otherwise require seven to ten years to reach the 50th percentile, generally need only four to seven years to reach the benchmark.

Accordingly, the conclusions of this longitudinal research, as reported in Thomas and Collier (1997, 2002), strongly indicate that the most effective programming for CLD students is bilingual education. Specifically, two-way developmental bilingual education programs were most effective in maintaining grade-level skills in the first language and in reducing the time needed to achieve at least the 50th percentile of NCE in the second language.

Bilingual Education and the SUP–CUP Distinction

Another strong rationale for bilingual education is provided by the SUP–CUP distinction, as proposed by Cummins (1981). According to Cummins, individuals who view the assimilation of immigrant students as a critical function of schools typically argue that the school must maximize experiences and practice with English if these students are to be successful in school. This view, according to Cummins (1981), is grounded in a perspective on language dynamics that he calls *separate underlying proficiency.*

As illustrated in Figure 4.2, the SUP perspective assumes that the two languages operate independently. Therefore, no transfer occurs between them. From this perspective, providing CLD students with resources, instruction, or literacy development in their native language would be a futile effort; increasing English language exposure is the path to English language development and, therefore, school success. This *interference hypothesis* holds that ongoing development in the first language so interferes with second language learning that effort should not be wasted in either native language support or ongoing development in the first language.

On the other hand, Cummins (1981) argues that although the two languages may seem separate on the surface, they are actually quite interdependent at the deeper level of cognitive functions. For example, it is a well-established finding that students who learn to read and write in their first language are able to readily transfer those abilities to a second language (Edelsky, 1982; Faltis, 1986; Hudelson & Serna, 1994; Krashen, 1996). This *transfer hypothesis* is equally valid in other subject domains, including math and science (Henderson & Landesman, 1992; Minicucci, 1996). Regarding the transfer of literacy skills, Brown (1994) has written:

> It has been common in second language teaching to stress the role of interference—that is, the interfering [e]ffects of the native language on the target (the second) language. . . . It is exceedingly important to remember, however, that the native

■ **f i g u r e   4 . 2**   Separate Underlying Proficiency (SUP)/ Common Underlying Proficiency (CUP)

Source: Adapted from Cummins (1981), pp. 23–24. Used by permission.

Relationships between First and Second Language Proficiency

When we build on the native language, we build on the potential for English language proficiency.

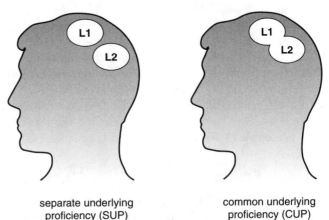

separate underlying proficiency (SUP)

common underlying proficiency (CUP)

theory *into Practice*

The *transfer hypothesis* (Cummins, 1981) holds that the CLD student who develops literacy in the first language is able to transfer those abilities to a second language. This transfer hypothesis is equally valid in other subject domains, including math and science (Henderson & Landesman, 1992; Minicucci, 1996). The transfer hypothesis is particularly important to the developing reading skills of CLD students. For example, research by Nagy, Garcia, Durgunoglu, and Hancin-Bhatt (1993) demonstrated a strong relationship between phonological awareness in Spanish and word recognition in English. Specifically, CLD students who could perform well on tests of phonological awareness in Spanish were more likely to demonstrate the ability to read English words and English-like pseudowords than were students who performed poorly on tests of phonological awareness in Spanish. The researchers have argued that this cross-language transfer pattern suggests that phonological awareness in L1 facilitates word recognition, schooling, and learning to read in L2.

■ *What classroom environment would you structure to foster cross-language transfer? What sorts of instructional strategies might build on the CLD student's literacy skills in L1 as a means to literacy development in L2?*

language of a second language learner is often positively transferred, in which case, the learner benefits from the facilitating effects of the first language. (p. 90)

For Brown, our natural tendency to notice the language errors that are inevitable for our CLD students often obscures our capacity to also notice the facilitating effects of the first language. Cummins (1981) maintains that these facilitating effects arise from a *common underlying proficiency* that, like an operating system, connects the two languages of a bilingual individual so that prior knowledge and academic skills in one language are transferable to learning and performance in another (see Figure 4.2).

A more graphic representation of these underlying and facilitating effects associated with CUP is provided by the *iceberg metaphor* (Cummins, 1981) of Figure 4.3. Moreover, these subsurface facilitating effects that may be associated with the notion of CUP also provide a strong rationale for bilingual education (Faltis & Hudelson, 1998) because what is learned well in one language need not be relearned in a second (Krashen, 1996).

Cummins (1981) has discussed this argument as a "less equals more" rationale for bilingual education. That is, CLD students will learn more English when they are first permitted to meaningfully participate in school activities that are provided in the language with which they are comfortable, the language that already equips them for oral and written communication. Thus, an environment that provides less English early on eventually leads to more English later, as students are able to first elaborate on shared language understandings, knowledge bases, and repertoires of literacy skills.

Nonetheless, there are at least two ways in which bilingualism, as a means to English (SLA) acquisition, may occur. *Subtractive* or *limited bilingualism* may

■ **figure 4.3** Iceberg
Metaphor of Second Language
Comprehension and Production

Source: Adapted from Cummins
(1981), p. 24. Used by permission.

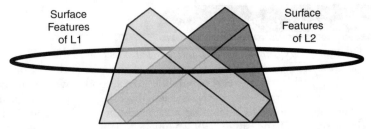

occur when the student's first language is gradually replaced by the more dominant
language (Cummins, 1979). In the case of subtractive bilingualism, students may
develop relatively low levels of academic proficiency in both languages. Conversely, *additive* or *proficient bilingualism* is associated with positive cognitive effects that enable the CLD student to attain high levels of proficiency in both
languages. Research has demonstrated that CLD students who are the product of
additive bilingualism outperform monolinguals on a variety of cognitive tasks
(Duncan & DeAvila, 1979; Kessler & Quinn, 1980).

■ When the Ideal Is Not Ideal

As the number of CLD students in the United States continues to grow at a phenomenal rate and the families of the students increasingly migrate to previously un-
affected regions of the country (as is increasingly the case with many midwestern
states), there are times, places, and situations in which the ideal is not always
ideal. That is, circumstances sometimes preclude the maximization of what research and analysis has demonstrated to be the most effective programming for
CLD students. Certainly, this scenario is often a frustrating, demoralizing set of circumstances. Such circumstances are especially exasperating for advocates of CLD
students and families who have dedicated their careers to making a difference for
these students. Nonetheless, it is a reality that must be reflectively and proactively

dilemmas *of Practice*

Mr. Jensen, a teacher at Great Plains High School,
offers his opinion about English language learners
while eating lunch in the teachers' lounge. He believes that students should be immersed in English-
only classes in order to learn English as quickly as
possible. He argues that his ancestors from Europe

did not have special services and they "did just
fine."

■ *If you were a colleague of Mr. Jensen's with the
knowledge you have now of additive and subtractive bilingualism, how would you respond?*

addressed if existing school-specific circumstances are to be confronted in a manner that maximizes the possibilities for CLD students.

Complicating Variables

As these dynamics manifest themselves each day in school systems throughout the nation, a variety of variables complicate the implementation of ideal programming for CLD students. These variables include the following examples.

Complicating Geographic Variables

Implementing the most effective programming for CLD students is difficult in rural school systems in which:

- The population of CLD students is increasing, but the population size remains insufficient to enable bilingual programming or program models.
- The increasing numbers of CLD students who speak a common first language (e.g., Spanish) would enable bilingual programming, but qualified bilingual teachers either do not reside in the region or community or cannot be successfully recruited to that rural region.
- The CLD student numbers justify bilingual programming, but the school system is geographically isolated from four-year degree-granting institutions to which paraprofessionals, who are interested in teacher education careers, can be persuaded to matriculate after their community college experiences.

Implementing the most effective programming for CLD students is difficult in urban school systems in which:

- The number of languages represented among CLD students is too varied to enable bilingual programming.
- The student distribution patterns across schools (court-ordered attendance patterns) preclude bilingual programming.

Complicating Sociopolitical Variables

National Level Sociopolitical initiatives at the national level, including the English-Only Movement/U.S. English (U.S. English, 1990), have argued that the nation confuses immigrants by offering them any language option except English—in schools, voting, documentation materials, and so forth. More recently, such groups have (despite the studies highlighted in this chapter) begun to argue that "no research" exists that supports bilingual education (Stevens, 2002).

State Level In states such as California, Arizona, and Colorado, repeated initiatives have sought to limit or eliminate bilingual education through referenda (Crawford, 1992b). In some states (e.g., California), such initiatives have limited, at least by title, the range of program models that can be implemented for CLD students (Crawford, 2000). Some states either do not offer a bilingual education endorsement or certification for school educators or have eliminated it from the endorsements or certificates that school educators can acquire. These circumstances limit the pool of qualified educators available to implement bilingual education.

Local Level   In certain regions and localities of the country, the lack of advocacy for the rights of CLD students to an appropriate education has fostered district programming policies that have effectively limited the availability of appropriate program models for CLD students. For a variety of reasons, many parents of CLD students are unable to successfully advocate for appropriate and effective programming for their children (de Lopez & Montalvo-Cisneros, 1986; Escamilla, 1999; Kang, Kuehn, & Herrell, 1996; Ovando, Collier, & Combs, 2003). Reasons for this situation include:

- Language differences
- Parental or caregiver work schedules
- Parent–teacher conference schedules and limited home visits by school educators and counselors
- Prior negative experiences with schools or teachers
- Culture-based deference to teachers in matters of schooling, instruction, and assessment
- Perceptions of cultural or language deficiency
- Shortage of school educators of that cultural or ethnic group, especially school counselors or outreach staff
- Perceptions that school is not a welcoming environment

As these examples demonstrate, although research has informed our understanding of effective and ideal programming for CLD students, other variables of environment, circumstance, and situation sometimes limit our capacity to implement the ideal. Therefore, it is important for us as educators to become acquainted with the more inclusive range of program models available for CLD students.

■ Range of Program Models for CLD Students

Although the range of program models available to CLD students across the United States is broad, it is perhaps not as diverse as the many titles by which similar programs are often labeled. Accordingly, the subject of programming for CLD students may at times seem complex and confusing. Yet a foundational understanding of program models is essential to the selection of appropriate instructional methods for CLD students.

This description of program models endeavors to simplify the seeming complexities of program labels while focusing on four basic aspects of each program model described: (a) the *foundations* of the program model, (b) key program *characteristics,* (c) *essentials* of program implementation, and (d) *concerns* regarding that program model. Consistent with the findings on program effectiveness described by Thomas and Collier (1997) and illustrated in Figure 4.1, these descriptions of program models proceed from least effective to most effective. Four general-use program models are discussed in detail, followed by an overview of two additional, limited-use program models.

English as a Second Language (ESL)

ESL programs, also referred to as ESOL (English to speakers of other languages) models are, in the literature of the field, variously considered (a) crucial components of any bilingual program (Ovando & Collier, 1998), (b) programs of a transitional perspective, grounded in a philosophy suggesting that the use of native language retards English development (Faltis & Hudelson, 1998), or (c) a model of immersion (that is, immersion in L2) education (Linquanti, 1999). Various types of ESL programming exist. ESL content models are typically (but not necessarily) implemented in self-contained classrooms (e.g., structured immersion), usually for the full school day. ESL pull-out models require auxiliary classrooms and teachers for varying periods of time during the school day and are therefore the most expensive (but least effective—see Figure 4.1 program models [Crawford, 1997; Thomas & Collier, 1997]). Last, ESL subject models are less frequently implemented and require from one to two periods of classroom instruction a day.

ESL program models, although less effective with CLD students than certain bilingual education programs (e.g., two-way bilingual), often arise as a result of complicating variables, including geographic and sociopolitical variables. For example, at the geographic level, bilingual program models are often not possible in rural school districts that have moderately high numbers of CLD students but are unable to recruit qualified bilingual educators. Sociopolitical variables may also complicate the use of bilingual program models. For example, some midwestern states do not offer school educators an endorsement in bilingual education. Therefore, even when districts have a sufficient number of interested local and bilingual educators (e.g., paraprofessionals) for the development of a self-generated certification program, these states preclude the endorsement of educators in bilingual education. In such districts, an ESL program model (or such a model bolstered by auxiliary native language support) is sometimes the only adequate alternative.

Foundations

ESL programming tends to be grounded in the philosophy that through appropriate instructional support (including scaffolding, guarded vocabulary, conceptualization, hands-on cooperative learning, etc.), CLD students can be transitioned to an instructional and learning environment that offers no significant first language support (Faltis & Hudelson, 1998; Linquanti, 1999). Therefore, the model is grounded in the premise that the teacher need not be fluent in the student's first language and that comprehensible input in L2 will carry the day. Although stronger types of ESL programming emphasize second language learning through content-area instruction, other types treat language learning in isolation from content-area learning. ESL pull out, though it is the most implemented type of ESL, is also the least effective (Thomas & Collier, 1997).

Characteristics

ESL program models vary significantly in the extent to which they emphasize clearly delineated language and content objectives. Certain types, including integrated content-based ESL and sheltered instruction, strongly emphasize both categories of objectives. Others, most notably ESL pull out, typically treat language learning in isolation and as a compensatory issue, paying little or no attention to content objectives (Chambers & Parrish, 1992; Faltis & Hudelson, 1998).

In contrast to "sink or swim" or extremely limited ESL programming, effective models of ESL programming (e.g., CALLA instruction [Chamot & O'Malley, 1994], sheltered content instruction [Echevarria & Graves, 2003], etc.) typically emphasize frequent opportunities for language interaction, the scaffolding of instruction, and constructivist activities focused on the derivation of meaning from context, language, and support structures (Echevarria & Graves, 2003; Linquanti, 1999). A focus on language interactions typically involves frequent and sometimes extended opportunities for teacher–student and student–student communication at all literacy levels: listening, speaking, reading, and writing. A language interaction environment that reduces the affective filter and emphasizes the construction of meaning from these experiences is most favorable.

Through scaffolding, teachers restructure instruction to a level that encourages student success until the learner is ready for increasingly higher levels of understanding. Scaffolding might involve contextualization of the lesson, peer-to-peer interactions, elaboration of prior knowledge or student responses, outlines of the material to be covered in a lesson, and more. Constructivist student activities in an ESL environment are made meaningful through the use of hands-on or application activities that directly relate to the grade-level or content-area curriculum. For example, a lesson on estimation can be rendered more meaningful when enriched by a hands-on activity involving estimates about the number of items in a jar, followed by the actual counting of those items.

Essentials and Concerns

Effective ESL program models demand a number of prerequisites to ensure the likelihood that CLD students are able to comprehend the instruction and prove successful in both content-area and language learning. To achieve this level of effectiveness, it is first essential that ESL instruction be intentionally grounded in the grade-level or content-area curriculum. Second, school educators must receive adequate professional development to deliver appropriately restructured instruction that scaffolds or shelters the curriculum to ensure comprehension, learning, and application (Herrera & Fanning, 1999; Murry, 1996; Murry & Herrera, 1999). Finally, authentic alternative assessments are crucial to the measurement of both process and product gains in language, acculturation, and content-area learning among CLD students. At minimum, such assessments should encompass criterion-referenced, incremental, and informal measures, including rubrics, self-assessments, and portfolios. Whenever possible, alternative assessments in L1 should also be incorporated, including journals, one-on-one (translated) discussions, interviews, and so forth.

Administrative buy-in and support of the program model is essential to the effectiveness of ESL programs. Site-based administrators must prove at least as well informed and trained as the school and classroom educators who are serving CLD students. Informed administrators are capable of creating a vision for the program, monitoring its appropriate implementation, and evaluating both classroom assessments and program effectiveness (Herrera & Fanning, 1999).

The following represent some of the concerns regarding ESL program models. Such programs, especially ESL pull out, can prove costly because resource teachers must be recruited, trained, supported, and evaluated. Additionally, although a few ESL programs make provision for some level of auxiliary native language support, typically these programs do not support or further students' ongoing CALP development in L1. The potential consequences of this omission are one reason why ESL pull-out programs are the least effective of all program models. ESL pull-out programs also tend to stigmatize CLD students while isolating them from critical content-area instruction. Finally, some ESL programs may not be focused on both literacy development and language development in L2, and ESL educators may inadvertently engage in assumptions about the student's level of BICS versus CALP proficiency in L2.

Transitional Bilingual Education

Largely due to long-standing patterns of federal funding for bilingual education, transitional programs (also referred to as early-exit programs [Ramírez, 1992]) are the most common form of bilingual programming. In the United States, transitional bilingual programs provide students with instruction in their native language for all subject areas, as well as instruction in L2 (English) as a second language. Nonacademic classes such as music, art, and physical education might also be delivered in L2 (Medina, 1995). However, this program of transitional instruction is sustained for only a limited number of years (typically two to three years in the United States). Students are then gradually transitioned into L2-only instruction. Although the native language of CLD students is transitionally supported by this program model, most transitional bilingual programs favor a goal of instruction in L2 (English) as soon as it is feasible (Genesee, 1999; Ovando & Collier, 1998).

Foundations

Transitional bilingual education emphasizes the mastery of grade-appropriate academic skills and knowledge that are initially attained through the student's first language. Concomitantly, the model seeks to accelerate English (L2) language development so that students can be transitioned to English-only grade-level classrooms more rapidly. As with other bilingual programs, one key rationale for the transitional model rests with the SUP–CUP distinction and the transfer hypothesis (Cummins, 1981, 1991). That is, many literacy skills and a great deal of knowledge acquired in the first language will transfer to the second. In particular, students learn to read and write with the least degree of difficulty when they learn to do so in the language they already know. Too often the reading and writing aspects of literacy development are postponed until the student can comprehend and speak English (Anderson, 1999; Cooper, 1986; Cummins, 2001b; Cunningham, Moor, Cunningham, & Moore, 1995; National Reading Panel, 2000; Peregoy & Boyle, 2001; Pearson, 1984; Snow, Burns, & Griffin, 1998). In a transitional program, students can begin to read and write immediately in their first language as part of content-area learning. Moreover, the literacy skills attained by this approach will transfer to English (Cummins, 1981), according to the dynamics of the transfer hypothesis.

The content-area instruction of CLD students through their first language as they are gradually learning English allows the students to perform on par with their grade-level peers in the content areas because they are learning in the language with which they are already comfortable. This transitional support in the early years of schooling not only lowers the affective filter but also increases motivation and confidence in academic learning. Furthermore, Genesee (1999) has noted that early instruction in the student's first language increases the likelihood that the student's parents, who often speak no English, will be involved in the educational process. The native language support provided in the content areas by the transitional model allows the student to maintain ongoing CALP development in L1 as he or she transitions into literacy development in the second language (Cummins, 1981, 1991; Thomas & Collier, 1997).

Characteristics

Transitional bilingual programming provides students with native language support in the content areas as they are learning English. Along with this provision of the model, content-area instruction is also typically sheltered during the transition period (Genesee, 1999). The subsequent transition is often initiated with mathematical instruction in L2 (especially computations), followed by reading, then writing and science, and then social studies. Most transitional programs begin in kindergarten or first grade and target oral proficiency in L2 within two years. These programs also typically target all-English instruction by the third grade for those who began in kindergarten, and the fourth grade for those who began transitional bilingual education in the first grade.

Essentials and Concerns

Transitional bilingual education is built on the premise that CLD students can learn to read and write in their first language and master grade-level skills, content, and concepts from subject-area instruction in that language. Accordingly, skillful and effective instruction in the first language is a programming prerequisite of paramount importance. This model relies on effective transitional instruction that (a) is gradual, (b) capitalizes on the transfer of reading and writing skills, and

fallacies AND facts

Mrs. Bodoni is in her second year as an eighth-grade social studies teacher. She has had limited experience working with CLD students since her district implemented an ESL pull-out program. Now the school district has informed grade-level content-area teachers that all CLD students will be transitioned to grade-level classrooms. She is panicking because she feels she will need to "dumb down" the curriculum for the CLD students in her content area and provide lower-level texts in order for them to be able to understand social studies content. She wonders how she can continue to provide challenging content for her native English speakers while having to provide easier content for her CLD students.

Fallacy: When CLD students are in the content-area classroom, content has to be watered down through the use of lower-grade-level material and simple, easy-to-complete exercises. Otherwise, CLD students will not find academic success.

Fact: CLD students typically bring a rich academic background with them when they have been schooled in their native countries up to grade level. The aca-

demic language (cognitive academic language proficiency) is what must be developed and scaffolded, not the curriculum. CLD students continue to need challenging content as much as native-English-speaking students. Higher-level thinking must also be a target of classroom instruction for all students. As for Mrs. Bodoni, she should first review the content of her current social studies curriculum. She can then use other proficient bilingual peers to help in the clarification of concepts, or ask a bilingual paraprofessional or parent volunteer to assist her in making instructional connections for her CLD students.

■ *What key concepts, ideas, and relationships should all students learn from Mrs. Bodoni's social studies class? These should be the focus of her instruction, with appropriate adaptations and modifications for language learning among CLD students. Among such instructional adaptations that have proven effective with CLD students are cooperative learning, hands-on experiences, role playing, visuals, reenactments, and outlining of key concepts and relationships to be learned.*

(c) minimizes the risk of raising students' affective filters. Ultimately, instruction must also be scaffolded or sheltered so that the academic content is made comprehensible to the students while the skills to be developed are introduced in an incremental, process-oriented manner. For these reasons, highly qualified instructors are essential to the effective implementation of transitional bilingual education.

Successful transitional programming also requires a challenging curriculum, demanding standards, and accurate assessment. Because students are receiving content-area instruction in their native language, and because this structure is provided for a limited period, the curriculum that grounds the instruction should stretch the learner toward new levels of performance (Ramírez, 1992; Linquanti, 1999). Rigorous standards and expectations are one way to better ensure that students attain such performance. Nonetheless, student assessments, particularly in the area of second language development, must be carefully implemented and accurately interpreted in order to ensure that students are progressing and to gauge what additional support will be needed when the students exit from the program.

Perhaps the most worrisome problem with transitional bilingual education is the limited time the students are allowed to transition to L2 (English). The premises on which this aspect of the model rests are not consistent with the research (please refer to Figure 4.1 for an illustration of these findings) regarding the time required for CLD students to attain grade-level proficiency and skills in the second language (Thomas & Collier, 1997, 2002). Also of concern is the fact that transitional bilingual programs are often perceived, by both students and staff, as segregated, compensatory education (Faltis & Hudelson, 1998; Ovando & Collier, 1998). Such programming may be viewed as stigmatizing, maintaining the status quo, or perpetuating a perception of a lower-class status among CLD students.

Developmental Bilingual Education

Developmental bilingual education, unlike the transitional program model, is more consistent with what we know about how long it takes CLD students to reach high levels of CALP development in L2 (Thomas & Collier, 1997, 2002; Ramírez, 1992). Despite the fact that developmental bilingual programming is far less prevalent than either the transitional bilingual or ESL program models, it is more effective (Thomas & Collier, 1997—see Figure 4.1) and less likely to foster a perception of compensatory education (Genesee, 1999; Linquanti, 1999). Also referred to as maintenance or late-exit (Ramírez, 1992) bilingual education, developmental programming enriches the education of CLD students by using both L1 and L2 for academic instruction. First introduced in the 1960s, the title was changed from "maintenance" to "developmental" (approximately 1984) in order to avoid negative political interpretations of the model as a perpetuator of first language maintenance (Genesee, 1999). In a developmental program, CLD students receive content-area instruction in their first and second languages through all grade levels provided by their school system. Most studies of the model indicate that a minimum of five to six years in such a program are required to demonstrate high academic achievement among participating students (Collier, 1992; Cummins, 1996; Thomas & Collier, 1997). Some developmental program models are implemented in grades K–12, and a smaller number also enrich the curriculum with lessons from the study of cross-cultural dynamics.

Foundations

At the foundational level, developmental bilingual education is well grounded in each of the dimensions of the prism model, a holistic model for CLD student education developed by Thomas and Collier (1997) and detailed in Chapter 1. From a sociocultural perspective, developmental programming clearly communicates to CLD students the value of both the cultural and the linguistic resources they bring to the classroom (Cummins, 1998). The model also better facilitates the involvement of parents (who may not speak English) in the student's socialization and education. At the cognitive and academic levels of the prism model, developmental bilingual education acknowledges and builds on research (Ramírez, 1992; Thomas

& Collier, 1997, 2002) that stresses the importance of using L1 to develop cognitive capacities and academic knowledge and skills, which may then be transferred to the second language. From a linguistic viewpoint, developmental programming is consistent with what we know about CALP development in L1, language transfer, the threshold hypothesis, and second language acquisition.

Characteristics

Typically, developmental programming begins with kindergarten or first grade, and the program expands to include one additional grade each year thereafter. The critical subject areas are taught through both English (L2) and the student's first language (L1) for as many grades as the structure of the school system can support. Although most developmental models emphasize Spanish and English, other first languages can also be supported, including Chinese, Korean, Navajo, and Vietnamese. Whatever the primary language of programming, students at virtually any level of proficiency in L2 can be served in the same developmental classroom. Moreover, full academic language proficiency in both languages is the goal of developmental programming. The exploration of information and knowledge across academic domains is targeted in both languages, as sheltered instructional techniques are often used to scaffold academic instruction in L2.

Developmental bilingual education also seeks to minimize perceptions of subtractive, compensatory education by emphasizing content-area learning in two languages, with proficiency in each valued as an additive objective. The first language is no longer treated merely as a bridge to the second, but is valued as an asset with various unique advantages (Cummins, 1998; Padilla & Gonzalez, 2001). The developmental model can also prove especially beneficial to students in those regions of the country where multilingualism reaps certain economic rewards.

Essentials and Concerns

First and foremost, school educators who are critical to developmental programming must receive adequate professional development in effective methods, strategies, and techniques of language and content-area instruction. Teachers who instruct in effective developmental programs use content-area curriculum, content-based instruction, hands-on and scaffolding materials, presentations that target a variety of learning strategies, peer and mixed groupings, extensive collaboration with paraprofessionals, multimodal presentations, computer resources, interactive and discovery learning techniques, multicultural resource tools, and more (Genesee, 1999; Moll, Amanti, & Gonzalez, 1992). Therefore, ongoing professional development for all staff, including qualified bilingual educators, is essential to classroom effectiveness in developmental bilingual education.

Successful implementation of developmental programming also requires both integration and separation. On the one hand, students must be integrated, regardless of their language proficiency in the language of instruction, in order to maximize learning from more capable peers. Heterogeneous student groupings are often essential in the content areas. On the other hand, the languages of instruction must be clearly separated in developmental programming. Language mixing and concurrent translation should be avoided in order to maximize the development of proficiency in each language of the program model. Most important, these two seeming disparate goals of integration and separation must remain the target for the duration of the program. Research has consistently demonstrated that CLD students need four to seven years in such a program to acquire full proficiency in all aspects of both languages and to attain full parity with language majority students in the content areas (Collier, 1992, 1995b; Ramírez, 1992; Thomas & Collier, 1997).

Among general concerns associated with developmental bilingual education are those regarding the following groups of students: (a) students who enter the program late, (b) students who are highly transient, and (c) students who exit the program early. It is often difficult to maintain the continuity of the program model across grade levels and schools. Certainly, a district-level coordinator is critical. A developmental program coordinator who collaborates closely with program teachers, program support staff, building-level administrators, and resource agents for the district is even more beneficial.

Two-Way Immersion

Two-way immersion programs, also known as two-way bilingual or dual language immersion programs, are an increasingly popular way to attract public support for multilingualism. The two-way model offers integrated language and academic instruction for both CLD students and native English speakers. Among the objectives of two-way programming are first and second language proficiency, strong academic performance in the content areas, cross-cultural celebration, and crosslingual understandings (Christian, 1994; Cummins, 2001b).

Cummins (2001b) has argued that two-way programs may offer advocates the best hope of transforming the rhetoric of what he calls the "Us versus Them" discourse, which characterizes the bilingual debate. In making this argument, Cummins cites the work of Porter (1990) and Glenn and LaLyre (1991) in noting the mutually beneficial advantages of two-way programming, including a language-rich environment, a climate of cross-cultural respect, high expectations for every child, genuine bilingualism for the majority population, mutual learning and enrichment, and comparatively manageable implementation costs.

Two-way programming integrates language learning with content-based instruction. Subject-area instruction is delivered to all students through both English and the language of CLD students. Most two-way programs begin in kindergarten or first grade and extend through the completion of elementary school. All students enrolled benefit from an additive bilingual environment because each language is engaged in the development of content knowledge.

Foundations

In general, two-way immersion programs are grounded in research and analysis pertinent to both first and second language acquisition (Bley-Vroman, 1988; Chomsky, 1966; Ney & Pearson, 1990; Ramírez, 1992; Thomas & Collier, 1997) and the dynamics of cross-cultural and multilingual interactions (Gleason, 1961; Lindholm, 1992; Veeder & Tramutt, 2000; Whorf, 1956). From the linguistic perspective, research has indicated that instruction in the second language, which is balanced with first language support, tends to yield higher levels of achievement among CLD students than instruction delivered only in the second language (Genesee, 1999; Thomas & Collier, 1997). Second, academic knowledge and skills acquired in the first language facilitate the acquisition of new knowledge and skills in the second language (Collier, 1989b). Additionally, research indicates that a second language (i.e., English) is best acquired by CLD students, especially non-English-speaking (NES) students, only after their first language is firmly established (Edelsky, 1982; Lanauze & Snow, 1989; Saunders & Goldenberg, 1999). Quality immersion programming for native English speakers enables students to develop advanced levels of L2 proficiency without compromising academic performance or their first language development (Genesee, 1983, 1987; Swain & Lapkin, 1982).

From the sociocultural perspective, two-way immersion programming builds on the notion of mutually more capable peers (Vygotsky, 1978). That is, CLD students who are acquiring English will benefit from social and academic interaction with native-English-speaking students who are more capable in English. In like manner, native-English-speaking students who participate in a two-way program benefit from their CLD peers, who are more capable in their first language and more knowledgeable about their native culture and life outside of the United States. At the same time, CLD students serving in this capacity for native-English-speaking students gain self-esteem, motivation, and an enhanced level of pride in their own culture (Lindholm, 1992).

Characteristics

Two basic versions of the two-way model have gained popularity in the United States—the 90–10 model and the 50–50 model. Both versions target bilingualism as the ultimate goal, and both focus on the core academic curriculum. The 90–10 version of two-way programming first targets development in the language of the CLD student. For example, in a Spanish–English program, grade 1 students would receive 90 percent of their instruction in Spanish from their classroom teachers. The remaining 10 percent of instruction, delivered in English, would emphasize oral language development in English. Grade 2 instruction in English would increase to 20 percent, with the addition of special courses such as music or art, taught in English. Nominal literacy development activities in English would also be initiated and might stress choral reading or chants. By the end of the school year for grade 2, English instruction time would increase to 30 percent with the addition to the curriculum of formal English instruction. Over the course of grades 4, 5, and 6, the instructional time devoted to English would increase to 50 percent. However, initially, math, language arts, and special courses would receive English instruction, while science and social studies were taught in Spanish. Gradually, each of the subject-area domains would be taught in English. Ultimately, the program will attain a 50:50 ratio of language instruction and maintain that level for the duration of the program. The 50–50 version of two-way programming is similar in all respects to the 90–10, except that initial instruction begins at a 50:50 ratio.

Essentials and Concerns

Critical to either version of two-way immersion programming are carefully planned lessons to maintain the ratio of instruction in each language, as well as the separation of languages. Concurrent translation should not be employed and lessons should never be repeated. Nonetheless, concepts taught in one language may be reinforced in another through a spiraling curriculum and thematic units. The time of day or subject areas might be used to alternate the language of instruction (Ovando & Collier, 1998).

Among other criteria integral to the success of two-way programming are the following: instruction that is grounded in the core academic curriculum, a minimum of four to six years of bilingual instruction, language arts instruction in both languages that targets all four aspects of literacy development, the instructional separation of the two languages, instruction in the non-English language for at least 50 percent of the time (up to a maximum of 90 percent in the early elementary grades), administrative understanding of and support for the program model, an additive bilingual learning environment, high levels of parental involvement, and highly qualified instructional personnel (Christian, 1994; Lindholm, 1990; Genesee, 1999). Also important to the success of this program model is a balanced ratio of students who speak each language. Although local dynamics may make it difficult to comply with this criterion, a 50:50 ratio of students is ideal, and a 70:30 ratio should not be exceeded.

Although this is the most effective of the program models discussed in this chapter (Thomas & Collier, 1997—see Figure 4.1), certain concerns related to two-way immersion programming are worth noting. First, some programs experience great difficulty with the recruitment of native-English-speaking students and greater difficulties with retention. Likewise, the parents of these students may prove enthusiastic at program conception and belligerent or apathetic as the program progresses. Second, native-English-speaking students may acquire a privileged status as the program progresses, to the detriment of the CLD students involved (Valdes, 1997). Finally, the instructional language used in the early grades of the two-way program may be inappropriately or inadvertently modified by classroom instructors in order to accommodate native-English-speaking students (Valdes, 1997). Such a situation is detrimental to participating CLD students, who may be shortchanged in their L1 literacy development.

Limited-Use Program Models

This section discusses two limited-use program models that are often the subject of literature and discussion in the arena of second language learning. Newcomer programs are frequently a response to unexpected demographic trends in the United States, especially in rural school systems. Second or foreign language immersion programs are most prevalent in Canada, but they have also been established in the United States, particularly in Hawaii.

Newcomer Programs

Newcomer programs are often a response to increasing numbers of CLD students, especially secondary students, in school systems that have previously experienced little or no cultural or linguistic diversity in classrooms. Some newcomer programs serve CLD students for as long as four years, others for as little as forty-five days. Although there are some programs at the elementary school level, many more are a response to increasing numbers of middle and high school immigrant students who have limited proficiency skills in their primary language (Genesee, 1999; Short & Boyson, 1998). Some newcomer programs are housed in the student's home school (by designated attendance area), and students in these schools also participate in special classes outside the program (e.g., art and music). Others are housed in separate locations; in these situations, CLD students are not transitioned to the home school until the newcomer program is considered complete. Most employ a set of courses distinct from those of traditional language transition programs. Many of these courses are designed to facilitate students' social and cultural integrations into U.S. life; others are formulated to instruct students with limited literacy skills (Genesee, 1999; Linquanti, 1999).

A variety of concerns are associated with newcomer programs (Feinberg, 2000; Linquanti, 1999; Trueba, 1994). Some programs approach complex content-area subject matter in a diluted manner. Other newcomer models target rapid mainstreaming without sufficient time for the development of English language proficiency. Some programs are largely a variation of the sink-or-swim method. Several recent variations of this program model focus on a social skills–school rules orientation to English language learning but neglect literacy development. Finally, some newcomer programs offer insufficient access to academic content while segregating students from their grade-level peers.

Ovando and Collier (1998) report that because some newcomer programs purport to implement a Canadian model but omit native language support for CLD students, they are in effect mislabeled as *structured immersion programs*. Such programs might substitute materials designed for students with learning disabilities for materials specifically designed to introduce students to the English language in a structured, step-by-step manner. Programs such as these have not proven effective with CLD students in the United States (Ovando & Collier, 1998).

Second or Foreign Language Immersion

Second or foreign language immersion is similar to two-way immersion in that native-English-speaking students are immersed in a second language as the medium of academic instruction and social interaction. It differs from two-way in that CLD students are not involved in the program. In second or foreign immersion programs, the second language is used for at least 50 percent and up to 100 percent of the academic instruction and the program may be implemented in the elementary or secondary grades (Genesee, 1999). Such programs promote second language literacy, cultural enrichment, and grade-level achievement in the academic content areas. The findings of research on the model indicate that long-term program participation does not interfere with first language development or academic achievement for native-English-speaking students (Genesee, 1987; Swain & Lapkin, 1991).

Nonetheless, it should be noted that, unlike CLD students, grade-level students who typically participate in such immersion programs (many of which have been implemented in Canada) frequently exhibit the following characteristics: (a) they have been socialized in the dominant (not the subordinate) culture, (b) their first language is the dominant language, and (c) many have already experienced significant levels of literacy acquisition in their first language before undertaking the immersion program. Indeed, although second language immersion programs were not specifically designed for CLD students, such programs have on occasion been inappropriately implemented with CLD students whose first language is not the dominant language.

Early immersion programs are initiated in kindergarten and typically extend through the end of elementary school. Late or secondary immersion programs offer intensive academic instruction through the second language for one to two years and usually begin in the seventh grade. Among concerns associated with second or foreign language immersion programs are the following: Teachers must demonstrate nativelike proficiency in the target language, inaccurate translations may cause problems in creating challenging instructional materials, such programming is sometimes inappropriately applied to CLD students, and support from the home and community are critical to program success.

Are You Aware?

Tamara Lucas (1999) argues that successful secondary schools proactively address the needs of adolescent CLD students by providing opportunities for CLD students to develop both their English proficiencies and their native language proficiencies as part of the challenging expectations in the content areas. Lucas also asserts that concentrating solely on the development of English language proficiency creates an academic gap that continues to widen as secondary students fall further and further behind their native-English-speaking counterparts. Unfortunately, this academic gap may be a contributing factor to the dropout rate.

Crandall (1998) discusses the characteristics of effective secondary programs for second language learners. Among these identified characteristics are the following:

- The program emphasizes native language literacy skills for students with less prior education.
- The program offers grade-level content courses in students' native languages for students with more developed literacy skills in the native language.
- The program offers ESL courses to all English-language-learning students, regardless of schooling background.
- The program offers CLD students the opportunity to move into sheltered instruction classes, in which subject matter is taught through strategies that make content more comprehensible.

■ Voices from the Field

"As a school leader it is very important to find out exactly what type of programs are being implemented in the school for ELL [CLD] students. It is important to understand which programs are developing and which are transitioning. We must know if these programs are designed to develop basic intercommunication skills only, or adding cognitive and academic skills.

I will make sure that my bilingual program is not subtractive but additive. This program will develop first language through content areas so that knowledge will simply transfer with the acquiring of the second language.

I will ask that teachers not only align their teachings with the standards and benchmarks but that they also use their experience and creativity to enrich lessons. These brain-based lessons will promote higher levels of critical thinking.

I will set high expectations of all students and staff. Staff will receive professional development on best programs, methodologies, and practices that will support ELL students. I will personally keep my staff up-to-date with research that supports our vision. Parents will be informed of our goals and mission to reconstruct our school to meet their children's needs. They will play an active role as supporters and consultants."

■ *Wriel Chavira, educational leadership candidate, Project SILTS, Las Cruces, NM; Manhattan, KS; Portales, NM*

■ Sociopolitical Foundations of Quality Programming

Several pieces of federal legislation have laid a foundation in law and policy for quality programming in the service of CLD students. Among these is the Bilingual Education Act of 1968. It authorized federal funding to develop instructional materials for use in bilingual education; provide professional development for teachers, aides, and counselors; and establish, implement, and maintain special programs for second language learners. The 1984 reauthorization of this act added several new categories of funding, including monies for family literacy, special populations (e.g., bilingual special education), academic excellence (to replicate exemplary models), developmental bilingual education, and special alternative programs (e.g., for low-incidence language groups). Title VII of the Improving America's Schools Act (IASA, formerly ESEA, the Elementary and Secondary Education Act) moved programming away from remedial, compensatory models of bilingual education toward enrichment and innovation, comprehensive school reform, and the systemwide integration of ESL/bilingual programs into the core of the schooling system.

Nonetheless, much of the impetus behind quality programming for CLD students in the United States rests with the court precedents established by a number of critical rulings over the past forty or more years. Among these judicial precedents,

The English-only movement (EOM) poses a substantial threat to bilingual education and equitable education for all students. English-only ideology directly contradicts the American democratic ideals of social justice and equality that supposedly unite our society despite our differences (Mora, 2002). In 1998, English-only advocates persuaded California voters to pass Proposition 227, also known as "English for the Children" or the Unz Initiative, which banned bilingual education or instruction in any language other than English in California public schools (Mora, 2002). Such legislation ignores current research regarding appropriate programming for CLD students and prohibits quality programming that is essential to second language acquisition and academic success among these students. The widespread attempts to pass legislation similar to Proposition 227 reveal the sociocultural and sociopolitical threats that exist to the appropriate education for CLD students in U.S. society.

at least three have been pivotal in the development of quality programming standards for CLD students, and they arise from the following cases: *Lau v. Nichols* (1974), *Castañeda v. Pickard* (1981), and *Plyler v. Doe* (1982). An overview of the rulings established in each of these cases follows, with an emphasis on foundations for quality programming.

Lau v. Nichols (1974)

In what began as a class action suit filed on behalf of Chinese-speaking children attending San Francisco schools, the case of *Lau v. Nichols* eventually proceeded to the U.S. Supreme Court, which, on the basis of the Civil Rights Act of 1964, rendered the following opinion:

> There is no equality of treatment merely by providing students with the same facilities, textbooks, teachers, and curriculum; for students who do not understand English are effectively foreclosed from any meaningful education.
>
> Basic English skills are at the very core of what these public schools teach. Imposition of a requirement that, before a child can effectively participate in the education program, he must have already acquired those basic skills is to make a mockery of public education. We know that those who do not understand English are certain to find their classroom experiences wholly incomprehensible and in no way meaningful. (*Lau v. Nichols*, 1974)

Although this ruling did not define "meaningful education" and did not mandate bilingual education, the ruling had a direct and immediate impact on the proliferation of bilingual education programming in the United States (Teitelbaum & Hiller, 1977). Additionally, this judicial precedent provided a powerful impetus for the passage of the Equal Educational Opportunity Act (1974). This act not only provided legislative support for the Court's ruling in *Lau,* but it also prompted the U.S. Office for Civil Rights (OCR) to enhance the oversight of programming designed for CLD students and funded with federal support.

Castañeda v. Pickard (1981)

The *Castañeda* case charged the school district in Raymondville, Texas, with violation of CLD student rights under the Equal Educational Opportunity Act. The court's ruling in this case was the first to establish specific criteria for quality programming and for determining a school district's degree of compliance with the Equal Educational Opportunity Act. Reversing an initial ruling in federal district court, the Fifth Circuit Court of Appeals agreed with the Mexican American plaintiffs and formulated a criterion-based test to determine the degree of school district compliance. This compliance test, which has become known as the Castañeda Test, requires the satisfaction of the following three criteria for quality programming for CLD students:

- Theory: The school program must be based on *sound educational theory.*
- Practice: The program must be implemented effectively with adequate resources and personnel.
- Results: The program must be evaluated and proved effective, not only in the teaching of language, but also in access to the full curriculum—math, science, social studies, and language arts (Alexander, Alexander, & Alexander, 2000; Crawford, 1995).

Subsequently, the Castañeda Test has not only become the basis of the court's ruling in other cases, but it has also been used as a compliance standard in OCR guidelines for quality programming.

Plyler v. Doe (1982)

The U.S. Supreme Court's ruling in the case of *Plyler v. Doe* was based on the Fourteenth Amendment to the U.S. Constitution. This judicial precedent effectively guarantees the rights of undocumented immigrants to a free public education and, by implication, to quality programming that meets the Castañeda Test as the benchmark standard. According to the Court's ruling in this case, U.S. public schools are prohibited from denying students admission to school on the basis of their undocumented status or that of their parents, requiring students or parents to disclose their immigration status (i.e., by requiring the proof of documented status), or demanding that all students or parents show proof of a social security number (Alexander et al., 2000; Carrera, 1989). Therefore, the case of *Plyler v. Doe* is crucial to quality programming for CLD students because the Court's ruling in the case better ensures that these students are not denied admission to the school's provisions for programming.

tips for practice

Elementary Education

1. Provide your CLD students with graphic representations of the concepts they are learning (e.g., a diagram or graphic organizer) to help them make connections between content and language. For instance, if the water cycle is the concept to be taught, incorporate a diagram of the steps involved in this process (e.g., evaporation, condensation, and so forth) with labels in the first and second languages.

2. To enhance the linguistic development of your CLD students in both English and their native language, create word walls in your classroom. To effectively implement this strategy:
   - Provide word walls in your students' first and second languages in different locations in your classroom. Placing word walls side by side could promote confusion among your CLD students because of different vowel sounds and the temptation for students to rely heavily on literal translation between the two languages.
     —Create word walls that depict uppercase and lowercase letters (*A/a, D/d*).
     —Display word walls that demonstrate word patterns and word organization.

3. Select curriculum materials that emphasize multicultural perspectives in lessons about famous personalities, nutrition, philosophies of science, and so on. This will validate the importance of diversity in the classroom and affirm the cultural heritages of your students.

4. Judiciously provide your students with CD-ROM reading and learning programs, such as *WiggleWorks: Scholastic Beginning Literacy System* (Scholastic, 2000), *Reader Rabbit: Learn to Read with Phonics 1st & 2nd Grade* (Broderbund, 2003), or *Kurzweil 3000* (Kurzweil Educational Systems, 2002). Such programs often help CLD students with language transitions because they are not required to actually produce language when they are using the computer.

5. Create learning centers in your classroom that emphasize:
   - Computer software, access to the Internet, and multimedia in different languages. This will provide students with continuous support for ongoing native language development.
   - Activities connecting reading and writing in both languages.
   - Volunteers from the community who provide support to the students in their native languages. This not only nurtures the development of the native language but also provides a source of positive role models.

Secondary Education

1. Make classroom and schoolwide activities structured and predictable in the following ways:
   - Ensure that CLD students have a clear sense of their daily schedules, even if they vary from day to day. Students will be less able to focus on instruction when they are concerned about where they should be or what they should be doing.
   - Give your students advance notice when a change of schedule is needed. Do not rely on simply telling students. Add other ways of letting students know about the change (e.g., different types of schedules on color-coded paper, schedule changes in a particular area of the room, or crossing off a regularly scheduled activity and the addition of the new activity).

2. Pair your less English proficient CLD students to work with other, more language proficient students.

3. Provide extensive opportunities for CLD students to use oral and written language as they define, summarize, and report on activities through both their native and English language capacities. Students will enhance their literacy skills by including illustrations and descriptions when they report their observations.

4. When teaching social studies concepts, such as world war or economic differences in various countries, ask open-ended questions that invite comparison and contrast and that prompt students to integrate what they have observed and learned in their native countries.

5. If an ESL program is used in your school, collaborate with the ESL teacher to make connections between content learned in the grade-level classroom and in the ESL classroom.

6. Help students relate to scientific terms and concepts in the new language by incorporating hands-on activities such as class projects. Have students identify outside resources available in the community, experts who can visit the classroom, and organizations that can be visited.

7. Teach CLD students how to recognize cognates (e.g., animals–*animales,* exploration–*exploración*) common to their L1 and L2 so that connections can be made within the content area.

General Education

1. Involve CLD students in extracurricular activities and lower their affective filters by doing the following:
   • Showcase the talents of various cultural groups at assemblies and school activities.

• Foster a student government body that includes the participation of culturally and linguistically diverse students.
• Publish bilingual student newspapers.
• Organize international clubs, intramural sports, and festivals.

2. Create a positive environment in your school and classroom with the following:
   • Consistently encourage the use of positive language, especially that which is free of untoward racial, ethnic, and linguistic connotations.
   • Learn about the demographic groups represented in your school and validate each by correctly identifying the associated ethnic groups and their home countries.
   • Promote cross-cultural appreciation among staff members by informing them of what you have learned or know about the cultures represented on campus, as well as the positive outcomes possible in a diverse school environment.
   • Develop a guiding mission statement that reflects the diversity of your school and your classroom and is displayed in the languages represented in your classroom.
   • Advocate for a schoolwide environment that provides equality of materials, facilities, and resources for all nationalities represented.

■ key theories and concepts

additive bilingualism
Bilingual Education Act (1968)
Castañeda Test
Castañeda v. Pickard
common underlying proficiency (CUP)
complicating geographic variables
complicating sociopolitical variables

developmental bilingual education
English as a second language (ESL)
English-only movement
iceberg metaphor
interference hypothesis
Lau v. Nichols
"less equals more" rationale
multilingualism

Plyler v. Doe
separate underlying proficiency (SUP)
subtractive bilingualism
transfer hypothesis
transitional bilingual education
two-way immersion

professional conversations on practice

1. Discuss recent research on program and instructional variables that influence the academic achievement of CLD students. What variables are predictors of academic success among these students? What program models were found most effective?

2. Discuss the BICS–CALP distinction and the way it provides a rationale for bilingual programming with CLD students.

3. Compare and contrast the interference hypothesis and the transfer hypothesis. Discuss the role of each of these in the SUP–CUP distinction.

4. Discuss the pros and cons of widespread program models for CLD students. What role do complicating variables play in a school district's selection among available program models?

5. Discuss the key court cases that have influenced programming for CLD students. In what ways has the Castañeda Test been used to ensure appropriate education for CLD students?

questions for review and reflection

1. Reflect on key predictors of academic success among CLD students. In what ways would you plan instruction to address these predictors?

2. According to recent research, what factors enhance the effectiveness of developmental bilingual education programs? What role would home visits play in bolstering the role of these factors?

3. What are the sociopolitical implications of the interference hypothesis?

4. What is the SUP–CUP distinction and what should teachers know about it?

5. Reflect on the transfer hypothesis. What is the role of this hypothesis in reading instruction for CLD students?

6. According to Cummins (1981), in what way does less English early on lead to more English later?

7. List at least five complicating geographic variables and explain the ways in which each may operate to preclude a school district's use of bilingual education. What other types of native language support for CLD students might the

district provide through whatever program model it selects?

8. List at least five complicating sociopolitical variables and explain the ways in which each may operate to preclude a school district's use of bilingual education.

9. First, explain some of the foundations of ESL program models. Second, what are some of the characteristics associated with these models?

10. Discuss the most effective model of programming for CLD students. Identify a few of the reasons that make it the most effective.

11. Why might the use of ESL pull-out programs be so widespread when research has found them to be the least effective program model for CLD students? Explain your answer.

12. Discuss the pros and cons of newcomer programs. What would you say to a school district that is contemplating the use of such a program?

13. What three court cases have significantly influenced programming for CLD students? Briefly discuss the highlights of the court's decision in each of these three cases.

suggested activities

Preservice Teachers

1. Investigate the types of programs for CLD students within a nearby school district. Determine the effectiveness of these models within an elementary, a middle, or a high school by dialoguing with CLD students, their teachers, and their parents.

2. Interview a non-native-born, non-native speaker of English. Discuss with this person the kind of school experiences he or she has had in the United States. Focus particularly on what type of programming was available to him or her in the development of the second language. In collaboration with this person, try to identify the societal and classroom implications of the various English-only movements in states such as California and Arizona.

3. Survey district and community members about their attitudes toward and perceptions about what services should be provided for CLD students. Write a mock proposal to the district's school board and city council to advocate for the most effective and realistic program model for CLD students. This proposal should be supported by current research and theory.

In-Service Teachers

1. It has been one week since Kim Dao, a recent immigrant from Vietnam, arrived in your classroom. She is schooled in her native language up to the fifth grade and has had a disrupted education because of the political turmoil and unrest in her home country. She has come to the United States with her parents and two younger siblings. With these factors in mind, what types of modifications and cross-cultural adaptations would you provide for Kim Dao in teaching a social studies lesson on climate and its relation to geographical regions?

2. Soultana has lived in the United States for almost one year. She has some oral language skills in Greek (her native language) and can understand the language perfectly. Her father is bilingual and well versed in the linguistic patterns of both Greek and English. Soultana's mother is only literate in Greek and has no English language skills. Soultana loves to socialize and does well in cooperative learning situations. She is currently in the speech emergence stage of second language acquisition. Her teachers are pleased with her work given the limited amount of time she has been in this country. How would you capitalize on the strengths of the parents in order to assist Soultana in the ongoing development of her native language as she becomes more proficient in English?

3. Survey fellow colleagues about their attitudes toward and perceptions of CLD students. Do they believe that current programming is effectively serving this population? If they believe current services could be improved, ask them what suggestions they might have. With this information and the current research on best programming for CLD students in mind, provide a short in-service within a staff meeting as a means toward voicing recommendations for improvements in current practices.

The information provided in this chapter will help the educator to:

- Contrast one-way and mutual accommodation.
- Draw and specify the six levels of the accommodation readiness spiral.
- Describe the differences between the two helices of the accommodation readiness spiral.
- Discuss readiness for critical reflection on practice.
- Explain how critical reflection is essential to readiness for critical reflection on practice.
- Describe readiness for CLD students and families and the critical role of home visits.
- Compare and contrast external and internal assessments of environmental readiness.
- Discuss the ways in which an understanding of curriculum trends and curriculum essentials contribute to the educator's capacity for curricular readiness.
- Compare and contrast decision making with and without a program model as aspects of programming and instructional readiness.
- Describe readiness for application and advocacy using the three components of advocacy.

A Framework of Accommodation Readiness

Although organizations certainly exert powerful influences on the people who inhabit them . . . organizations are human creations guided by human intentions and decisions. . . . Thus, if organizations are human constructions, the people in them should be the ones to determine what is needed and how to bring about meeting those needs. . . . Organizational change is a result of people changing themselves.

—K. F. Osterman & R. B. Kottkamp, *Reflective Practice for Educators: Improving Schooling through Professional Development*

critical standards *Guiding Chapter Content*

TESOL/NCATE teacher standards reflect professional consensus on standards for the quality teaching of pre-K–12 CLD students. Additionally, the CEEE Guiding Principles and their accompanying indicators serve as a framework to assist practitioners, policymakers, and clients as they collaborate to enhance academic enrichment and language acquisition among CLD students. Therefore, in order to help educators understand how they might appropriately target and address national professional teaching standards in practice, we have designed the content of this chapter to reflect the following standards.

TESOL ESL Standards for P–12 Teacher Education Programs

TESOL ESL—Domain 2: Culture. Candidates know, understand, and use the major concepts, theories, and research related to the nature and structure of culture to construct learning environments that support ESOL [CLD] students' language and literacy development and content-area achievement. (p. 15)

- **Standard 2.a. Nature and role of culture.** Candidates know, understand, and use the major concepts, principles, theories, and research related to the nature and role of culture in language development and academic achievement that support individual students' learning. (p. 15)

    2.a.3. Understand and apply knowledge about home/school communication to enhance ESL teaching and build partnerships with ESOL families. (p. 17)

Note: All TESOL/NCATE standards are cited from TESOL (2001). All Guiding Principles are cited from Center for Equity and Excellence in Education (1996).

TESOL ESL–Domain 5: Professionalism. Candidates demonstrate knowledge of the history of ESL teaching. Candidates keep current with new instructional techniques, research results, advances in the ESL field, and public policy issues. Candidates use such information to reflect upon and improve their instructional practices. Candidates provide support and advocate for ESOL students and their families and work collaboratively to improve the learning environment. (p. 38)

- **Standard 5.c. Professional development and collaboration.** Candidates collaborate with and are prepared to serve as a resource to all staff, including paraprofessionals, to improve learning for all ESOL students. (p. 41)
  - 5.c.1. Establish professional goals and pursue opportunities to grow professionally in the English language teaching field. (p. 42)
  - 5.c.2. Work with other teachers and staff to provide comprehensive, challenging educational opportunities for ESOL students in the school. (p. 42)

CEEE Guiding Principles

Guiding Principle #3: Limited English proficient students are taught challenging content to enable them to meet performance standards in all content areas, including reading and language arts, mathematics, social studies, science, the fine arts, health, and physical education, consistent with those for all students.

3.5 Schools provide professional development opportunities for teachers, paraprofessionals, and other educators to prepare them to meet the instructional and assessment needs of limited English proficient students. (p. 7)

Guiding Principle #4: Limited English proficient students receive instruction that builds on their previous education and cognitive abilities and that reflects their language proficiency levels.

4.11 All teachers understand and value the linguistic backgrounds and cultural heritages of their students' families and use this information to enrich classroom instruction and to facilitate limited English proficient students' learning of academic content. (p. 8)

Even a cursory examination of each of the dimensions of the CLD student biography—the sociocultural, the cognitive, the academic, and the linguistic—demonstrates the many complex challenges and processes through which CLD students must navigate to be successful in school and in life. Necessarily, these multifaceted complexities point to the need for professional readiness, which school educators should be able to demonstrate in order to appropriately accommodate these learners.

In this sense, we are targeting not one-way but mutual accommodation (Díaz, Moll, & Mehan, 1986; Nieto, 1992). The notion of *one-way accommodation* explains the tendency among some educators to assume that unsuccessful students are either "genetically inferior or culturally deprived" (Nieto, 1992, p. 258). That is, when certain students, especially CLD learners, do not automatically accommodate to the culture of the school, the result is often questions about their intelligence, assumptions about their abilities, or suspicion concerning the capabilities of family members.

Conversely, the perspective of *mutual accommodation* expects complete accommodation from neither the student nor the educator. Instead, they each collaborate to maximize the resources each brings to the educational process and to select from among "the best strategies at the disposition of each" (Nieto, 1992, p. 258). Accordingly, in mutual accommodation:

- Home languages are affirmed and supported.
- Funds of knowledge, which students bring to the classroom and families bring to the school, are elaborated on.
- The methods and strategies of instruction are adapted and closely monitored for effectiveness with the student.

Mutual accommodation thus defines a process in which both teacher and student are enriched. As the CLD student biography is maximized, the teacher's professional responses to that biography typically include intentional preassessment, differentiated instruction, alternative assessment of efficacy, and critical reflection on practice. Throughout the remainder of this text, we use the terms *mutual accommodation* and *accommodation* synonymously.

As a foundation for understanding the professional readiness that must be demonstrated for mutual accommodation, Chapters 1, 2, and 3 detail many of the complexities, theories, and research associated with each of the four dimensions of the CLD student biography. Chapter 4 further explores the programming and sociopolitical contexts of accommodation for the CLD student. This chapter examines the levels of readiness that school educators should demonstrate in order to appropriately (and mutually) accommodate CLD students and deliver effective instructional methods for these learners.

■ The Accommodation Readiness Spiral

Preparedness to accommodate the CLD student is demonstrated by the six levels of the accommodation readiness spiral, summarized in Figure 5.1. The *accommodation readiness spiral* is an emergent framework for readiness that has been developed by the authors and is based on over seven years of field experience and evolving research with CLD students and their educators. The spiral ranges from the initial readiness level, readiness for critical reflection on practice, to readiness level 6, readiness for application and advocacy. Each of the six levels illustrated is sequential and increasingly indicative of an educator's capacity for effective praxis with CLD students.

Levels of Readiness

The six levels of readiness constitute a spiral because the process of capacity building for each subsequent level is progressive, but recidivism or regression is always

■ **figure 5.1** Accommodation
Readiness Spiral

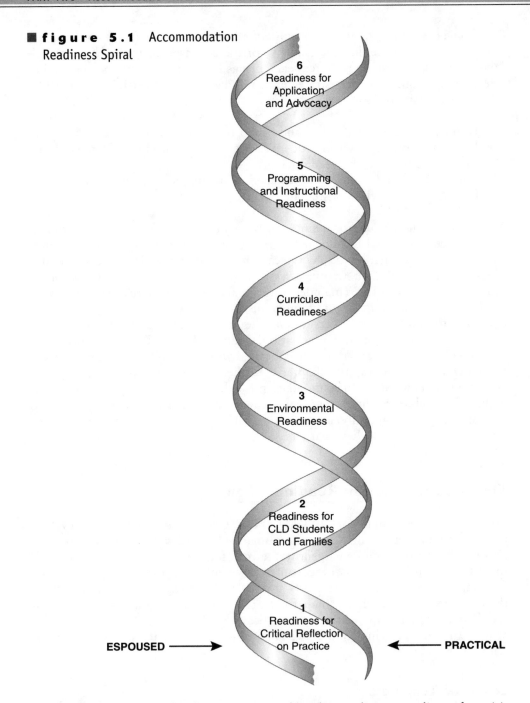

6
Readiness for
Application
and Advocacy

5
Programming
and Instructional
Readiness

4
Curricular
Readiness

3
Environmental
Readiness

2
Readiness for
CLD Students
and Families

1
Readiness for
Critical Reflection
on Practice

ESPOUSED ⟶   ⟵ **PRACTICAL**

a possibility. For example, the attainment of level 1 readiness, readiness for critical reflection on practice, serves as essential preparation for level 2 readiness, that
is, readiness for CLD students and families. This is the case because effective and

productive interactions with CLD students and families require reflection on the range of cross-cultural assumptions in which teachers may engage as they interact with individuals of a culture different from their own.

Such interactions also require a capacity for critical reflection because, as discussion to follow explores, it is one's prior socialization in a particular culture (a culture different from that of the CLD student) that is typically at the core of misconceptions and incorrect assumptions about CLD students and their family members. For example, school educators often assume that Asian students will, despite any language differences, prove successful in mathematics. In reality, this assumption is quite often incorrect for a variety of reasons, including the sociopolitical environment in the home country, the level of schooling attained in the home country, the educational levels of the parents, and more. In any case, a capacity for critical reflection among school educators is essential to readiness for CLD students and families. Similarly, level 2 readiness of the accommodation readiness spiral is essential to a capacity for level 3 readiness, and so on, through level 6 of the spiral.

Regression or recidivism is always a possibility because capacity building for any given level of the spiral is not always sufficient to enable progression to the next level. For example, building a capacity for consistent critical reflection on practice often requires a resocialization in thinking as well as a great deal of reflective practice with CLD students in the school or in the classroom. None of us was born a reflective thinker. Each of us must build this capacity through focus, practice, and experience. At any given point in time, the capacity may prove sufficiently strong to enable the next level of professional readiness and upward movement along the spiral. Nonetheless, as the practice dynamics change, the educator's capacity may become insufficient to enable effectiveness at the next level of readiness. In this case, the educator may temporarily regress along the spiral.

Forms of Readiness

Figure 5.1 also demonstrates the fact that the accommodation readiness spiral is a double helix. This configuration is appropriate because readiness for accommodation may occur in two forms: espoused readiness and practical readiness. *Espoused readiness* defines what the educator says, and may believe, about her or his level of readiness for accommodation. Espoused readiness operates at the conscious level and can fluctuate or change rather easily in response to new information or ideas. Although the educator may believe that espoused readiness guides his or her actions, this is often not the case.

Practical readiness, on the other hand, is so deeply ingrained in the educator's consciousness that the educator may not be able to fully articulate the nature of that readiness. Unfortunately, practical readiness is often indicative of frequently unchecked assumptions and beliefs that tend to shape and guide actions in practice. Unlike espoused readiness, an individual's level of practical readiness is formulated over years of socialization before and during professional practice. Therefore, one's level of practical readiness is not so easily recognized or changed.

Not infrequently, the decisions the educator makes, the actions that he or she takes, and the accommodation performance that he or she demonstrates in practice are governed by these two forms of readiness. At times, despite the level of espoused readiness, the assumptions the educator holds tend to be reflected in the practical readiness demonstrated in praxis. In these instances, the educator's practical level of readiness may not match the level espoused. When such discrepancies exist, deeply ingrained practical readiness prevents the new intentions of espoused readiness from appropriately guiding the educator's professional actions in practice. If the discrepancy between espoused and practical readiness grows sufficiently large, the double helix of the accommodation readiness spiral soon becomes so distorted that the spiral collapses. This situation is indicative of the educator's need to personally and professionally reconstruct her or his readiness for accommodation.

In the following discussion, we explore each of the six levels of the accommodation readiness spiral, as illustrated in Figure 5.1. As each is explored, the reader is encouraged to periodically review the spiral as a framework for self-examination of accommodation readiness. At the same time, the reader should recall that espoused readiness may significantly differ from practical readiness. Moreover, critical reflection is central to the alignment of these two forms of readiness in practice with CLD students and families.

■ Readiness for Critical Reflection on Practice

An educator's prior experiences and prior socialization concerning cultural and linguistic diversity can and will influence school and classroom practice with CLD students. Beginning teachers typically bring at least twenty-three years of prior socialization and experiences in a particular culture to the classroom. More experienced educators may bring forty or more years of their own socialization to their practice with CLD students. If this socialization did not significantly involve prior experience with cultural and linguistic diversity, especially with those cultures and languages of the CLD students in the school, cross-cultural and crosslinguistic ambiguity, assumptions, miscommunications, attributions, and tensions are inevitable (Herrera, 1996; Murry, 1996). Effective school educators learn to reflect as well as *critically reflect* on their perspectives about, their planning for, and their practice with CLD students and families.

Reflection in this sense involves validity testing, preceded by assumption checking (Murry, 1996), and this reflection lies at the heart of self-readiness for the accommodation of diversity. It should also be mentioned at this point that reflection defined as validity testing is a uniquely adult phenomenon (Mezirow, 1991; Murry, 1996). Most texts, especially texts of the cognitive approach that suggest that K–12 students should reflect (as in metacognitive learning strategies) are referring to a different notion of reflection. This different notion is one that we would define as *introspection*. One might further define this K–12 notion of reflection as thinking about one's thinking or actions.

Adult or teacher reflection, on the other hand, involves developing a capacity for confronting assumptions and testing the validity of those assumptions. The subsequent act of critical reflection emphasizes validity testing (i.e., reflection) that is specifically focused on one's prior socialization. The value of both reflection and critical reflection in preparing school educators for appropriate accommodative practice with CLD students is well documented (Herrera, 1996; Herrera & Murry, 1999; Murry, 1996; Murry, 1998; Murry & Herrera, 1999). As illustrated in Figure 5.2, a teacher's readiness for critical reflection on practice with CLD students is demonstrated by a capacity for the confronting/checking of assumptions in practice, validity testing on those assumptions (reflection), and reflection on the influence of prior socialization on the origin of any assumptions made.

As an example of these processes, let us examine the case of Soledad as a basis for understanding readiness for critical reflection in practice with diversity (see Figure 5.3). Soledad's case is complex but not unusual among educators of CLD

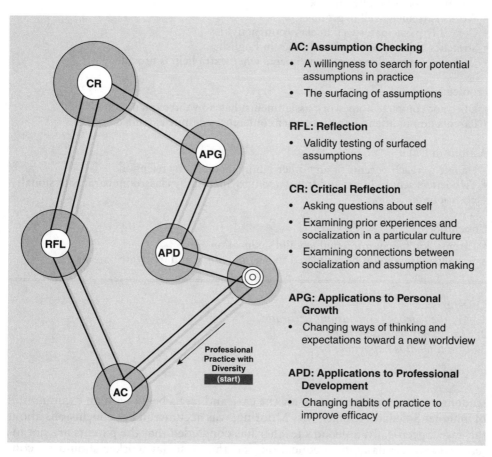

AC: Assumption Checking
- A willingness to search for potential assumptions in practice
- The surfacing of assumptions

RFL: Reflection
- Validity testing of surfaced assumptions

CR: Critical Reflection
- Asking questions about self
- Examining prior experiences and socialization in a particular culture
- Examining connections between socialization and assumption making

APG: Applications to Personal Growth
- Changing ways of thinking and expectations toward a new worldview

APD: Applications to Professional Development
- Changing habits of practice to improve efficacy

Professional Practice with Diversity (start)

■ **figure 5.2**   Readiness for Critical Reflection on Practice

■ **figure 5.3**   The Case of Soledad

Soledad

Biography:
- Fifth-grade, female, Hispanic
- Family emigrated from the state of Zacatecas, Mexico, two years ago
- Three years prior schooling in Mexico
- One year of schooling in Texas
- Early production stage of SLA
  —Reads phonetically, listens with understanding to contextualized communication, repeats memorable and some nonmemorable language, recognizes language connections, will use contextual clues to aid understanding and facilitate reading
- Parents work at local beef-packing plant; father was a ranch foreman in Mexico

Classroom Behaviors:
- Attentive and generally on task
- Works extremely well in groups
- Generally participates well in classroom activities
- Stretches her communicative abilities in English
- Completes most classroom assignments when extra help is provided

Problems:
- Does not complete homework assignments; has no valid explanation
- Parents do not attend parent–teacher conferences despite extended hours

Actions to Date:
- Unable to reach parents or any other family members by telephone
- Two letters sent to home and translated into Spanish by classroom paraprofessional; no response

Conclusions:
- Parents don't seem interested in child's education
- Social worker should be contacted to visit the home and motivate parents

Questions:
1. *Are the teacher's conclusions accurate?*
2. *If so, what should be done?*
3. *If not, what is happening here?*

students. Take a moment to review the case and let us begin with an examination of whether Soledad's teacher, Ms. Mooring, was accurate in her conclusions about the case. Specifically, Soledad's teacher has concluded that the parents are not interested in their daughter's education and that a social worker should be contacted to motivate the parents. To reflect on the case, Soledad's teacher must first ask: "Based on the facts of the case, did I make an *assumption* that the parents don't care about Soledad's education and must be motivated to do so?" This is assumption checking, in the sense that the teacher has surfaced a potential assumption in her practice. She can then test the validity of that sociocultural assumption by examining whether she was correct in making that assumption.

Reflection

Ms. Mooring can reflect on (validity test) her assumptions by asking herself such questions as: "What other reasons might account for the problems I have recorded in the Soledad case summary? Could it be that Soledad's parents work very long hours for many days of the week just to survive as a family? Could it be that they read my letter but are afraid to contact or visit the school because of their prior negative experiences with schools and school educators? What about the parents' literacy levels? Could it be that Soledad's parents neither understand English nor are able to read written Spanish?" As a teacher who is willing to reflect on her professional practices, Ms. Mooring might explore any one or more of these alternative explanations. If she finds any one or more of these correct, she has made an invalid assumption.

That is *not* to say that Ms. Mooring was wrong or is a poor teacher. Instead, her reflection simply suggests that she made a cross-cultural assumption that may have limited the effectiveness of her practice. Such assumptions are common in cross-cultural encounters, especially those in which educators have limited experience with cultures other than the one in which they were socialized. The more appropriate measure of professional effectiveness for Ms. Mooring is her willingness to validity-test (reflect on) any assumptions she surfaces by assumption checking. Through reflection, she will eventually improve the effectiveness of her practice with CLD students (Herrera, 1996; Murry, 1996; Murry, 1998).

In this case, professionalism on the part of Soledad's teacher yields positive implications. That is, through reflection on the case and a home visit, Ms. Mooring finds that her assumptions were invalid. Soledad's parents do indeed care very much about Soledad's education and wish to be involved as much as possible in her academic success. However, both parents work very long hours, seven days a week, and neither is sufficiently literate to read written Spanish. Therefore, as a result of reflection, Ms. Mooring is better able to understand the actions of both Soledad and her parents. She is now in a better position to structure appropriate teaching accommodations to improve her instructional effectiveness with Soledad.

Critical Reflection

After reflecting on assumptions in practice, Ms. Mooring's next professional step is to engage in critical reflection. Critical reflection begins with the self and one's socialization. That is, what in her prior experiences or prior socialization in a particular culture might have prompted Ms. Mooring to make an invalid cross-cultural assumption? Could it be that in her culture most parents have more time for their children—time to help the student with homework, time to attend parent–teacher conferences, and time to visit the school at the teacher's request? Could it be that because of her socialization to that perspective, Ms. Mooring expected a more immediate and visibly concerned response from Soledad's parents on their receipt of the teacher's letter? From such efforts at critical reflection, teachers can learn the many ways that primary socialization acts as a cultural filter on perspectives, expectations, and actions in practice with diversity. Eventually, the teacher builds the capacity and the self-readiness to recognize such influences in cross-cultural encounters *before* making assumptions or engaging in actions in practice that are counterproductive.

Figure 5.2 summarizes the various steps of readiness for critical reflection in accommodative practice with diversity. As depicted in this figure, the cyclic nature of the processes involved illustrates that critical reflection must be an ongoing aspect of readiness for accommodation.

■ Readiness for CLD Students and Families

Insufficient time is often the bane of a teacher's existence. There never seems to be enough of it. Time for planning, time for instruction, time for assessment, time for paperwork, time for grading, time to breathe—it always seems to be in short supply. Yet a little time invested in semistructured conversations with CLD students and their families will yield surprisingly useful, and sometimes unexpected, rewards. These rewards, which result from a readiness for CLD students and families as depicted in Figure 5.1, include, but are by no means limited to, enhanced teaching efficiency, improved student performance, and a reduction in the time required for instructional planning.

CLD students bring a variety of schooling, cultural, and language experiences to the classroom. Teachers can effectively maximize these experiences to focus instruction for cognitive and academic growth, reduce or eliminate reteaching, increase the perceived relevancy of instruction, keep students interested and motivated to learn, and more. Too often the tendency is to assume that limited English proficiency also implies limited schooling or an inadequate knowledge base. As a result, secondary-level CLD students who have taken calculus in Mexico have actually been placed in beginning mathematics classes in U.S. high schools. Such invalid assumptions are commonplace when time is not taken to explore the student's background through conversations with the student and with family members.

Teachers who enhance their readiness for CLD student accommodation through semistructured conversations increase both their effectiveness as teachers and their available time in the classroom. These insightful teachers collaborate with bilingual paraprofessionals or parent and community volunteers as needed to conduct these essential conversations. Time is further maximized when such conversations are undertaken as part of a home visit. Through home visits, the teacher learns about the student, the parent(s) or guardian(s), the community, and sometimes extended family members who are key stakeholders in the CLD student's educational aspirations. In turn, parents and family members learn that the teacher values their participation in the educational process, is interested in the academic success of their child, and is willing to seek them out as valuable resources in accommodation. Table 5.1 further illustrates the many advantages of home visits

■ **t a b l e   5 . 1**   Parent–Teacher Conferences versus Home Visits—Comparisons and Contrasts

	In-School Parent–Teacher Conference	In-Community Home Visit
Typically accommodates CLD parents' work schedules		✓
Typically accommodates CLD parents' prior experiences with schooling		✓
Typically accommodates CLD parents' transportation issues		✓
Typically encourages involvement of extended family members (e.g., *abuelos* [grandparents], *padrinos* [godparents]		✓
Provides contextual information on the student's socialization in a particular culture		✓
Provides contextual information on family language biographies, literacy levels, and literacy access		✓
Provides contextual information on the community and culture(s) surrounding the school		✓
Provides contextual information on the CLD student's level of acculturation		✓
Provides contextual information about economic and acculturation stressors on the CLD student and family		✓
Typically lowers the affective filter for CLD parents		✓
Provides a contextualized opportunity to test assumptions about student and family		✓
Sends a message that the educator truly values the participation of parents, families, and community members		✓
Sends a message that the educator is truly concerned with the academic and transitional successes of the CLD student		✓
Sends a message that the educator is willing to seek out parents and family members as valuable resources		✓
Is typically student- and family-centered		✓
Is typically teacher-centered	✓	
Typically accommodates the educator's schedule and preferences	✓	
Typically follows the educator's agenda as a conversational focus	✓	

compared to parent–teacher conferences. These proactive visits provide educators with an outstanding venue for teacher–student conversations.

Semistructured Conversations

Because these teacher–student or teacher–parent conversations are only semistructured, the affective filter is kept at a low level and the teacher remains free to further explore any information that surfaces as a means of enhancing teaching effectiveness with the CLD student. For the school educator, such conversations begin to establish an inclusive understanding of the students who will be accommodated in the school or the classroom. Following are some of the questions that will be answered through these conversations:

- What cultures are represented by students in the school and in the classroom?
- What native languages do students bring to the learning community?
- How many students will need accommodation and at what levels?

Although the conversations are semistructured rather than structured (i.e., they do not follow a strict protocol), questions asked at various points of the conversation (or at various iterations of conversations) should generally address at least three domains related to the prior experiences, knowledge, and capacities of CLD students. Perhaps the most central of these domains arises from the sociocultural dimension of the CLD student biography and emphasizes the student's acculturation experiences and level of acculturation. Typical questions that may be incorporated into teacher–student or teacher–parent conversations that address this domain include the following: From what country did the student emigrate? What is her or his recency of immigration? To what extent has the student's family migrated within the United States? Where do the parents work and according to what typical schedules? What cultural transition stresses have been difficult for the CLD student and his or her family? How has the student coped with these stresses?

Such questions, when incorporated into a nonthreatening conversation (or home visit discussion), begin to paint an informative picture of the student's current level of acculturation. As previously discussed, the student's level of acculturation, especially acculturation stressors, may profoundly influence such concerns as interest levels, motivation levels, attention span, language transitions, classroom behavior, and more. Table 5.2 suggests additional sources of information relevant to the student's level of acculturation. Nevertheless, there is no comparable substitute for the teacher–student conversation because it not only yields valuable information but it also demonstrates the teacher's interest in what the CLD student brings to the classroom.

A second domain of guiding questions for conversation is directly related to the academic dimension of the CLD student biography and addresses the CLD student's experiences, knowledge, and skills in the content areas. The academic performance of CLD students is significantly affected by the extent to which content-area instruction is perceived as relevant; builds on prior knowledge, skills,

■ **t a b l e   5 . 2**   Checklist: Readiness for CLD Students and Families

Has the teacher or school educator, through teacher–student or teacher–parent conversations or other sources of information, explored the following concerns to enhance readiness for the accommodation of CLD students and their families?

Readiness Concern	Sources of Information
Student's Level of Acculturation	
Informal assessment of level of acculturation (selected aspects)	Primarily teacher–student (T/S) and teacher–parent/family (T/P) conversations
• Circumstances/culture in home country prior to immigration	CLD student, parent(s)/guardian(s), extended family members
• Recency of immigration	CLD student, parent(s)/guardian(s), extended family members
• Current home dynamics	CLD student, parent(s)/guardian(s), extended family members
• Parents' work obligations	Parent(s)/guardian(s)
• Acculturation stressors	CLD student, parent(s)/guardian(s), extended family members
• Coping strategies	CLD student, parent(s)/guardian(s), extended family members
• The student's involvement in language brokering dynamics	CLD student, parent(s)/guardian(s), extended family members
• Proximity/transportation issues	Parent(s), social worker, school records
Formal assessment of level of acculturation	Acculturation quick screen (AQS) (C. Collier, 1987)
Student's Content-Area Knowledge/Capacities	
Informal assessment of:	Primarily T/S and T/P conversations
• Prior schooling in home country	CLD student, parent(s)/guardian(s)
• Prior schooling in the U.S.	School records, CLD student, parent(s)/guardian(s)
• Content-area experiences/levels	CLD student, parent(s)/guardian(s)
• Parent/family beliefs about schooling and educators	CLD student, parent(s)/guardian(s), extended family members
• Student's preferred and most difficult subject areas	CLD student, parent(s)/guardian(s)
Formal assessment of: criterion-referenced and norm-referenced assessments of content-area knowledge	Modified district tools or pretests

(continued)

■ **t a b l e   5 . 2**   Continued

Readiness Concern	Sources of Information
Student's Language Biography	
Informal assessment of:	Primarily T/S & T/P conversations
• Dominant language of first schooling in home country	CLD student, parent(s)/guardian(s), extended family members
• Dominant language spoken at home	CLD student, parent(s)/guardian(s), extended family members
• Extent of L2 schooling in U.S.	School records/CLD student
• Apparent CALP v. BICS development in L1 and L2	CLD student, parent(s)/guardian(s), extended family members, paraprofessionals
Formal assessment of:	
• L1	Translated LAS, Bilingual Verbal Ability Tests (BVAT), etc.
• L2	Idea Proficiency Test (IPT), LAS, etc.

or capacities; and accommodates the construction of new meanings derived from connections to prior knowledge and concepts (especially connections fostered by hands-on, interactive learning experiences). Among guiding questions of the content-area or academic domain that may initiate purposeful conversations with students and families are the following:

- Was the CLD student schooled in the home country and to what extent?
- What content areas were emphasized and at what level?
- What are the beliefs of family members about schooling and the role of school educators?
- What are the student's preferred subject areas?
- With what subject area(s) does he or she have difficulties?

Table 5.2 provides a checklist that teachers can use as a primer in developing appropriate, site-specific questions for the semistructured conversations of this domain.

Teacher–student and teacher–family conversations should discuss the linguistic dimension of the CLD student biography by surfacing the CLD student's prior language biography. Accordingly, the student's language exposures, experiences, and development in L1 and L2 should be explored. Teachers and school administrators should be aware that families are often surprised and motivated by the educator's interest in their native language. When such an interest extends to a home visit by the school educator, the conversation also provides the opportunity to reinforce for the family the well-established finding that the CLD student can benefit from conversations and learning in the home that are grounded in the native or home language (Beck, n.d.; Diaz-Rico & Weed, 2002; Fern, Anstrom, & Silcox,

1994; Kober, n.d.; Parker, 1997; Samway & McKeon, 1999). Among pertinent and guiding questions that may establish this language biography are the following:

- What was the dominant language(s) of communication and education in the home country?
- Was the student schooled in the dominant language and to what level?
- What is currently the dominant language in the home and is it supported for the student by the parent(s) or guardian(s)?
- To what extent has the student been schooled in L2 in the United States?
- If the student demonstrates some proficiency in L2, to what extent does she or he exhibit CALP versus BICS proficiency?
- What family literacy levels are suggested by the conversation, and is future follow-up (to gain more thorough information) needed?
- What literacy resources exist in the home and in the community?

Again, Table 5.2 provides a checklist that school educators can use as a tentative guide in developing questions for their semistructured conversations related to this language domain. Nonetheless, effective teachers will pursue and elaborate their conversations with the recognition that all of the domains to be explored are interrelated.

In summary, teacher–student (and teacher–family) conversations, especially those that surround a home visit, are powerful paths to teacher readiness for CLD student accommodation. The information obtained from these conversations will enhance teaching effectiveness. The messages transmitted by these interactions tend to encourage parental or guardian involvement and to motivate CLD students.

Environmental Readiness

Environmental readiness for best practice in the accommodation of CLD students, illustrated in Figure 5.1, demands an analysis of the external and internal environments that may affect professional effectiveness. Both of these environments constitute the context in which instruction will take place. In a classroom where students appropriately draw from their experiences, learning, and interactions to construct meaning, context is powerful.

The External Environment

Most of us, as teachers, would prefer to believe that the environment that seems external to our practice is generally inconsequential. After all, we are typically taught to focus on such internal factors as the curriculum, instructional planning and delivery, monitoring, and evaluation. Yet research and analysis in education has repeatedly highlighted the powerful impact that the external environment can have on professional practice for an educator (Hargreaves & Fullan, 1998; Herrera, 1996; Herrera & Fanning, 1999; Routman, 1996). No program, no classroom, no instruction is an island unto itself. Rather, each is surrounded by an external context that can powerfully influence the success of the educator in practice.

Accommodative school educators enhance their readiness for CLD students and families in order to enhance the academic success of these students in the classroom. Yet, for Ladson-Billings (1995), such efforts are not accommodative unless CLD students are permitted to target academic success "while retaining their cultural identities" (p. 477). This *culturally relevant pedagogy*, as defined by Ladson-Billings, exhibits at least three notable characteristics. First, teachers, as members of the school community, develop fluid, reciprocal, and equitable relationships with their students and their communities. Second, these teachers tend to view knowledge as dynamic, shared, constructed, and recycled. Third, culturally sensitive teachers foster an aca-demic community that promotes individual self-concepts, fosters a sense of belonging, honors human dignity, and values cultural competence alongside academic success.

■ *What are the potential consequences of asking CLD students to sacrifice their cultural identi-ties in order to be academically successful in school? What do you know of the cultural backgrounds of the CLD students you teach or plan to teach? What aspects of their cultural identity tend to support their academic achieve-ment? In what ways can teachers increase their capacities for student and family readiness and culturally relevant pedagogy?*

Of particular importance in the external environment is the sociopolitical con-text of schooling and teaching in the service of CLD students. ESL and bilingual education are politically volatile topics at the national, state, and local levels. The Unz Initiative in California is one glaring example of an external sociopolitical fac-tor that impacts what is possible and what is not for CLD students in the classroom (Herrera & Murry, 1999). Accordingly, external politics can influence funding for CLD student education, programming possibilities, public reaction to classroom instruction, and so on.

Equally influential on appropriate practice for CLD students is the status of students' native languages in the learning community. Escamilla (1994) has demon-strated that the English language can exert such a force (hegemony) within the school or in the community of the school that bilingual education or, in some cases, native language support for CLD students is effectively precluded. Even among children in a bilingual school, Escamilla found notable discrepancies be-tween the status afforded Spanish and English. Essentially, students in the school tended to interpret these discrepancies as a message that Spanish was useful, but solely as a transition to English.

Ultimately, external environmental readiness is concerned with the degrees of parent or guardian, family, and community involvement in the appropriate education of CLD students. Once again, our experience with teachers and building adminis-trators who teach in highly diverse schools has repeatedly demonstrated that no sin-gle act is as effective in promoting family and community involvement as the home visit (see Table 5.1). These home visits provide a site-specific opportunity for school educators (including teachers, administrators, counselors, and paraprofessionals) to learn about the key stakeholders in the CLD student's educational aspirations—the student, the parent(s) or guardian(s), extended family members, and the community.

At the same time, family and community members learn that the school educator values their participation in the educational process, is interested in the academic success of CLD students, and is willing to become a part of their world in order to collaborate in the planning of accommodations for these students. Lucas, Henze, and Donato (1990), who conducted ethnographic research with secondary-level Hispanic students and families, also recommend the following strategies to promote family and community involvement:

- Offer ESL classes to parents.
- Conduct monthly parent nights with scheduling to accommodate parent workloads.
- Schedule neighborhood meetings.
- Consider rescheduling parent–teacher conferences to morning hours. Additionally, seek out and enlist the collaboration of *padrinos* (godparents) as valuable resources in the education of Hispanic CLD students.

Table 5.3 provides a checklist for school educators of potential external variables and professional actions in practice that may affect student success or the effectiveness of professional practice with CLD students. Although this checklist is by no means exhaustive, it does provide a sample range of the external environmental factors that may influence a teacher's effectiveness or schoolwide effectiveness with CLD students.

The Internal Environment

At the same time, informed educators of CLD students are concerned with the internal environment of the school and classroom. Again, research and analysis in the field has repeatedly emphasized the potential influence of the internal context on CLD student success, especially literacy development in L2 (Baker & Freebody, 1988; Hamayan, 1994; Perez & Torres-Guzman, 2002). Of particular importance is the internal environment of the classroom, where primary accommodations for CLD students will take place. At one level, we are concerned with questions such as the following:

- Is the classroom a welcoming environment?
- Does the classroom affirm or celebrate the cultures and languages represented?
- Are bulletin boards and word walls thoughtfully designed to promote literacy in the content areas and to affirm the cultures and languages of CLD students?
- Does the classroom arrangement promote discovery, cooperative, thematic, and center-based learning?

At a more interactive level of the classroom or internal environment, we are concerned with other questions. Does the classroom encourage and promote social, cognitive, academic, and linguistic interactions as a means to learning? Does this internal environment facilitate homogeneous and heterogeneous peer groupings? Does the classroom environment enable independent or collaborative hands-on learning through such provisions as centers, manipulatives, realia, and more?

■ **t a b l e   5 . 3**   Checklist: Environmental Readiness

To enhance environmental readiness, consider the following variables and actions that may affect either CLD student productivity or professional practice with CLD students.

Readiness Concern	Appropriate Readiness Actions
External Environment	
Sociocultural mores/patterns of the community surrounding the school	Shop in the community, attend community functions, conduct schoolwide celebrations of other cultures, invite community members to present on their cultures
Socioeconomic characteristics of the community	Seek out demographic information, shop in the community, avoid assumptions, conduct free lunches or dinners
Perceptions of the school and educators	Conduct home visits, shop in the community, attend community functions, conduct functions to draw in the community
School/media relations	Invite local reporters to the classroom/school, highlight the positives, write to/for the newspaper, videotape best practices
Relationship to school board	Invite members to the classroom, attend meetings, talk to members
Relationship to district/committees	Talk to administrators/members, participate, present, dialogue, persuade
Relationship to democratic process	Voice informed opinion, invite representatives, vote, advocate
Internal Environment	
Multicultural and multilingual classroom library	Collaborate with school librarian to check out books or write proposals to buy books, use books from home
Environmental print in students' native languages	Translate and post labels, create separate word walls in L1 and L2, create content-based boards in L1 and L2
Classroom arrangement	Structure to enable cooperative learning, heterogeneous and homogeneous grouping, centers, etc.
Learning centers	Structure around need, including literacy, science, math, technology, native language, etc.
Literacy support materials	Picture dictionaries, realia, magazines, newspapers, how-to books, etc.
Examples of (all) student productivity	Designate areas, post in any language, include motivating feedback, incorporate process and product, invite parents/community

Where CLD students are to be accommodated, teachers must be concerned with the capacity of the internal environment to promote content-based literacy development in both L1 and L2. Table 5.3 provides a summary of internal environmental factors that may affect student success or effectiveness in practice with CLD students, especially effectiveness in literacy development. Of particular concern are a multicultural and multilingual classroom library, environmental print in students' native languages, and literacy support materials.

Literacy support materials, especially those applicable to the elementary classroom, support either reading or writing as a focus of literacy development. For example, developmentally appropriate literature promotes a reading focus and is suitable for read-alouds. Likewise, dialogue journals can be used to enhance a writing focus. Other literacy support materials such as posters, ads, or brochures can be maximized in choral or buddy reading activities or the development of a classroom newspaper. Pattern books can also be used to promote reading and writing literacy, and they are very effective when used for shared reading activities.

■ Curricular Readiness

Traditionally, curricular readiness for school educators has involved a basic understanding of such curricular issues as planning, scope, sequence, and consistency. Nonetheless, more recent curriculum trends have necessitated a grasp of other, more complex dynamics such as the degree of alignment between the curriculum and selected standards for concept or context coverage and quality, the degree to which the curriculum encourages parental or caregiver involvement, and the cross-cultural sensitivity of the curriculum.

Diaz-Rico and Weed (2002) have cautioned that teachers who lack a solid foundation in multiculturalism are sometimes guilty of "trivializing the cultural content of the curriculum" (p. 262). That is, cultural references or affirmations might be limited to ethnic months, bulletin boards, holidays, or meals. Seldom are books about other cultures or books in other languages available. Seldom are persons from other cultures illustrated in any fashion except provincial dress. Seldom are persons from other cultures accurately represented in the curriculum.

One way to avoid the trivializing of the curriculum is through building a capacity for critical reflection. Readiness for critical reflection serves as the foundation for (i.e., level 1) of the accommodation readiness spiral depicted in Figure 5.1. Previously, we discussed critical reflection as validity testing (or reflection) on the influences of one's prior socialization on assumptions in practice. School educators who critically reflect on their curriculum are less likely to engage in assumptions that might lead to a trivializing of the curriculum. When engaging in critical reflection on the curriculum, school educators should begin with reflection or validity testing that focuses on questions such as the following:

- Do my texts, bulletin boards, and classroom discussions appropriately include and represent groups from nondominant cultures?

- Are the challenges faced by individuals of nondominant groups presented in a realistic fashion?
- Are persons of color and women discussed or presented in a manner that is positive and inclusive of the full range of possibilities?
- Are multiculturalism and multilingualism presented as assets or liabilities?

Teachers should validity-test the presentations, treatment, and discussion of persons and groups throughout the curriculum. If this reflection uncovers shortcomings, then curricular accommodations should appropriately adapt and modify for these shortcomings. At the level of critical reflection, teachers are often concerned with reflecting on the extent to which their own prior socialization may not prompt them to immediately locate shortcomings in the curriculum, especially those that are crossculturally or crosslinguistically insensitive.

Curriculum Trends

Emergent trends in curricular readiness have also necessitated new competencies among school educators. For example, many school educators are now asked to review, analyze, and even vote on certain curriculum initiatives at the district or school levels (e.g., Success for ALL). Such initiatives may or may not be normed on schools with high levels of cultural or linguistic diversity. Some curricular initiatives stress particular philosophies such as a back-to-basics perspective, a phonics orientation to literacy development, or a promise of enhanced efficacy with at-risk students. Reflective decision making amid such initiatives (e.g., Reading Recovery, No Child Left Behind) demands new capacities and skills in curricular readiness, including critical review skills, a capacity to surface assumptions inherent in the initiative (e.g., assumptions about the needs of CLD students), and a capacity to reflect on the potential impact of an initiative on CLD students.

Inevitably, then, curricular readiness as illustrated in Figure 5.1 must encompass an understanding of and reflection on the current curriculum, recent curricular trends, and the potential impact(s) of emergent curricular initiatives. For teachers of CLD students, the many complex and differential learning, language, and adjustment needs these students bring to the school necessitate this curricular readiness. Such readiness should be highly and intentionally focused on the essentials of whatever curriculum is currently adopted.

Curriculum Essentials

Curricular readiness is suggested by critical reflection on each of the following questions concerning curriculum essentials:

- Has the educator of CLD students identified and refocused instructional planning and methods on the core of the currently adopted curriculum?
- Has the educator identified those standards of academic achievement that must be targeted by the curriculum and then appropriately modified the curriculum for CLD students in order to target those standards?

- Has the educator assessed the extent to which CLD students are provided access to an appropriate curriculum?

At minimum, curricular readiness that effectively answers these fundamental questions involves certain specific understandings and proactive actions, each focused on the differential learning and adjustment needs of CLD students. These understandings and subsequent actions then form a foundation for curricular accommodations specific to the CLD student.

Curriculum Essential 1: Identify and Focus on the Core Curriculum

Effective teachers of CLD students are proactive in addressing the issues involved in identifying and focusing on the core curriculum. Recent work by George Gonzalez (2002) suggests that lessons, most texts, and curricula can be examined and refocused to those critical concepts or premises that are essential to understanding and learning. These critical concepts or premises carry the essence of what a student would need to learn in order to know that material. When the curriculum and instruction for CLD students are focused on these critical concepts or premises, the teacher has established the *core*, content-based curriculum that may then also serve as the context for appropriate second language acquisition in the classroom setting. The teacher can then analyze the core curriculum to determine the critical vocabulary CLD students will need to learn and the discourse, genre patterns, and schemata associated with the content that may prove difficult for CLD students.

Several consequences are typical outcomes of such a process of emphasizing and targeting curriculum essentials. First, the curriculum is not watered down for CLD students because it has been appropriately modified to refocus instruction on the critical concepts and premises that students should learn. Second, classroom instruction that also targets second language acquisition among CLD students is centered not on basic skills or concepts but on the core curriculum that students must learn in order to prove academically successful in the classroom. Third, the teacher remains free to elaborate on the core curriculum as CLD students gain in L2 proficiency. Similarly, the grade-level teacher, with the collaboration of a paraprofessional, parent volunteers, or more capable peers, is free to elaborate on the critical concepts and premises of the curriculum by maximizing the CLD student's proficiencies and understandings in her or his native language.

Curriculum Essential 2: Concentrate on Standards of Academic Achievement

Having focused their curriculum modification efforts on an appropriate response to curriculum essential 1, most teachers have little difficulty in addressing the second curriculum essential because most local standards are derived from the local curriculum, which in turn has typically been designed to conform to some similar set of standards at the state level. Therefore, if appropriate curriculum modifications for CLD students focus on the core curriculum, then by inference these modifications also target critical standards for academic achievement. However, specific lesson plans for CLD students should still be directly linked to specific standards for academic achievement. Moreover, effective teachers of CLD students also monitor their teaching practices to ensure that their curriculum and their instruction are consistent with national standards of best practice with CLD students. Among such standards are the *ESL Standards for Pre-K–12 Students* (TESOL, 1997) and those of the National Board for Professional Teaching Standards for CLD students (NBPTS, 1998).

Curriculum Essential 3: Ensure That CLD Students Are Provided Access to an Appropriate Curriculum

As we reiterate throughout this text, CLD students do not compete with their native-English-speaking peers from a level playing field. Each of these CLD students faces singular sociocultural, cognitive, academic, and linguistic challenges that grade-level students do not typically confront. Yet most school systems and their curricula are based on the notion of meritocracy, which is grounded in the assumption that the playing field *is* level. In turn, these structures and assumptions lead to other assumptions that tend to deny CLD students access to an appropriate curriculum. For example, because a CLD student may demonstrate a limited ability to read and write in L2 (English), school officials and educators often tend to assume that the student is not capable of adequate academic performance in a grade-level classroom where instruction uses the grade-level curriculum. Accordingly, such a student is sometimes placed in a separate ESL or immersion classroom where the content-area curriculum is watered down to basic skills and concepts, most instruction is focused on language learning, and the texts and materials used bear little or no relationship to the grade-level curriculum.

Recognizing the dangers of such assumptions and situations, the national organization of Teachers of English to Speakers of Other Languages (TESOL) has, based on extensive research (Christian, 1994; Clegg, 1996; Genesee, 1994; Leone & Cisneros, 1995; McLaughlin, 1995; Pease-Alvarez & Hakuta, 1992; Thomas & Collier, 1995), developed a set of ESL standards for pre-K–12 students (TESOL, 1997). Along with these standards for professional practice with CLD students, TESOL has developed certain access guidelines in the form of questions, which are designed to ensure quality educational experiences for CLD students (TESOL, n.d.). These access guidelines include access to a positive learning environment, an appropriate curriculum, full delivery of services, and equitable assessment. Those access guidelines applicable to curriculum essentials suggest that educators of CLD students must be concerned with the extent to which CLD students are offered accommodative access to:

- Special instructional programs specifically designed to promote the CALP development in L2 necessary for participation in the full range of grade-level instruction offered to grade-level students.
- A core curriculum intentionally adapted to encourage the exchange, affirmation, and development of first and second languages and cultures among not

just CLD but all students, and the development of those higher-order thinking skills necessary for grade-level performance across the curriculum.

- Instructional programs and associated services that seek to identify differential students, provide curricular and instructional support, and monitor the efficacy of those services. Such programs encompass, but are not limited to:
  —Early childhood education
  —Special education (only as determined to be appropriate by means of formal assessments, informal assessments, and a placement team)
  —Gifted and talented education (especially programs that use linguistically and culturally adapted acceptance or referral criteria)
  —Diverse education (e.g., migrant, recent immigrant or newcomer, Title I)

These access guidelines, as developed by TESOL, suggest that curriculum access is a complex yet significant component of what teachers should consider curriculum essentials. As we reiterate throughout this text, the differential learning and adjustment needs of CLD students are complex, and therefore diverse programming, curriculum modifications, and instructional adaptations are essential to best practice for these students.

Programming and Instructional Readiness

In some school districts, increasing cultural and especially linguistic diversity in the schools is an extremely new phenomenon. Educators in such districts have unique opportunities. For example, in regard to programming, these educators are more or less free to select among the range of available program models, depending on their district dynamics.

Decision Making without a Current Program Model

In schools or school districts where a programming model has not yet been adopted, educators are more at liberty to examine the research on effective models before making their programming decisions. They are also at greater liberty to examine the current demographics of their schools in order to better maximize programming decisions. Ideally, programming decisions should account for a variety of significant factors, including:

- CLD student numbers
- Variety of languages represented
- Recency of immigration among CLD students
- Teacher capacities to implement program models under consideration
- Recruiting potentials
- Available facilities
- Collaboration potentials across classrooms
- Latest research on programming

dilemmas *of Practice*

Ms. Nuveau has just joined the faculty at Huron Elementary in August of this school year. She had been an educator of CLD students in her previous seven years of practice as a third-grade teacher in another state. This will be her first year as a second-grade teacher. The student body of the school is approximately 7 percent Mexican American, 1 percent African American, and 92 percent European American. Of the Mexican American children in Ms. Nuveau's class, about 35 percent speak no English and none are performing at grade level. During her first week of teaching, she learns that all Mexican American children in her class, as well as CLD children in all classes at her grade level, will be pulled out of the classroom for thirty minutes total each week for

ESL instruction. Otherwise, grade-level teachers are responsible for meeting the needs of these students. Although her school has already adopted a very limited form of the ESL pull-out program model, Ms. Nuveau is certain that this level of ESL instruction will be insufficient to accommodate the language transition needs of her CLD students.

■ *In what ways might this program model be problematic for CLD students at this school? In what ways can Ms. Nuveau advocate for a change in program model at the school? What theory, research, or best practice arguments can she use to rationalize her advocacy?*

In making such programming decisions, it is essential that educators are reflective, site-specific, and student-centered. Reflective decision making will ensure that potential assumptions about student dynamics, staff readiness, and district infrastructure are surfaced and challenged.

In these school districts where educators have options in programming decisions, the program selection process should maximize the range of instructional methods available to classroom teachers. That is, the program model chosen should not limit the ability of teachers to use a variety of methods that are consistent with that model in order to address the particular needs of CLD students at their site. Educators have many options when appropriate models of ESL programming are selected as an umbrella under which a variety of classroom instructional methods can be pursued, including content-based ESL, sheltered instruction, and CALLA.

Decision Making with a Current Program Model

In other schools or school districts, overarching programming models for CLD students have already been selected, usually at the administrative or central office level. These selection decisions tend to frame and sometimes limit the range of classroom instructional methods from which teachers may choose in serving their CLD students. For example, many Great Plains school districts have mandated ESL pull-out programming in all schools that serve CLD students. Decisions of this nature not only limit the range of instructional models available to teachers, but they also tend to disinvolve grade-level teachers from the education of CLD students. Teachers in such districts who are unaware of the significant limitations on their instructional choice should be informed. Moreover, these teachers should still endeavor to vary and augment instruction (e.g., with auxiliary native language support) so that it better reflects research and targets maximum effectiveness within the bounds of such programming constraints.

Programming and Instructional Readiness through Advocacy

Educators in school districts where programming has already been determined may also choose to collaborate in advocacy for programming changes toward models that are more consistent with the latest research on programming and more enabling of a variety of appropriate instructional methods in the classroom(s) where CLD students are served. For example, the research of Thomas and Collier (1997) demonstrates the limited effectiveness of ESL pull-out programming with CLD students compared to other program models. Such research can be used as a foundation for collaborative advocacy among schools and educators in order to encourage changes in district or school-level programming.

Similarly, in districts with rapidly increasing numbers of CLD students, the pursuit of ESL pull-out programming quickly becomes unrealistic, as the number of CLD students pulled out soon exceeds the number of students remaining in the classroom. These sorts of changing demographics may provide a basis for teacher and administrator advocacy that encourages conversions in CLD programming. The best ESL conversions move programming toward models that emphasize the instruction of CLD students in grade-level classrooms through research-driven approaches, methods, and strategies.

Accordingly, classroom teachers benefit from an awareness of programming dynamics at the school or district level. Such readiness among classroom teachers enables more informed decision making about appropriate instructional models for the particular CLD population served. Through readiness, informed teachers are able to remain consistent with programming limitations while also maximizing site-specific effectiveness with CLD students in the classroom. Effective programming and instructional readiness as illustrated in Figure 5.1 encompasses, but is not limited to:

- An understanding of which program models would be effective with and feasible for CLD students in a given school.
- An awareness of programming dynamics at the district and school levels.
- An understanding of the manner in which district and school programming dynamics can frame or limit decisions about instructional approaches or methods for CLD students in the classroom.
- A grasp of which instructional methods would be effective with and realistic for CLD students in a given classroom.
- An examination of opportunities for teacher-based, administrative, or collaborative advocacy to improve programming and classroom instruction for CLD students.

■ Readiness for Application and Advocacy

Ultimately, personal and professional development, as well as capacity building for the accommodation of CLD students, must involve the application of what a teacher has learned about self, professional readiness, and CLD students in the school or classroom. Yet, as Figure 5.1 illustrates, the processes involved in this transition to applications also necessitate a certain application readiness.

Readiness for Theory-into-Practice Applications

This transition will necessarily involve the question of readiness for theory-into-practice applications. That is, to what extent is the educator ready to apply theory to the accommodation of CLD students? First and foremost, this readiness level of the accommodation spiral must encompass a realization that not all theories or models that have been proven effective in classrooms will also prove effective with CLD students. Many highly publicized theories or popular models of education fail to account for either cultural or linguistic diversity in the classroom (Cummins, 2001b; Valdes, 1996; Vavrus, 2002). As a result, some theories, although supported by extensive research, will not prove applicable to the differential learning and adjustment needs of CLD students. Likewise, not all theories are applicable to the student dynamics at a particular school. It is regrettable that this argument is more often used as an unsubstantiated rationale for nonaccommodation. Therefore, effective teachers of CLD students are critical readers of research on and theories of teaching (Angell, 1997; Mettetal & Cowen, 2000; Routman, 1996; Weedon, 1993). These effective teachers are also advocates for theory- and research-driven practice with CLD students.

Second, effective teachers of CLD students realize that flexibility in theory-into-practice applications for CLD students must be a goal of readiness. When theories do prove promising for the accommodation of CLD students, the application of these must first maintain essential consistency with the theoretical model yet also allow for flexibility in site-specific adaptations. Classroom practice with CLD students must be grounded in, and remain true to, the particular needs and dynamics of the site-specific population to be served.

Third, readiness for effective theory-into-practice applications necessarily highlights the teacher's understanding of sociocultural dynamics. No application of theory, no matter how robust the framework for effectiveness, will be successful with CLD students if that application is not cross-culturally and crosslinguistically sensitive. Culture and language are not only linked in an integral manner but they are central to what the CLD student brings to the classroom. Just as the teacher's cultural and language socialization filter her or his perceptions and actions in practice, the CLD student's socialization will filter his or her response to classroom praxis. Culturally or linguistically insensitive accommodations with CLD students can result in a number of untoward consequences, including affective filter–based interferences with learning, withdrawal, anxiety, lack of motivation, anger, resentment, and more.

Are You Aware?

The values and perspectives of the community typically shape policies at the school district level. Diaz-Rico and Weed (2002) have argued that teachers can provide a leadership role in helping to shape the community's perspectives:

Many opportunities exist for such [community] service. Service clubs such as rotary and Kiwanis provide opportunities for speakers: What better way to reach the business leaders of the community with current information about multicultural and linguistic issues? These activities deliver the message that teachers are knowledgeable and interested in the community at large. (p. 277)

■ *In what ways will you shape the opinions about and attitudes toward CLD students and families in your community? What is your readiness for advocacy in professional practice?*

Readiness for Differentiated Instruction

Application readiness is also a function of the teacher's preparedness to deliver *differentiated instruction,* which is central to the accommodation of the CLD student. This preparedness first demands an understanding that appropriately differentiated instruction for CLD students must be student-centered and grounded in a foundation of student or family preassessment. A teacher's readiness for CLD students and families is essential to his or her readiness for differentiated instructional applications.

Teachers who appropriately differentiate instruction for the CLD student are also aware of the need to incrementally implement that instruction, not by template, but by student response. Differentiated instruction, by definition, does not imply recipes, disconnected sets of strategies and activities, or quick fixes. Therefore, reflective teachers realize that differentiated instruction, when appropriately and incrementally implemented, must be process and product focused, reflectively monitored for student response, and intentionally refined (based on the findings of evaluation).

Above all, insightful teachers know that appropriately differentiated instruction for CLD students is *atypical.* The classroom may be loud as students maximize their social and linguistic interactions toward development. The environment for learning may look different as seating arrangements are modified to accommodate various peer groupings and cooperative learning. The room may be bustling with activity as students construct new knowledge from hands-on or thematic applications of learning.

Somewhat ironically, the reactions of building administrators, parents, community members, and fellow teachers to differentiated instruction, especially its atypical characteristics, are not always positive. In fact, some may argue that there is no classroom management. Others may bemoan the lack of classroom structure as demonstrated by the atypical seating arrangements and seemingly random use of learning centers. Still others may go so far as to assert that such accommodations are highly problematic because students are not treated as equals, according to certain educators' notions of meritocracy.

Readiness for Advocacy

Such difficult and often inexplicable challenges of accommodation are but one reason why preparedness for CLD student accommodation must involve a readiness for advocacy among school educators (see Figure 5.1). Elsewhere, we detail the consequences that may arise when educators fail to advocate for their CLD students, and we provide a framework for student advocacy both inside and outside the school (Herrera & Murry, 1999). Essentially, this framework suggests that teachers who demonstrate a readiness for advocacy share three common and critical characteristics: currency, defensibility, and futurity.

Advocacy as Currency

Currency, as a component of advocacy in practice, is concerned with the extent to which the teacher is current about best practice for CLD students and is aware of potential threats to appropriate services and accommodations for CLD students and families. A teacher's best efforts to differentiate instruction for CLD students in the grade-level classroom may be short-circuited by a community initiative that results in a school board decision to adopt an ESL pull-out model of language programming. Therefore, effective teachers of CLD students maintain currency regarding best practices and the internal and external environments of the school, especially the sociopolitical climate of accommodation. These proactive teachers establish and maintain their currency through such efforts as:

- Periodically reviewing appropriate educational literature.
- Attending local, state, and national conferences.
- Paying attention to local and state issues in the media.
- Inviting the media to document effective student accommodation in practice.
- Attending local school board meetings.
- Discussing their practices with the school administrator, board members, and others.

One powerful path to teacher readiness for currency is participation in a collaborative learning community of teachers and other educators who meet to discuss issues, literature, research, and best practice in the accommodation of CLD students. Hargreaves and Fullan claim that:

> In complex, rapidly changing times, if you don't get better as a teacher over time, you don't merely stay the same. You get worse. . . . Professional learning and collegiality can therefore no longer be an optional luxury for course-going individuals, or a set of add-on workshops to implement government priorities. Professional learning must be made integral to the task of teaching as a basic professional obligation

of teachers themselves. Only then will teachers be able to deal effectively with the numerous new challenges they face. (1998, p. 48)

These comments further demonstrate the critical role of ongoing professional learning in the complex accommodation of diverse student populations.

Advocacy as Defensibility

Defensibility, as a component of a framework for advocacy, is concerned with the extent to which the teacher is capable of (a) self-examination and self-reflection on practice, (b) articulating research- and theory-based rationales for accommodations in practice, and (c) the reflective development of a personal platform for best practice. Routman (1996) has argued that teachers must be able to articulate what they know and the rationale behind what they have implemented as best practice in the classroom. When the school administrator arrives to act on the complaints of fellow teachers that the accommodative classroom is too loud and disorganized, in what ways will the teacher be prepared to defend her or his classroom accommodations as best practice for CLD students? Will she or he be able to articulate the theory or research that supports hands-on, cooperative, and highly interactive learning for these students? Such questions illustrate why teachers must prove capable of defending their practices and demonstrate a readiness for advocacy in the accommodation of CLD student needs.

One of the best ways for teachers to ensure their capacity for advocacy is to challenge whether they are able to articulate their professional learning into a defensible position for accommodative practice with diverse populations. An effective way to document such learning and to synthesize it into an articulate defense for practice is the teacher's development of a best practice platform. Necessarily, such a platform expresses one's philosophy of practice in appropriate accommodations for CLD students. However, the platform also includes a defensibility component in that it provides a theory or research-based rationale for the educator's philosophy and defines what this philosophy means for critical aspects of effective practice with CLD students. A quality platform for best practice with CLD students should include the following sections: preinstructional assessment, methodology and instruction, postinstructional assessment, and reflection on effectiveness and cross-cultural sensitivity in practice (Murry & Herrera, 1999).

Interacting with other teachers within a collaborative learning community is also a critical way in which educators can enhance their capacity for defensibility of professional practice. As teachers dialogue with one another regarding the ways in which they successfully accommodate CLD students, they have opportunities to practice articulating rationales for their classroom practices. Therefore, effective educators maximize professional learning and collaboration with others in at least two ways. First, they use these to enhance their knowledge of best practice and potential threats to best practice. That is, they maximize professional learning and collaboration with others toward enhanced currency. Second, proactive educators synthesize professional learning, collaboration with others, and knowledge of their own practice environment and circumstances to both adapt practice in accommodative ways and articulate sound rationales for the defensibility of that praxis.

For example, Mr. Kowalski maximizes the advocacy components of currency and defensibility in the appropriate accommodation of learners in his second-grade class at Hesston Elementary. Because his class is composed of over 40 percent CLD students who are non-English proficient (NEP), he uses his professional learning about language dynamics and his collaboration with fellow teachers to advocate for appropriate instructional practices in his classroom and in his school. Specifically, his professional knowledge of first language acquisition and second language acquisition informs him that these NEP students will need ongoing native language support as a means to literacy development.

Therefore, in order to target the currency component of advocacy in practice, Mr. Kowalski remains informed and current about best practices to enhance first and second language acquisition, as well as potential threats to such practices. For example, the threats specific to his site include a sociopolitical environment in the community that favors an English-only perspective on the education of these students. Additionally, he collaborates with other teachers in the school to maintain and enhance this currency.

In order to bolster the defensibility of his practices in native language support, Mr. Kowalski works with colleagues to maximize his knowledge of common underlying proficiency (CUP) (Cummins, 1981). The SUP–CUP distinction rationalizes the ways in which well-developed CALP skills in L1 will transfer to emergent literacy development in L2 (English). Accordingly, this distinction provides him with a foundation from which to articulate a rationale for native language support in his classroom.

Advocacy as Futurity

Futurity, as a component of advocacy in practice, reflects the extent to which teachers are able to demonstrate a readiness to step out of the box in professional actions for CLD students and families.

> In action for advocacy, educators engage in futurity in order to better serve student/family needs, and to insure the long-term viability of appropriate efforts to deliver needs-appropriate, culturally-relevant, and student-centered practices and programs within the school. . . . This notion of teacher leadership redefines the teacher's role in the learning community as one which influences and engages people to take individual and collaborative actions to prompt appropriate change and improvements in professional practice. (Herrera & Murry, 1999, p. 127)

Thus, in at least one sense, futurity involves teacher leadership in appropriate accommodations for CLD students. Indeed, teachers who step out of the box on a regular basis are often the teachers who are the most effective with, and the most motivating to, their CLD students. The teachers who risk the misunderstandings of their colleagues in order to provide hands-on instructional accommodations for their CLD students are often the ones who sufficiently shelter the curriculum so that instruction is at last made comprehensible to their CLD students.

Futurity in the form of teacher leadership is increasingly an expectation of best practice with and advocacy for CLD students. Among examples of such futurity in practice are the following:

- Ms. Quintanilla frequently collaborates with parent and community volunteers to enhance the level of native language support she is able to offer her sixth-grade CLD students. Yet she knows that many of her fellow teachers within the school believe there is little they can do to provide such support to their language-learning students. Moreover, many of these teachers hold inaccurate assumptions regarding the willingness of CLD parents to support the education of their children. Therefore, at a recent grade-level meeting, Ms. Quintanilla offered to accompany those of her colleagues who are willing to make home visits to meet with the parents of their CLD students and to learn about the home lives and cultures of these students. She and a bilingual paraprofessional volunteered to translate as needed during such visits. As key aspects of these visits, parents will be encouraged to articulate their beliefs about education for their children, and they will also be encouraged to volunteer in the classroom.
- Mrs. Claymore, a fifth-grade teacher who recently completed her ESL endorsement, strongly believes that changing demographics in the classroom indicate that her school should move from an ESL pull-out programming model to the delivery of sheltered instruction in grade-level classrooms. She knows that most teachers in her grade level are now ESL endorsed and capable of serving the needs of CLD students in the classroom. Therefore, she meets with her building-level administrator and proposes that she and two other teachers attend an upcoming institute, which will deliver in-depth professional development regarding the sheltered instruction observation protocol (SIOP). Further, she argues that she and her colleagues are willing to, and will be capable of, serving as trainers of trainers to other teachers within her grade level regarding the SIOP model of instruction for CLD students. Accordingly, she encourages her principal to consider a fifth-grade-level pilot of SIOP instruction for CLD students in grade-level classrooms.
- Mr. Erichsen, a tenth-grade history teacher, has noted a recent and significant increase in the number of Mexican American CLD students in his classes. He knows little about the culture and language of these students, but he knows that most of them live in a small inner-city community near his high school. He decides that he will begin to shop in that community at least once a week and attend some of the community functions in order to learn more about these students, their parents, and their community. Based on these experiences, Mr. Erichsen has decided to propose at the next faculty meeting that the school begin to serve as a host for some of these community functions. He will argue that this hosting will provide teachers and administrators valuable opportunities to meet and collaborate with parents, extended family members, and community leaders.

The following voice from the field was recorded by an in-service teacher as part of her ESL endorsement preparation sequence at Kansas State University. The format of the journal was developed by Murry (1996) and is designed to promote critical reflection on practice with CLD students.

Behavior/Event

"I would like to share a personal experience I had with an ELL [CLD] student from my first year of teaching. During my first year of teaching, I taught Interrelated Education. I had a two-year teaching provisional in Special Education in addition to my Elementary Education degree. My caseload consisted of 10 fourth and fifth grade Hispanic boys, 1 Hispanic Down syndrome girl, and one mentally retard Caucasian boy. During this time, I had some intense and challenging teaching experiences with one of my fifth grade Hispanic boys whom we will call Dan for the remainder of this journal.

Dan was in fifth grade and had just recently moved to Ulysses from Dumas, Texas. Prior to living in Texas, Dan had been placed in a different school every 6–8 months. Dan came to our school on an IEP [individual education plan]. His goals were to identify letters and sounds by the end of fifth grade. With the High Plains Educational Cooperative, Dan would receive pull-out time as well as in classroom time. His daily pull-out was 180 minutes and his in-class time was 120 minutes, with 0 minutes of ESL. The only time during the day I was not with Dan was during P.E., Music, Lunch, Library, and recess. With all the moving his family did [and] with each school district having different ESL programs and different Special Education programs, Dan was placed in a Special Education program.

Dan's basic integrated communicative skills were able to get him his needs in a school setting, but were not very clear for communicating to [the] public as to what he needed. In Dan's home they spoke Spanish. His Dad knew very little English. The English Dan picked up was from being placed in a Public School at the age of 7 and then trying to survive. Dan was not an IEP child, he was an ELL student with 0 minutes of ESL. Dan knew he was not a Special Education student. He had phenomenal math skills, [and was] just waiting for someone to help him communicate with others what he knew. He had a drive to succeed and determination to prove to everyone he was as good as the rest of the fifth grade class. My goal for the duration of his stay was to teach him to read and to communicate with others. I also wanted to put him with his class in a fifth grade curriculum, modified just for him so that he would get the content needed and maintain his status of being a fifth grade student.

After 8 months of intense work with Dan, he had to move on with his family to his new home. Dan would leave his new school in hope of finding a school that would recognize his abilities. He could now sit in a fifth grade classroom and do fifth grade math, he could read at a second grade level, and comprehend stories on a fourth grade level. Dan was exited from Special Education after 6 months and placed in an ESL classroom. All Dan needed was to be bathed with the English Language, given a modified curriculum, supportive teachers, and he could accomplish anything. Dan felt good about exiting the Special Education program and was ecstatic about being with his peers who shared the same type of lifestyle that he did.

Feelings

- Compassion
- Caring
- Empathy
- Determination
- Discouraged
- Excited

Thoughts

I wondered how Dan could have been in school for five years and never been given the opportunity to be in an ESL program. I wondered if any teacher in the past had sat down with Dan and looked in his eyes and noticed his determination to succeed. I wondered how Dan felt being shifted from school to school every 6–8 months. After Dan left my school he would call once or twice a year and just say, "Mrs. Fischer, Mrs. Fischer, um, um, it's Dan," and then hang up. I wondered why he had called, or if something had happened good or bad. I wanted to know if every time I poured my heart and soul into helping a child if the family would pack up and leave. I wondered if it was worth my time and effort to really help the children if they were just going to be leaving anyway. I wondered if this is what the schools prior to Ulysses had done or thought about Dan.

Learnings

Step One I assumed that Dan's prior schools had placed him in Special Education for lack of knowing Dan. I assumed all ELL learners would pack up after 6–8 months and leave. I wasn't sure if it was worth my time, effort, and tears to help them with everything I had.

Step Two I'm not sure if my first assumption is valid or invalid due to the fact that I don't know for sure the reasoning behind Dan's prior schools' justification of putting Dan in Special Education. I would assume that my assumption is valid and the teachers did not take the time to look at the Language Development of the Prism Model. The Language Development part of the Prism Model makes it clear that students do have a traditional language used at home but it may not be the language used at school. In the process, teachers need to honor the silent period and allow them to participate when he/she is ready. The silent period should be just that, a silent period, and not be thought of as a learning disability. My second assumption is invalid. Not all ELL learners pack up and leave after 6–8 months, but the reasoning behind the majority of ELL students packing up and leaving is due to their SES [socioeconomic status].

Step Three I believe my first assumption has originated from Dan being put in Special Education and not ELL. Until I took this class, I didn't realize some of the complex things I expected out of my ELL students. Looking back at my first year of teaching I was blind to the fact that Dan's real problem was his language. I just took him under my wing and started from point A and tried to get him to point B in the quickest way I could. I didn't look at Dan as a Special Education child ever, but I also didn't look at him as benefiting from an ESL program until 3 months with Dan. So I did my best with bathing him in as much English as I could and hoped for the best. After putting him in the ESL program I did start to see more gains than with just being with me. I believe my second assumption has originated after my six years of teaching ELL learners. Each year I find that I lose at least two children leaving with their family for the sake of having a job and providing for their families.

Applications

Step One What I have gained from this journal is realizing that I shouldn't give up on my ELL learners. So what if they move away after 6–8 months; at least I have given them a small foundation for the next teacher to build on. They deserve everything I can give them. My hope for all other teachers (not enrolled in this class) is for them to open their eyes and see the same thing. I don't want them to give up on their ELL learners, water their material down to nothing, and allow them to just be a warm body in the classroom.

Step Two I believe after writing this paper I learned even more about Dan and understand a few more things about him than I did 6 years ago. In discovering this, I will try even harder to help my ELL learners in order to help build their self-esteem, confidence, and limit their stress from their home lives. They need to succeed and feel the success of life just as any other child in my classroom."

■ *Tamara Fischer, Ulysses, KS*

tips for practice

Elementary Education

1. Complete the following steps in order to enhance your readiness for critical reflection on practice:

   A. First, select one of your CLD students to profile. Briefly note what you know about the background knowledge and experiences of this student in each of the following areas:
      - Language Development
        —Approximately what level of BICS and CALP language proficiency does this student possess in L1 and in L2?
      - Academic Development
        —What prior schooling has this student experienced in the home country and in the United States?
        —Does the student have the knowledge and skills base to perform academically at grade level with appropriate language-transition support?
      - Acculturation
        —What challenges and setbacks has this student experienced in adjusting to life and schooling in this country?
        —What impact are these challenges and adjustments having on his or her classroom performance?

   B. Try to carry out one of the following, which are listed in the order of preference: (i) conduct a home visit with the parents, guardians, or family members of the selected student, or (ii) interview the student (with a translator, if necessary).

   C. Compare your notes on the background knowledge and experiences of this student with what you learn from either a home visit or an interview with the student.

   D. Reflect on any assumptions you made about the student's background and experiences. Were these assumptions confirmed by the findings of your home visit or interview? Why might any differences between the two exist?

   E. Critically reflect on what experiences or factors in your prior socialization might have prompted you to make certain assumptions about this student's background. Think about the implications of this exercise for reflective practice with all CLD students.

2. Although you may not speak the native language(s) of your CLD students, consider multiple ways to provide ongoing native language support for these students as a means to CALP development in L1 and L2; such efforts will enhance your readiness for CLD students and families. One way to accomplish this is by maximizing the capacities of a bilingual paraprofessional. When it is feasible, effective teachers plan and intentionally collaborate with bilingual paraprofessionals in the delivery of accommodative instruction for CLD students. Parents, guardians, or caregivers who are encouraged to volunteer in the classroom and build on classroom instruction in the home are also excellent sources of native language support. Such caregivers (as well as extended family members) should definitely be strongly encouraged to continue CALP and literacy development in L1 in the home. Finally, CLD students' bilingual peers are an excellent resource for native language support in the classroom. Heterogeneous peer groupings for cooperative learning are effective ways to maximize these resources.

3. Children's first teachers are their parents or guardians, and these individuals are certainly the most influential. What they do in aiding academic success for their child is crucial. Therefore, as a means to readiness for students and families, it is essential to make that connection as soon as possible. Visit the home of your CLD students before school begins to lower the affective filters of the student and of the parents or guardians. Provide the following in the native language of the student: a welcome letter, a list of expectations for the classroom, and possible ways the parent(s) can be helpful within the classroom and school. Review each document with the parents or guardians using an interpreter as necessary. In this way, the parents or guardians will be able to understand and discuss your classroom expectations. Additionally, such visits encourage dialogue about student

and parent or guardian strengths that may be capitalized on in the classroom and school.

4. Investigate possible ways to adapt and modify your current curriculum so that you can continue to challenge your CLD students effectively. Such efforts will enhance your curricular readiness for professional practice with CLD students. Begin by asking yourself questions such as: What are key concepts, ideas, and relationships that *all* students should learn from my curriculum? How might I adapt and modify this curriculum so that CLD students are challenged to learn these key concepts, ideas, and relationships yet are appropriately supported in their ongoing second language development? Experiment with ways to scaffold the curriculum. Among ways to scaffold the key components of the curriculum are:
   - Supplement the curriculum through *separate* word walls in L1 and L2, illustrations of concepts, posters, bulletin boards, and realia.
   - Enrich the curriculum through an auxiliary classroom library of books, pamphlets, and other sources of literature in the language(s) of CLD students.
   - Specify the curriculum through outlines, concept maps, Venn diagrams, and so forth.

Secondary Education

1. Although parents or guardians of CLD students are external to the classroom, their involvement can provide consistent links in the effort to support the native language and culture of the student. The following can promote such involvement and enhance the teacher's readiness for CLD students and families:
   - A family night in the classroom or school, such as a family math night, a family writing night, a family career fair, or even a family physical fitness fair. In order to validate the native cultures and languages of CLD students and their families, include flexible activities in the first languages of your CLD students. Quality activities also function to lower the affective filter for risk taking among CLD caregivers and extended family members.

2. As a means to programming and instructional readiness, visit with the ESL coordinator for your district to investigate and become informed about programming options for CLD students

you currently serve. Next, visit the homes of your CLD students and consult with their parents or guardians. If feasible, take time to explain school classroom procedures that might be difficult and inform them about the following:
   - An explanation of the placement process for CLD students, including procedures for language proficiency testing.
   - The insight that parents or guardians can provide regarding native language proficiency, previous schooling experience, behavioral and cultural patterns of the CLD student, and any information that may be of help to the teacher in instructional planning.
   - The value of their input in both the placement process and the planning for appropriate classroom instruction.

   Later, compare the information provided by the parents or guardians of CLD students with that of the ESL coordinator to see if additional insight provided by the parents or guardians can enrich programming decisions or inform instructional needs, modifications, and accommodations necessary to foster student success in your classroom.

3. Paraprofessionals often play a key role in helping CLD students gain the most from their educational experiences. Additionally, collaboration between the teacher in the classroom and the school administrator is often crucial for CLD student success. As a means to readiness for application and advocacy, the following tips are designed to foster an effective collaborative relationship between the teacher and the bilingual paraprofessional:
   - Get to know each other and discuss your perspectives on ESL or bilingual education and favored approaches.
     —Hold scheduled planning conferences or meetings.
     —Occasionally have lunch or dinner together for discussion.
   - Learn about each other's background experiences with CLD students.
     —Discuss at school or after school.
     —Share knowledge bases about the home cultures of CLD students.
   - Attend community functions together.
   - Learn about the home environment of CLD students together.

- Collaborate in conducting home visits.
  —Collaborate in conducting preassessment and monitoring conversations with parents or guardians and students.
- Plan instruction together in order to capitalize on the potential contribution each of you can bring to appropriate and accommodative instruction for CLD students. Among enabling questions to ask are the following:
  —How can the paraprofessional support the teacher's plan for CLD student learning?
  —What ideas does the paraprofessional have about instructional modifications the teacher may not have considered?
  —What alternative learning contexts can the paraprofessional generate to reinforce the teacher's lesson?
  —What sort of instructional modifications do the CLD student's language assessment scores suggest are needed?
  —Does the paraprofessional need to provide an overview or preview of the day's lesson in the native language prior to the teacher's instruction in English?
  —Can the paraprofessional offer auxiliary instruction on the topic to a mixed group of CLD and grade-level learners in order to reinforce learning and promote an inclusive learning environment?
- Collaborate to extend the teacher's ability to conduct ongoing informal assessment and monitoring of CLD student progress. The following are quality questions to ask:
  —What assessments can the teacher and the paraprofessional both conduct?
  —What assessments are better conducted by the paraprofessional than the teacher?
  —What assessment environments capitalize on the power of each or both?
  —Does the paraprofessional need to conduct informal postinstructional assessments in the native language as a check on learning?
- Collaborate to encourage, promote, and enhance CLD parental or caregiver involvement in the instructional goals of the class. The following are guiding questions to ask:
  —What cross-cultural concerns among parents or guardians can the paraprofessional help the teacher identify and address?

—In what ways can parents or guardians become directly involved with the paraprofessional and teacher in native language and instructional support?

General Education

1. Create a "Welcome to School" video in the native language of your CLD population. This will help acquaint new students and their families with the school environment, procedures, and special events. Students who are bilingual and of the same background can narrate this video. Some of the topics to be included could be school staff, registration and enrollment procedures, cafeteria procedures, and available community services.

2. Have bilingual personnel available during enrollment and registration of CLD students to explain the policies and expectations of the school to parents or guardians in the native language and in English. Provide professional development for such personnel before the beginning of school each year or at various times throughout the year to ensure understanding of such policies and expectations and to address and clarify any possible questions or posed dilemmas by the personnel.

3. In order to make the classroom environment inviting and welcoming for CLD students and their parents or guardians, teachers can do the following:
   - Invite the parents or guardians of CLD students and the extended family to share aspects of their culture and language with the whole class. This may include specific traditions and customs, clothing, food, rituals, and more.
   - Label vocabulary words and pictures in both English and the native languages of your students.
   - Encourage students to use their native language in pairs and in heterogeneous cooperative groups when working on projects or for simple clarification of a concept taught.
   - As a means to environmental readiness for CLD students, create a positive, engaging atmosphere in which students are guided to contribute to presentations and discussions from their own unique cultural perspectives. For example, if the class is studying the geo-

graphy of the Middle East, ask students of this cultural background to share any photos or pictures they may have from their homeland.

4. Reflect high expectations for all students through the alignment of lessons and curriculum with local and state standards. Such efforts on curricular readiness greatly enhance the teacher's capacity to argue best practice in the classroom. Adapt and modify the curriculum linguistically when necessary for CLD students rather than watering it down or simplifying the content to a lower grade level. For example, when addressing local

and state standards regarding historical concepts within the fourth-grade social studies curriculum, you can provide (a) visuals such as outlines and graphic organizers, (b) hands-on manipulatives such as salt maps, and (c) activities that involve cooperative groups for problem solving and aid in concept understanding. Technology-based activities, such as the computer program "Oregon Trail," may also prove effective. Such activities and programs provide CLD students with opportunities to demonstrate understanding, declarative knowledge, and a capacity for application.

key theories and concepts

accommodation readiness spiral
critical reflection
curricular readiness
curriculum essentials
environmental readiness
espoused readiness
mutual accommodation

one-way accommodation
practical readiness
programming and instructional readiness
readiness for application and advocacy
readiness for CLD students and families

readiness for critical reflection on practice
recidivism
reflection
semistructured conversations
socialization
theory-into-practice applications

professional conversations on practice

1. Discuss one-way and mutual accommodation, with an emphasis on reasons why the mutual accommodation of CLD students is not more widespread in schools.

2. Discuss reflection and critical reflection, with an emphasis on the ways in which each contributes to a practitioner's readiness for critical reflection on practice.

3. Discuss the six readiness levels of the accommodation readiness spiral and your reflections on your preparedness for each.

4. Discuss the advantages of a home visit over a parent–teacher conference in promoting both parental or caregiver involvement and readiness for CLD students and families.

5. Discuss the components of advocacy and the ways in which each contributes to the educator's readiness for application and advocacy.

questions for review and reflection

1. Explain the notion of critical reflection. In what ways does critical reflection differ from reflection?

2. In what ways must readiness for critical reflection on practice serve as a foundation for all other levels of the accommodation readiness spiral?

3. In what ways would you prepare for a home visit to the family of a CLD student whose culture and language were different from your own? In what ways would you avoid inappropriate cross-cultural and crosslinguistic assumptions about the student, his or her parents or caregivers, and extended family members?

4. List at least five advantages of using a home visit versus a parent–teacher conference as a means to readiness for CLD students and families.

5. Reflect on the environments internal and external to the school. What factors should be assessed in the external and internal environments as a means to environmental readiness? (List and discuss at least four each.)

6. What are curriculum essentials? Discuss the significance of these curriculum essentials to curricular readiness.

7. What are two ideals in programming for CLD students at the district or school level? In what ways can teachers contribute to the attainment of these ideals?

8. What are at least two crucial factors to consider in ensuring that theory-into-practice applications for CLD students contribute to readiness for application and advocacy? Discuss why each is crucial.

9. Reflect on accommodations for CLD students. What are at least two critical factors to consider in ensuring that differentiated instruction contributes to readiness for application and advocacy? Discuss why each is critical.

10. What are the three essential components of effective advocacy for CLD students and families? Discuss why each is essential to effectiveness.

suggested activities

Preservice Teachers

1. An important aspect of serving the needs of CLD students is understanding and acknowledging how your personal values influence the way you teach. Figure 5.4 is a chart that you can use to gain insights into the ways in which your personal beliefs might affect your interactions with students and parents of different cultures. Please complete this chart and reflect on its various sections.

2. Obtain a copy of a school's handbook of policies and procedures that is given to parents. Put yourself in the shoes of parents of CLD students. How well would you be able to understand this handbook? Identify the gaps and barriers they may encounter when attempting to understand the school's expectations. How can these be addressed?

3. During a practicum experience, you walk into the teacher's lounge and overhear a teacher discussing how a particular student never completes his work and is always talking in Hindi to his best friend in class. According to her, it is not in her job description to teach a student who cannot speak or understand the English language. How would this comment make you feel? Would you address this situation? If so, how?

In-Service Teachers

1. When preassessing CLD students, it is important to make modifications that support their native languages and take into consideration their sociocultural backgrounds. Figure 5.5 is a chart that can help you understand whether educators in your school are making such culturally responsive modifications.

2. Judy is a ninth-grade Hmong student who is doing very well in her courses. However, her parents have not participated in school activities, nor have they responded to any of the teacher's letters or phone calls home. Make a list of possible reasons you think may be contributing to this "lack of involvement." Discuss this list with a colleague and identify any possible assumptions you may have made.

3. Ask your students to journal about the value they and their family members place on education. Compare their responses to your own upbringing, values, and views about the importance of education. What sociocultural factors may play a part in the difference you see between the viewpoints you and your CLD students hold?

figure 5.4 Personal Perspectives Self-Reflection Tool

EFFECTIVENESS INDICATORS	ACTUAL SITUATION		EVALUATION			NEEDS			FUTURE GOAL
	In Progress	In Place	I Do This Well	I Do This So-So	I Need Improvement	Technical Assistance	More Time	Resources	
1. I am aware of my culture's dominant traditions, attitudes, interaction styles, and educational viewpoints.									
2. I am aware of situations in which my values, interaction styles, beliefs, and attitudes may be positively affecting my interactions with cultures different from mine.									
3. I am also aware of situations in which my values, interaction styles, beliefs, and attitudes may negatively affect these interactions.									
4. One of my primary goals when interacting with people of different cultures is to convey empathy and acceptance of their world as they define it.									
5. Another primary goal to further developing cross-cultural competence is: _____ _____ _____									

figure 5.5 Culturally Responsive Preassessment Tool

EFFECTIVENESS INDICATORS	ACTUAL SITUATION		EVALUATION			NEEDS			FUTURE GOAL
	In Progress	In Place	We Do This Well	We Do This Somewhat	We Need Improvement	Technical Assistance	More Time	Resources	
1. Our team regularly conducts preevaluation conferences to inform the family about the assessment process and to learn their concerns, goals, and observations about their child.									
2. ESL and/or bilingual educators are an inherent part of the preevaluation process.									
3. Our team uses various strategies to prepare the family for the actual evaluation (e.g., home visits).									
4. At the end of the preevaluation, our team provides the family with both a verbal and written summary of any information obtained in both English and the native language.									
5. Questionnaires for parents regarding information about their child's academic and linguistic background are provided in both English and the native language.									

Professionalism in Practice

In Part III, we recommend a professional approach to the instructional accommodation of CLD students. This professionalism is conceptualized as involving three sequential components: planning, implementation, and evaluation. In Chapter 6, we provide and rationalize recommendations for planning appropriate practices for CLD students. In Chapters 7 through 9, we discuss and detail three contemporary and robust methods of effective instruction. Finally, in Chapter 10 we discuss ways to appropriately engage in the evaluation of prior instructional planning and implementation. These processes of evaluation use nationally recognized standards of best practice with CLD students as touchstones of comparison.

The information provided in this chapter will help the educator to:

- Describe the ways in which consistency among instructional terms enables communication and collaboration.
- Differentiate among the terms *approach, method, strategy,* and *technique.*
- Discuss three dominant approaches to language instruction for CLD students.
- Differentiate among the philosophical foundations for the grammatical, communicative, and cognitive approaches to language instruction.
- Summarize the history and evolution of the grammatical, communicative, and cognitive approaches to language instruction.
- Summarize the noteworthy methods of the grammatical approach.
- Differentiate between early and contemporary communicative methods.
- Summarize early methods of the communicative approach.
- Discuss contemporary methods of the communicative approach.
- Describe the influences of the cognitive model of learning on the cognitive approach.
- Differentiate between metacognitive knowledge and metacognitive regulation.
- Summarize and highlight key features of the CALLA method.

Planning and Grounding Instructional Methodology

It is the action, not the fruit of the action, that's important. You have to do the right thing. It may not be in your power, may not be in your time, that there'll be any fruit. But that doesn't mean you stop doing the right thing. You may never know what results come from your action. But if you do nothing, there will be no result.

—Mohandas K. Gandhi

critical standards *Guiding Chapter Content*

TESOL/NCATE teacher standards reflect professional consensus on standards for the quality teaching of pre-K–12 CLD students. Additionally, the CEEE Guiding Principles and their accompanying indicators serve as a framework to assist practitioners, policymakers, and clients as they collaborate to enhance academic enrichment and language acquisition among CLD students. Therefore, in order to help educators understand how they might appropriately target and address national professional teaching standards in practice, we have designed the content of this chapter to reflect the following standards.

TESOL ESL Standards for P–12 Teacher Education Programs

TESOL ESL—Domain 1: Language. Candidates know, understand, and use the major concepts, theories, and research related to the nature and acquisition of language to construct learning environments that support ESOL [CLD] students' language and literacy development and content-area achievement. (p. 1)

- **Standard 1.b. Language acquisition and development.** Candidates understand and apply concepts, theories, research, and practice to facilitate the acquisition of a primary and a new language in and out of classroom settings. (p. 6)

  1.b.4. Create a secure, positive, and motivating learning environment. (p. 9)

  1.b.9. Understand and apply knowledge of the role of individual learner variables in the process of learning English. (p. 11)

TESOL ESL—Domain 5: Professionalism. Candidates demonstrate knowledge of the history of ESL teaching. Candidates keep current with new instructional techniques, research results, advances in the ESL field, and public policy issues. Candidates use such information to reflect upon

Note: All TESOL/NCATE standards are cited from TESOL (2001). All Guiding Principles are cited from Center for Equity and Excellence in Education (1996).

and improve their instructional practices. Candidates provide support and advocate for ESOL students and their families and work collaboratively to improve the learning environment. (p. 38)

- **Standard 5.a: ESL research and history.** Candidates demonstrate knowledge of history, research, and current practice in the field of ESL teaching and apply this knowledge to improve teaching and learning. (p. 39)
  - 5.a.1. Demonstrate knowledge of language teaching methods in their historical contexts. (p. 39)

CEEE Guiding Principles

Guiding Principle #4: Limited English proficient students receive instruction that builds on their previous education and cognitive abilities and that reflects their language proficiency levels. (p. 8)

4.1 School districts take into consideration the whole profile of a student, including language/cultural background, native language literacy, and appropriate and valid student assessment data when making decisions about the placement and provision of services to limited English proficient students. (p. 8)

4.6 Teachers identify and design comprehensible instruction that is appropriate to limited English proficient students' developmental levels as well as to their stages of first and second language acquisition. (p. 8)

4.9 Teachers use instructional approaches, such as cooperative learning and experiential learning, that are sensitive to the multiple experiences of learners and that address different learning and performance modes. (p. 8)

After coming to the decision that they would like to enhance their practice to better accommodate the varying assets and needs of their students, many educators are at a loss as to where they should turn or what they should do first. Some practitioners have heard about new activities that they think might be useful in their classrooms. Others have read articles concerning wonder-working methods that promise miracles overnight. What *is* the first step on the path to creating long-lasting, systematic change in practice?

Essential to the successful implementation of any program is a logical plan of action. Effective educators first critically think about and reflect on their personal beliefs about the overall goals of education before determining the actual changes they will implement in the classroom. Randomly incorporating new activities into instruction most often does not lead to eagerly anticipated positive results with students. Rather, the effective educator demonstrates logic-, theory-, and research-based reasons for the selection and sequence of actions that he or she chooses to incorporate in classroom instruction. Such practitioners choose a sound approach around which they can structure their teaching. Then, they choose an appropriate method and consider specific strategies and techniques. But what is meant by an *approach,* and aren't *methods, strategies,* and *techniques* basically the same thing? Although these terms are often interchanged in everyday speech, such inconsistency in terminology leads to confusion in the field of education. In this chapter, we discuss the need for consistent nomenclature among educational terms, and we provide an organizing framework for the conceptual definitions of *approach, method, strategy,* and *technique.* Because choosing an approach is the first step in developing a plan for accommodative instruction, we also explore various approaches to second language acquisition.

■ Consistency in Nomenclature — names or terms Enables Communication

The educational field has evolved tremendously in the recent years of incredible technological advances. Educators are now able to communicate with one another across state and national boundaries with ease. Information resources that were once available only to those with funds for numerous literary subscriptions, or those who had the benefit of a nearby university library, are now available to educators through the Internet. For this reason, practitioners have greater access to the growing body of research and theory regarding the most effective instruction for students. Consequently, many educators are beginning to implement changes in their curriculum and instruction in order to better accommodate students and prepare them to meet the evolving challenges of society. With increasing frequency, educators are discussing, comparing, contrasting, and evaluating instructional ideas that were used in the past, those that are used in classrooms today, and those that represent the cutting edge of theory-based classroom practice.

Along with these emergent conversations about systemic change in education is a growing need for consistent terminology. Educators are often caught in a quagmire of competing terms and left wondering how everything fits together. For example, the cognitive academic language-learning approach (CALLA) is one of the most promising new methods of instruction for CLD students. Yet it is variously referred to in the literature and in classroom practice as a model, a method, and an approach. A similar problem arises with the integrated skills approach, which we would tend to characterize as a method of instruction. Indeed, it is difficult for educators to effectively communicate with one another about ideas for instructional practice when each person is relying on a different conceptual understanding of or nomenclature for the same term.

As Oller (1993) relates, the quest to find a suitable form of organization for educational nomenclature began with the efforts of Ed Anthony (1963), who suggested that a distinction between an approach, a method, and a technique was necessary. As such, he described an *approach* as something similar to a theory, a *method* as the type of curriculum, program, or procedure that a school or educator chooses to adopt, and a *technique* as the specific actions taken in the classroom setting that put the method into practice (Oller, 1993). Further attempts to clarify educational concepts have been numerous. Indeed, multiple definitions and relationships among *methods, techniques, procedures, designs, activities, tactics, strategies, curricula,* and other such terms have been variously proposed (Anthony & Norris, 1969; Richards, 1983; Richards & Rodgers, 1982; Strain, 1986; Strevens, 1980).

We argue the need to provide educators with consistent terminology that is organized to afford clear direction for conceptualizing the pedagogical terms educators will use when referring to their practices. Accordingly, based on our review of the literature and our experiences with instructional methods in practice, we have developed operational definitions for the instructional terms outlined in Figure 6.1. These terms are used throughout the remainder of this text and ground our discussions of appropriate instructional methods for CLD students. By sharing identical concept definitions of the type outlined in Figure 6.1, practitioners in different classrooms, schools, districts, and states can effectively communicate and collaborate with one another to share information, as well as plan, implement, and evaluate ideas that lead to improved classroom instruction and enhanced student achievement.

To accommodate the assets and differential learning needs of *all* students, effective educators provide instruction that is grounded in theory and practice. Such educators first examine their beliefs concerning human and mental development, learning, and language acquisition. They review literature and research to acquire an understanding of the theories that guide contemporary understandings regarding essential aspects of successful instruction. With the best interest of their students in mind, effective educators then choose an approach on which they will base their instruction.

Approach

An *approach* is the philosophical orientation to instruction that serves as a guide for choosing among methods that are considered to be consistent with the tenets of the theory and research that ground the philosophy. As such, the instructional and related decisions an educator makes regarding the manner in which practice takes place in the classroom ultimately find their rationale in the chosen approach. Accordingly, the choice of an approach should not be a rash decision. An educator's approach should be theory- and research-based and should reflect his or her personal philosophy of education. Later in this chapter, we detail three instructional approaches. Although the grammatical approach is discussed primarily for historical purposes, the communicative and cognitive approaches are contemporary approaches that reflect what we know to be true about quality methods of instruction for CLD students.

Method

After deciding on the approach that will provide the basis for actual classroom practice, effective teachers choose a method. A *method* is a body of philosophically grounded and purposively integrated strategies and techniques that constitutes one translation of an approach into professional practice. That is, appropriate methods fit under the umbrella of a particular approach. Figure 6.2 illustrates this and other relationships among the practice-based definitions explored in this chapter. A method represents the practical or applied aspect of the instructional approach and therefore must be consistent with the chosen approach.

■ **figure 6.1**   Comparisons in Nomenclature among *Approach, Method, Strategy,* and *Technique*

Approach
(Broadest Category)

An approach *is the philosophical orientation to instruction that serves as a guide for choosing among methods that are considered to be consistent with the tenets of the theory and research that ground the philosophy.*

- Approaches are grounded in a research-based or theoretical framework for practice.
- Approaches to instruction reflect philosophies of human and mental development, learning, and language acquisition.
- Approaches guide the choice of related methods that are consistent with the theory and research that ground the philosophy.

Method

A method *is a body of philosophically grounded and purposively integrated strategies and techniques that constitutes one translation of an approach into professional practice.*

- Methods are consistent with a practitioner's approach to instruction.
- Methods represent the practical or applied aspect of an instructional approach.
- Methods are the umbrella for the strategies that one selects and uses because of their consistency with one's philosophy of instruction.

Strategy

A strategy *is a collection of philosophically grounded and functionally related techniques that serves as an implementation component of an instructional method.*

- Strategies are consistent with the practitioner's method, just as the method must prove consistent with the approach to instruction.
- Strategies represent an implementation component of a method, as applied to field practice.
- Strategies are the umbrella for techniques that are selected and used in practice.

Technique
(Most Specific Category)

A technique *constitutes specific actions or action sequences that have been designed to achieve a defined, strategic objective.*

- Techniques must be consistent with the strategies that are chosen for their applicability to particular student populations.
- Techniques represent action subcomponents of strategies.
- Individual techniques may be combined with other related techniques to achieve effective implementation of a particular strategy.

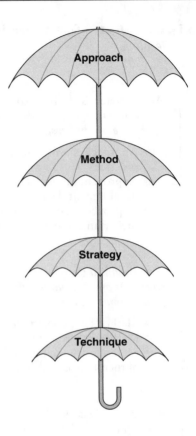

■ **figure 6.2** Illustration of the Relationships among Approach, Method, Strategy, and Technique

For example, some educators decide to adopt the communicative approach, which emphasizes the need for student interaction opportunities. If this is the case, a method comprising various strategies and techniques that promote student interaction is needed. The sheltered instruction method, which is discussed extensively in Chapter 8, is an example of a research- and theory-based method grounded in the communicative approach. This particular method emphasizes the incorporation of both teacher–student and student–student interactions. In contrast, the implementation of a method that lacks interaction strategies and techniques will result in instruction that is not consistent with the practitioner's personal philosophy of education. Such inconsistencies can lead to mixed messages, student confusion, and inconsistent student performance.

Strategy

In implementing their chosen method, which is purposefully aligned with their adopted approach, effective teachers choose appropriate strategies. A *strategy* is a collection of philosophically grounded and functionally related techniques that serves as an implementation component of an instructional method. Consequently, strategies fall under the umbrella of a specific method, as depicted in Figure 6.2. The strategies selected by an effective teacher are philosophically consistent with his or her chosen method of classroom instruction. For example, the sheltered instruction method highlights the incorporation of hands-on activities. The use of hands-on activities is a particular strategy that educators employ when using the sheltered instruction method with their students. Another strategy of this method is the use of cooperative learning.

Technique

Finally, effective educators determine the specific ways in which the chosen strategies will manifest themselves in the classroom—that is, they choose appropriate techniques. *Techniques* are specific actions or action sequences that have been designed to achieve a defined, strategic objective. As such, techniques fall under the umbrella of chosen strategies, as illustrated in Figure 6.2, and represent action subcomponents of strategies. For example, if educators decide to use the strategy of cooperative learning, they may decide to have students collaborate by doing think-pair-share, jigsawing, or group problem solving. Actions such as these constitute the techniques with which educators put the cooperative learning strategy into practice with their students.

Individual techniques can also be effectively combined with other related techniques to achieve successful implementation of a particular strategy. For instance, a practitioner may want to combine the think-pair-share technique with the group problem-solving technique to effectively implement the cooperative learning strategy. In such a case, the teacher might group CLD students heterogeneously according to high and low English proficiency. Within each group, the students first read the selection of text. They then form pairs (two per group) and share their personal ideas. At this juncture, the more English proficient CLD students may serve as more capable peers for students who are less proficient in English. As a whole group, the students then problem-solve together. Finally, each of the groups shares its ideas with the rest of the class.

■ Consistency: In Practice

In creating a plan for student instruction that best accommodates the needs and assets of every student, effective teachers use theory and research to make informed accommodative decisions regarding their instructional approach, method, strategies, and techniques. As Figure 6.1 illustrates, the effective teacher begins with the broadest category, which involves choosing an approach that reflects his or her personal philosophy of instruction. The educator will then choose a method that is consistent with the chosen approach and determine particular strategies that are aligned with his or her method. Ultimately, the teacher will focus on the choice of specific techniques that support the strategies chosen. Techniques are the most specific category of instructional actions. Because the first step in planning for language instruction involves the choice of an instructional approach, the subsequent sections of this chapter present an overview of the three dominant approaches to second language instruction.

■ Three Dominant Approaches to Second Language Instruction

For more than two thousand years, language teachers have been debating what the nature of second language instruction should be: deductive or inductive (Howatt, 1984; Kelly, 1976). In *deductive language instruction,* students learn the rules and patterns of the second language as a means of learning the language. Deductive instruction is structure-based. Conversely, *inductive language instruction* emphasizes authentic uses of the second language as a means of naturally acquiring the rules and patterns of the language. Inductive instruction is meaning-based.

As illustrated in Table 6.1, dominant language instruction methodology falls into one of three approaches: the grammatical approach, the communicative approach, or the cognitive approach. Of these approaches to language instruction, the grammatical approach fits into the structure-based deductive category of language instruction. The communicative and cognitive approaches, on the other hand, correspond to the meaning-based inductive language instruction category. These differing approaches to language instruction evolved from different philosophies of human development, learning, and language learning. These philosophies are comparatively distinct and inform the methodology of each approach. In choosing appropriate second language approaches for CLD students, educators must understand the philosophies and research that support and challenge the usefulness and educational value of each approach.

Grammatical Approach

The *grammatical approach* is a teacher-centered means of providing second language instruction. The underlying philosophy of the approach assumes that learners acquire language most efficiently by memorizing language rules and sentence patterns in a methodical, sequenced curriculum. Learners study these rules and patterns in ways that are often isolated from a meaningful context. For example, the sequenced curriculum of the grammatical approach typically begins with nouns, then verb conjugations, adjective use, possessives, and pronouns. Subsequent instruction, as well as drill and practice, tends to emphasize sentence structure, agreement rules, and idiomatic usage. Amidst this sequential learning, a learner's first language is viewed as interfering with second language acquisition because differences in structure and syntax rules are considered points of confusion. According to the tenets of the grammatical approach, these points of confusion become the emphasis of instruction. At a superficial level, these propositions might seem logical. However, as this chapter explains, the nature of language belies this recipe approach to language acquisition.

■ **table 6.1**   Dominant Philosophical Approaches to Language Instruction

APPROACHES		
Grammatical/ Grammar-Based	**Communicative**	**Cognitive**

History

Origins in nineteenth-century classical Greek and Latin instruction	Primary origins in 1960s and 1970s research on language learning through communication, constructivism, and social interaction	Origins in 1980s and 1990s research on learning functions, memory, and cognition

Characteristics

Teacher-centered Emphasis on the rules and structure of target language	Student-centered Emphasis on communication and meaningful acquisition of knowledge	Learner-centered Focus on explicit teaching of learning strategies (LS) in communicative ways

Methods

Grammar-Translation (Historical) • More emphasis on development of reading, writing, and grammar • Less emphasis on oral language development • Rules of grammar are taught holistically Direct (Historical) • Focus on total immersion in L2 • No use of L1 allowed in the classroom • Involves an open-ended response to materials the teacher brings into the classroom Audiolingual (Historical) • Grammar structures are carefully sequenced and taught • Minimal use of L1 • Emphasizes error correction, drills, and repetitive practice	Silent Way (Historical) • Teacher modeling/talk • Reinforcement through repetition/signals • Seldom content-based Natural Way (Historical) • Stresses comprehensible input • Minimal error correction/production • Acceptance of students' L1 • Not necessarily content-based Suggestopedia (Historical) • Emphasis on relaxed physical setting • Minimal error correction • Use of L1 for explanations • Not necessarily content-based Integrated Content-Based • Emphasizes L2 development • Focus on content and language integration • Subject area integrated into thematic units Sheltered Instruction • Grade-level modified curriculum • Scaffolded instruction • Visuals, cooperative learning, and guarded vocabulary	CALLA • Developmentally appropriate language instruction • Intentional focus on CALP development in L1 and L2 as related to content areas • Focus on prior knowledge • Explicit instruction in the following learning strategies: — Metacognitive — Cognitive — Social/Affective

(continued)

■ **t a b l e 6 . 1**   Continued

APPROACHES		
Grammatical/ Grammar-Based	**Communicative**	**Cognitive**
	Strategies	
Examples from the direct method: • Drill and practice • Rote memorization	Examples from the sheltered instruction method: • Scaffolding • Guarded vocabulary • Cooperative learning • Hands-on activities	Examples from the CALLA method: • Cooperative learning • Explicit LS instruction • Maximizing content and language objectives
Techniques		
General examples: • Dialogue memorization • Repetition • Mnemonics • Kinetics	General examples: • Reduced use of idioms • Manipulatives and realia • Simulations/big books • Heterogeneous grouping	General examples: • KWL chart • Questioning • Word walls • Outlines

[handwritten annotation: Phonecis]

Grammatical Approach: History and Evolution

The grammatical approach has been the predominant means of teaching a second language for several thousand years. This approach was originally used in early Greek and Latin instruction, which focused on language learning as a mental discipline. Evidence of the use of the grammatical approach in bilingual glossaries dates back to 2500 BC in Mesopotamia (Kelly, 1976). However, the use of the grammatical approach was most prevalent during the Middle Ages, the eighteenth century, the nineteenth century, and the first half of the twentieth century. Given the findings of recent research and analysis, most second language researchers and linguists now consider the grammatical approach a historical artifact (Canale, 1983; Cummins, 2001a; Krashen, 1981; Ovando & Collier, 1998; Wong Fillmore & Valdez, 1986). At least at the level of the public school classroom for CLD students, communicative and cognitive approaches have essentially replaced the grammatical approach as philosophical foundations for language instruction.

Grammatical Approach: Philosophical Foundations

In the past, some theorists such as John Locke and David Hume believed that all human knowledge was the product of interaction with the world outside the individual—that is, the environment. Such knowledge, it was believed, was gained through the senses. These and other philosophers maintained that individuals acquired knowledge through what they tasted, touched, saw, heard, and felt. Later, John Watson and B. F. Skinner further developed this idea that the environment shapes human behavior through a series of environmental stimuli and responses that shape, or condition, human behavior. They believed that the environment shapes behavior by rewarding desirable behavior and punishing undesirable behavior. They proposed that behaviors that are rewarded increase in frequency and behaviors that are punished decrease in frequency (Moshman, Glover, & Bruning, 1987). This theory of human behavior is called behaviorism, or behavioral psychology. Table 6.2 illustrates the influences of these and other theorists on the grammatical approach.

Educators who subscribed to the beliefs of behavioral psychology contended that language-learning experiences must emphasize the explicit teaching of grammar. Moreover, consistent error correction was considered essential to shape *correct* language acquisition among second language learners. Because the assumption of this perspective was that a person's language learning is shaped exclusively through explicit grammar- or rule-based instruction and correction and not by any instinctive language ability, language instruction occurred in a fixed scope and

■ table 6.2   Philosophical Approaches to Language Instruction and Their Foundations

Philosophical Approach	Grammatical (Historical)	Cognitive (Contemporary)	Communicative (Contemporary)
Perspectives on Human Development	Fixed/staged/predictable	Typically staged but environmentally variable	Interactively variable
	Locke Hume Watson	Piaget	Vygotsky Bakhtin
Perspectives on Learning	Behaviorist	Cognitivist	Social Constructivist
	Stimulus-response (S-R)	Guided or independent construction of meaning	Guided or independent construction of meaning
	Skinner	Gazzaniga; Edelman	Bruner; Ansubel; Papert
Perspectives on Language Learning	Deductive (specific to general)	Inductive (general to specific)	Inductive (general to specific)
	Rule/structure driven	Interaction/guidance driven	Interaction driven
	Memorizing language rules and/or sentence patterns with drill-and-practice emphasis	Explicit teaching/modeling of learning strategies and language for communication	Language learning through and for authentic communication
	Palmer; Fries; Oller; Obrecht	Oxford; Chamot; O'Malley; Hakuta; Bialystok	Krashen; Terrell; Echevarria; Vogt; Short

sequence. From this deductive view of language instruction, students first learned grammatical and syntactical rules. They then used these rules as a guide for producing language. Students began learning a second language by memorizing and practicing basic rules for common language uses. As the students progressed through each step in the language-learning process, they memorized and increasingly practiced the complex language structures. Educators following this grammatical behavioral philosophy believed that language does not develop from exposure alone. Instead, they believed that the student learns best through sequenced patterns of instruction, the reinforcement of correct language use, and the correction of erroneous language production.

Grammatical Approach: Methods

The grammatical approach to second language instruction has taken many forms over the past two thousand years. Until the eighteenth century, the disputation method of the approach, which emphasized the memorization and application of language rules and structures, was the most prevalent venue for language instruction. The instructors would first read language treatises to the students explaining each point in simple language. Next, the instructor would present a series of questions and then subsequently answer the questions through instruction. Finally, the instructor would pose questions to the students, and the students would respond with memorized answers to demonstrate their mastery of language rules (Kelly, 1976). The disputation method diminished in popularity and eventually disappeared completely with the development of the grammar-translation method. This and other methods of the grammatical approach are summarized in Table 6.1 and discussed in the following sections.

Grammar-Translation Method   The grammar-translation method of language instruction developed during the eighteenth century and became popular during the nineteenth century (Kelly, 1976). In this method, the teacher first presented language rules to students. Then the students memorized a vocabulary list. Finally, the students applied the language rules and exceptions, as well as the vocabulary terms, to the translation of written text. At beginning levels of instruction, language learners often translated isolated sentences. As students became more proficient, they would translate increasingly complex classical texts (Howatt, 1984; Kelly, 1976). Translation was not for meaning. Instead, the grammar-translation method focused on grammatical accuracy (Kelly, 1976). The direct method replaced the grammar-translation method by the 1940s.

Direct Method   Among the grammatical approaches of the twentieth century, the direct method and the audiolingual method focused less on explicit instruction of grammar rules and structures and more on the repetition and memorization of language patterns. The direct method originated in the late nineteenth century and experienced popularity during the first half of the twentieth century (Kelly, 1976). The developers of the direct method—Harold Palmer, for example—sought to create a scientifically based teaching method for second language instruction (Palmer & Palmer, 1925). Behaviorist psychology and *ergonics,* the association of words with the specific contexts in which they were learned, formed the basis of the direct method (Kelly, 1976), which was most closely associated with the Berlitz language schools (Richard-Amato, 1996). In the direct method, students inferred grammar through exposure to carefully sequenced guided instruction in the target language. According to this method, teachers would model and students would practice language patterns, with the goal of internalizing grammatical patterns. Vocabulary was taught in context through dialogues and choral responses (Brooks, 1960). Because direct methodologists viewed a learner's first language as interfering with his or her ability to learn the target language, they heavily discouraged translation. However, the direct method did place some emphasis on context through the use of objects, photographs, diagrams, and drawings (Kelly, 1976).

Audiolingual Method World War II brought a new emphasis on language learning. U.S. military troops who were bound for destinations overseas needed a rapid means of learning foreign languages. The audiolingual method was developed in response to this need. The audiolingual method presented pattern drills and dialogue designed to develop grammatical structures and vocabulary in a highly sequential manner. Teachers reinforced accurate production and error correction through consistent feedback (Terrell, Egasse, & Voge, 1982). Developers of the audiolingual method believed that when language learners practiced pattern drills and dialogue designed to develop particular language structures, the new language structures would become a habit. They viewed language acquisition as the memorization and recall of language patterns.

Grammatical Approach: Synopsis

Given that the grammatical approach has since been superseded by other approaches more robustly grounded in research and public school practice, this text emphasizes more contemporary approaches to language instruction for CLD students. The evolution of the grammatical approach is presented for historical purposes. Although some public school educators continue to use the grammatical approach, primarily in foreign language but also in some ESL classrooms, the approach is no longer considered the best available philosophical grounding for language education among CLD students. Several reasons account for the conclusion that the grammatical approach fails to offer the best available language instruction for CLD students. First, the approach focuses on knowing about a language instead of emphasizing how to use the language for the intended purpose of language, which is communication. In fact, most CLD students study the target language for the express purpose of being able to use the language for social and academic purposes, not to learn the structure of the language (Krashen, 1981, 1982). CLD students must learn a second or third language (i.e., English) in order to discuss, understand, read, write, and think for academic, social, and work-related purposes. Moreover, conjugating verbs, practicing contrived sentence patterns, and memorizing lists of decontextualized vocabulary words does little to promote authentic language use for critical purposes. Second, grammar-based drills and exercises do not provide CLD students with comprehensible input. Drills are often far removed from a communicative context and provide no real motivation for CLD students to communicate. Finally, educational research on second language acquisition programs reveals that CLD students who receive grammar-based ESL instruction do much worse on standardized tests that assess reading capacities in English than their CLD peers who participate in dual language and content-based ESL programs (Thomas & Collier, 2002).

Communicative Approach

A more research- and theory-based approach to second language instruction is the *communicative approach*. As detailed in Table 6.1, the communicative approach emerged in the 1960s. The change in language teaching philosophy came from international concerns over the ineffectiveness of the grammar-based approaches in developing language learners who could actually use the target language in real-life situations (Blair, 1982). As the name implies, the communicative approach focuses on learning language through and for communication. The communicative approach assumes that language production contains an infinite number of possible language combinations, so memorizing patterns and rules does little to prepare language learners for authentic language use. In other words, language learners use language to communicate for a purpose. The role of the teacher (and the classroom) is to provide a context for authentic communication. From a communicative point of view, language acquisition is not a linear, sequential progression. Instead, language development occurs as a language learner receives comprehensible input and creates or tests hypotheses regarding language use as she or he interacts in authentic, language-rich, low-anxiety language acquisition environments (Blair, 1982; Terrell, 1991).

Communicative Approach: History and Evolution

Although certain premises and applications derived from a communicative approach date back to the fourth century and enjoyed some popularity during the height of Greek and Roman world influences, the Renaissance, and the last half of the nineteenth century, this approach was not widely adopted until the last half of the twentieth century (Kelly, 1976). Initially, the communicative approach was used primarily as a basis for modern language teaching, with an emphasis on using target languages for authentic purposes. However, in the 1960s and 1970s, the communicative approach emerged as the foundation for a more natural way to learn language. That is, it served as an approach that fostered second language acquisition methods and strategies that more closely emulated the way in which children learn their first language. In the 1980s and 1990s, as researchers and educators began to realize that the primary communicative environment for CLD students was the classroom, the communicative approach evolved to encompass constructivist language instruction in the context of the content-area curriculum.

Communicative Approach: Philosophical Foundations

The communicative approach differs from the grammatical approach in that it does not subscribe to the behaviorist perspective (see Table 6.2). According to Blair (1982):

> Part of the blame for current [1980s] inefficiency in language training must be laid at the door of a misguided faith that stimulus-response psychology, linked with sophisticated linguistic analysis, provides a scientific basis for language pedagogy. Conventional methods of language learning [grammar-based approaches], based on what must now be regarded as outmoded and unacceptable views of learning, may actually place formidable barriers in the path of learners. (p. viii)

The communicative approach represents a revolution in thought regarding language teaching. Instead of the more traditional viewpoint of behaviorism, constructivism serves as the theoretical foundation of the communicative approach.

Constructivism represents a theoretical body of literature that views the human brain as having certain fundamental structures of understanding that enable it to draw meaning from experience (Kukla, 2000; Searle, 1995). According to this developmental view of learning, people are born with the capacity to acquire specific abilities such as language comprehension and production. Although the behaviorists believed that learning occurs through environmental stimuli and a learner's responses to those stimuli, the social constructivists believe that learning occurs as a result of interactions between the environment and the learner's mind. In describing this interaction, Vygotsky (1978) stated: "The mastering of nature and the mastering of behavior are mutually linked, just as man's alteration of nature alters man's own nature" (p. 55). He claimed that the interaction between thought and language leads to higher-order thinking. In other words, rather than the mind being a passive recipient of input (a behaviorist perspective), the mind actively gathers information and constructs meaning (a constructivist perspective) (Moshman et al., 1987). Although the brain contains structures for language learning, the environment or context shapes the course of language and cognitive development (Vygotsky, 1978). The context provides a wide range of information, but the learner selects information and synthesizes that information with what he or she already knows to create a new understanding.

Social constructivists believe that interpersonal interaction leads to language and cognitive development and that all learning is socially constructed (Derry, 1999; Hacking, 2000; Kukla, 2000; Vygotsky, 1978). Vygotsky proposed that optimal learning occurs in a zone of proximal development, the gap between what a learner already knows and the upper limit of what a learner can accomplish with expert assistance (Vygotsky, 1978). The optimal level of instruction is a level just beyond what a learner can accomplish independently.

Vygotsky's theories of learning and development have helped shape constructivist perspectives as well as methods of the communicative approach. Vygotsky (1978) maintained that learning is more than mirroring. He subscribed to the idea that children actively construct knowledge by collecting information from the environment of the learning situation in order to build meaning and understanding.

Vygotsky proposed that learning can actually lead development. In discussing the processes of learning and development, he differentiated between the external and the internal interactions in which the learner participates. To explain, the "expert" in the learning situation shares his or her own ways of knowing by externally modeling his or her thought processes for the learner. Then the learner externally manipulates the information the expert provided. The external learning interactions between the learner and the information may require the learner to question the expert or ask the expert to rephrase or repeat ideas for clarification. When the learner is able to take possession of the information, the new knowledge becomes internalized. This internalization of external learning is referred to as development (Vygotsky, 1978).

Vygotsky also developed his theory of the *zone of proximal development*. He defined this zone as the area between the level of independent performance and the level of assisted performance. He argued that learning occurs when new information and skills fall within the zone, or the space between

what the learner already knows and what he or she can do with the help of an expert. The zone of proximal development shifts as the individual learns more complex concepts and skills and becomes capable of independently achieving the tasks that once required the assistance of another (Vygotsky, 1978).

Finally, Vygotsky viewed language as a mechanism for thinking. Language is the means by which we express what is learned and understood. When children face a cognitively difficult task, they often talk out loud as a means of gaining control over the cognitive processes that are necessary to accomplish the task. Although adults may not verbally express this type of self-talk, they continue to use inward, private speech (Lantolf & Appel, 1996).

Within your own classroom practice:

- *In what ways do your CLD students construct knowledge?*
- *How do you target the zone of proximal development with your CLD students?*
- *How do you use more capable or language proficient peers to encourage learning in the zone of proximal development?*
- *What role does cooperative learning offer for the support of potential development?*
- *How are parents or guardians of CLD students welcomed and maximized in ways that increase the CLD students' potential development?*

In addition to constructivism, the idea that people are born with a genetically predetermined capacity to learn language also contributed to the foundation of the communicative approach. This belief in a person's inherent capacity to develop language was the product of the work of Noam Chomsky (1986) and his theories of first language acquisition. Chomsky proposed that all people are born with a language acquisition device (LAD) that serves as an inherent mental system specifically devoted to language development and use (Akmajian, Demers, Farmer, & Harnish, 1995). According to Chomsky, the structure of the LAD provides the learner with an innate understanding of what he has referred to as *universal grammar*. This universal grammar consists of the rules and structures common to all languages (Akmajian et al., 1995). Another way to conceptualize universal grammar is as the logic of language.

Chomsky has argued that language acquisition is a natural process in which the LAD interacts with context to collect the linguistic information necessary to develop a particular language of thought and communication. He maintains that second language acquisition follows a similar developmental path to first language acquisition (Chomsky, 1986). In a speech to the Northeast Language Teachers' Association in 1965, Chomsky explained:

> A good deal of the foreign language instruction that is going on now . . . is based on a concept of language . . . [which assumes] that language is a system of skills and ought to be taught through drill and by the formation of S-R [stimulus-response] associations. I think the evidence is very convincing that that view of language is entirely erroneous, and that it's a very bad way—certainly an unprincipled way—to teach languages. If it happens to work, it would be an accident for some other reason. Certainly it is not a method that is based on any understanding of the nature of language. Our understanding of the nature of language seems to me to show quite convincingly that language is not a habit structure, but that it has a kind of a creative property and is based on abstract formal principles and operations of a complex kind. (Blair, 1982, p. 5)

Chomsky asserts that explicit instruction in the structure of language is pointless because all people are born with an innate understanding of grammar—a universal grammar. Like the constructivists, Chomsky maintains that languages develop as the brain gathers and uses linguistic information. He argues that the LAD, through communicative interaction, gathers the linguistic evidence necessary to derive the structure of a specific language (Chomsky, 1986).

The constructivist point of view led many educational theorists and researchers to conclude that environmental exposure to the target language and social interaction in that language is sufficient to prompt a learner's innate ability to develop the capacity to comprehend and produce that language. Nonetheless, this point of view does not negate the fact that educators may play a significant role in language acquisition. Instead, this perspective argues that the appropriate role of the educator shifts from purveyor of all knowledge (a behaviorist perspective) to enabler or facilitator of meaning construction (a constructivist perspective). Therefore, the communicative-constructivist perspective asserts that a language-rich instructional environment is necessary to activate a learner's genetic predisposition for language development. Figure 6.3 provides a graphic illustration of additional suggestions for the creation of a language-rich environment for language acquisition.

Accordingly, learners do not need explicit instruction in the structure and vocabulary of the language in order for the language to develop. Instead, they need meaningful social and communicative interaction in the target language. Furthermore, learners do not need explicit error correction, because errors are recognized as developmental in nature and a part of language learners' efforts to create and test hypotheses about how the target language works. Therefore, the role of the

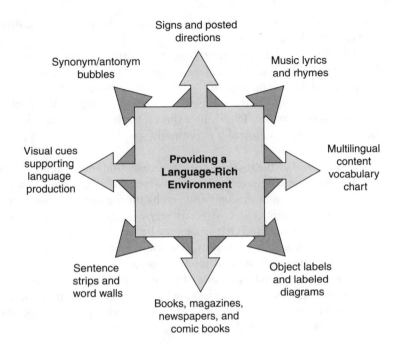

■ **figure 6.3** Suggestions for the Creation of a Language-Rich Environment for Language Acquisition

effective educator is to foster a communicative environment conducive to social interaction and the construction of meaning in context. That is, language, thought, meaning, and use should not be isolated as separate, disconnected components. Instead, they should be integrated in ways that emulate the natural progression of communication.

Communicative Approach: Methods

Perhaps the most common theme shared among methods derived from the communicative approach is their greater or lesser emphasis on communication as the primary purpose of language. Diaz-Rico and Weed (2002) conclude that these methods, most of which have evolved as a response to changing theory and research, reflect fundamental changes in perspectives on the appropriate nature of second language teaching. These methods increasingly acknowledge and elaborate on (a) language as embedded in social contexts, (b) the multiplicity of language functions, (c) the need for student-centered, teacher-facilitated language instruction, and (d) the need to stress communication versus rules in language teaching. The early methods derived from the communicative approach—the silent way, the natural way, and suggestopedia—targeted social language development as a goal of instruction. Contemporary methods, including integrated content-based (ICB) instruction and the sheltered method, strongly emphasize interactive, communicative, and contextual language acquisition through adaptations and modifications of the grade-level curriculum. The following overviews first summarize early communicative methods and follow with those methods that are considered contemporary. Table 6.1 provides an illustration of these relationships among communicative methods.

Early Methods of the Communicative Approach Early methods of the communicative approach are primarily presented for historical purposes. Each of these early communicative methods was part of the evolution of the communicative approach toward a more inclusive, content-based, and interactive philosophy of instruction for language instruction. Accordingly, each of these early methods is briefly summarized in order to provide the reader with a sense of the foundation on which more contemporary, communicative methods were designed (see Table 6.1). This and forthcoming chapters emphasize the more contemporary methods of the communicative approach, many of which are in widespread use in public school classrooms.

Silent Way The silent way presented learners with simple linguistic situations that they were to observe and then describe in the target language, focusing especially on the actions they witnessed. The first language of learners was not used, and the teacher emphasized the pronunciation and word flow of the learner's descriptions while encouraging target language production. Unlike the protocol of grammatical methods, learners who learned according to the silent way developed their own criteria for the quality of language acquisition functions (listening, speaking, and correction) in which they engaged. In fact, the teacher's silence was intentionally designed to encourage student initiative, language production, and linguistic interactions (Gattegno, 1982).

Natural Way The natural way, another method of the communicative approach, is sometimes referred to as the natural approach. Nonetheless, as Richard-Amato (1996) reminds us, "Krashen and Terrell (1983) developed the natural approach [way] as a *method*" (p. 128). Accordingly, this chapter refers to this method as the *natural way*. This early communicative method was based on four general premises:

- Comprehension precedes production.
- If allowed to proceed naturally, language production will emerge in stages.
- Communicative goals should guide instruction.
- Interactive communicative activities should be designed to lower the affective filter.

Although the method did not include the content-based emphasis of its successors, it nonetheless did much to refine and extend the philosophy of the communicative approach to second language instruction.

Language instruction in the natural way followed a specific order. First, the teacher created a situation in which communication was made meaningful. Then the teacher communicated information in the target language. The teacher simultaneously modified the language to a level at which the learners could understand the messages of instruction. One way the teacher accomplished this was to ensure that instruction was adapted in such a way that language input was comprehensible (see Figure 6.4). Moreover, instruction through the natural way ensured that the silent period was recognized and respected. Accordingly, language-learning students spent much of their time building comprehension skills before they were prompted to produce language. Consequently, language instruction usually began with student understanding of oral language and then speaking, reading, and writing (Terrell, 1991). Although the natural way is still used in some foreign language classrooms, its incidence in public school classrooms is not widespread. To a considerable extent, the natural way created the foundation for the sheltered method of instruction.

■ **figure 6.4** Providing Comprehensible Input

Providing Comprehensible Input

Speak Slower
- Avoid an exaggerated slow pace.
- Use longer natural pauses between sentences and ideas.

Speak Clearly
- Use fewer reduced vowels.
- Use fewer deleted consonants.
- Use fewer contractions.
- Use fewer fused forms (*want to*, not *wanna*).
- Use key words stressed to support meaning.

Select Vocabulary Carefully
- Use high-frequency words.
- Use cognates.
- Use fewer idioms.
- Use less slang.
- Use fewer pronouns and more referents.

Use Visuals to Support Meaning
- Objects
- Pictures
- Gestures
- Labeled diagrams
- Body language and movement
- Videos
- Role playing
- Demonstrations

Simplify Syntax
- Use shorter sentences.
- Use fewer clauses.

Suggestopedia The communicative method of suggestopedia was designed to place as much language teaching emphasis on learner personality and motivation as that typically placed on intellect. In particular, Georgi Lozanov (1982) was interested in what could be learned intuitively and spontaneously. He believed that fear of language learning often inhibited the rapid acquisition of the language. Consequently, he advocated the creation of a relaxing, stress-free environment that would, in his view, enhance language acquisition. A suggestopedia lesson typically involved music playing in the background. First, students would read a translation of text in their first language. Then the instructor would remove the translation and present the same text in the target language. Visual aids would support the meaning of the text. Students would work with the text through conversation, retelling, and role playing. By working with the target language text through multiple modalities used in a relaxing environment, language learners would acquire the target language rapidly (Lozanov, 1982). Although suggestopedia never experienced widespread use, the idea of a relaxing, low-anxiety environment for language acquisition is a purposive component of most contemporary methods of the communicative approach (see Figure 6.5).

Contemporary Methods of the Communicative Approach Contemporary communicative methods involve content-based language instruction. The communicative environment in which CLD students must excel is most often that found in

■ **f i g u r e 6 . 5**   Suggestions for Providing a Low-Anxiety Language Acquisition Environment

- Develop choral reading experiences and chants to lessen CLD students' apprehensions about taking risks in L2 (English).
- Seek out and structure opportunities for the use of the target language in interpersonal communications.
- Attend to the needs, desires, and individual aspirations of students.
- Accept and do not constantly correct all attempts at target language production.
- Accept the use of the students' native languages in the classroom and encourage parents to support ongoing CALP development in L1 at home.
- Exhibit an interest in the home culture and languages of CLD students.
- Allow CLD students with very limited English proficiency to communicate through gestures, including nodding, pointing, gesturing, or drawing.
- Allow more capable or bilingual peers to assist in the completion of outlines, KWL charts, Venn diagrams, etc.
- Write language and content objectives on the board and refer to them throughout lessons.
- Develop a predictable daily routine to enhance students' understandings of expectations, instructional protocol, and means of evaluation.

content-area classrooms. Consequently, second language researchers and educators developed content-based communicative methods to help CLD students acquire the language they need to be academically successful. The most common methods for teaching CLD students academic language are the integrated content-based (ICB) method and the sheltered instruction method. Because these methods are detailed in Chapters 7 and 8, the following discussions provide only overviews of each of these contemporary communicative methods.

The Integrated Content-Based (ICB) Method   The ICB method involves the concurrent teaching of academic subject matter and second language acquisition skills. The language curriculum is based directly on students' academic and linguistic needs. At the secondary level, grade-level teams of educators are often formed to collaborate in the development of thematic units and the planning of instruction that emphasizes content and language objectives across subject areas. This communicative and cross-curricular method of instruction is new to many secondary teachers and requires a commitment from school faculty as well as administrators.

The Sheltered Instruction Method   The sheltered instruction method can be implemented in either a grade-level or a second language classroom. Sheltered lessons integrate language and content objectives into the same lesson. Content objectives are typically derived from the curriculum, as aligned with local, state, or national standards. Language objectives are best derived from practice standards for CLD students, such as the TESOL standards (TESOL, 1997). Language objectives are functionally linked to the CLD student's level of L2 (English) proficiency. Students receive grade-level content, but teachers scaffold their instruction in order to provide comprehensible language input and a modified grade-level curriculum.

Although there are several variations of sheltered instruction, each of these tends to share certain common themes, which are also strategies of the method. Among these common strategies are hands-on applications and social interactions, cooperative learning, guarded vocabulary, and visual support. The dominant model of sheltered instruction is the sheltered instruction observation protocol (SIOP) (Echevarria, Vogt, & Short, 2000, 2002), which uses thirty indicators of best practice with CLD students. Although the sheltered instruction method of the communicative approach is a widely implemented method of language instruction in public school classrooms, new understandings of the learning process have also fostered the development of a third approach to language instruction: the cognitive approach.

Cognitive Approach

The cognitive approach (see Table 6.1) is an emergent product of efforts to examine and analyze the cognitive psychological side of learning, language learning, and instruction to promote language learning (Awh & Jonides, 1998; Banich, 1997; Elman et al., 1997; Gilhooly, Logie, Wetherick, & Wynn, 1993; Johnson, 1996; Just

■ Voices from the Field

"I am an elementary school counselor, and the students I work with are pre-school to second grade. I work with all the ESL students in classroom guidance, which involves friendship and social skills. Reading instruction is difficult for our ESL students because letter sounds or phonemes may be different in their native language. The illustrations used in tests and textbooks are often difficult because of cultural differences. Consequently, I invite other students to the guidance office and teach the ESL child board games so they understand the rules and they can begin to use illustrations to make connections between their native language and English. We also have the ESL children teach us games they play at home. These types of peer groups also help the ESL students' social skills. Young children are very accepting of each other, so we utilize peer partners a great deal. This is very helpful for both the ESL student and their peer partner. The parents have a great deal of difficulty helping the students with their homework and projects. They have a difficult time in understanding the students' progress. With a great deal of support, however, these students progress rapidly. I try to help the parents feel acceptance in the school environment. I make home visits with the child and help explain what the child is doing in school and how the parent can help. Digital cameras are great, enabling us to make a movie of the child's day at school and share it with the family. We invite the parents to explain their culture to the other children in the classroom. For example, the parents may cook a native dish for the classroom to try. Sometimes, we will have one of the parents be a parent helper in the classroom; this helps the parents feel part of the school. If we realize the child is not progressing, we always try a child study in order to develop a formal plan to help the child be more successful."

■ *Donna Jackson, primary school guidance counselor, Poquoson, VA*

& Carpenter, 1992; Kim & Hirsch, 1997; Newell, 1990; O'Malley & Chamot, 1990; O'Malley, Chamot, Stewner-Manzanares, Russo, & Küpper, 1985a, 1985b; Paris & Winograd, 1990; Zimmerman, 1990). Cognitive psychology is essentially concerned with the structure and nature of comparatively complex knowledge processes (such as discovering, recognizing, conceiving, judging, reasoning, and reflecting) and their influences on or relationships to actions (Gagné, 1985; Shuell, 1986; Elman et al., 1997).

Cognitive Approach: History and Evolution

The history and evolution of the cognitive approach is integrally connected to that of cognitive psychology and the acceptance of trends in that discipline among educational psychologists (see Table 6.2). In particular, we are concerned with the evolution of the cognitive model of learning and perspectives on learning among the disciplines of psychology. Recently, Mayer (1998) summarized the evolution of these learning perspectives according to three general metaphors.

During the first half of the twentieth century, the metaphor of *learning as response acquisition* dominated psychological theory and educational practice (Mayer, 1998). Grounded in a history of research on animals, learning was perceived as a mechanical process wherein successful responses were more or less automatically strengthened and those that were unsuccessful were summarily weakened. This behaviorist metaphor tended to perceive the learner as a passive recipient of information whose repertoire of behaviors was determined by rewards and punishments encountered in the environment. Not surprisingly, drill and practice served as the epitome of instruction based on this learning perspective.

A new learning metaphor, *learning as knowledge acquisition,* was the product of the cognitive revolution of the 1950s and 1960s. According to this view, the learner was a processor of information and the teacher a dispenser of information. In education, the curriculum thus became the focus of instruction. This curriculum-centered approach subdivided topics into studies, studies into lessons, and lessons into facts and formulas. Because the goal became the amount of knowledge the learner possessed, standardized testing became the assessment of choice.

The metaphor of *learning as knowledge construction* was the outcome of efforts to refine and enhance cognitive theory during the 1970s and 1980s. Research evolved to emphasize subject-area learning in realistic situations. The perception of the learner changed from one of recipient to a constructor of knowledge. Instructionally, the focus changed from curriculum-centered to child-centered. Assessment matured from its preoccupation with quantitative measurements to an acknowledgment of the merit of qualitative evaluation.

Today, this child-centered perspective on learning has led to the recent development of six learner-centered principles that guide the ongoing research, theoretical, and practical efforts of the American Psychological Association (APA, 1995). Thematically, these six principles, summarized below, are focused on the notion that learning can be a meaningful activity.

1. The learning of complex subject matter is most effectively accomplished when understood as an intentional process of constructing meaning from information and experience.
2. Through support and instructional guidance, over time the learner is capable of creating meaningful, coherent representations of knowledge.
3. The successful learner is capable of linking new information to existing knowledge in meaningful, relevant ways.
4. The successful learner has the capacity to create and use a vast array of thinking and reasoning strategies in order to target complex learning goals.
5. Higher-order strategies designed to enhance the selecting and monitoring of mental operations facilitate creative and critical thinking.
6. Learning is influenced by a variety of environmental factors that include, but are not limited to, culture, prior socialization, technology, and instructional practices.

Are You Aware?

Computer assisted language learning (CALL) is capitalizing on the digital revolution in order to enhance the language acquisition and academic success of CLD students in the classroom. At the level of language acquisition among CLD students, CALL enhances the student's capacities in all four domains of literacy development. Word-processing programs that are capable of processing multiple languages enhance writing development. Language-learning programs for auxiliary, center-based instruction in language arts, such as Rosetta Stone (Fairfield Language Technologies, 2000), support and enhance listening and reading skills and are used in ESL, bilingual, or dual language programming. Programs such as WiggleWorks (Scholastic, 2000) enhance speaking ability among CLD students.

Yet CALL technology is not intended to replace the classroom teacher or accommodative classroom instruction. Instead, CALL is a resource that the professional educator must organize, plan, implement, monitor, and evaluate. Hanson-Smith (1997) describes three levels of CALL implementation in the classroom, each of which is summarized below. Each of these levels has added suggestions for the teacher's appropriate role(s) in facilitating the CALL resource.

- A passive listening experience supported by a search engine that allows students to repeat a passage, search for the meaning of the passage, analyze its syntax, see a related illustration or photo, or scan a related text
  —Teacher's Role(s):
    - Monitor student progress, encourage risk taking, instruct, and model as necessary.
- A vehicle through which CLD students can listen to a sentence, compare their language production to that of a computer model, or have the computer assess the accuracy of their responses
  —Teacher's Role(s):
    - Guide students through the use of CALL.
    - Suggest strategies for maximizing supplemental references.
    - Assess students' weekly progress reports.
- A tool used to research current events, cultural and historical topics, business reports, climate, or a variety of other content-based topics
  —Teacher's Role(s):
    - Encourage metacognitive regulation concerning the effective use of CALL.
    - Assess students' products and outcomes generated as a result of CALL access and maximization.

Cumulatively, these six principles suggest a reconceptualization of meaningful learning as a process that is as much cognitive as it is biological, cultural, social, interactive, motivational, and affective.

At the level of instruction for language acquisition, the cognitive approach traces the efforts of theorists, researchers, and practitioners to incorporate much of what has been learned from the evolution of cognitive learning theory. At the theoretical level, one example is the efforts of Ellen Bialystok to develop a model of second language acquisition. Her model, sometimes referred to as an *information-processing model* of second language acquisition, incorporates three components related to specific types of knowledge, including implicit and explicit linguistic knowledge (Bialystok, 1990a). At the level of research and analysis, recent work on the cognitive side of language, language learning, and language instruction has contributed to the evolving foundations of the cognitive approach (Elman et al., 1997; Johnson, 1996; Kim & Hirsch, 1997). Finally, at the practical level, recent efforts to apply the cognitive model of learning to language instruction have resulted in the development of CALLA (Chamot & O'Malley, 1994; O'Malley & Chamot, 1990; O'Malley et al., 1985a, 1985b), which is the dominant contemporary method of language instruction grounded in the cognitive approach.

Cognitive Approach: Philosophical Foundations

Wittrock (1998) and Mayer (1998) have argued that a renewed interest in cognition marks a fundamental shift in psychological research, especially that of educational psychology, from a behaviorist to a cognitive perspective on learning. Each of these analyses has variously argued that the behavioral perspective on learning tended to (a) deny attention to the learner's active role in the learning process, (b) study learning in isolation from the school tasks it helped accomplish, and (c) inadequately account for the role of background knowledge in the learning process. Today, the cognitive perspective is more directly tied to the challenges and processes confronted by the learner, as well as to the teaching and instructional protocols designed to address these issues. Among the emphases of the new cognitive perspective (Chamot & O'Malley, 1994; Kroll, 1998; Mayer, 1998; Wittrock, 1998) are the following:

- The learner's background knowledge and socialization experiences in a particular culture, especially the ways in which these may facilitate connections to new learning
- The learner's strategies for knowledge acquisition, especially cognitive, metacognitive, and social affective strategies
- The learner's metacognitive processes, especially his or her emergent capacities for introspection
- The learner's interaction with text relationships, such as cause and effect and sequence
- The learner's interaction with certain text structures, including enumeration, classification, and generalization
- The learner's perceptions of and interaction with discourse structure (e.g., expository and narrative) and certain genres of writing (e.g., indirect and linear)
- The learner's affective processes
- Means to research the learner's thought and affective processes
- Types of constructivist teaching procedures
- Ways to teach comprehension, analysis, critical thinking, and application

As these emphases demonstrate, the cognitive perspective affects a considerable variety of educational interests relevant to the CLD learner, including cultural and cross-cultural dynamics, learning in the content areas, critical thinking, literacy development, sociocultural and social affective effects on learning, constructivist learning environments and teaching, and the learner's application of acquired knowledge in different contexts.

Cognitive Model of Learning

Fundamentally, the cognitive approach is grounded in a cognitive model of learning. This perspective on learning is similar to that of Mezirow (1991) and views the learning process as active versus passive, dynamic versus static. Furthermore, this view holds that learning (at minimum) involves (a) information selection from the environment, (b) information categorization and organization, (c) the relation of new information to known concepts, categories, and premises, (d) the use of information in appropriate contexts, and (e) metacognition on the process (Chamot & O'Malley, 1994; Gagné, 1985; Mezirow, 1991; Shuell, 1986).

Role of Memory in Learning The cognitive perspective on learning is grounded in a differentiation among three types of memory: long-term, short-term, and working memory. Chamot and O'Malley (1994) have characterized these functions as mental operations based on developmental, cognitive, and information theories. Although the conceptual definitions for the first two types of memory are comparatively self-evident, the study of working memory is a relatively new line of research (Awh & Jonides, 1998; Gilhooly et al., 1993; Johnson, 1996). Working memory describes a system for temporarily holding and manipulating information for a brief period during the performance of an array of cognitive tasks including, but not limited to, comprehension, learning, and reasoning (Baddeley, 1986; Just & Carpenter, 1992; Newell, 1990). Working memory is characterized by limited storage capacity and rapid turnover, as differentiated from the larger capacity and archival system of long-term memory. When we engage in the literacy skill of listening, we tend to use the temporary storage capacity of working memory to hold segments of sentences online. We also use working memory like a mental blackboard to associate these sentence segments with verbs and objects in order to comprehend the messages and meanings of the sentences we hear.

The Role of Knowledge in Learning We may also associate functions of memory with types of knowledge processed or stored. In fact, most of the stored information we can recall from our prior socialization and classroom instruction is stored in long-term memory as declarative or procedural knowledge. *What* we know—that is, what we can declare—is stored as *declarative knowledge*. Memory frameworks or *schemata* serve as the storage venues for declarative knowledge. These frameworks enable declarative knowledge to be stored as interconnected concepts and ideas that can be recalled as isolated facts or as structured associations among ideas. New experiences, especially learning experiences, tend to alter our existing schemata by adding to, expanding on, or challenging previously stored information. Because these existing schemata can be altered, effective teachers first surface these knowledge banks before providing their students with new information. Through such elaboration of prior knowledge, effective classroom instruction purposively adds to or expands on existing schemata rather than constructing entirely new banks of associated information.

What we know *how* to do has been stored in long-term memory as *procedural knowledge.* Procedural knowledge can be used to accomplish either simple or complex mental procedures (e.g., solving a word problem in algebra) or physical procedures (e.g., learning how to swing a golf club for maximum drive distance). According to Chamot and O'Malley (1994), procedural knowledge is stored in memory as *production systems.* The systems consist of a series of steps or phases, which include a condition and an action that can be conceptualized, as connected through an if–then sequence. For example, *if* a CLD student targets as a goal verbal collaboration in cooperative learning with a more English proficient peer, *then* the student might set as a subgoal or objective the task of interacting as comprehensibly as possible in L2 (English). *If,* on the other hand, she experiences difficulty in language production regarding certain concepts, *then* she might set as a subgoal the use of code switching between L1 and L2 in order to communicate (which, after all, is the purpose of language).

A third type of knowledge, *conditional knowledge,* involves knowing *when, why,* or *where* to use information and skills. Conditional knowledge is also stored in long-term memory as schemata. Ehren and Gildroy (2000) have argued that this type of knowledge may be the most important and the most difficult for both students and teachers. They state that information and skills are of little use unless an individual has a critical sense of when and where to use them, as well as when *not* to use them. For example, a farmer may have declarative knowledge of what a herbicide is. He may also possess procedural knowledge of appropriate ways to apply the chemical for maximum effectiveness. Yet, if he does not have knowledge about *why* herbicides are used, he may randomly apply the chemical without a genuine purpose. If he does not possess conditional knowledge of *where not* to apply the herbicide, he may destroy valuable field crops even though he was effective in applying the chemical.

Johnson (1996), has argued that second language teaching can be structured so as to encourage the transfer of knowledge stored as schemata or production systems in one language to new learning tasks in a second language. He concludes that declarative and procedural knowledge are especially important aspects of language competence. He asserts that these two types of knowledge are at the crux of the language learner's ability to achieve the automatization of frequently used items of information or skill bases. *Automatization,* in this sense, refers to the integration of large amounts of information into a readily accessible whole or sequence through a process of restructuring (Anderson, 1983; Bialystok, 1990a). Such restructuring requires that the knowledge base be updated or reorganized for ready access, or that the skills base be reorganized to enable a more efficient procedure.

For Johnson (1996) automatization is as crucial to language learning and language transfer as many other skills typically emphasized because it liberates the learner's conscious attention so that it becomes available for the high-level skills necessary for language acquisition, production, and pragmatics. He argues that second language teaching strategies too often build declarative knowledge first (i.e., the rules and structure of the language, which are emphasized by the grammatical approach) on the assumption that language learning will best proceed from declarative knowledge to the skill building necessary for procedural knowledge. He maintains that language acquisition must be able to proceed from either direction, declarative to procedural (proceduralization) or procedural to declarative. Accordingly, he concludes that there are two distinct roles for declarative knowledge in language acquisition. First, declarative knowledge serves as a starting point for proceduralization. Second, declarative knowledge provides the individual with a generative knowledge base for transfer and production. Johnson also notes that communicative language instruction (as in the methods of the communicative approach) is in fact a set of techniques for the proceduralization of language.

Finally, the cognitive model of learning is also concerned with *metacognitive knowledge.* Livingston (1997) notes that a considerable degree of confusion exists as to what constitutes metacognition and metacognitive knowledge. Livingston defines *metacognition* as "higher-order thinking that involves active control over the cognitive processes engaged in learning" (p. 1). She concludes that much of the confusion arises from the interchangeable use of a variety of terms (e.g., *executive control, self-regulation,* and *meta-memory*) with metacognition. Metacognition is most often associated with Flavell (1979), who tended to be more precise in differentiating among terms applicable to metacognition. According to Flavell, metacognition consists of both metacognitive knowledge and metacognitive experiences or regulation. Therefore, Flavell has argued that *metacognitive knowledge* can be conceptualized as acquired knowledge about cognitive processes that may be used to control or regulate cognitive processes.

Metacognitive Knowledge Flavell (1979) divided metacognitive knowledge into three categories: knowledge of person variables, knowledge of task variables, and knowledge of strategy variables. The main category, knowledge of person variables, refers to a general awareness about the ways in which human beings learn and process information and an individual's knowledge of her or his own learning processes. For example, CLD students may be aware that they are more successful in learning a lesson when they preview that lesson with their parents in their native language. Knowledge of task variables encompasses knowledge about the nature of the task and the processing demands it may place on the individual. For instance, CLD students are often aware that it will take them more time to read and comprehend a chapter in a science text than it will to read a chapter in a novel. Knowledge relating to strategy variables surrounds an awareness of both cognitive (thinking) and metacognitive (thinking about thinking) strategies, as well as conditional knowledge about when and where such strategies are appropriate.

Metacognitive Regulation Flavell (1979) conceptualized metacognitive regulation as the use of metacognitive strategies to control cognitive activities and to ensure that a cognitive goal (e.g., the understanding of a text written in L2) is attained. As such, metacognitive regulation supervises the planning, implementing, and evaluating of cognitive activities. CLD students do not need to know just about a strategy—declarative knowledge—they also need to know how to apply the strategy—procedural knowledge—and when to use the strategy—conditional knowledge (Butler & Winne, 1995; Pressley, 1995).

Anderson's Model of Metacognition   Anderson (2002) provides a model of meta-cognition that guides students to incorporate the following five components into their learning processes: prepare and plan, select and use learning strategies, monitor use of strategies, orchestrate various strategies, and evaluate strategy use and learning. The first of the components, prepare and plan, emphasizes the need for learners to think about what they need to do in order to accomplish the goals set by the teacher or to accomplish their personal learning goals. Students then must select strategies pertinent to the task and apply them appropriately. For learners to successfully incorporate this second component of the metacognition model, teachers must instruct students on specific types of strategies—what they are, how to use them, and when to use them.

The third component of Anderson's model of metacognition involves the monitoring of strategy use. For students to be able to effectively use strategies, educators must teach learners to periodically stop what they are doing, reflect on the manner in which they are actually using a particular strategy, and determine if they need to realign their actions in order to employ the strategy more accurately. Orchestrating various strategies, the fourth critical component of Anderson's metacognition model, calls attention to the fact that some situations and tasks require the use of more than one strategy. Students must be able to evaluate their progress toward achieving the determined goals and realize when a strategy is not working for them. A new strategy or, as is often the case, a combination of strategies may be more effective for the situation (Anderson, 2002).

The fifth component of the metacognition model, evaluate strategy use and learning, guides learners to reflect on their progress in the learning process. Teachers help students develop the ability to ask self-directed questions similar to the following:

- What goals am I trying to accomplish?
- Which strategies am I currently using?
- How effectively am I using the strategies?
- What other strategies might work for this task?

In this way, the metacognitive model, which is graphically depicted in Figure 6.6, enables students to take control of their learning. While the teacher provides necessary instruction, modeling, and support, the students work to develop the metacognitive skills necessary for independent problem solving (Anderson, 2002).

Cognitive Approach as Cognition and Communication

Ultimately, the cognitive approach is an amalgamation of what we have learned from cognitive psychology and the cognitive learning model, as well as what we

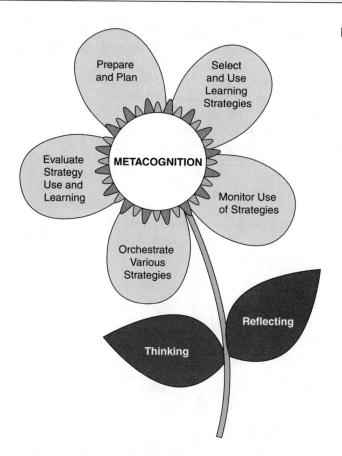

■ **figure 6.6**   Cognitive Growth

have learned about communication as the purpose of language and language acquisition. From the perspective of the former, the cognitive approach places a strong emphasis on the learner's background, interactions, memory, knowledge, thinking process, and capacity for self-regulation as foundations for language acquisition and success in the academic context. To this end, explicit instruction in learning strategies, including cognitive, metacognitive, and social/affective strategies, is a crucial focus of pedagogy according to the approach (each of these strategies is detailed in Chapter 9).

From the perspective of the latter, the cognitive approach also builds on what we already know about pedagogy that targets communication as the purpose of language and language acquisition. Accordingly, the cognitive approach to instruction for CLD students, as illustrated in Tables 6.1 and 6.2, variously emphasizes:

- Social interaction and communication in the environment for language acquisition
- Communication as the purpose of language and the motivation for language acquisition

- Attention to the affective motivators or inhibitors of language acquisition
- Elaboration of the student's prior knowledge of cognitive academic language in L1 and L2
- Collaboration with and maximization of parents or caregivers as valuable language resources and as partners in the reinforcement of classroom instruction
- Meaningful and relevant language instruction
- Scaffolded instruction for language acquisition
- Active, dynamic, learner-centered language instruction
- Content-area integration with language instruction
- Thematic instruction and cooperative learning
- Comprehensible input for language acquisition

According to Genesee (2000), the cognitive perspective on language acquisition and language instruction further enhances our recognition that provisions for learning and language learning must account for:

- Individual differences in learning styles by structuring alternative grouping arrangements, offering variation in the type and use of instructional materials, and modifying time frames for learning and response.

dilemmas *of Practice*

Mrs. Cooper, an educator of twenty years, teaches fifth grade in a rural community where the number of CLD students has increased steadily over the last fifteen years. Every fall and spring, all educators in her building are required to hold parent–teacher conferences. Her frustration relates to problems in scheduling conferences with parents of her CLD students and problems encountered when parents of CLD students do not show for these conferences at the time indicated. Instead, these parents tend to arrive at odd times when Mrs. Cooper is either teaching or meeting with other parents. She feels that these families are inconsiderate and do not think about her schedule and the rules for parent conferences. What actions should Mrs. Cooper take regarding these problems?

■ *Mrs. Cooper needs to reflect on and address her own assumptions about parents of CLD students and her beliefs that they are inconsiderate about attending parent conferences. She should try to understand the scheduling conflicts for families of*

CLD students and that these parents need to work to survive and provide for their families' needs. To this end, she could find out where the families that are not attending parent conferences live and visit their homes during her conference time, before or after school, or on weekends. If she takes her own child or spouse, she could possibly break down a barrier of anxiety for these families because they would be able to see her as an individual with a family as well. Mrs. Cooper could ask about the educational experiences and challenges the CLD student has had with prior or current schooling and any other information that could be of help when accommodating the student's needs in the classroom. She could also ask the parents about the skills or cultural traditions and customs that the student could share with the class. Although such home visits take extra time and effort on Mrs. Cooper's part, they are essential to establish positive relationships with the parents or caregivers of her CLD students.

- The second language learner's need for context-rich, meaningful learning environments.

Accordingly, cognitivists argue that the ongoing developmental needs of students who are acquiring language are best addressed by attending to their primary patterns of prior socialization in a particular culture, especially the preferred learning styles they demonstrate as a result of that socialization. CLD students will exhibit more or less favorable responses to certain types of learning environments, strategies, and relevancy. Again, as with instruction designed to target multiple learning style preferences, variation is the key to effectiveness. Ultimately, CLD students bring to the classroom singular language acquisition needs that are best served through highly contextualized learning environments and constructivist, meaning-focused instruction that targets cognitive academic language proficiency.

Cognitive Approach: Methods

As illustrated in Table 6.1, although recent research and analysis (Cummins, 2001a; Johnson, 1996) suggest ongoing efforts to connect cognitive theory and perspectives and premises for language instruction, to date only one compilation has been characterized in the literature as sufficiently robust to constitute a method of the cognitive approach. Indeed, through their development of the CALLA method, Chamot and O'Malley (1994) have achieved a groundbreaking integration of cognitive theory with mostly communicative strategies for language instruction.

The CALLA Method The CALLA method (Chamot & O'Malley, 1994) is designed to enrich the language that CLD students can use for academic communication (see Table 6.1). Concomitantly, CALLA is designed to further the abilities of CLD students to comprehend the discourse of the various content areas and to enhance their capacities to be academically successful in those subject areas. CALLA is considered applicable to CLD students at beginning, intermediate, and advanced levels of target language proficiency. The CALLA method, which is detailed in Chapter 9, includes three primary components: topics from the major content areas, the development of academic language skills, and explicit instruction in learning strategies. Content topics are incrementally introduced and scaffolded with extensive contextual supports and reduced linguistic demands. The emphasis on the development of academic language skills targets all four literacy domains (listening, speaking, reading, and writing) in daily content lessons. Explicit instruction in learning strategies targets both content and language acquisition. Among learning strategies emphasized are cognitive, metacognitive, and social/affective strategies.

tips for practice

Elementary Education

1. While assessing your CLD students scaffold assessment tasks in a contextualized manner by:
   - Incorporating easily accessible classroom materials such as brief quotations, charts, graphics, cartoons, and works of art.
   - Including questions for small-group discussion and individual writing.
   - Enhancing the students' understanding of assessment processes by modeling the steps involved. For example, you can use the six-trait model checklist to walk students through the writing process.

2. Incorporate cloze exercises to help your students understand a lesson. For such an exercise, teachers write a summary or take an excerpt of a reading passage, lesson, or class activity and then delete every *nth* word. Students then "fill in the blank" with an exact word or related word.
   - The following is an example of a cloze passage taken from "The Marble Champ."

     The truth was that Lupe _____ no good in sports. She could not catch a _____ or figure out in which _____ to kick the soccer ball. _____ time she kicked the ball _____ her own goal and scored a _____ for the other team. (Soto, 2000, p. 268)

3. In order to affirm the identity and culture of students, have them keep reflective journals in which they write daily. You can provide a topic for them to write about or give them the freedom to write about their thoughts and feelings concerning personal and cultural issues and events in their lives. Encourage CLD students to write in either their native language or English. When they write in English, do not correct grammatical errors. In this way, the students focus on personal expression versus the conventions of writing.

Secondary Education

1. Design authentic assessment tasks such as exhibits, dramatic interpretations, interviews, observations, self-reflections, and a variety of writing samples that require different ways of demonstrating knowledge or skills. For example, students in mathematics can be assessed on their comprehension of math concepts through word problems, oral presentations, and written explanations of their thought processes on a problem.

2. To help your students acquire language in a contextualized manner, incorporate process writing in your classroom. Process writing provides opportunities for students to comprehend and acquire language in a meaningful and motivating manner. It targets listening and speaking as well as writing and reading. Provided below are some things that can be done in the classroom to initiate process writing as a series of literacy development activities:
   - Have your students do some prewriting activities such as viewing a film or sharing the reading of an article that sets the stage for the content-area topic.
   - Have your students review key concepts and vocabulary to incorporate in their writing.
   - Use word-processing programs if they are easily accessible. These programs facilitate the draft and edit stages of the writing process and also allow students to concentrate on their writing style and organization instead of their handwriting.

3. In order to promote cultural awareness and understanding in your classroom, have your students create personal time lines. By doing this, students can learn how their own lives and the lives of their classmates are tied to various political, cultural, and historical events. You can incorporate the following steps when having your students create time lines:
   - Model a time line of your own life, expanding on events that you know will trigger ideas for students (e.g., when you met your best friend, your first day of school, your

first day at work, times you have traveled, birth or death of a family member, when you learned a second language).

- Add significant historical and cultural events that also took place during your time line, such as the fall of the Berlin Wall, the civil rights movement, and scientific advances such as cloning and space travel.
- Have students create their own time lines by interviewing family members to learn about events that took place in previous generations. When did parents or grandparents get married or come to the United States (or other milestones in their lives)?
- Combine the student and teacher time lines into a collective class time line. This can be illustrated with drawings or bar graphs. Add key historical, cultural, and political events to the personal or collective time lines so that students can understand the relationship between their lives and these events.

4. Plan lessons that will promote higher-order thinking skills among students. For example:
- Ask students to take a stance on a particular historical issue that has variable levels of cultural and political significance for different groups of people. For example, around the time of Columbus Day, provide two newspaper articles or other forms of public opinion regarding the discovery of the Americas. One article might support the celebration of this day as the founding of a new country. Another article might denounce the celebration of this day, asserting that America was invaded rather than discovered and that many Native Americans unjustly lost their lives and their land.

General Education

1. In order to understand the academic and social needs of your CLD students, consult their par-

ents when making placement decisions. During these discussions with parents or caregivers, you can ask questions related to the student's prior educational experiences, extent of native language proficiency, and the parents' involvement in literacy development.

2. Meet and collaborate regularly with the other teachers in your building to develop a purposeful, meaningful variety of formal and informal assessment measures for CLD students, such as interview protocols, questionnaires, observation checklists, rating scales and criteria, holistic scoring, and other methods for evaluating student work samples. You can also use these planning times to analyze test results and to recommend changes in programs that serve CLD students. These meetings can be held during staff development time or planning periods.

3. Teachers can select assessments that are appropriate for the developmental level and linguistic background of the students by connecting these assessments to state or district standards. To do so, educators may elect to ask themselves the following questions:
- Is the assessment linked to high content and performance standards that describe what all students should know and be able to do?
- Are the standards clear to the students and teachers involved?

4. In order to help your students adjust to a new classroom environment:
- Write the language and content objectives of the lesson on the board and review them orally with your students before class begins (ask more capable peers, parent volunteers, or paraprofessionals to translate as necessary). This helps teachers demonstrate to their students what is expected of them throughout a lesson. It is also helpful to preview upcoming lessons and link new lessons to prior concepts.

■ key theories and concepts

approach	CALLA method	cognitive approach
behaviorist	cognition	cognitivist

communication as the purpose of language

communicative approach

conditional knowledge

constructivist

declarative knowledge

grammatical approach

integrated content-based (ICB) method

language acquisition device (LAD)

learning as knowledge construction

learning strategies

metacognition

metacognitive knowledge

metacognitive regulation

method

procedural knowledge

production systems

schemata

sheltered method of instruction

strategy

student-centered

technique

thematic units

working memory

■ professional conversations on practice

1. This chapter reviews the grammatical approach and associated methods for historical purposes. Discuss, in detail, at least two major reasons why the methods of the grammatical approach are problematic for CLD students in public school classrooms.

2. The need to establish a common, consistent nomenclature to be used in instructional planning for CLD students is a benchmark of this chapter. Discuss the need for such consistency in terminology and the ways in which it enables communication and collaboration among policymakers, educators, and staff.

3. This chapter summarizes the philosophical foundations of the grammatical, communicative, and cognitive approaches to language instruction, as well as methods, strategies, and techniques associated with each approach. Discuss the unfavorable effects that can be anticipated when classroom instruction for CLD students mixes philosophical approaches or uses methods that are not consistent with a selected philosophical approach to language instruction.

■ questions for review and reflection

1. In what ways would you define and differentiate among the terms *approach, method, strategy,* and *technique?*

2. What are the three dominant approaches to language instruction?

3. In what ways would you summarize the philosophical foundations of the grammatical approach?

4. In what ways would you summarize the philosophical foundations of the communicative approach?

5. In what ways would you compare and contrast a behaviorist and a constructivist perspective on learning?

6. In what ways would you summarize the philosophical foundations of the cognitive approach?

7. What are the noteworthy features of at least two methods of the grammatical approach?

8. Which methods of the grammatical approach are contemporary versus historical?

9. In what ways would you compare and contrast early and contemporary communicative methods?

10. What are the noteworthy features of at least two early methods of the communicative approach?

11. What are the noteworthy features of the integrated content-based (ICB) method of the communicative approach?

12. What are the noteworthy features of the sheltered instruction method of the communicative approach?

13. What three types of memory are explored by the cognitive perspective?

14. In what ways would you differentiate among declarative, procedural, and conditional knowledge?

15. In what ways would you differentiate between metacognitive knowledge and metacognitive regulation?

16. What three types of learning strategies are explicitly taught by the CALLA method?

17. What are the noteworthy features of the CALLA method of the cognitive approach?

18. In what ways would you describe meaningful learning?

19. In what ways did Chomsky describe the role of the LAD in language acquisition?

20. What does it mean to ground language instruction in a philosophical approach?

suggested activities

Preservice Teachers

1. After reading the following vignette, identify the instructional approach used. What are some of the characteristics of this approach? Identify the method(s) associated with the approach found in the vignette. What are some of the characteristics of the identified method(s)?

The twenty students in Mr. Brown's sixth-grade class are engaged in writing a book report on ancient Egypt. The room is overflowing with posters, illustrations, hieroglyphics, books, and student work related to ancient Egypt. The class has been studying ancient Egypt for two weeks and their book reports are a culmination of their studies. Rather than having students turn in individual book reports, the teacher has required the students to work in collaborative groups of three to four in which they will write, design, and present their report to the class.

Half of the students in Mr. Brown's class are classified CLD (the other half are English-only), and several languages can be heard in the classroom. Students in all parts of the classroom are talking excitedly while they are writing rough drafts, discussing their ideas with other students, and editing the work of their classmates. The teacher wanders from group to group in order to observe and provide assistance when necessary.

One of the student groups, led by Van, a CLD Vietnamese student, is ready to present

the group book report at the end of the day. Mr. Brown has the group go to the front of the room where they proceed to present their book report. Van begins by presenting a time line on a large piece of chart paper. He describes the relevant events that took place during each of the dates his group has included, using vocabulary he has learned over the course of the two-week unit. Margarita follows by presenting a visual representation of what homes were like in ancient Egypt. Ben then goes on to discuss the class system of ancient Egypt with a Venn diagram of the similarities and differences between the class system of ancient Egypt and the purportedly classless system of twentieth-century America.

In-Service Teachers

1. After reading the following vignette, identify the instructional approach used. What are some of the characteristics of this approach? Identify the method(s) associated with the approach found in the vignette. What are some of the characteristics of the idenitfied method(s)?

In his science classroom, Mr. Babcock displays posters, several of which are written in Spanish and in English, of scientists and inventors from diverse cultures. His third-period physical science class is mostly made up of sophomores, with a few juniors and seniors who need the class to graduate. The students have a wide range of English language proficiencies. Mr. Babcock has carefully structured the lab groups to include both native English speakers and CLD students who demonstrate limited English proficiency. Students with a stronger command of English are placed in groups with CLD students to act as peer coaches.

The content and language objectives on the board cover the scientific method and related terminology. Each group is given a number of tools that students have used in previous work: a graduated cylinder partially filled with water, a ruler, a balance, a table of densities, and a piece of aluminum foil. Mr. Babcock has the students read the daily objectives aloud and gives the students the task of determining the thickness of the piece of aluminum foil. Students review on the board the steps they will take as scientists to design an experiment and predict the outcome. Each group has a leader, a recorder, a timekeeper, and a materials keeper.

The ensuing discussion is animated as the groups tackle the activity. The students within each group come to a consensus on the method of measurement, and the recorder writes down the plan. The leader calls on the materials keeper to begin the process. While the activity proceeds, the recorder keeps careful record of the steps taken, questions, and results. The timekeeper calls time. Then the leader from each group explains to the class their method of testing the thickness of the aluminum foil, the questions that the group members developed, and the results determined. As a class the students review the content and language objectives on the board and explain to Mr. Babcock how they met the objectives or why they believe more practice is necessary to meet the objectives.

assessment tips and strategies

The following assessment tips and strategies are drawn from the content of Chapters 4 through 6.

ASSESSMENT

Formal and informal assessments are crucial to the measurement of process and product gains in language, acculturation, and content-area learning among CLD students. Student assessments in the area of second language development must be carefully implemented and accurately interpreted in order to ensure that students are progressing and to gauge what additional support will be needed. Furthermore, alternative and authentic assessments require CLD students to demonstrate their knowledge or skills in a variety of ways. Effective teachers select assessments that are appropriate for the developmental levels and linguistic backgrounds of the students by connecting these assessments to state or district standards.

Assessment Tips

- An informal assessment of a CLD student's language biography should include the following factors:
  —Dominant language of first schooling in native country
  —Dominant language spoken at home

  —Extent of L2 schooling in the United States
  —Actual CALP versus apparent BICS development in L1 and L2
- A formal assessment of a CLD student's language biography can be done by using the following tests:
  —To determine L1 proficiency—use the translated LAS, BVAT, etc.
  —To determine L2 proficiency—use the IPT, LAS, and so on.
- An informal assessment of a CLD student's level of acculturation should include the following factors:
  —Circumstances and culture in home country prior to immigration
  —Recency of immigration
  —Current home dynamics
  —Parents' work obligations
  —Acculturation stressors
  —Coping strategies
  —The student's involvement in language brokering dynamics
  —Proximity to school and issues of transportation (check with parent, social worker, school records)

- A formal assessment of a CLD student's level of acculturation can be done through the acculturation quick screen (AQS) (C. Collier, 1987).
- When teaching key concepts, teachers should assess student understanding by:
  —Asking open-ended questions that invite comparison and contrast.
  —Prompting students to integrate what they have observed and learned in their native countries.
- Informal content-area assessments should encompass measures such as rubrics, self-assessments, and portfolios.
- Assessments should be incremental and criterion referenced.
- Alternative assessments in L1 should include journals and one-on-one discussions.
- Assessment tasks should be scaffolded in a contextualized manner in order to accurately assess CLD students.
- A formal assessment of a CLD student's content-area knowledge and capacities should be done through modified district tools or pretests.

Assessment Strategies

- Informal assessment of the level of acculturation is primarily done through teacher–student (T–S) and teacher–parent or family (T–P) conversations.
- Scaffold assessments by incorporating easily accessible classroom materials such as brief quotations, charts, graphics, cartoons, and works of art.
- Scaffold assessments by including questions for small-group discussion and individual writing.
- Scaffold assessments by modeling the steps involved.
- Use alternative assessments that require CLD students to demonstrate their knowledge and skills in different ways, such as:
  —Exhibits
  —Dramatic interpretations
  —Interviews
  —Observations
  —Self-reflections
  —Writing samples
- Meet and collaborate regularly with the other teachers in your building to develop multiple formal and informal assessment measures for CLD students, such as:
  —Interview protocols
  —Questionnaires
  —Observation checklists
  —Rating scales and criteria
  —Holistic scoring

The Integrated Content-Based Method of Instruction

The most important single factor influencing learning is what the learner knows. Ascertain this and teach accordingly.

—David Ausubel, *Educational Psychology: A Cognitive View*

critical standards *Guiding Chapter Content*

TESOL/NCATE teacher standards reflect professional consensus on standards for the quality teaching of Pre-K–12 CLD students. Additionally, the CEEE Guiding Principles and their accompanying indicators serve as a framework to assist practitioners, policymakers, and clients as they collaborate to enhance academic enrichment and language acquisition among CLD students. Therefore, in order to help educators understand how they might appropriately target and address national professional teaching standards in practice, we have designed the content of this chapter to reflect the following standards.

TESOL ESL Standards for P–12 Teacher Education Programs

TESOL ESL—Domain 1: Language. Candidates know, understand, and use the major concepts, theories, and research related to the nature and acquisition of language to construct learning environments that support ESOL (CLD) students' language and literacy development and content-area achievement. (p. 1)

- **Standard 1.b. Language acquisition and development.** Candidates understand and apply concepts, theories, research, and practice to facilitate the acquisition of a primary and a new language in and out of classroom settings. (p. 6)
  - 1.b.5. Understand and apply current theories and research in language and literacy development (p. 9)
  - 1.b.9. Understand and apply knowledge of the role of individual learner variables in the process of learning English. (p. 11)

CEEE Guiding Principles

Guiding Principle #2: Limited English proficient students develop full receptive and productive proficiencies in English in the domains of listening, speaking, reading, and writing, consistent with expectations for all students. (p. 6)

2.7. English language arts teachers and specialists in English language collaborate with each other and with teachers in other core content areas to design instruction that supports students' learning of English as well as core content. (p. 6)

Note: All TESOL/NCATE standards are cited from TESOL (2001). All Guiding Principles are cited from Center for Equity and Excellence in Education (1996).

Guiding Principle #3: Limited English proficient students are taught challenging content to enable them to meet performance standards in all content areas, including reading and language arts, mathematics, social studies, science, the fine arts, health, and physical education, consistent with those for all students. (p. 7)

3.8. English language arts teachers and specialists in second language acquisition coordinate their instruction with teachers in other content areas to assure that students are acquiring the language necessary to participate fully in classroom activities that involve critical thinking (e.g., analysis, synthesis) and problem solving within the content disciplines. (p. 7)

3.11. Students who are in the process of acquiring proficiency in English recognize the importance of performing in all content areas at a level comparable to that expected of students who are native speakers of English. (p. 7)

Much debate has surrounded the question of whether students can learn academic content if they do not yet have a high level of proficiency in the English language. The previous chapters of this book present the theoretical and research-based rationales for the use of content-based instruction to promote both the linguistic and academic development of CLD students. This chapter explores why the integrated content-based (ICB) method of instruction provides an excellent venue for language learning. Although the types of strategies and techniques associated with this method may prove beneficial with native-English-speaking students, they are crucial to the academic success of CLD students.

For second language learners, language proficiency involves more than basic interpersonal communication skills (BICS). Because language learners must develop the cognitive academic language proficiency (CALP) to succeed in grade-level academic classes in English, content classes such as biology, physics, calculus, economics, world literature, and U.S. history become their communicative environment (Mohan, 1986). The assumption that CLD students must speak English before they can learn academic content is a serious threat to their potential academic success. For example, as discussed in Chapter 3, CLD students need one to three years to acquire basic interpersonal communication skills and five to seven or more years to acquire cognitive academic language proficiency (Cummins, 1981; Thomas & Collier, 1997). If a school waits until CLD students have acquired CALP to begin content instruction, then CLD students are at least five years behind their age-appropriate grade level academically. Even if a school waits until CLD students have acquired a BICS level of proficiency, these students are still two to three years behind their peers academically. As Collier (1995a) noted, "When the context of second language use is school, a very deep level of proficiency is required" (p. 2).

The Council of Chief State School Officers (CCSSO) argues that for CLD students to be academically successful in school, they must continue to learn and expand their knowledge of new content so that they do not fall behind their monolingual English-speaking peers (CCSSO, 1992). One way that educators can minimize the gap between monolingual English-speaking students and their CLD peers is to link language development with academic content (Short, 1993b). This practice of integrating grade-level language and content objectives presents a positive solution to the dilemma of how to prepare CLD students who are not proficient in English vis-à-vis grade-level curricula.

Research related to CLD students further indicates that language learning and content-matter learning are interrelated and must be taught simultaneously if CLD students are to achieve both academic success and high levels of second language proficiency (Cummins, 2000; Cummins, 1996; Freeman & Freeman, 1998; Freeman, Freeman, & Mercuri, 2002; Thomas & Collier, 1999). When CLD students learn English through content-based instruction, they attain a higher level of second language proficiency faster than when they study English as the focus of instruction (Dulay, Burt, & Krashen, 1982). In a synthesis of the findings of a longitudinal study on second language acquisition program effectiveness, regarding the CALP development of CLD students, Collier (1995a) observed,

> Students do less well in programs that focus on discrete units of language taught in a structured, sequenced curriculum with the learner treated as a passive recipient of knowledge; students achieve significantly better in programs that teach language through cognitively complex academic content in math, science, social studies, and literature, taught through problem solving, discovery learning in highly interactive classroom activities. (p. 2)

Consequently, CLD students learn their second language most effectively when academic content rather than the structure of the language itself is the context of language instruction.

The ICB method is a means of providing content-based second language instruction using academic thematic units. The theme of the unit provides a context for academic and language development (Brinton, Snow, & Wesche, 1989). A thematic unit can be defined as "a set of related learning activities and experiences that effectively support teaching multiple content areas and skills organized around a central topic, idea, or theme" (Gardner & Wissick, 2002, para. 3). The classroom, the environment, and the target culture are sources that can provide ideas for the unit's focus. Activities that integrate the teaching of content and language concepts are then incorporated into instruction, which is structured around the unit's topic, idea, or theme (Curtain & Haas, 1995). As Haas (2000) notes, thematic units planned in this manner facilitate the incorporation of a variety of language concepts into a topic area that is interesting and worthy of study, thereby giving meaning to the language that CLD students are learning. Finally, thematic units specifically benefit CLD students because learning language through specialized content-based instruction allows CLD students to acquire cognitive academic language proficiency in a natural way and in a communicative environment. In the content-based second language classroom, CLD students receive comprehensible input to facilitate the mastery of key content concepts while learning the language necessary for academic survival in the mainstream classroom (Mohan, 1986).

ICB instruction is grounded in the communicative approach, which was introduced in Chapter 4 and discussed in Chapter 6. The primary ways in which ICB instruction reflects the communicative approach include, but are not limited to, an emphasis on communication, the authentic use of literacy in context, and the cultivation of all literacy domains (listening, speaking, reading, and writing). This chapter explores the evolution of the ICB method and its emphasis on the interrelation between second language acquisition and academic development. In this chapter, we describe and provide examples of how this method works in practice in elementary and secondary settings. A brief discussion also explores the implementation of this method in different classrooms and teaching situations.

■ Evolution of Content-Based Instruction

The research base for ICB instruction can be traced to a movement known as *language across the curriculum*. This movement espouses a reciprocal relationship between language and content learning (Brinton et al., 1989). The language-across-the-curriculum movement found that directing the attention of learners to content language more specifically addressed the language acquisition needs of CLD students in the academic context. This integration of content and language instruction occurred through the teaching of specific content with language teaching aims (Brinton et al., 1989). By proposing the integration of content and language instruction, the language-across-the-curriculum movement provided a methodological foundation for teachers of CLD students to provide content-based language instruction. This new method of second language instruction provided CLD students with varying levels of second language proficiency with comprehensible content-based instruction so that the successful acquisition of academic content could take place.

For decades, foreign language departments, adult education programs, and military programs have been teaching content classes for specific purposes. These programs, often referred to as English for specific purposes (ESP) or language for specific purposes (LSP), seek to prepare students to learn language for different environments, including the fields of medicine, engineering, computer science, and others (Brinton et al., 1989). ESP and LSP instruction use specially designed content-based texts and lectures to assist adult CLD students in developing speaking, listening, reading, and writing skills in English. Using content curricula allows educators to provide language instruction that focuses on the language-learning needs of adult CLD students who are preparing to enter professional studies or the workforce. Through multiple strategies and techniques, ESP and LSP instruction introduces students to vocabulary, syntax, and discourse styles of the target area. Materials and activities that reflect the target area and represent the key concepts are used in instruction. As Brinton and colleagues (1989) note, "In LSP courses, the primary emphasis has traditionally been on the 'what' of language instruction—language content which reflects the second language needs of learners 'for whom the learning of English is auxiliary to some other professional or academic purpose'" (p. 7).

Similarly, content-based instruction in foreign language programs, often referred to as *immersion instruction,* has focused on teaching students a new language through the medium of academic content areas (Brinton et al., 1989). Immersion instruction uses strategies and techniques to ensure that the academic content language of instruction is comprehensible to the learner. With immersion instruction, success is almost exclusively linked to language majority students—those whose native language is that of the majority group—thereby making this model most successful in foreign language teaching (Brinton et al., 1989). However, CLD students who do not enjoy extensive native language support in this type of model do not receive adequate support or sufficient comprehensible input to be academically successful.

Content-Centered Methods of Instruction

More recently the field of education in the United States has witnessed a search for alternative programs to serve culturally and linguistically diverse student populations. Programs with a focus that goes beyond language in isolation, life skills vocabulary, or redundant content already known in the CLD students' first language are emerging, with promising results. This search for alternative programs has focused on instruction that integrates linguistic modifications, meaning making through conceptualization, real-life applications of content, and a period of "bathing" students in the rhythm of the new language. Accordingly, these elements are central to teaching and learning using ICB instruction.

Although many language teaching programs focus on the integration of language and content as the vehicle for reaching the maximum academic potential of CLD students, the method that is the focus of this chapter is the integrated content-based method of instruction with a thematic focus. In recent years, research on the ICB method has provided a solid theoretical framework for instruction that has proved effective at both the elementary and secondary school levels. ICB instruction is often found in the following learning environments:

- Classrooms in which a language teacher and a grade-level teacher are collaborating to meet the needs of CLD students
- Pull-out programs in which the CLD specialist closely aligns instruction with local and state academic content standards
- Schools in which the curriculum for all grade levels is based on themes aligned with local and state academic content standards
- Middle school and high school classrooms in which content-area teachers are teaming to collaborate and integrate themes and topics from different subject areas

■ Integrated Content-Based Instruction

In ICB instruction, language acquisition and content learning are not separate acts of teaching. Rather, language serves as a medium of instruction and learning.

Context, thereby, functions as the central component of interactions between teacher and student. Cazden (1977) notes:

> We must always remember that language is learned, not because we want to talk or read or write about language, but because we want to talk and read and write about the world. Only linguists have language as their subject matter. For the rest of us—especially for children—language is the medium of interpersonal relationships, the medium of our mental life, the medium of learning about the world. (p. 42)

This integration of language acquisition and content learning provides the framework for ICB instruction and provides CLD students with learning experiences that facilitate language acquisition and contextualize academic content.

The ICB method challenges the myth that academic instruction needs to be delayed until CLD students have developed a high level of English language proficiency. With ICB instruction, the CLD student immediately receives instruction rooted in the academic content of the lesson while simultaneously learning English. As Short (1991) notes, by providing CLD students with the opportunity to use language in meaningful contexts while studying the academic subject matter, teachers create an ideal learning environment for facilitating language development and academic learning. When language instruction concentrates on subject matter, the learner has the advantage of a familiar extralinguistic context. This familiarity with context can be a tremendous facilitator of comprehension and thus of language acquisition among CLD students. The more the CLD student learns and comprehends language related to a specific content area, the more likely he or she is to comprehend future instruction in that content area.

Are You Aware?

Walqui (2000) argues that the departmentalization of secondary education tends to result in the fragmentation of learning for all students. In response to Walqui's argument, many middle and high schools help students make the connections in their learning through content-based or interdisciplinary instruction. Many campuses across the nation are starting to organize their teaching around multidisciplinary teams of teachers who share the same group of students. For secondary CLD students, the connections in learning greatly help to reinforce the students' development of academic language. Teachers who collaborate and coordinate grade-level content instruction with the academic needs of their students consistently use academic language in content instruction. These teachers also maintain consistency through constant communication regarding social and cultural factors, student learning styles, and student language proficiency levels that can inhibit or support academic success for adolescent CLD students. Walqui (2000) asserts that a change to this type of instruction takes time and energy. However, once planned and implemented, this type of collaboration among secondary educators provides more meaningful learning connections not only for CLD students but also for all students.

■ *How can teachers who share the same CLD students communicate more effectively? List how elementary and secondary teachers can tie various content areas together in meaningful ways for CLD students.*

ICB instruction engages CLD students in authentic activities linked to specific subject matter that is incorporated within a theme. Teachers integrate language and concept development by providing CLD learners with real-world experiences through hands-on activities. In this way, the ICB method reflects a whole language approach. ICB instruction stimulates CLD students to use targeted academic language for relevant, cognitively demanding purposes.

Benefits of ICB Instruction for CLD Students

Research by Caine and Caine (1991) suggests that learning facts and skills within a meaningful context rather than in isolation enables the individual to store the material in memory with less time required for practicing and rehearsing the information. This is particularly true for CLD students who are simultaneously learning both academic content and language. Therefore, when teachers present lessons that integrate academic content and language development across the curriculum, the CLD student enjoys an enhanced opportunity to internalize and process new learnings and language. Table 7.1 provides a brief summary of the similarities and differences between segregated and integrated skills instruction.

Using the ICB method, the integration of language and content instruction is done by incorporating subject-area content into early language programs (Curtain & Haas, 1995). Curtain and Haas suggest that language and content instruction are also integrated by putting language into a larger, more meaningful context and by providing situations that require authentic language use. ICB instruction also allows for the concurrent teaching of academic subject matter and second language learning skills. Thus, when using the ICB method, teachers create an ideal learning environment for facilitating the acquisition of content knowledge among CLD students (Short, 1993a).

With ICB instruction, the language emphasized in the curriculum is based directly on the academic needs of the students. For example, the sequence of skills and language introduced is structured to reflect the needs of the CLD student by bridging gaps and making concrete connections to background knowledge. In this manner, students acquire content information while simultaneously developing their CALP in the target language. Furthermore, through repeated exposure to academic language, CLD students begin to transfer second language skills to other academic subjects areas.

Vygotsky (1978) proposed that through increased social interaction and scaffolding of instruction, students are better able to contextualize and comprehend new learnings. The ICB method not only provides CLD students with the opportunity for increased social interaction with their peers but also scaffolds learning by providing repeated exposure to content and language that is meaningfully contextualized for CLD students. Thus, the ICB method eliminates any artificial separation between language instruction and subject-area classes.

Attention to each of the four domains of the CLD student biography—language, cognitive, academic, and social development—increases CLD student

■ **t a b l e 7.1**   Segregated versus Integrated Skills Instruction: Comparisons and Contrasts

Criterion	Integrated Skills Instruction		Segregated Skills Instruction
	ICB	SI	
An ESL certified/endorsed teacher typically delivers classroom instruction.	+		
Emphasis on all literacy skills of language.	+	+	
L2 development is a goal.	+	+	
Content knowledge/skills and L2 development goals.	+	+	
Focus on requisite terminology for content.	+	+	
Focus on core, grade-level curriculum.	+	+	
Content and ESL standards guide instruction.	+	+	
Classroom instruction typically follows the scope and sequence of a grade-level class.	+	+	
A subject-area certified teacher, with professional development for CLD student needs, typically delivers classroom instruction.		+	
Focus on isolated/discrete language skills.			x
Language and content learning are separated.			x
Basic skills orientation of instruction.			x
A subject-area certified teacher with no professional development for CLD students may lead instruction.			x

Legend
ICB—Integrated content-based method
SI—Sheltered instruction method
x—Not appropriate for CLD students
+—Appropriate for CLD students

achievement. Nonetheless, Genesee (1994) suggests that language instruction is often an isolated part of the student's day when conventional language instruction methods are used. Moreover, the student's learning of language concepts and skills is commonly segregated from her or his development of social, cognitive, and academic understandings. In contrast, the ICB method integrates these four aspects of the CLD student biography. For the CLD student, this integration of language learning and content-area instruction facilitates language acquisition as well as cognitive development (Curtain & Haas, 1995).

Furthermore, ICB instruction motivates learners because language becomes the medium through which all students have access to meaningful and developmentally appropriate content material (Genesee, 1998; Grabe & Stoller, 1997; Met, 1991). Therefore, the ICB method decreases perceptions of marginalization

dilemmas *of Practice*

Ms. Reyes is a sixth-grade English teacher at an urban middle school. Many CLD students at this school do not yet exhibit high levels of English proficiency. On a weekly basis, Ms. Reyes reads a list of vocabulary words and their definitions to the students but does not provide any opportunities for student discussion or dialogue about them. Rather, she asks students to write down the definitions and then write sentences using each word appropriately. She is disappointed with her CLD students who are having difficulty completing the sentence writing homework and are not prepared for the weekly vocabulary tests. What can Ms. Reyes do to create a more successful language acquisition process for her struggling CLD students?

■ *The way that Ms. Reyes has designed her vocabulary instruction does not include strategies to present these words in a meaningful and relevant way for CLD students. Without being able to form a connection between the new vocabulary terms and their existing schemata, Ms. Reyes's CLD students are likely to feel overwhelmed by this information that has little meaning for them. It's important for Ms. Reyes to understand that vocabulary development is best accomplished through activities that promote listening, speaking, reading, and writing in meaningful contexts. Such activities might include student presentations, collaborative group work, think-pair-share activities, jigsaw reading, and more. Ms. Reyes could also plan with other content-area teachers who share the same students. These collaborating educators could decide which themes would indicate the necessary vocabulary to be acquired to ensure academic success. Meaningful connections could then be established across content courses and with those teachers.*

among CLD students (Short, 1993a). Additionally, content-based instruction capitalizes on the content knowledge, expertise, and background knowledge that CLD students bring to a lesson. According to Genesee (1994, 1998), this connection makes language acquisition more concrete by placing language into an authentic and meaningful context.

ICB instruction promotes the negotiation of meaning in context among CLD students (Grabe & Stoller, 1997). When meaning is negotiated, the CLD student and the teacher (or other students) work together to ensure the student's comprehension of the language or content material. The teacher tries to present the information in multiple meaningful ways, and the student tries to construct meaning from the multiple interactions. Such meaning negotiation is known to enhance language acquisition as the CLD student learns how to engage in communication, focusing on both form and content (Grabe & Stoller, 1997). Accordingly, this negotiated meaning provides a forum for teaching more complex language in authentic contexts.

Finally, incorporating opportunities for higher thinking instruction using the ICB method develops a wider range of discourse skills among CLD students than does traditional segregated skills language instruction (Crandall, Spanos, Christian, Simich-Dudgeon, & Willetts, 1987). As suggested by the Center for Advanced

Research on Language Acquisition (CARLA, n.d., General Principles), the ICB method provides teachers with opportunities to integrate the following cognitive skills, each of which enhances language development (Curtain, 1995; Met, 1991):

- *Information-gathering skills*—absorbing, questioning
- *Organizing skills*—categorizing, comparing, representing
- *Analyzing skills*—identifying main ideas, identifying attributes and components, identifying relationships and patterns
- *Generating skills*—inferring, predicting, estimating

■ Delivering Integrated Content-Based Instruction

According to Short (1991), the ICB method places an emphasis on three key factors that are each applicable to both language and content teachers: (a) the use of a variety of media, (b) the development of students' thinking skills, and (c) the use of student-centered instruction. By using multiple media, the content-area teacher is able to increase CLD students' comprehension of key content through the presentation of information in a variety of ways. Moreover, a targeted focus on thinking skills in ICB instruction increases CLD students' comprehension of content. Finally, the student-centered organization of the ICB method builds on the existing background knowledge that CLD students bring to the classroom.

Consequently, the implementation of the ICB method requires teachers to select rich content that drives language instruction and contextualizes learning. ICB instruction also necessitates a commitment on the teacher's part to adapt and modify curriculum materials so that student needs guide curriculum development. To maximize the effectiveness of implementation, language teachers and content-area teachers often work collaboratively to ensure learner success.

ICB teachers understand that the CLD student takes on the role of an active constructor of meaning. Consequently, language learning is most likely to occur when the CLD student actively participates in meaningful, content-based contexts. Thus, delivering ICB instruction requires the teacher to create an environment for learning that not only reflects the goals and objectives of instruction but also promotes the integration of language, content, and the culture of the CLD student. When planning, instructing, and assessing an ICB lesson, effective teachers consider several components. The following sections explore each of these components and their related subcomponents in greater detail (see Figure 7.1 for an outline of the components of the ICB method).

Planning an ICB Lesson

Planning an ICB lesson for CLD students requires special attention to the linguistic and academic needs of these students. Creating a context for the development of language and content understandings is of utmost importance. Consequently,

I. **Planning**
   A. Select the theme.
   B. Choose topics relevant to the theme.
   C. Create language and content objectives.
   D. Gather appropriate instructional materials.
   E. Arrange the classroom environment.

II. **Instruction**
   A. Preteach key content vocabulary.
   B. Build background.
   C. Facilitate collaborative learning.
   D. Use authentic activities for integrating literacy.
   E. Engage CLD students cognitively.
   F. Provide visual support and graphic organizers.
   G. Develop learning centers.

III. **Assessment**
   A. Provide formative assessment.
   B. Provide summative assessment.

■ **f i g u r e   7.1**   The Process of Creating and Implementing an ICB Lesson

ICB lesson planning begins with choosing an overarching theme. Other elements of the planning phase of ICB lessons include choosing topics related to the theme, creating language and content objectives, designing meaningful student-centered activities, gathering appropriate materials, and arranging the classroom environment. These elements of the planning phase should all support the development of CLD students' deep conceptual understandings of the theme and their capacities to communicate these understandings. Necessarily, therefore, this discussion of planning an ICB lesson begins with selecting a theme.

Selecting a Theme

A theme in ICB instruction provides the framework on which the teacher can map the identified needs of the CLD students in the classroom. The theme is the overarching idea that shapes the unit, lessons, and topics that constitute the ICB method. Although themes require time, in terms of curriculum development and adaptation as well as in the coordination of materials, the impact on CLD student motivation and academic achievement is well worth the effort.

In ICB instruction, selecting a theme often requires a new way of thinking about instructional delivery and student learning. This selection process acknowledges the interrelationships of various bodies of knowledge and demonstrates the relationship between principles and processes. Selection of the theme is important in setting the vision for the unit. For the teacher, the theme becomes the framework within which to begin reflecting on instruction. For the student, the theme is a frame of reference from which connections are made to prior knowledge, personal interests, and academic content.

Themes selected are based on deep conceptual issues inherent in content-area curricula as well as on the linguistic and academic needs of the CLD students being served. Theme selection first considers what the students already know and what is of interest to them. Additionally, teachers reflect on the relation of the theme to the grade-level curriculum and the backgrounds of students. Teachers also consider the cultural relevancy of the theme to CLD students as well as their own knowledge base and interest in the theme and possible topics. Pesola (1995) suggests that as teachers begin to consider choosing a topic, they think about questions similar to the following:

- What learner characteristics, such as developmental level, learning style, experiential background, and culture, describe the students as individuals?
- Does the classroom environment support the proposed theme?
- What understandings about the culture and the subject content will the students develop?
- Are materials available to support a given range of activities related to the theme and associated topics?

Selecting a Theme: In Practice   For the purpose of illustrating how to design an ICB lesson, this chapter presents a practical scenario highlighting the salient points of the ICB method. In this example, Ms. Gallardo is a high school teacher who teaches a government class the first period of every day. Of the total of twenty students, thirteen are culturally and linguistically diverse and the remaining seven are native English speakers. As Ms. Gallardo plans her instruction for the two weeks to follow, she considers the population she is serving and the content area she teaches. It has been her experience with this particular class that her students tend to learn best when exposed to concepts that can easily be related to prior knowledge. This tends to be true for any learner, even though the high school–level instruction tends to be more context-reduced, or abstract. Because many of the students in her class are neither completely proficient in English nor familiar with many of the cultural norms of the United States, Ms. Gallardo decides to teach rights, privileges, and responsibilities in the weeks to follow. This theme allows for a great many enriching activities that foster the transfer of concepts from one culture to another. Opportunities for expression through dialogue and other forms of communication and exploration with language are ample.

Ms. Gallardo chooses to teach the theme of rights, privileges, and responsibilities because this theme directly correlates with the standards she must address during the first quarter of her government class. She is aware that in planning instruction she must first consider standards that need to be addressed in her content area as well as the needs of every student in her classroom. By aligning instruction with grade-level standards, Ms. Gallardo increases CLD student engagement and motivation by providing them with challenging academic and linguistic content.

Choosing Topics Relevant to the Theme

The selection of a theme sets the stage for topic development and decisions regarding the linguistic and academic objectives that will allow for optimal language development and content learning. When beginning the task of choosing topics, effective teachers consider the following question: Which topics related to the theme would maximize learning, capture student interest, and motivate student involvement? Topics are critical to planning lessons that reflect the integration of language and content at multiple levels. Topics become the backbone of the theme selected and will influence all future decisions about the most appropriate instruction for the CLD learner.

Topics align with the selected theme and are revisited as the theme progresses over time. The scope and sequence of the grade-level or content curriculum should be analyzed when selecting topics within a theme. Topics dictate the language and academic syllabus and provide a map for the delivery of instruction. They also determine how grade-level and content-area texts, authentic literature, and materials will be used to maximize integration of content and language objectives.

Once the teacher decides on the number of topics to use and selects those that are most appropriate, he or she begins thinking about a time line for delivery. Additionally, the teacher considers specific ways in which each topic will address local and state standards. The topics provide the focus for individual lessons and the language and content objectives that are written for each lesson. In turn, these objectives support language development and academic success among CLD students.

Making decisions regarding the most appropriate topics that align with the overarching theme involves multiple considerations. The following suggestions may assist educators in the selection of topics that effectively guide the successful delivery of an ICB lesson for CLD students:

- The topic must be selected for its linguistic, cultural, cognitive, and academic merits, as well as its timeliness, student appeal, and potential for enhancing the future academic success of CLD students.
- The topic must reflect the identified theme.
- The topic selected should also provide coherence and continuity across skill areas and encourage progress in higher-level language skills.
- Topics need to engage the students academically as well as linguistically.
- Availability of varied materials that match the students' proficiency levels should also be considered when selecting topics.

Once the topics have been identified, the teacher generates lessons to provide instruction on the topics that she or he has selected.

Choosing Topics Relevant to the Theme: In Practice Now that Ms. Gallardo has decided on the theme of instruction for the weeks to follow, she must reflect on the topics related to the theme. Ms. Gallardo's class begins first thing in the morning, and she wants to choose topics that are interesting and relevant to her students' lives. She considers the fact that many of the students are new to the United States. She also considers how various topics that deal with rights, privileges, and responsibilities relate to the national and state standards that her government class must address.

The topics Ms. Gallardo chooses to focus on include the nature of human rights, the U.S. Constitution with an emphasis on the Bill of Rights, and the evolution of civil and human rights in the United States and other selected countries. Ms. Gallardo purposely selects topics that potentially involve meaningful language experiences in context. In order to provide topics that benefit the population she serves in a meaningful and rich manner, Ms. Gallardo presents topics that facilitate the content and language concepts that specifically relate to rights, privileges, and responsibilities.

The first topic to be covered in Ms. Gallardo's class is the nature of human rights. She plans to use each topic as a building block for the subsequent topic while reintroducing each topic strand throughout the instruction of the entire theme. Common language that is used and revisited throughout the unit will be valuable to the CLD students in her classroom and will help reinforce new concepts taught. In this way, she facilitates the construction of new knowledge from prior knowledge for all students. This structure serves as the foundation on which subsequent instruction will be built.

Given the topics that Ms. Gallardo will deliver throughout the time line of the theme at hand, she decides to seek out literature that encourages meaningful connections to students' prior experiences. Some of the literature she chooses includes information regarding human rights in the home countries of her CLD students. Ms. Gallardo plans to use the information from these readings to maximize higher-level questioning with her students. Such questioning is designed to prompt her students to think about the topics presented and extend their learning as they question and investigate the nature of human rights.

Using the ICB method, Ms. Gallardo has decided to allow ample time for the coverage of each topic so that her students form a solid grasp of content vocabulary and concepts. She will gauge her students' progress with each topic and ensure that her students are reaching at least 80 percent mastery of content concepts before she moves on to a new topic. As Ms. Gallardo considers the topics chosen, time line developed, level of student interest, language enrichment needs, and cognitive challenges for her students, she places herself in a much better position to begin planning smaller elements of instruction.

Creating Language and Content Objectives

Once the theme has been chosen and the topics selected, teachers that use the ICB method begin the decision-making process regarding both language and content objectives designed to maximize language acquisition and academic development. When selecting language and content objectives, attention should be given to their specific connections to the topic. Additionally, a comprehensive examination of students' linguistic, academic, cognitive, and sociocultural needs provides guidance in developing appropriate objectives. In this way, language and content objectives are compatible with the curriculum selected and reflect the needs of the students. When considering which content and language objective to develop for a lesson, Table 7.2 may be a useful tool in ensuring that lessons include objectives that reflect a variety of activities and levels of cognitive complexity.

■ **table 7.2**   Lesson Plan Word List

Content Objectives	Language Objectives
Contrast	Listen to
Reflect	Write
Justify	Describe
Select	Clearly articulate
Reflect on	Define
Generate	List
Rationalize	Inform
Apply	Summarize
Analyze	Discuss
Identify	Rewrite
Compare	Recommend
Demonstrate	Convince
Examine	Explain
Cooperate	Clarify
Judge	Support
Use reference materials to	Differentiate
Distinguish	Monitor
Demonstrate	Paraphrase
Modify	Defend
Relate	Debate
Classify	Argue
Integrate	Propose
Create	Comprehend
Design	
Invent	
Formulate	
Prepare	
Decide	
Differentiate	
Plan	
Predict	
Organize	
Self-assess	
Make connections between	
Use a rule to	
Make a rule about	
Visualize	
Infer	

Language Objective Development   The design of ICB instruction begins with student needs and culminates with an understanding of the unique linguistic challenges CLD students face within the target subject. Mathematics, science, language arts, and social studies all have specific vocabulary, syntax, semantics, and discourse features that are particular to the subject area. Consider the words of Morris (1975) regarding the teaching of mathematics:

> The problems of teaching in a second language are accentuated when mathematics is the context of dialog. This is due essentially to the abstract nature of mathematics and the difficulties, which arise in absorbing abstract concepts. Also, the language used has to be precise, consistent and unambiguous, if mathematical ideas are to be explored and described effectively. And for dialog to become possible, the child must be equipped with a basic repertoire of linguistic concepts and structures. (p. 52)

Morris has cogently argued the need for students to understand the linguistic concepts and structures of academic content lessons and the implications of this argument for the teaching of mathematics. However, his statement could fundamentally apply to any content area. Given these implications, designing clear language objectives is paramount in the planning of ICB instruction. Understanding the interrelationship between CLD student needs and the linguistic challenges they face in academic contexts prepares the teacher by enabling him or her to design clear language objectives for specific content-area lessons.

The process of determining appropriate language objectives is typically initiated through the teacher's reflections on the proficiencies of students in each of the literacy domains of listening, speaking, reading, and writing. Understanding the implications of each of the different levels of language proficiency in these areas for student engagement and academic performance makes it much easier for the teacher to make decisions regarding appropriate language objectives. Effective teachers of the ICB method also coordinate both language and content objectives in planning for the implementation of daily lessons. This coordination facilitates planning for activities that support and complement both linguistic and academic processes. Consequently, teachers preparing to write language objectives reflect on the language proficiency of their CLD students and the language of the targeted content or grade-level curriculum.

In designing instruction using the ICB method, teachers differentiate instruction for CLD students who are at differing levels of second language proficiency. For example, language objectives are designed to address the needs of CLD students at the speech emergent stage as well as at the preproduction stage of second language acquisition. Additionally, teachers plan language objectives to support CLD students in developing the cognitive academic language proficiency necessary to succeed in content-area classes. Language objectives are carefully designed to stretch CLD students a step beyond their current level of language proficiency. The teacher supports CLD students in reaching language objectives by providing them with comprehensible input, as discussed in Chapter 6. This teacher-supported challenging of CLD students' linguistic abilities scaffolds and accelerates the students' development of language skills necessary for academic success in the content areas.

Of the linguistic factors affecting academic achievement in the content areas, Saville-Troike (1984) has written that knowledge of vocabulary is the most critical aspect of the academic success of CLD students. Knowledge of specific content vocabulary is far more important to comprehension than morphology and knowledge of syntactic structures. Therefore, targeting language objectives that focus on vocabulary development in every lesson is a prerequisite to the integration of language and content. For example, when writing language objectives in social studies, the teacher considers the fact that CLD students may be unfamiliar with specialized vocabulary related to social studies content as it pertains to events in the United States.

Reflecting on the following questions will facilitate the decision-making processes involved in writing language objectives that will guide successful lesson delivery:

- What are your CLD students' proficiency levels in listening, speaking, reading, and writing?
- In what ways can listening, speaking, reading, and writing in English be developed?
- What language knowledge is necessary for CLD students to understand the language structures of the content area you are teaching?
- What vocabulary is necessary for CLD students to express themselves in the target content area?
- How does the structure of the text influence reading comprehension in the content area?
- Do the symbols or language of the content area have a different meaning in other countries?
- Will the inferences drawn from the readings differ based on cultural background?
- How can the linguistic load be scaffolded to support CLD student learning?

Language Objective Development: In Practice The language objectives of Ms. Gallardo's ICB instruction are determined based on a number of factors. She ensures that all facets of literacy are addressed as she plans to deliver the topics that fall under the theme of rights, privileges, and responsibilities. All the students in her room, particularly those who are CLD students, must be meaningfully engaged in the listening, speaking, reading, and writing aspects of the instruction she provides. Because the content area of social studies lends itself to expanding the opportunities for CLD students to learn the second language naturally, social studies provides a perfect setting in which to capitalize on language building.

During the planning stages of instruction, Ms. Gallardo uses her knowledge of the students' academic backgrounds. Students' prior educational experiences are key to helping her plan the direction of her lesson so that all her students are receiving instruction that is appropriate for their level as well as adequately challenging. Although she will be making some modifications to text when it is too structurally or linguistically complex for her CLD students, she is committed to ensuring that all of her students receive the full benefit of the lessons' objectives. Therefore, when she writes language objectives she is careful not to reduce the academic or cognitive challenge of the curriculum.

Fortunately, Ms. Gallardo understands that her content area offers CLD students the perfect opportunity to learn government concepts as well as to work with language in ways that enable them to manipulate language concepts and extend their linguistic understandings. Using the ICB method, Ms. Gallardo does not have to specifically focus on separating the language objectives from the content-area material because they naturally serve each other. Her students will become interested and engaged in the lessons as they increase their understanding of social studies concepts using the second language.

Keeping the aforementioned factors in mind, Ms. Gallardo decides on the following language objectives for her ICB instruction. Each student will be able to:

- Read and comprehend an article about the rights that people in different countries enjoy.
- Define *rights* in her or his own words.
- Write an essay about a fundamental human right in which the student provides three reasons why all people should be afforded the right (adaptations include prewriting graphic organizers and paragraph frames).

Content Objective Development   Teachers often struggle with the development of content objectives that target the CLD students in their classrooms and are rigorous as well. Thinking about and writing content objectives for a new population requires a paradigm shift in one's conceptualization of what is relevant within a content-area curriculum. By taking a new perspective and integrating language and content, effective teachers identify and align essential content objectives to ensure the academic success of all students.

One of the most difficult tasks teachers must face is deciding on the essential academic content to include in a lesson. When planning ICB instruction, teachers ask questions about the most critical concepts necessary for CLD students' full access to and conceptualization of the grade-level academic content. These concepts are then negotiated with students to connect what is taught with their prior knowledge and cultures. Effective teachers also show how previously studied academic material aligns with the new topic so that CLD students develop an understanding of the relationships among concepts within a content area.

For certain academic content areas, effective teachers may also find it necessary to think about content objectives in relation to the sequence of the curriculum. For example, in the mathematics curriculum, making decisions about content objectives is easier when the teacher refers to the district, state, and national content standards for guidance. Then, after compiling a list of possible content objectives, the teacher can collaborate with other professionals in the content area to determine which objectives would best address the mathematics concepts that are essential for the academic success of CLD students in the classroom.

When writing content objectives, teachers who use the ICB method recognize the critical role that cognitive academic language proficiency (CALP) plays in the academic achievement of CLD students. Therefore, as teachers develop the content objectives within a topic, they consider the multiple cognitive and academic needs of their CLD students. Knowledge of CLD students' backgrounds in the targeted content area is crucial when making decisions regarding content objectives. Students' previous schooling experiences and knowledge bases determine what academic content to target and for what purposes. For example, in science education some terminology and symbol systems are recognized internationally. Therefore, knowing if CLD students have strong backgrounds in specific science concepts will help guide the teacher in making decisions for the lesson in a selected topic area.

Equally important is the teacher's understanding of how the content of the subject area is taught in a student's country of origin. This consideration is necessary because pedagogy differs from country to country and can influence motivation and engagement in the classroom setting. Giving thought to the impact that a student's academic background and educational experiences may have on her or his learning will help the teacher write content objectives. When such aspects of the student biography are taken into consideration, the teacher can create content objectives that build on the strengths of the CLD student in relation to the specific content area of instruction.

Reflecting on the following questions will facilitate the decision-making processes involved in writing content objectives that guide succesful lesson delivery for CLD students:

1. What is the academic knowledge base of my CLD students in this content area?
2. How is this content area taught in my students' countries of origin?
3. What are the critical concepts necessary for the future success of my CLD students in this content area?
4. What are the critical concepts that my CLD students need to know before learning the new content material?

Content Objective Development: In Practice In teaching according to the ICB method, Ms. Gallardo targets specific content objectives she will use to assess her students. She has consulted both national and state standards as a starting point for developing the academic objectives she selects. In order for Ms. Gallardo to approach her ICB lessons effectively, she focuses carefully on what her students bring with them to the academic setting. Ms. Gallardo asks herself about her students' prior knowledge that can relate to the content instruction she is planning. She considers the prior experiences that may facilitate or hinder learning in her classroom. This type of knowledge helps Ms. Gallardo decide on appropriate content objectives that are suitable for her students.

Given the standards that Ms. Gallardo must address throughout the thematic unit, she carefully examines the course materials. She finds that the literature directly relates to her students' previous lives and educational experiences in their respective countries of origin. Ms. Gallardo builds capacity for future learning in her classroom by tying the critical concepts her CLD students have learned in their home countries to those that will be presented in the following weeks. Her CLD students will learn how to make connections between their prior knowledge and the new understandings they are constructing, and they will become more proficient at identifying how they can make such connections when new themes and topics are presented to them. After giving the matter considerable thought, Ms. Gallardo chooses the following content objectives:

- Each student will choose one right that he or she believes should be a fundamental human right and justify why that right should apply to all people.
- Each student will compare and contrast the rights and privileges afforded residents of the United States and those of at least one other country.
- Each student will identify how particular types of government can affect the rights that citizens within the country experience.

Gathering Appropriate Instructional Materials

When gathering materials to support the selected topic of instruction, the teacher considers the overall goal and objectives of the lesson. Each of the materials the teacher selects needs to reflect the critical concepts in the lesson as well as support CLD students' comprehension of and engagement in the lesson. Therefore, when selecting materials, effective teachers remember to consider the following questions:

1. In what ways does the material support and enhance the content of the lesson?
2. How might technology be used to reinforce student learning?
3. In what ways can visuals, realia, and discovery learning be used to reinforce the content of the lesson?
4. How might native language resources be identified and incorporated into the lesson to support and facilitate CLD students' comprehension?

By considering each of these factors, the teacher is able to better plan instruction that will build student capacity toward higher-level thinking and language processing. The following principles, suggested by Brinton and colleagues (1989, p. 34), offer guidelines for materials development:

1. Theme and content (specified in terms of communicative goals) are of primary importance.
2. The language exercises are derived from the text rather than imposed on it.
3. The texts are authentic—they have been produced for and by native speakers of English; in other words, they have not been simplified for pedagogical purposes.
4. Texts used represent all the media (e.g., print, audio and video recordings, together with slide or tape presentations) and, when presented in the course, retain as many features of their original presentations as possible.

Because the texts used in the classroom often guide activity development as well as class discussions, teachers carefully choose appropriate texts for ICB instruction. The following considerations by Brinton and colleagues (1989) may aid the teacher in the selection of texts:

- Student interest level
- Difficulty level of the text
- Accessibility of the text in terms of student comprehension
- Availability of the text
- Flexibility of the text (i.e., Does it allow for the integration of multiple skills and activities?)

When appropriate text selection guidelines are taken into consideration, the opportunities for student learning are enhanced. The teacher is able to provide content material that is not only comprehensible for students but also sufficiently challenging to interest and motivate them to participate in the learning process.

theory *into Practice*

Preview, view, and review is an effective instructional strategy in which content is *previewed* in one language, presented (*viewed*) in the other, and *reviewed* in the first (Freeman & Freeman, 1998; Lessow-Hurley, 1990). The following vignette illustrates an appropriate use of this strategy in practice.

Preview, View, and Review in Action in a Science Classroom

Mrs. Rodriguez is introducing Newton's Three Laws of Motion, a very abstract and complex lesson for all students. She uses preview, view, and review to help her CLD students with comprehension of the lesson.

- **Preview:** CLD students are provided the text of the lesson in their native language the night before the lesson is implemented. The text has been summarized to highlight key concepts and key vocabulary.
- **View:** Mrs. Rodriguez presents the lesson in English and encourages her CLD students to use their native language resource as a guide.

- **Review:** At the end of the week, Mrs. Rodriguez reviews for the test on Friday. This review is conducted in the native language of the CLD students, in this case Spanish. She groups her students heterogeneously by second language proficiency and ability level. The groups then discuss and record their responses to the review questions on chart paper. This collaborative review allows the CLD students to clarify content and vocabulary with one another. Groups are also encouraged to include visuals such as graphic organizers and illustrations to represent their learning.

■ *How might a teacher who does not speak a language other than English use preview, view, and review? How could you evaluate the effectiveness of preview, view, and review with CLD students?*

Gathering Appropriate Instructional Materials: In Practice In planning materials for the ICB lesson that she will teach her students as an introduction to the theme of rights, privileges, and responsibilities, Ms. Gallardo considers all of the language and content objectives she has already outlined. For the introductory lesson to the theme, she chooses to touch on the rights of Americans that are outlined in the Bill of Rights. In considering how to make the concepts comprehensible to her CLD students, Ms. Gallardo decides to highlight important aspects of the document by using them as realia. She will also use translations of the Bill of Rights she found on the Internet in the students' native languages. She accommodates her CLD students by modifying the language of the Bill of Rights in English so that CLD students are able to comprehend the document in the second language after having read it in their native languages.

During this lesson, the students will have the opportunity to explore how the Bill of Rights compares to a document that describes the rights of citizens in their home countries. In this way, Ms. Gallardo will guide her students to elaborate on their background knowledge as they make meaningful connections to new information. Ms. Gallardo decides she will also use a film about the Bill of Rights that the students will view during the introductory lesson. This film will give the CLD students a visual representation of the events that surrounded the Bill of Rights in the 1700s and help the students understand the significance the document holds for Americans today.

Arranging the Classroom Environment

The classroom environment plays a pivotal role in the success of any ICB lesson because the classroom environment sets the stage for the lesson. When planning a lesson according to the ICB method, effective teachers consider various ways in which the classroom environment might affect student dynamics and engagement. For example, the environment of the classroom should accommodate multiple types of student groupings (e.g., collaborative, one-on-one, small group, and whole group). Each type of student grouping needs to reflect the goals and objectives of the lesson. Furthermore, items such as bulletin boards that support student learning and are placed strategically in the classroom can be valuable additions to the classroom environment.

Within the instructional design of an ICB lesson, effective teachers seek to create a learning environment in which respect and rapport are paramount. Such an environment is characterized by the following traits:

- The learning culture reflects the importance of the content as well as the learning needs of CLD students.
- The classroom is a safe environment in which the opinions and insights of every student are valued and respected.
- Teacher–student interactions reflect the willingness of each to learn from the other.

Arranging the Classroom Environment: In Practice The environment of the classroom plays a significant role in the instructional process for Ms. Gallardo. Maximizing the ICB method, she first thinks about the possible ways in which she can make learning as conducive as possible for the students in her class as they work with the theme at hand. Ms. Gallardo then lists ways in which she will specifically give attention to the details of the environment in her classroom.

The physical arrangement of the desks and chairs in her classroom is one of the ways in which the environment reflects the language and content objectives Ms. Gallardo has outlined. The desks in her classroom are arranged so that she has easy access to all of her students and her students can easily dialogue and interact with one another. Grouping desks in numbers of no more than five helps her accomplish this goal. Ms. Gallardo's grouping allows the CLD students of varied levels of proficiency in English to help one another, and it maximizes the input and helpfulness of more capable peers. At the same time, native English speakers serve as models who support the acquisition of English for the CLD students. The environment Ms. Gallardo creates is designed to lower the affective filters of the CLD students and provide a positive environment in which to learn.

On the walls of the classroom, Ms. Gallardo places visual representations that relate to the theme. For example, representations of the Bill of Rights are posted on the walls and accompanied by rich descriptions. Additionally, in one area of the room, Ms. Gallardo has created and made available an interactive bulletin board for her students. This bulletin board will serve as a questioning and evaluation tool for her students. The interactive bulletin board includes questions that correspond to the language and content objectives she will target throughout the lesson. Each of the questions has a visual aid next to it that signifies its meaning. The students will reach into a pocket that contains the answers to the questions and must post the answers alongside the questions to which they correspond. Ms. Gallardo will change the questions and answers once she observes that all students have had an opportunity to use the interactive bulletin board.

Copies of texts and other literature that support the theme are placed around the room. Ms. Gallardo also makes sure to provide opportunities, such as small-group activities, for students to interact as much as possible within the context of what she is teaching. Additionally, she posts websites at each of the four computers in the room so that students have the opportunity to use technology as a resource to access information.

Instruction

As discussed in Chapter 1, curricula in U.S. schools tend to assume that students are fluent in English, and they reflect a middle-class, Eurocentric point of view. Consequently, for White, middle-class, native-English-speaking students, these curricula often reflect their prior knowledge and experiences, culture, and levels of English language proficiency. However, CLD students bring other prior school and life experiences, cultures, and languages to U.S. classrooms. Therefore, Eurocentric,

English-based curricula do not always coincide, and sometimes conflict, with the wealth of knowledge and experiences of CLD students. This difference in knowledge and experience requires teachers of CLD students to devote special consideration to CLD students' prior knowledge and experiences, cultures, and levels of native and English language proficiency.

When delivering an ICB lesson to CLD students, effective teachers (a) preteach key content vocabulary, (b) build on the background knowledge of students, (c) facilitate collaborative learning to promote linguistic and conceptual development, (d) integrate the four literacy domains, (e) ensure CLD students' cognitive engagement, (f) provide visual aids and graphic organizers to support student comprehension, and (g) develop centers that encourage active student learning.

Preteaching Key Content Vocabulary

In an ICB lesson, the use of content language that targets both academic and linguistic development is critical. In fact, the consistent and comprehensive use of the target language facilitates and increases CLD students' understanding of the lesson. To enhance students' comprehension of the content material, effective teachers select principal vocabulary terms from the lesson and preteach them to CLD students. This preteaching of key vocabulary helps CLD students prepare for the lesson as well as make critical connections to their existing background knowledge. Strategies for preteaching vocabulary to CLD students include:

- Using graphic organizers, such as semantic webbing or vocabulary maps, to graphically illustrate for CLD students how they might associate new vocabulary words with background knowledge.
- Selecting high-frequency words to add to a word wall (using separate English and L1 word walls when possible).
- Associating vocabulary words with concrete objects.
- Having students act out or role-play vocabulary words.
- Using visual cues to assist CLD students as they make connections to and develop an understanding of key vocabulary.

Once the key vocabulary words have been selected and taught, the teacher reiterates and incorporates these key terms throughout the lesson. This repetition of vocabulary reinforces language acquisition and the comprehension of academic content among CLD students.

Preteaching Key Content Vocabulary: In Practice   Ms. Gallardo wants to ensure that her students are using a common language as they study the theme of rights, privileges, and responsibilities. Using a common language in ICB methodology is important because it enables students to communicate more effectively with one another as they share their thoughts on thematic topics. Consistency in language also facilitates future learning in subsequent themes by providing students with a knowledge foundation they will be able to use to understand new ideas and concepts they encounter. Consequently, Ms. Gallardo uses graphic organizers and the vocabulary posted throughout the room as consistent references during her lessons. She also uses the texts in the room and the bulletin boards to reinforce key vocabulary terms that may be abstract for CLD students. The visuals around the room further support the key concepts and vocabulary of the lesson.

Ms. Gallardo's students become more familiar with the vocabulary words and learn to purposively interact with key vocabulary terms in various contexts. After the students dialogue in groups and as a whole class, Ms. Gallardo asks them to role-play the creation of the Bill of Rights. As they dramatize this activity, the students interact using the common language that they will continue to share throughout the thematic unit.

Building Background

When presenting an ICB lesson, effective teachers guide CLD students to make connections between the content-area curriculum and their past experiences and knowledge. Making such connections to prior knowledge and experiences can be beneficial to CLD students for both academic and social affective reasons. First, these connections cognitively engage CLD students in the learning process by creating a meaningful context from which they can understand the lesson. Additionally, the attention given to CLD students' past experiences and knowledge validates their background and culture as worthy of attention and study.

Strategies to incorporate and build on CLD students' background knowledge include but are not limited to:

- Posing questions to the CLD students about their past experiences.
- Asking CLD students what they know about the key concepts.
- Having CLD students freewrite about the topic so that the teacher can assess their knowledge and understanding of the lesson material before teaching.
- Providing visual cues and examples to promote meaningful connections between the content and the CLD students' background knowledge.
- Inviting family or community members to share information about the topic with the class.

Building Background: In Practice One of the most important elements Ms. Gallardo emphasizes in her ICB lesson is that of connecting new information or concepts to the prior knowledge her students possess. This helps her develop a deeper understanding of what her students know and makes her better able to determine the best way to approach instruction. She also validates her students by inviting them to share their expertise. Ms. Gallardo begins by asking her students about the rights they have in any realm of their lives. These rights might pertain to the contexts of home, school, or other organizations and activities in which they may be involved. Ms. Gallardo encourages her students to discuss what they know about the rights of citizens in their native countries and what they know about the rights of U.S. citizens. The discussion also centers on the idea of the necessity to delineate rights for a country's citizens and the idea that these rights are crucial to the success and continuous development of any country. Ms. Gallardo asks students to write a paragraph describing what having rights means for a citizen of a country. She also asks the students to explain why those rights may be the same or different across countries.

Facilitating Collaborative Learning

When presenting an ICB lesson, the structuring of a variety of student collaborative learning groupings facilitates content and language development among CLD students. Vygotsky (1978) proposed that children learn as a result of social interaction. Cooperative learning allows CLD students to interact with one another using language that pushes them beyond basic interpersonal communication to develop their cognitive academic language proficiency. Cooperative learning groups also encourage the active engagement of CLD students in content instruction. Students in heterogeneous language and content proficiency groups are prompted to negotiate the meaning of language and content using the target language. A CLD student's peers can enhance his or her comprehension by clarifying information, providing academic dialogue to deepen conceptual understandings, and enabling transfer from L1 to L2.

Using multiple forms of grouping allows CLD students to experience a variety of linguistic and cognitive supports and challenges. Additionally, when CLD students have the opportunity to apply their learning in cooperative settings, the content is shared at a developmentally appropriate level. In comparison to whole-group activities, smaller groups provide CLD students with more opportunities to communicate as well as a less intimidating context in which to use the target language as a tool for negotiation and learning.

The primary considerations for educators when creating cooperative learning groups include the following:

- Make sure group work is developmentally appropriate.
- Provide multiple opportunities for CLD students to discuss the material orally.
- Use a variety of grouping organizations (one-to-one, small group, whole group, etc.).
- Foster interdependence among students by structuring groups so that no one individual can complete the task alone.
- Motivate groups to work together by making sure that each member of the group is held accountable for his or her tasks.
- Create a group setting in which communication in any language is accepted and respected. Use more capable peers to scaffold language transitions.
- Work with groups to ensure that students are being supportive of one another.
- Provide rich feedback that acknowledges the efforts of the entire group.

Facilitating Collaborative Learning: In Practice

At the beginning of the ICB lesson, Ms. Gallardo addresses the whole class when eliciting prior knowledge. She makes sure that everyone understands what the topic is and what the collaborative group activity will entail. After the class discusses the nature of rights and the students share what they know about individuals' rights, Ms. Gallardo asks the students to work in their groups. She structures each group in a purposeful way with the goal of ensuring that the CLD students feel comfortable taking risks as they engage in learning concepts and language simultaneously. To this end, Ms. Gallardo notes several factors, including the linguistic abilities of her CLD students. Grouping a CLD student who has less proficiency in English with a student who is more proficient reduces the anxiety levels of CLD students who are new to the English language and enhances language transfer potential. Ms. Gallardo also places native English speakers in these groups because they model the English language in a nonthreatening manner for CLD students. Other factors to consider when grouping students include gender, maturity, ability, and the likelihood for positive student interaction.

Using Authentic Activities for Integrating Literacy

Activities in an ICB lesson allow the teacher to create authentic experiences that involve speaking, listening, reading, and writing throughout the lesson. These activities reflect the interests, developmental levels, experiences, and various learning styles of CLD students. In addition, authentic activities provide CLD students with many opportunities for hands-on involvement through discovery learning. When creating activities to engage CLD students, teachers might consider the following recommendations of Curtain and Haas (1995, Suggestions section, para. 2):

- Use the students' prior knowledge and personal experience.
- Use holistic strategies that integrate listening, speaking, reading, and writing that naturally connect language and content.
- Challenge the students to think critically.
- Address the students' multiple ways of learning.

By following these guidelines, teachers are better able to provide CLD students with opportunities to engage in authentic, content-specific activities that challenge them not only academically but also linguistically.

Using Authentic Activities for Integrating Literacy: In Practice

For the introductory lesson and for subsequent lessons, Ms. Gallardo includes a variety of activities to engage her students in learning content concepts and language. Maximizing the ICB method, she uses whole-group instruction to cultivate prior knowledge through discussion and visuals. She also uses small groups for writing and role-plays, and allows time for individual reading of text. As they participate in activities that require them to recall, evaluate, synthesize, and apply new information, students develop sophisticated understandings of human rights. They compare what they know about this theme in their home countries to what they are learning about this theme in the United States. After analyzing this comparison, students practice articulating the fundamental concept of human rights. Finally, each student chooses one right

■ Voices from the Field

"In the Spring of 2000, it was determined that our high school would create a team of teachers to teach a randomly selected group of students over a two-year period, integrating the subjects of Math, English, and Science. For this team, four teachers were selected. Three content area teachers and one Special Education resource teacher comprised the team. When assigned this endeavor, we were both anxious and nervous about trying this instructional method at our high school for the first time.

Our first objective as a team was to find a way to integrate the different content areas. Since Earth Science and Algebra must follow a logical sequence, it was decided that the teachers of those two classes would provide for me an outline of their projected monthly lessons. Using their outlines as a guide, I developed my English lessons. While it was fairly easy to find literary selections to coincide with Earth Science ("The Perfect Storm" during the weather unit), Algebra proved to be a little harder to integrate into English. I eventually did discover that some of the stories lent themselves to the creation of graphs and charts: If eight percent of the population of London died from the plague during Shakespeare's time, how many people from our community or school would that be? History was also fairly easy. The Montagues and the Capulets from *Romeo and Juliet* can easily be equated with the Israelis and the Palestinians or the Puritan thought from *The Crucible* can be compared with the beliefs of the Taliban.

Literature was not the only way we integrated the subjects, though. A required research paper for Earth Science was written in the English classroom with students receiving both English and Science credit. The science teacher graded for content, while I graded for the composition traits. Another paper required that data taken from sources be put into a graph. Another paper required that the students use a modified version of the inquiry method of research, a method they had previously used in science. Although American History was not a class included on the team, we did request and receive a course syllabus from a teacher of that subject which I tried to follow with American literature during the sophomore year. The Special Education teacher's degree in Social Science came in very handy when integrating history into the English curriculum.

Everyone in the team had skills, expertise, and knowledge in various areas that contributed to a successful year. I never felt like I was alone. I had three other colleagues by my side in this endeavor. Students really enjoyed the class discussions and made connections with concepts previously discussed in other classes. I've had a renewed interest in teaching high school English because I'm covering new topics in creative and exciting ways."

■ *Karen Myers, high school English teacher, Emporia, KS*

that he or she believes is fundamental to human existence and writes an essay to justify why all people should be afforded that basic human right.

Engaging CLD Students Cognitively

In addition to creating activities that are content specific and academically challenging, effective teachers find ways to cognitively engage their CLD students during ICB lessons. One of the primary ways to create more cognitively engaging and intrinsically motivating lessons is to relate academic content and language tasks in ways that guide students to use higher-order thinking skills. For example, students initially strive to understand the literal meaning of the lesson's grade-level content. The teacher may then ask students to relate what they are learning to their previous experiences. She may ask them to share their insights with the class. CLD students are validated and motivated when they know that their input is as salient and relevant to the academic content as that of their native-English-speaking peers. Finally, the teacher may prompt the students to use higher-order thinking skills by asking them to evaluate the validity of the information (that is, reflect on the lesson). For example, students might be prompted to engage in a debate that centers on the following questions:

- Is the information true in every situation?
- Which situational factors influence or determine the validity of this information?
- From whose point of view is this information presented?
- Might others have different opinions?

Specific considerations for providing cognitively engaging and intrinsically motivating lessons for the CLD students according to the ICB method include:

- Foster opportunities for CLD students to engage in extended discourse.
- Increase the percentage of questions asked of CLD students that require the use of inferential and higher-order thinking skills.
- Develop activities that engage students in cognitively challenging academic tasks, such as doing research projects, problem solving that pertains to student-relevant issues, and writing essays, plays, and poetry.
- Engage students in activities that require them to use metacognitive, cognitive, and social affective learning strategies.

Engaging CLD Students Cognitively: In Practice   As Ms. Gallardo thinks about the ways in which her students process new concepts, she reviews the topics, objectives, literature, activities, and groupings she selected for teaching the theme. She knows that her ICB content objectives hold CLD students to the same grade-level expectations as their native-English-speaking peers. Additionally, because Ms. Gallardo ensures that the authentic activities address the language and content objectives, she is confident that her students are sufficiently challenged to question, apply, analyze, and reflect on what they are learning. Ms. Gallardo wants her students to interact with new vocabulary and concepts in a rigorous yet nonthreatening way.

As she thinks about future lessons using the ICB method, she decides that she will incorporate an activity that will require the students to work together as a class to develop a set of student rights. These rights will specifically address characteristics of interpersonal relationships among faculty, staff, and students; school and classroom environments; and services and resources provided by schools that enable students to learn most effectively. Ms. Gallardo may first ask the students to individually reflect on their academic progress thus far and write a one-page journal entry in which they discuss aspects of their education that have negatively or positively affected their success. Then she may encourage students to share their thoughts with the class as a whole. Finally, she may guide the whole class to a consensus on the specific rights that should be included in their set of student rights.

Providing Visual Support and Graphic Organizers

Visual aids and graphic organizers play a vital role in an ICB lesson because they provide the contextual cues from which CLD students can make meaningful connections to the content. Therefore, when teaching an ICB lesson, teachers plan for an increased use of visual support and realia throughout the lesson. Visual support can include items such as illustrations, maps, photos, and videos. Realia can include those authentic objects that accurately represent the key content and concepts of the lesson (e.g., food, animals, clothing). Graphic organizers used in a lesson may include, but are not limited to:

- Semantic webs
- KWL charts
- T-charts
- Venn diagrams
- Categorization or classification charts

These instructional aids help students focus their thoughts on the lesson material and make connections regarding relationships among interrelated pieces of information. Such tools also help students uncover and organize the topic-related understandings and ideas they bring from their prior experiences and background knowledge.

Providing Visual Support and Graphic Organizers: In Practice

Ms. Gallardo selects a myriad of visuals and graphic organizers that match the objectives and standards she is targeting during her coverage of the theme of rights, privileges, and responsibilities. Through the classroom environment, she immerses CLD students in the context of the concepts they will learn. Bulletin boards (both visual and interactive), maps, and documents (such as the Bill of Rights and those documents that highlight the functions of government in the United States) are posted around the room. Word walls that contain vocabulary terms for each topic are also displayed in three different areas of the room.

Ms. Gallardo uses a KWL chart at the onset of the introductory lesson to learn what the students already know about the topics to come. This KWL chart also functions as a metacognitive learning strategy. T-charts are used to compare the differences between governments of various countries, and Venn diagrams support CLD students in comparing, contrasting, and analyzing information. As is typical in teaching according to the ICB method, Ms. Gallardo clarifies the purpose of the visuals and graphic organizers for her students so they will understand how to use the tools to increase their knowledge of concepts and their knowledge about how they learn.

Developing Learning Centers

Centers offer CLD students the opportunity for extended explorations of theme-based instruction according to the ICB method. Using centers involves the formation of several small areas around a classroom that provide activities to promote independent, active student engagement. A class breaks into small groups and, while the teacher provides individualized instruction at one center with one group, other groups work at different centers. Centers assist CLD students as they make concrete connections to content and language, and centers provide CLD students with opportunities to practice and apply new concepts in a variety of settings and through a variety of media. For example, centers allow CLD students to work individually, in pairs, or even in small groups to practice and apply learning through hands-on activities. These hands-on activities require that students use their reading, writing, listening, and speaking skills. Additionally, through the use of media such as technology resources (computers, tape recorders, video), visuals (magazines, photos, pictures), realia (food, clothing, books), and manipulatives (Unifix cubes, counting bears, sentence strips, white boards), students develop thorough understandings of the lesson's concepts.

When planning centers, effective educators consider a variety of linguistic, academic, and cognitive factors. Among such factors are:

- The ways in which the centers intentionally reflect the language and content objectives of the lesson.
- Student interactions (e.g., how large or small and how collaborative do you want to make the centers to maximize the equipment needed for each center, including computers?).
- The familiarity of CLD students with the media of the centers.
- Levels of support that students may need to successfully complete center activities.
- Length of time necessary to complete center activities (keep in mind the developmental levels and the attention spans of students).
- Length of time needed for the setup and cleanup of the centers.

Developing Learning Centers: In Practice   After working with the students as a class to connect students' prior knowledge to new concepts, Ms. Gallardo uses centers, a reinforcing aspect of the ICB method, to help her students develop their understandings of the content material. She explains what the students will do when she breaks the class into smaller groups for center work. She discusses the activities to be done in each center, and she makes sure that all of her students are familiar with the texts they are to read, the way in which the role-plays are to be structured, and the expectations she has for the piece of writing they are to produce. At the teacher-facilitated center, Ms. Gallardo works with a group of five students on the history of the Bill of Rights. In this center, Ms. Gallardo's students work daily on their culminating project, an essay on a universal human right. She provides additional support to her CLD students as their essays evolve and as they maximize the centers.

At the interactive center, a group of five students uses text, reference materials, visuals, and their own prior knowledge to create role-plays that demonstrate the importance of individual rights within a given country. Students at the listening and reading center listen to a portion of a book on tape about the Bill of Rights. Ms. Gallardo has chosen an audiobook that contains vocabulary that is part of the common language her class is sharing. In this way, the information is rendered more comprehensible for her CLD students. In the current events center, students choose three (of several) newspaper or magazine articles on national or international human rights issues to read, and then they create a graphic organizer summary for each. These articles reflect a wide range of reading levels and several languages. (Ms. Gallardo collected the multiple language articles from her students.) At the writing center, students use text and varied literature around the room to write about the comparison of individuals' rights in their respective home countries (or a country of their choice) with those ensured to citizens of the United States.

Ms. Gallardo's school uses block scheduling, so she has a 100-minute span of time with her students every other day. Because there are five centers operative at the same time and all students are to receive the benefit of each, Ms. Gallardo spends twenty minutes in whole-group instruction at the beginning of each day, and the rest of her time is divided equally among the centers. Students rotate from center to center and begin their tasks immediately to maximize the time they have to work with the content of the theme. Ms. Gallardo leaves the center a few minutes before the end of each class period to bring closure to the lesson. When using the ICB method, such closure is crucial for students because it clarifies the key information they should have gleaned from the morning's events, and it informs students of the ways in which the subsequent lesson will connect to what they learned.

Assessment

Assessment is an integral aspect of every lesson. On the one hand, assessment provides teachers with valuable information regarding lesson effectiveness. On the other hand, assessment is a valuable source of information about the development of conceptual understandings among all students and language acquisition among CLD students. On-going, or *formative*, assessment is the feedback that the teacher gives the student to clarify misconceptions, affirm new understandings, and challenge the student to think more deeply about key content concepts. The feedback that teachers provide students on their learning logs, projects, and writing are examples of formative assessment. Formative assessment enables teachers to dispel misconceptions before they become too entrenched in students' conceptualizations. In this way, students can revise their understandings as they are learning. Culminating, or *summative*, assessment occurs at the end of lessons. Teachers collect evidence from sources such as finished projects and essays to determine the degree to which students attained the lesson objectives.

Providing Formative Assessment

Throughout the delivery of an ICB lesson, effective teachers conduct ongoing and regular evaluation of CLD student performance. This type of ongoing assessment allows the teacher to evaluate the effectiveness of the lesson and ensure CLD student comprehension. A primary way for the teacher to promote CLD student comprehension is to adjust and modify instruction as needed. Modifications to the lesson occur when the teacher observes student behavior or responses that are indicative of confusion or misunderstanding. The immediate modification of a lesson requires the teacher to be flexible and responsive to (that is, accommodate) the needs of CLD students.

Continuous feedback to the CLD student is another way in which ongoing or in-process assessment can be conducted. Ongoing assessments should be specific, constructive, and thorough. In this way, the CLD student is able to obtain a clear picture of teacher expectations and meet the lesson objectives. Ways in which the teacher can provide continuous feedback through the ICB method include, but are not limited to, the following:

- Offer feedback that focuses on one aspect or area of the lesson so as not to overwhelm the CLD student.
- Engage the CLD student in a brief discussion about the lesson to determine her or his comprehension of key concepts. Follow this discussion with specific recommendations or tips that the CLD student can use immediately to increase his or her understanding of the lesson.
- Pose constructive questions to help the CLD student assess his or her own comprehension of the lesson and derive longlasting meaning from the experience.
- Be sure to provide feedback that is comprehensive and comprehensible for the CLD student.

Finally, ongoing evaluation requires the teacher to make certain that the lesson itself aligns with the overall instructional goals and objectives of the lesson, as guided by the unit theme and topics. By continually checking instruction against these objectives, the teacher is able to ensure the congruence of the lesson with instructional goals.

Providing Formative Assessment: In Practice   The only way for Ms. Gallardo to make sure that her students are achieving mastery of the language and content objectives she delineated for the introductory lesson is to consistently monitor the ongoing progress of her CLD students. Ms. Gallardo carefully observes her students' responses, especially their responses to higher-order thinking questions, to ensure that they comprehend the language and concepts involved in the lesson. She notes body language and facial expressions to detect feelings of frustration or success among students. She also watches student dynamics during group work to gauge the effectiveness of activities associated with the use of the ICB method.

Ms. Gallardo facilitates the learning that occurs in her classroom by providing consistent and continuous feedback to her CLD students. Thus, her students become aware of her expectations, and this awareness fosters greater student success in mastering lesson objectives. All of the feedback Ms. Gallardo gives her students is positive and constructive. She also uses her feedback to model the appropriate use of common language the students of the class share regarding the theme of rights, privileges, and responsibilities.

Providing Summative Assessment

Summative assessment typically occurs at the end of a project or a lesson. During summative assessment, teachers and students examine revised and completed student work to collect evidence of language and content development. Summative assessment describes and documents students' proficiency levels in meeting lesson objectives. For CLD students, a teacher defines levels of acceptable language production based on the expected characteristics of the students' levels of second language proficiency. For example, language production from a CLD student who is at an intermediate level of English language proficiency will contain fewer errors, more complex sentence constructions, and more descriptive vocabulary than that of a CLD student at a speech emergent level of English language proficiency. Effective teachers of the ICB method are careful to avoid confusing limited language proficiency with difficulty in expressing oneself due to a lack of conceptual understanding.

Rubrics can be useful tools in summative assessment. When students help develop rubrics, they gain insight into the characteristics of quality products. To guide students in the creation of rubrics, a teacher may pass out work samples (without names or other identifiers, preferably from a different year or school) that reflect varying degrees of language and content proficiency. Groups of students review the samples and rank them according to levels of proficiency. As a class, the groups discuss why and how they ranked the samples. The teacher then guides the students to consensus regarding the ranking that most appropriately corresponds to each particular sample.

Next, students discuss in groups the defining characteristics of each level of ranking. The groups share their defining characteristics with the entire class and the class comes to consensus about the characteristics of each level of proficiency. The first several times the class creates a rubric in this manner, the teacher provides extensive modeling and support to help students define quality work. As the students continue to create and use such rubrics to assess their own work, the class creates a common expectation for quality academic work. Students can use these rubrics to reflect on their strengths and areas of inexperience in order to create goals for their own language and academic development.

Providing Summative Assessment: In Practice   Ms. Gallardo looks forward to having her CLD students write their essays as the culminating project for their unit on rights, privileges, and responsibilities. Before they begin their essays, the students create a rubric by which their essays will be evaluated. In creating this rubric, students examine exemplary, proficient, and basic sample essays to identify the key characteristics of each level of writing and the extent to which each level of content proficiency addresses the content-area concepts inherent in the lesson objectives. These students have experience with creating assessment rubrics, so they are able to tackle the challenge of creating rubrics for both content and language proficiency. When the time arrives to assess the students' essays, the students and Ms. Gallardo will collect evidence of language and content development from the essays to provide a basis for assessment. Subsequently, Ms. Gallardo will meet with each student to discuss the evidence and arrive at meaningful conclusions regarding the student's progress in language and content development. They will also explore areas in which the student needs to grow. Thus, Ms. Gallardo's students think about their own learning and the strategies and techniques they use to gain new understandings.

Concluding Thoughts

Effectively implementing instruction according to the ICB method takes time, practice, and critical self-reflection. Accommodatively planning for, instructing, and assessing CLD students requires special attention to their language development needs. For many ICB teachers, modifying the language of instruction without simplifying the grade-level content can prove to be a difficult skill to master. Yet, if educators do not provide CLD students with the support they need to reach the same high standards as their English-speaking peers, the achievement gap between these and grade-level students will continue to widen. By soliciting the help of teachers experienced in this method or by forming learning communities with other teachers who are implementing ICB instruction, educators find the support needed to change teaching practice.

tips for practice

Elementary Education

1. Invite a more language proficient CLD student to peer tutor and explain unfamiliar academic terms in the native language. This activity benefits the less proficient CLD students and at the same time enables the peer tutor to clarify her or his understanding of the key concepts.

2. Incorporate process writing into content-area classes. In process writing, the students begin with prewriting activities such as viewing pictures or sharing prior knowledge. Next the students write about their ideas and experiences. Then the students share this informa-

tion with the teacher, who writes the students' input on a large piece of chart paper. This sets the stage for the content-area topic. During the acquisition of knowledge, the students learn about language specific to the selected topic while making meaningful connections to the content.

3. Teach your students the strategy of going from general to specific as you study a concept in content-area textbooks. Demonstrate how to identify global concepts by using the table of contents, headings, subheadings, and illustrations in content-area chapters.

4. Use poetry, chants, music, demonstrations, and discussions of pictures and real objects to build language related to content concepts.

5. When teaching math, identify key terms and reinforce this new vocabulary throughout a lesson. Mathematical terms such as *altogether, more,* and *less* can clue students in to what is expected of them, especially when solving math word problems.

6. For the development of language through literature, use visuals such as pictures, diagrams, or realia and talk through a story or a particular chapter of a book to help CLD students grasp the story line first. Then read and reread the story or chapter to build vocabulary and foster comprehension.

Secondary Education

1. To make content and language acquisition meaningful, collaborate with other teachers and select a theme that can be transferred across content areas. For example, an environmental theme such as deforestation can be the focus of language arts, science, social studies, and literacy lessons.

2. Adapt or incorporate materials such as alternate versions of textbooks, newspaper articles, outlines, or magazine articles that enhance understanding and connect language learning to the real world.

3. Provide science students with specific, step-by-step experiment instructions. Post the instructions in a central location in the classroom so that CLD students can refer to them when doing the experiment. This will help CLD students focus on and comprehend the activity. Key terms and academic language should be central components of this chart.

4. Design a discovery learning lesson that allows students to research or solve a problem on their own. Students identify a problem, generate a hypothesis, design procedures or experiments to test the hypothesis, and conduct research to solve the problem. For example, while working on a lesson on soil erosion, organize a field trip to the local parks and recreation department. Students can prepare written questions about soil erosion and pose

these questions to a park official during the class trip. The multidimensional aspects of this lesson incorporate listening, speaking, reading, and writing in the content area.

5. Include information gap activities such as jig-sawing, problem solving, and simulations while working on difficult content concepts such as the civil rights movement. Set up these activities so that each student in a group has one or two pieces of information needed to complete the activity but not all the necessary information. This provides students a chance to work collaboratively, share information, practice their language skills, and implement critical thinking skills.

6. Collaborate with the high school English teacher to align various concepts across the content areas with literature that students are currently reading. This can help CLD students make connections between literature and content they are studying in other areas of the curriculum.

General Education

1. Collaborate closely with the ESL educator or with other grade-level educators when planning instructional modifications for CLD students. This can be helpful in identifying language or academic tasks with which CLD students might be having difficulty. Examples of such tasks might include reading textbooks, writing reports, or doing library research.

2. Clearly identify the academic and language objectives for each lesson and constantly reinforce them throughout the lesson to give CLD students a clear focus and an understanding of expectations. For instance, at the beginning of a lesson, write both the language and content objectives on the board and ask a student to read them aloud. Throughout the lesson, direct questions back to the objectives. At the end of the lesson, ask students questions directly related to the objectives as they go on break or leave the classroom. For example, one of the content objectives might include the following: *Compare and contrast the effects of the Industrial Revolution on the lives of city dwellers.* As each student leaves the room, orally elicit from him or her a positive and a negative effect the

Industrial Revolution had on the lives of people living in the city.

3. To enhance CLD student comprehension across the content areas, frequently summarize the most important ideas of a lesson by using visuals and graphic organizers, paraphrasing key ideas, or having students individually provide oral summaries. For example, when discussing photosynthesis, you may have diagrams on the wall depicting this cycle with words labeled in English on one diagram and in the native language(s) of your students on another diagram. After discussing this process, students can provide the class with either an oral or a written summary of this process in their own words. A limited English proficient student could describe this process in his or her native language while pointing to the different steps of the cycle on the diagram (a more capable peer, parent volunteer, or paraprofessional may translate if necessary).

4. Provide your students with ample opportunities to communicate about the concepts being covered in the classroom by:
   • Allowing students more time to speak (when they feel comfortable with doing so).
   • Encouraging small-group discussions.
   • Asking open-ended questions.

5. Provide contextual cues for CLD students by using multiple media in the classroom such as compact discs, the Internet, videos, and more. This allows you to place the information in concrete contexts that facilitate language acquisition. Furthermore, this allows you to compartmentalize language, thereby providing CLD students with the whole picture. For instance, before delving into a chapter on the Vietnam War, you can show students a video that emphasizes the key features of the war. You can subsequently discuss this video with students and check for understanding before beginning the chapter. Key vocabulary can also be reviewed at this time using background knowledge the students might have regarding similar wars that may have taken place in their native countries.

6. Extend explorations of themes by connecting the lessons to basal readers, trade books, and content tasks. Hands-on projects also help CLD students develop their understanding of the key topics and concepts within the theme. For example, when students are learning about the circulatory system and cardiopulmonary resuscitation (CPR), you can provide a mannequin on which students can perform CPR as they describe what they are doing.

▪ key theories and concepts

academic objectives
authentic activities
centers
cognitive tasks
content-based instruction
content language
English for specific purposes (ESP)

environmental factors
immersion instruction
integrated content-based instruction
integrated content-based language instruction
interrelating materials and content
language across the curriculum

language for specific purposes (LSP)
linguistic objectives
linguistic proficiency
student dynamics
thematic units
theme
topic

▪ professional conversations on practice

1. Discuss the challenges in selecting a theme in your content area. What considerations would you make to ensure cognitive engagement and interest in the selected theme?

2. Discuss how language and content are integrated to maximize learning for CLD students.

3. Discuss the process of decision making when planning an ICB lesson.

4. Discuss the challenges in implementing ICB instruction at the elementary, middle, and secondary levels.

5. Discuss how this method of instruction complements or challenges your current instructional practice.

questions for review and reflection

1. What is content-based instruction?

2. What are the benefits of content-based instruction for CLD students?

3. What are the primary differences between language across the curriculum, English for specific purposes/language for specific purposes, and immersion instruction? How did each of these contribute to the development of integrated content-based instruction?

4. What are thematic units? Why is it important to have a theme when planning ICB instruction?

5. How should you select a theme? What considerations should be given to the academic and experiential backgrounds of CLD students when selecting a theme?

6. What is a topic? How should a topic reflect the theme?

7. What is the difference between a language and a content objective? What role does each play in the development of an ICB lesson?

8. Why and how are materials and content interrelated in ICB instruction? What are the benefits

of this for CLD students? What considerations must the teacher make to interrelate materials and content?

9. What considerations should be given to student dynamics when planning an ICB lesson?

10. Why is it essential to include authentic activities in ICB lessons?

11. Why is it important to include higher-order thinking skills in ICB instruction? How can higher-order thinking skills be incorporated into instructional delivery?

12. What key factors should be considered when developing centers?

13. What approach does the ICB method reflect, and what are the implications of this philosophical orientation for how you approach instruction with your CLD students?

14. What are the steps that must be taken in planning ICB instruction? Is it necessary to include all of the steps? Why or why not?

suggested activities

Preservice Teachers

1. When planning a content-based unit on a particular topic, it can be helpful to create visuals. Visuals can suggest ways in which to integrate the topic across different content areas more effectively. Use Figure 7.2 to create an outline for a content-based unit. Target a specific theme and grade level and note these at the

bottom of the template. Identify and briefly describe at least two activities per box on your template.

2. Observe the classroom practice of an educator of CLD students. List at least five ways in which he or she successfully integrates content and language so that the key content is covered in ways that are meaningful to CLD students.

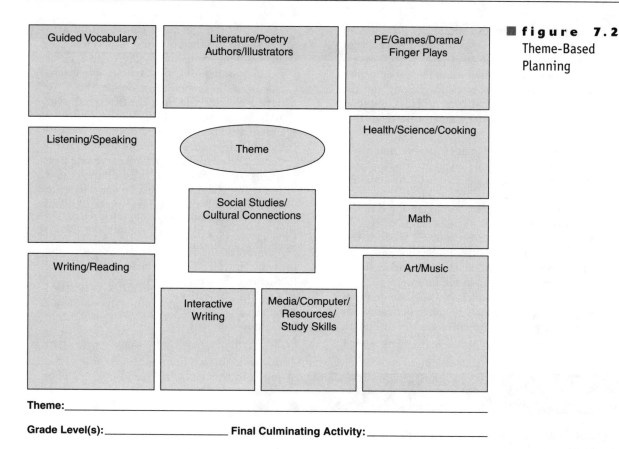

■ **figure 7.2**
Theme-Based
Planning

Theme:_____

Grade Level(s): _____ Final Culminating Activity: _____

Then identify ways in which you would target listening, speaking, reading, and writing if you were teaching the lesson.

3. With other preservice teachers of various content areas, identify and list ways in which a theme could be integrated in all of the represented content areas. Generate at least three activities that infuse literacy (listening, speaking, reading, and writing) across these content areas.

In-Service Teachers

1. Set up a miniconference with at least two other teachers in your school who share the same CLD students you have. Collaborate with these teachers to decide on a specific theme that can be integrated across all of your content areas. Next, decide on a topic related to the theme that

each of you could address throughout the semester. Discuss and share ideas on how and when you could integrate this topic in all the content areas. Additionally, share ideas about ways to integrate language skills into your lessons. What materials will you use? What key vocabulary will be emphasized? For example, the overriding theme of your lessons may be "Agriculture—Important Food Crops." The topic of your lessons might be "corn." For American history, you might incorporate this topic while discussing Native Americans, Pilgrims, or agricultural resources. For world social studies, you could discuss any corn-producing country's agricultural system, differences between agricultural and industrial economies, or current events regarding international trade.

Focusing on the math curriculum, students can estimate the number of kernels or the weight of corn. They might also create word problems incorporating the theme vocabulary. For health and science, incorporate discussions on the source of nutrition that corn provides, the food group to which it belongs, and the nutrients that corn contains.

2. Newspapers and magazines can be used effectively for integrating language development with content lessons. Select one of the activities below to implement in your classroom practice. What types of accommodations did you need to make for the various stages of second language acquisition of your CLD students? What were the activity's highlights and challenges for CLD students? How will you address these challenges in the future?

   • Plan a lesson in which you will use newspapers and magazines in your classroom for language and content-area development. For instance, if you are a political science

teacher, you might have students find articles related to the current content area you are studying. Students might write a paragraph summarizing this article, circle new words in the article and define them, or have a class debate on a controversial issue addressed in the article.

   • Classified ads can be used in many ways to make real-world connections for CLD students. For example, students can circle new words and define them, find abbreviations and define them, or write a business letter to apply for a job that has been advertised and practice interviewing for the job.

3. Develop an ICB lesson that links a variety of content areas and literacy skills. Consider and list ways in which this lesson addresses the following to enhance student success:
   • Academic objectives
   • Language objectives
   • Cognitive dimensions
   • Sociocultural dimensions

assessment tips and strategies

The following assessment tips and strategies are drawn from the content of Chapter 7.

ASSESSMENT
Formative assessments are a type of ongoing or in-process evaluation that allows the teacher to evaluate the effectiveness of the lesson to ensure CLD student comprehension. Summative assessments, on the other hand, refer to the culminating assessments that occur at the end of lessons. When conducting summative assessments, teachers might work with students to examine revised and completed student work or to collect evidence of students' language and content knowledge development. This latter type of assessment documents and describes students' proficiency levels in meeting lesson objectives.

Assessment Tips
• Formative assessments are used in order to:
   —Clarify misconceptions.
   —Affirm new understandings.

   —Challenge the CLD student to think more deeply about key concepts.
• Formative assessments rely on the teacher's feedback, which should be specific, constructive, and thorough.
• When modifying instruction according to assessment feedback, teachers must observe students and look for student behavior or responses, including body language and facial expressions, that are indicative of confusion or misunderstanding.
• Effective teachers are flexible and responsive to the needs of CLD students, as indicated by assessment feedback, and incorporate immediate modifications into a lesson.
• Use the evaluation from summative assessments to check the degree to which the lesson aligned itself with the overall instructional goals and objectives of the lesson.

Assessment Strategies

- Examples of formative assessments include learning logs, projects, and writing.
- Rubrics can be useful tools in summative assessments:
    - Rubrics grant the student insight into the characteristics of quality products.
    - Teachers pass out sample work at varying degrees of language and content proficiency.

- Groups of students review samples and rank them according to levels of proficiency.
- Teachers guide students to consensus.
- Students learn how to assess their own work.
- Class creates a common expectation regarding the quality of academic work.
- Students can reflect on their strengths and inexperience to create goals.

The information provided in this chapter will help the educator to:

- Discuss characteristics of sheltered instruction and its application to content-area instruction.
- Differentiate sheltered instruction from content-based ESL, segregated skill instruction, and integrated skills instruction.
- Describe the overarching themes and elements of sheltered instruction.
- Discuss similarities and differences between the SDAIE and SIOP variations of sheltered instruction.
- Describe the three aspects and eight components of the SIOP model.
- Explain ways in which each of the eight components of the SIOP model can be effectively implemented in practice.
- Develop curriculum adaptations to enhance the comprehensibility of material for CLD students.

The Sheltered Method of Instruction

América sits at the back of the room and says nothing. América used to talk all the time. In her village, she greeted the animals in Spanish mixed with a few Mixteco words. She sang to the morning. She recited the many poems taught her since she was a baby. She had a voice—strong, open, and free. Somehow, in Chicago, she has lost this voice. She thinks hard about her far-away home that is beginning to fade from her memory.

—Luis J. Rodríguez, *América Is Her Name*

chapter outline

Realities of Sheltered Instruction

Variations on Sheltered Instruction

Myths and Misconceptions Associated with Sheltered Instruction

Types of Students

Language Proficiency of CLD Students

Standards of Best Practice

Specially Designed Academic Instruction in English (SDAIE)

The Sheltered Instruction Observation Protocol (SIOP)

Preparation

Instruction

Review and Assessment

Closing Thoughts on the SIOP Model of Sheltered Instruction

critical standards *Guiding Chapter Content*

TESOL/NCATE teacher standards reflect professional consensus on standards for the quality teaching of pre-K–12 CLD students. Additionally, the CEEE Guiding Principles and their accompanying indicators serve as a framework to assist practitioners, policymakers, and clients as they collaborate to enhance academic enrichment and language acquisition among CLD students. Therefore, in order to help educators understand how they might appropriately target and address national professional teaching standards in practice, we have designed the content of this chapter to reflect the following standards.

TESOL ESL Standards for P–12 Teacher Education Programs

TESOL ESL—Domain 3: Planning, Implementing, and Managing Instruction. Candidates know, understand, and are able to use standards-based practices and strategies related to planning, implementing, and management of ESL and content instruction, including classroom organization, teaching strategies for developing and integrating language skills, and choosing and adapting classroom resources. (p. 21)

- **Standard 3.a. Planning for standards-based ESL and content instruction.** Candidates know, understand, and apply concepts, research, and best practices to plan classroom instruction in a supportive learning environment for ESOL [CLD] students. Candidates serve as effective English language models as they plan the classroom for multilevel classrooms with learners from diverse backgrounds using standards-based ESL content curriculum. (p. 21)

    3.a.3. Plan students' learning experiences based on assessment of language proficiency and prior knowledge. (p. 23)

Note: All TESOL/NCATE standards are cited from TESOL (2001). All Guiding Principles are cited from Center for Equity and Excellence in Education (1996).

- **Standard 3.c. Using resources effectively in ESL and content instruction.** Candidates are familiar with a wide range of standards-based materials, resources, and technologies and choose, adapt, and use them in effective ESL content teaching. (p. 26)

  3.c.2. Select materials and other resources that are appropriate to students' developing language and content-area abilities, including appropriate use of L1. (p. 27)

  3.c.3. Employ appropriate variety of materials for language learning, including books, visual aids, props, and realia. (p. 27)

TESOL ESL—Domain 4: Assessment. Candidates understand issues of assessment and use assessment as they relate to ESOL students. (p. 30)

- **Standard 4.c. Classroom-based assessment for ESL.** Candidates know and use a variety of classroom and performance-based assessment tools that are standards based to inform instruction. (p. 35)

  4.c.2. Use various instruments and techniques to assess content-area learning (e.g., math, science, social studies) for ESOL learners at varying levels of language and literacy development. (p. 36)

CEEE Guiding Principles

Guiding Principle #4: Limited English proficient students receive instruction that builds on their previous education and cognitive abilities and that reflects their language proficiency levels.

4.6 Teachers identify and design comprehensible instruction that is appropriate to limited English proficient students' developmental levels as well as to their stages of first and second language acquisition.

4.8 Teachers use instructional materials and resources that support English language learners in the classroom (e.g., properly translated native language materials, English language materials controlled for linguistic complexity).

4.11 All teachers understand and value the linguistic backgrounds and cultural heritages of their students' families and use this information to enrich classroom instruction and to facilitate limited English proficient students' learning of academic content. (p. 8)

The traditional school curriculum and most classroom instruction practices are grounded in the notion of a level playing field (Escamilla, 1994, 1999; Walqui, 2000). Yet Chapter 1 discussed the fact that CLD students do not participate on a level playing field when they attend public school in the United States. At the same time that they and their caregivers must often adapt to a new country, transition to a new culture, and rapidly learn a new language, these students are asked to perform, often at grade level, in the content areas. Therefore, unlike their grade-level peers, CLD students face singular challenges and processes that pose formidable obstacles to their success in school, as discussed in Chapters 1, 2, and 3. This is not to say that CLD students do not bring assets to the school. In fact, we can maximize these assets in ways that support the students as they compete with their grade-level peers. Yet the challenges and obstacles that contribute to the creation of an unlevel playing field are among just a few of the reasons why we recognize that CLD students arrive at school with differential learning and transition needs, which must be accommodated if these students are to reach their full academic and career potentials.

Sheltered instructional methods are specifically designed to target these potentials and to recognize these differential learning and transition needs. To shelter is basically to protect (Mish et al., 2001). Sheltered instructional methods protect or preserve the potentials of CLD students as they build the sociocultural, academic, cognitive, and linguistic (L2) knowledge, capacities, and skills their grade-level peers may already take for granted in classroom learning. More specifically, sheltered methods preserve student potentials such as:

- The potential for communicative, interactive, and literacy-focused language acquisition toward CALP proficiency in L2.
- The potential for academic achievement in the content areas based on elaborated background knowledge, exposure to the full scope and sequence of the curriculum, and alternative and equitable process and product assessment practices.
- The potential to live the American dream, in which an equitable education is for *all* students and is the foundation on which any individual can aspire to success.

Furthermore, sheltered methods protect the students from anxiety, ambiguity, confusion, frustration, and many other factors of the affective filter hypothesis (Krashen, 1982), factors that we know inhibit learning and language acquisition.

In this chapter, we first explore the realities of and variations on sheltered instruction. Second, various myths and misconceptions associated with the model are discussed. Third, alternate forms of sheltered instruction are compared and contrasted. Finally, the chapter details the sheltered instruction observation protocol (SIOP) model of sheltered instruction as a thoroughly comprehensive and sheltered variation, specifically designed for the differential learning and transition needs of CLD students.

■ Realities of Sheltered Instruction

Sheltered instruction is a method for combining philosophies, strategies, and techniques that appropriately recognize the multifaceted challenges that CLD students confront. At the same time, the method provides CLD students with instruction that is comprehensible, relevant, and motivating. Although sheltered instruction does focus on making grade-level content comprehensible, it is more than content-based ESL because it explicitly emphasizes language and content objectives. In some ways, sheltered instruction can be viewed as integrated skills instruction because it does not emphasize a basic skills curriculum or focus on the development of discrete language skills in isolation, as does segregated skill instruction. But, as illustrated in Table 8.1, sheltered instruction is also more than integrated skills

■ **table 8.1**   Comparison of Segregated and Integrated Skills Instruction

Criterion	Segregated Skills Instruction	Integrated Skills Instruction ICB	SI
Focus on isolated or discrete language skills.	x		
Language and content learning are separated.	x		
Basic skills orientation of instruction.	x		
A subject-area certified teacher, with no professional development for CLD students, may lead instruction.	x		
An ESL certified or endorsed teacher typically delivers classroom instruction.		+	
Emphasis on all literacy skills of language.		+	+
L2 language development is a goal.		+	+
Content knowledge and skills and L2 development are goals.			+
Focus on requisite terminology for content.		+	
Focus on core, grade-level curriculum.			+
Content and ESL standards guide instruction.			+
Classroom instruction typically follows the scope and sequence of a grade-level class.			+
A subject-area certified teacher, with professional development for CLD student needs, typically delivers classroom instruction.			+

Legend:
ICB   Integrated content-based ESL method
SI   Sheltered instruction method
x   Not appropriate for CLD students
+   Appropriate for CLD students

instruction because the full scope and sequence of curriculum is used to target academic language proficiency and a deeper conceptual understanding of the content material.

Variations on Sheltered Instruction

Although Echevarria and Graves (2003) argue that sheltered instruction was first introduced by Stephen Krashen in the early 1980s, this method has evolved through a variety of forms and has been identified by a number of labels. In fact, this type of support for CLD students has been variously labeled sheltered, sheltered instruction, sheltered English, integrated skills instruction, content-based English language teaching (CELT), scaffolding, specially designed academic instruction in English (SDAIE), and the sheltered instruction observation protocol

(SIOP). After first examining commonalities among variations of sheltered instruction, we briefly explore the SDAIE model of sheltered instruction, owing to its popularity in practice. However, we consider the SIOP model to be the most developed, explicated, and researched, and therefore we emphasize this variation in subsequent sections of this chapter.

Common Themes in Sheltered Instruction

Among the many variations of sheltered instruction that have evolved over time, most tend to share certain commonalities or themes in addressing the differential learning and transition needs of CLD students. At least four of these themes are relatively common across virtually all variations associated with the method. These four common themes are illustrated in Figure 8.1 and include hands-on activities, cooperative learning, guarded vocabulary, and the use of visuals. This particular figure is, for the purpose of illustration, grounded in the use of the sheltered method with secondary-level CLD students.

Hands-On The hands-on theme of sheltered instruction is also consistent with an emphasis on interaction, which is highlighted as a component of some sheltered variations. Such interaction (especially hands-on learning situations) is considered essential for CLD students as a means by which they can practice their emergent L2 skills. For example, a sheltered lesson on corn, delivered as part of a thematic unit on agriculture, might involve an interactive, hands-on activity in which CLD students (in groups) weigh ears of corn. They might then compare the weight of the ear with and without kernels to gauge yield. Activities that enable communicative, student-centered, student-to-teacher, and peer-to-peer interaction at appropriate language and content levels are crucial. These interactions may stress either homogeneous or heterogeneous student groupings, the latter of which allows students to benefit from the capacities of a more capable peer. Hands-on interaction also provides students with new ways to clarify concepts and to demonstrate what they have learned.

Cooperative Learning The cooperative learning theme of sheltered instruction builds on research that highlights the many benefits of such learning (Cohen, 1986; Kagan, 1986; Slavin, 1983), especially for CLD students (Hertz-Lazarowitz & Calderón, 1993; Slavin, 1995). Cooperative learning can be understood as a descriptor of the many ways in which students may be placed into small, primarily heterogeneous collaborative groups in ways that maximize interdependence and target either individual or group goals for learning. Positive interdependence is one valuable outcome of collaboration toward a common goal. It fosters the perspective that each student should care about another's learning. Research on cooperative learning has suggested a number of benefits for bilingual students that may be associated with this theme or strategy of sheltered instruction. Specifically, research indicates (Calderón, Tinajero, & Hertz-Lazarowitz, 1992; McGroarty,

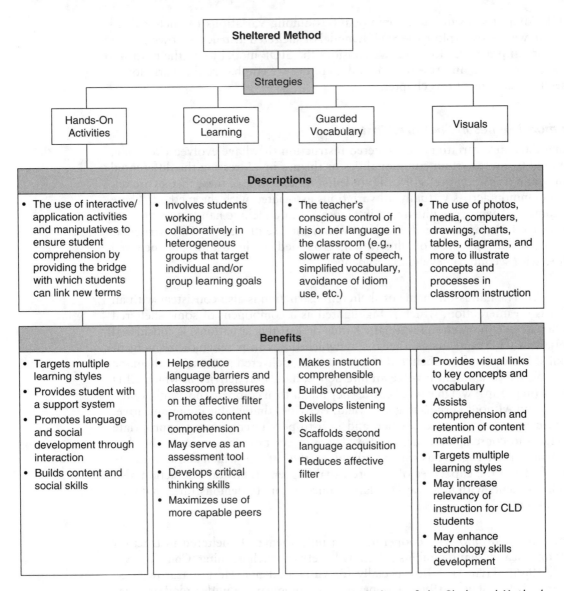

■ **figure 8.1**   Overview of Common Themes among Variations of the Sheltered Method

1989; Slavin, 1995; Tinajero, Calderón, & Hertz-Lazarowitz, 1993) that, for CLD students, cooperative learning:

- Enables students to act as mutual resources in active learning.
- Fosters opportunities to integrate language with content learning.

- Encourages the incorporation of a variety of curricular materials that enhance content learning and language production.
- Increases both the variety and frequency of L2 practice through a multiplicity of interaction opportunities.
- Enhances both L1 and cognitive development through social interaction.

Consequently, cooperative learning is typically understood as an essential theme of sheltered instruction that promotes the integration of language and content, the ongoing support of CALP development in L1, and active constructivist learning that is relevant to students' interests.

Guarded Vocabulary   As further illustrated in Figure 8.1, guarded vocabulary is a common theme among variations of sheltered instruction. Also sometimes referred to as reducing the linguistic load of instruction, guarded vocabulary does not involve actions such as unnatural speech or raising the volume of instruction. Instead, the strategy involves linguistic actions on the part of the instructor that increase the comprehensibility of instruction. These teacher actions involve linguistic controls on instructional delivery such as:

- Slowing the rate of speech.
- Emphasizing word enunciation.
- Simplifying the vocabulary used.
  —For example, to simplify the sentence, "Typically, to subtract two numbers, one places the subtrahend under the minuend and solves for the difference," one can reduce the linguistic load along the lines of, "To subtract one number from another, you can usually place the smaller number underneath the larger number to find the difference between the two."
- Using more consistent vocabulary with appropriate repetition.
  —For example, patterned stories, songs, raps, or chants can be used to emphasize linguistic repetition with students and thereby reinforce vocabulary, language structures, and intonation (Richard-Amato, 1996).
- Using shorter sentences with simpler syntax.
  —For example, to simplify the sentence, "At the autumnal equinox, not only do the periods of day and night equalize, but a seasonal transformation occurs as well," one can reduce the linguistic load along the lines, "At the autumnal equinox, the periods of day and night equalize. At this time, there is also a seasonal transformation."
- Inserting more pauses between phrases.

Accordingly, guarded vocabulary extensively emphasizes the linguistic dimension of CLD student learning and language acquisition. In particular, the strategy focuses on techniques that enhance the comprehensibity of linguistic input for students who are acquiring a second language (i.e., English).

Visuals   A fourth theme common among variations of the sheltered instruction method is visuals (see Figure 8.1). Basically, this theme is inclusive of what

■ Voices from the Field

Guarded Vocabulary and Social Studies: A Simulation

"When I teach how Africans came to America, I list out words like Africa, uncomfortable, pain, hurt, Middle Passage, slave, slave trade, ship, boat, American colony, economy, income, and money. I make sure that I use these terms, demonstrate the relationship of the synonyms, and use the support vocabulary to build CLD students' content vocabulary. Visual depictions of the Middle Passage help to convey the text material. I also bring in a refrigerator box and have students take turns getting in the box to demonstrate the limited amount of space that slaves had during the Middle Passage. In collaborative groups, students discuss how they personally and/or their families came to the United States. The adolescents begin to make connections to both the historic and current forms of immigration, which usually are precipitated by economic progress."

■ *Roger Syng, middle school social studies teacher, Garden City, KS*

Echevarria, Vogt, and Short (2000) refer to as supplementary materials, and it encompasses such instructional supports as commercial illustrations, big books, realia, overheads, multimedia presentations, demonstrations, graphics, bulletin boards, maps, and more. These visuals not only contextualize curriculum and instruction, but they also provide powerful visual links between language and content. Echevarria and Graves (2003) report that the graphic depiction of text, through such visuals as charts, diagrams, and webs, enables CLD students to modify difficult texts, organize thoughts in a meaningful way, and recap a theme or topic. For example, a story map not only reduces text to the most important points, but it also teaches students to expect certain recurring patterns in stories and books. Concept maps, such as the one depicted in Figure 8.2, enable students to visualize the relationships between the components of a process.

Scaffolding in Sheltered Instruction

Certain models of sheltered instruction also emphasize the notion of scaffolding. As discussed in Chapter 6, Vygotsky (1962) has argued that through social interaction and the assistance of an adult or a more capable peer, the learner may surpass his or her level of actual or predictable development to attain a new or potential level of development. The sort of support and assistance from adults or more capable peers that students might need to target the zone of proximal development has been referred to as scaffolding. Such scaffolding enables the student to be challenged to the next level of performance or development.

The notion of scaffolding is consistent with a constructivist perspective on learning (see Chapter 2) and the argument that students learn by constructing meaning from their experiences and interactions. Therefore, the concept of scaf-

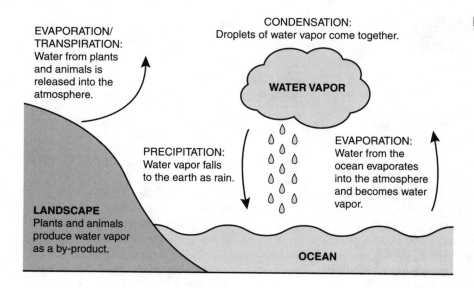

folding serves as a metaphor to compare the support offered to students through teacher–student and student–student interaction to the framework that supports the builders of a structure until they have fostered a new creation from their many shared efforts. As applied to language and literacy development through sheltered instruction, the scaffolding strategy provides the support, structure, and assistance that CLD students often require to construct meaning from the complex academic language of textbooks and that of instruction delivered in L2. For example, in sheltered instruction, new vocabulary is sometimes previewed in the native language, contextualized in English, and reviewed again in the native language (Herrera, 2001; Kole, 2003; Perez, 2002).

■ Myths and Misconceptions Associated with Sheltered Instruction

A variety of myths and misconceptions tend to be associated with the sheltered method of instruction. Similarly, the origins of these myths and misconceptions can be attributed to a variety of reasons, including:

- The broad range of evolving variations of the sheltered method that are discussed in the literature.
- Occasional misinterpretations and misapplications of the method in practice.
- Confusion among practitioners of this method and other methods of the communicative approach (see Chapter 6) about language development among CLD students.

Mr. Cottonware has been teaching biology in a rural high school for three years. During this time, he has become increasingly frustrated with the low performance of his fluent English-speaking CLD students. He does not understand why the CLD students are performing so poorly on assignments, because language does not seem to be a problem. These students have also been disrupting class by walking around and talking extensively to others. Because this is a content-based science course, it is necessary to work in the laboratory at least twice a week, which Mr. Cottonware schedules for every Tuesday and Thursday. Mr. Cottonware orally explains the experimental setup the day before everyone is to perform the experiment and then again right before breaking the students up into work groups the day of the experiment. He feels that the fluent English-speaking CLD students prevent everyone else from working productively because they continually ask others for directions.

■ *What should Mr. Cottonware do? Mr. Cottonware should heterogeneously group students according to proficiency level in both the English language and content-area understanding. It is evident that the CLD students are having a hard time understanding the procedures of experiments, which is causing them to constantly look to their peers for directions. Heterogeneous grouping can help minimize*

disruptions in the classroom by allowing students to dialogue with one another without having to walk around or try to converse with a peer across the room. This type of grouping will give CLD students an opportunity to articulate their knowledge and understanding of the content without getting off task and distracting others. More capable peers with higher proficiency levels who have a grasp of the language and content can aid CLD students struggling with their language by providing them with clear directions. This will not only minimize disruptions but also enhance learning for all students.

CLD students need frequent opportunities to visualize images related to language and content. A demonstration of the experiment beforehand can help the CLD students by providing them with step-by-step procedures to follow. Mr. Cottonware should also display or otherwise have available written instructions and the steps of the procedures for the experiment in simplified language. This will allow CLD students a chance to follow along and refer back to the steps when necessary. Incorporating these steps will enhance vocabulary and content learning for CLD students. At the same time, these students will be more interested and engaged in the procedure, and will thereby be less likely to get off task and disrupt others.

Additionally, many of the strategies and materials associated with the sheltered method have long been used in isolation with both CLD and grade-level students, but they have not always been integrated into a holistic method for second language learners.

Among myths and misconceptions concerning the sheltered method, some relate to the type of student for which the method is applicable. Others relate to the languages spoken by, or the language proficiencies of, the students to be instructed. Still others relate to connections between the method and standards for best practice with CLD students.

Types of Students

One commonly shared myth about the sheltered method asserts that sheltered instruction is designed only for self-contained classes of CLD students. In reality, the sheltered method uses strategies and techniques that are applicable to both CLD and grade-level students and therefore may be used in the grade-level classroom (Echevarria, Vogt, & Short, 2000; Sheppard, 1995). Necessarily, the teacher will need targeted professional development in methods, strategies, and techniques for instructing CLD students, but the sheltered method is regularly used in grade-level classrooms. For example, in secondary schools the sheltered method allows subject-area teachers who are trained in addressing the differential needs of CLD students to deliver courses that allow CLD students to participate in the regular content of the curriculum rather than in elective or pull-out courses for graduation. The method can also be used for self-contained classes of CLD students, where its various strategies and techniques of instruction and assessment are equally effective. For the grade-level student, the sheltered method shares many of the same characteristics of instruction that are considered effective for all students (Echevarria & Graves, 2003). Such characteristics include the following:

- A variety of grouping strategies
- An emphasis on higher-order thinking skills
- Clear explanations of learning tasks
- Links to prior learning
- The use of supplementary materials
- Consistent feedback on performance
- Student engagement

However, as Echevarria and Graves (2003) have noted, although sheltered instruction shares many of the characteristics of what we know about effective instruction, sheltered instruction "is more than simply good teaching—much more" (p. 53). Whereas sheltered instruction methods, strategies, and techniques are beneficial to all students, these types of accommodations are *essential* to the academic success of CLD students.

Language Proficiency of CLD Students

Some educators also believe that the sheltered method is designed solely for CLD students with intermediate or advanced language proficiency. In some cases, this misconception arises from the fact that the specially designed academic instruction in English (SDAIE) model of sheltered instruction (one variation among many) is limited to CLD students with these levels of proficiency in L2 (Russell, 2002). In other cases, this misconception arises from the reality that the sheltered method generally targets not just second language acquisition but also rigorous grade-level content-area learning. In fact, high-quality sheltered instruction is characterized by professional attention to the particular language development needs of CLD students, as well as the incorporation of both language and content objectives into curriculum and lesson preparation and instructional delivery. According to Echevarria, Vogt, and Short (2000):

> In model SI [sheltered instruction] courses, language and content objectives are systematically woven into the curriculum. . . . Teachers generally present the regular, grade-level, subject curriculum to the students through modified instruction in English, although some special curricula may be designed for students with significant gaps in their educational backgrounds or very low literacy levels. Teachers must develop the student's academic language proficiency consistently and regularly as part of the lessons and units they plan and deliver. (p. 11)

For CLD students whose L2 proficiency is not advanced, the teacher's level of English in classroom instruction is modulated or guarded to increase comprehensibility and reduce the affective filter. Moreover, quality sheltered instruction for CLD students emphasizes the explicit instruction of academic language skills, such as asking for clarification, confirming information, and persuading through language. Therefore, although accommodations must be implemented to enhance the comprehensibility of content material for students who possess beginning levels of English proficiency, the sheltered instruction method can be effectively used for the instruction of *all* CLD students.

Similarly, some teachers believe that sheltered instruction is specifically designed for CLD students who are homogeneously grouped according to the level of L2 (English) proficiency. Instead, sheltered instruction enables successful practice with either homogeneously or heterogeneously grouped CLD students. In some schools where CLD students are homogeneously grouped according to L1 or L2 proficiency, bilingual instructors are used (Sheppard, 1995). In other schools, these students are heterogeneously grouped, even in the grade-level classroom, and ESL or trained content-area teachers provide instruction (Echevarria, Vogt, & Short, 2000).

Standards of Best Practice

A final myth of sheltered instruction concerns the belief that such instruction is not grounded in standards of best practice with CLD students. In reality, Echevarria, Vogt, and Short (2000) report that high-quality sheltered instruction, especially its emphasis on academic language development in the content areas, targets at least three of the nine ESL standards for pre-K–12 students developed by the Teachers of English to Speakers of Other Languages (TESOL) organization (TESOL, 1997). That is, CLD students who are guided to target academic language proficiency in L2 through content-focused sheltered instruction should be able to:

- Interact in the classroom toward language development.
- Obtain, process, construct, and provide subject matter information in spoken and written form in L2.
- Use appropriate learning strategies to draw meaning from and apply academic knowledge.

Specially Designed Academic Instruction in English (SDAIE)

A particularly popular variation of sheltered instruction in certain regions of the United States is known as *specially designed academic instruction in English* (SDAIE) (California State Department of Education, 1994). For CLD students who have attained an intermediate or advanced level of proficiency in L2 (English), SDAIE emphasizes cognitively demanding, grade-level appropriate core curricula. Among the objectives of SDAIE that are applicable to CLD students are:

- Opportunities for social interaction as a means to cognitive and language development.
- Access to the core curriculum.
- Variable English (L2) language development.

As with other sheltered variations, SDAIE stresses comprehensible input, guarded vocabulary, hands-on interaction, and the use of supplementary materials, especially visuals. Additionally, the following elements of the SDAIE variation of the sheltered method are generally incorporated:

- Goals and Objectives
  —Language, content, and social affective
- Cooperative Learning
  —Small homogeneous or heterogeneous groups that target collaborative learning
- Modified Instruction
  —Thematic units taught through scaffolding strategies and language-level-appropriate lesson modifications
- Multifaceted Assessment
  —Formal and informal assessments that evaluate process and product, with a process emphasis on portfolios, running records, and anecdotal records

The primary goal of SDAIE is to teach content as CLD students continue to improve their capacities for speaking, reading, and writing in L2 (Rohac, 2000; Russell, 2002). Nonetheless, CLD students who learn this content through SDAIE will "still need support in acquiring academic English that intermediate and advanced ELD classes will provide" (Russell, 2002, p. 41). Therefore, Russell reports that SDAIE, despite the many ways in which it has been applied in field practice, was never intended for use with remedial students or with CLD students who are at beginning stages of second language acquisition.

The Sheltered Instruction Observation Protocol (SIOP)

As distinct from the SDAIE variation, we consider the SIOP model of sheltered instruction to be the most researched, developed, and explicated of the sheltered instruction variations. Consequently, we devote the remainder of the chapter to a brief history of the model's development and a detailed exploration of the model and its application in practice.

After five years of collaboration with practicing teachers, Center for Research on Education, Diversity & Excellence (CREDE) researchers Jana Echevarria, MaryEllen Vogt, and Deborah Short developed a high-quality model of sheltered instruction known as the sheltered instruction observation protocol (SIOP). They specifically designed this variation of sheltered instruction to provide an explicit and consistent framework grounded in research and field-tested by teachers to identify effective practices for sheltered instruction. The SIOP model is a professional development instrument for teachers in culturally and linguistically diverse school settings (Echevarria, Vogt, & Short, 2000). SIOP is the most comprehensive form of sheltered instruction because it goes beyond strategies and techniques to include the major indicators of well-developed lessons for CLD students. Such indicators include language and content objectives, supplementary materials, connections between content and the prior knowledge and experiences of students, vocabulary development, appropriate speech, learning strategies, interaction with teachers and other students, activities that require students to apply knowledge of content and language, and a cycle of review, feedback, and assessment (Echevarria et al., 2000).

Many devoted teachers have tried to find ways to make their instruction more comprehensible for culturally and linguistically diverse learners. Yet, for all of their efforts and best of intentions, these teachers are often unable to find resources that demonstrate exactly *how* they can modify curriculum and instruction to meet the needs of their students. In providing a rationale for their development of the sheltered instruction observation protocol, Echevarria and colleagues (2000) explain,

> Traditionally, to meet the needs of students who struggle with grade-level reading materials, texts were rewritten according to readability formulae (Gray & Leary, 1935; Ruddell, 1997). The adapted text included controlled vocabulary and a limited number of concepts, resulting in the omission of critical pieces of information. We have learned that if a student's exposure to content concepts is limited by vocabulary-controlled materials, the amount of information they learn over time is considerably less than that of their peers who use grade-level texts. The result is that the "rich get richer and the poor get poorer" (Stanovich, 1986). (p. 17)

For these authors, such reductionistic curricular adaptations do not succeed in closing the gap between native speakers and CLD students. Instead, this gap is actually expanded and eventually contributes to schooling attrition rates among CLD students. Therefore, effective teachers plan lessons that are accommodative but also challenging for students who are acquiring English. Appropriately adapted lessons include and do not omit age-appropriate content and materials. The SIOP model of the sheltered instruction method provides teachers with a research-based tool for effecting these appropriate accommodations and for making grade-level content comprehensible for all students.

In the design and implementation of appropriate content-based lessons for CLD students, the SIOP model considers the following three critical aspects of the teaching process: preparation, instruction, and review and assessment. SIOP explores the spectrum of teaching practices through the examination of thirty essential indicators, each of which pertains to one of the three critical aspects of the teaching process illustrated in Figure 8.3. Throughout this chapter, the examples provided clarify the many ways in which teachers can effectively implement the various indicators of the SIOP model of sheltered instruction. All of the examples pertain to an eighth-grade science lesson on the planets in our solar system. Ms. Nygaard, a teacher at Konza Middle School, develops and delivers this hypothetical science lesson.

Preparation

Of the three critical aspects of the SIOP model, perhaps the most fundamental is preparation. Effective teachers in schools with culturally and linguistically diverse

■ **f i g u r e 8 . 3**   Critical Aspects and Indicators of the SIOP Model

Aspect of Preparation
- Content objectives
- Language objectives
- Content concepts
- Supplementary materials
- Adaptation of content
- Meaningful activities

Aspect of Instruction

Building Background *(category of instruction)*
- Students' life experiences
- Students' prior learning experiences
- Key vocabulary

Comprehensible Input *(category of instruction)*
- Appropriate speech
- Techniques to clarify content concepts
- Clear explanations of academic tasks

Strategies *(category of instruction)*
- Opportunities for students to use strategies
- Use of a variety of question types
- Scaffolding techniques

Interaction *(category of instruction)*
- Discussion and in-depth responses about concepts

- Sufficient response wait time
- Appropriate grouping configurations
- Clarification of lesson material in L1

Practice and Application *(category of instruction)*
- Hands-on materials and manipulatives
- Activities requiring students to apply knowledge of content and language
- Activities that use all literacy domains

Lesson Delivery *(category of instruction)*
- Support of content objectives
- Support of language objectives
- Appropriate engagement of students
- Appropriate pacing

Aspect of Review and Assessment
- Review of key vocabulary
- Review of content concepts
- Ongoing feedback to students regarding language production and the application of new content concepts
- Formal and informal assessment of student progress toward attaining content and language objectives

populations consider many different factors when creating lesson plans. In a SIOP lesson, student needs and characteristics drive the ways in which teachers design their content-area lessons. Therefore, six SIOP indicators guide teachers to do the following:

- Write content objectives for the lesson.
- Write language objectives for the lesson.
- Select content-area concepts appropriate for the grade level and educational background of the students.
- Gather supplementary materials that give students comprehensible input by contextualizing information.
- Develop ways to adapt content to the language proficiency levels of all students.
- Create meaningful activities that allow students to practice and apply content knowledge using all four language domains (listening, speaking, reading, and writing).

Integrating Content and Language Objectives

The first two indicators of quality preparation are integrating content and language objectives. For several decades, researchers in the field of second language acquisition have recognized the need for educators of CLD students to integrate content and language objectives into their lessons (Cantoni-Harvey, 1987; Chamot, 1985; Cummins, 2001a; Enright & McCloskey, 1988; Mohan, 1986; Thomas & Collier, 1997). Content objectives clarify the essential information and understandings that students should glean from the lesson. With the overarching goals of the lesson in mind, students have a framework within which to organize specific details of the lesson. Language objectives help CLD students focus on acquiring the academic language they need to develop the vocabulary, language structures, and cognitive language necessary to perform well in school.

When developing content and language objectives, an effective teacher selects appropriate objectives derived from local, state, and national grade-level content and language standards. Throughout lessons, the teacher shares the objectives with his or her students by posting the objectives in a visible place in the classroom and explicitly relating lesson content and activities to the posted objectives. The teacher encourages students to self-assess their progress toward meeting the lesson objectives as they proceed through each lesson.

Integrating Content and Language Objectives: In Practice In order to get a better sense of what content and language objectives might actually look like, let us examine the efforts of Ms. Nygaard, our hypothetical science teacher at Konza Middle School. Ms. Nygaard is confident that her content objectives are appropriate for the grade level of her students. She has ten years of teaching experience with eighth-grade science, and she wrote her objectives using her school district's curriculum frameworks for eighth-grade science and middle school English as a second language. Additionally, she talked to the school's ESL teacher about

Are You Aware?

Is ESL content-based instruction more effective than ESL pull-out?

Yes. Ovando and Collier (1998) have argued that students have access to more of the curriculum while they are learning English if the instruction and curriculum are properly and appropriately structured. Also, content-based instruction can be seen as a much more cost-effective program than ESL pull-out. Content-based instruction provides content-area teachers an opportunity to collaborate with ESL teachers in making curricula more adaptable according to the needs of CLD students. To understand a comparison between content-based instruction and ESL pull-out, refer to Table 8.2.

■ **table 8.2**   Comparison of Content-Based Instruction versus ESL Pull-Out Program

Content-Based Instruction	ESL Pull-Out
Students remain in grade-level content-area classroom.	Students lose access to content while in ESL class and are therefore often confused on returning to the classroom.
Students remain with peers (nonstigmatizing).	English learning is isolated (many times with grammatically based exercises that are not often effective).
Teacher is trained with best practices for CLD students.	Lack of interaction with native-language-speaking peers.
Lessons are modified within the content area to meet student needs.	Fosters relationships among immigrants from various linguistic and cultural backgrounds.
Students achieve academically and linguistically while progressing in their grade level.	No training for classroom teacher.
Native language support is more easily incorporated through proficient bilingual peers and through supplemental material that the grade-level content teacher can provide.	Perceived as remedial instruction.
All students benefit by reaching their potential through cooperative learning and by becoming more appreciative of cultural and linguistic differences.	Students feel stigmatized.
Most effective model.	Seen as review year after year and often devalued as compared to grade-level content material.
Least expensive with the ESL teacher in the classroom as an additional resource teacher.	Minimal native language use.
	Students limited to this programming take longer to develop language skills because there is no meaningful connection to content or context.
	Must hire an extra resource specialist (e.g., the ESL teacher).
	Most expensive model.
	Least effective model.

the language objectives. She wrote three content objectives and two language objectives.

Content Objectives for Students
- List the names of the planets in the order that they orbit the sun.
- Describe three ways in which the inner and outer planets are different from each other.
- Explain the unique characteristics of Earth that allow the development and sustenance of life.

Language Objectives for Students
- Using ordinal numbers, list the planets in the order that they orbit the sun.
- Compare and contrast the inner and outer planets using comparative and superlative adjectives.

Although her class includes CLD students at varying levels of proficiency in English, Ms. Nygaard knows that most of the CLD students will be able to list the planets in their order from the sun using ordinal numbers. However, as some of the newer CLD students may experience difficulty using comparative and superlative adjectives, she will have them focus more on using descriptive adjectives. All of the materials, concepts, adaptations, and activities used in the SIOP lesson will support the CLD students in attaining the lesson objectives.

Content Concepts

When preparing a SIOP lesson, a third indicator of quality preparation addressed by effective teachers is the choice of content concepts. Accommodative teachers use the lesson objectives to develop content concepts that are central to the unit's theme and are appropriate for the grade level and educational backgrounds of the students (Echevarria et al., 2000). Some teachers mistakenly underestimate the cognitive and academic abilities of CLD students because many do not speak much English. However, limiting CLD students to a remedial curriculum based on assumptions negatively affects their academic achievement (Thomas & Collier, 2002). It is essential to keep the quality of the content intact.

In order for students to comprehend grade-level content concepts, they must have the prerequisite knowledge base essential to the concepts covered. This means that when planning a lesson, the effective teacher examines the basic understandings, theories, and premises on which the specific content concepts are based. If students lack such background knowledge, the teacher incorporates the necessary explication before covering the actual concepts of the lesson (Echevarria et al., 2000).

Content Concepts: In Practice After analyzing the content objectives she has written, Ms. Nygaard determines that the lesson will focus on the following two grade-appropriate content concepts:

- Each planet in the solar system has a unique set of characteristics.
- The Earth has characteristics that make the development and sustenance of life possible.

Ms. Nygaard then reflects on the background information that is essential for her students' understanding of the concepts.

Although she knows that all of her students have the capacity to understand the concepts of the lesson, Ms. Nygaard is aware that some of her CLD students have no background knowledge of the basic components of an atmosphere. Many of her students are also unaware of how an atmosphere influences a planet's environment. Therefore, to ensure that all students will be able to fully understand the lesson's content concepts, Ms. Nygaard develops a short introductory lesson that explains key information relevant to an atmosphere.

Supplementary Materials

A fourth indicator of quality preparation according to the SIOP variation of sheltered instruction involves the use of supplementary materials. CLD students need opportunities to use supplementary materials, including many hands-on, visual, and kinesthetic materials, in order to practice and more fully understand key grade-level content concepts (Echevarria et al., 2000). Supplementary materials also provide students with the chance to practice new vocabulary and language structures. Not surprisingly, in a long-term longitudinal research project Thomas and Collier (2002) found that lessons making use of multiple media, a natural learning environment, real-world problem-solving applications of content concepts, and unifying themes facilitated the second language acquisition and academic achievement of CLD students.

Supplementary Materials: In Practice   For visual support, Ms. Nygaard turns her classroom into a representation of our solar system. Using supplementary materials to enhance her instruction, she hangs representations of the sun and planets across the back of her classroom. Each planet has note cards hanging from it on a string. The top note card for each planet has its ordinal number describing its position from the sun. Each of the other note cards states a key fact about the planet. She also displays a pictorial word wall with the key content vocabulary as well as descriptive adjectives related to the planets.

To supplement her course materials and support her content and language objectives, Ms. Nygaard chooses several alternative texts and hands-on materials. The textbook set for eighth-grade science came with a Spanish text and recording of the chapter that her Spanish-speaking students can use, but not all of her CLD students speak Spanish. So she instructs her CLD students who do not speak English to find readings on the Internet at the technology center in the classroom. She encourages her CLD students to read their first language texts at home or in groups during their resource period before they read and discuss the text in English during class.

When students have finished their work and during designated reading times, students can choose reading materials from the classroom's solar system library. Ms. Nygaard and the school media specialist collaborated to assemble a space-related collection of fiction and nonfiction books, comic books, and magazines at different reading levels and in different languages.

Adaptation of Content

The adaptation of content is a fifth indicator of quality preparation using the SIOP model of sheltered instruction. Grade-level texts and lectures are often difficult for CLD students to understand. However, using texts from lower grade levels and more simplified lectures does not provide CLD students with age- and grade-appropriate concepts and vocabulary. Therefore, in order to make grade-level texts and materials accessible to CLD students, teachers need to scaffold the content before, during, and after reading.

Adaptation of Content: In Practice Ms. Nygaard understands the importance of using grade-level text with her CLD students. However, she knows that the CLD students, as well as many native-English-speaking students, experience difficulty when trying to fully comprehend the grade-level texts. Therefore, Ms. Nygaard provides students with activities before, during, and after reading a text to help all her students better understand the key concepts. The following paragraph highlights some of these adaptations, and other accommodations appear in subsequent sections.

Ms. Nygaard knows that her CLD students can understand grade-level text better if she contextualizes information, so she decides to show a video about the planets in the solar system before the students read the grade-level text. Throughout the video, she frequently pauses the VCR and asks the students to describe the main ideas. Then she clarifies any misunderstandings and explains any unmentioned but important key concepts. In their learning logs, the students record what they are learning using the language they know best.

In the days after the video showing, the students read the text. They preview the text by looking at all the pictures and headings. Ms. Ramirez, a Spanish-speaking paraprofessional, also takes a few moments to preview the material in Spanish, the language spoken by the majority of the CLD students. As the class is previewing, the students share what they know about the topics and predict what the chapter will say. While the class then reads and discusses the English text, Ms. Nygaard and the students create a table that summarizes the characteristics of each planet. Ms. Nygaard consistently refers students to pictures, tables, and figures as well as the text while the students are gathering information and discerning main ideas. The students add the Planets of Our Solar System table (see Table 8.3) and their own additional insights to their learning logs.

Meaningful Activities

A sixth indicator of quality preparation involves incorporating meaningful activities. Meaningful activities that provide CLD students opportunities to read, write, listen, and speak promote their cognitive, linguistic, and academic development. Saunders, O'Brien, Lennon, and McLean (1999) found that when CLD students have many opportunities to use writing, speaking, and listening to help them work with information from text, they have a much greater understanding of the content

■ **table 8.3**   Planets of Our Solar System

Planet	Position Relative to the Sun	Diameter	Composition	Distinguishing Features	Temperature	Atmosphere
Mercury	Inner planet	4,880.0 km	Terrestrial	Craters and plains	90–700 K	Thin atmosphere; planet atoms
Venus	Inner planet	12,103.6 km	Terrestrial	Rolling plains	740 K	Dense atmosphere; carbon dioxide and sulfuric acid
Earth	Inner planet	12,756.3 km	Terrestrial	71% water	288–293 K	77% nitrogen and 21% oxygen
Mars	Inner planet	6,794.0 km	Terrestrial	Mountain, bulge, canyons, and crater	186–268 K	Thin atmosphere; carbon dioxide
Jupiter	Outer planet	142,984.0 km	Gas	Great Red Spot and small, faint rings	288–293 K	Hydrogen and helium
Saturn	Outer planet	120,536.0 km	Gas	2 distinct rings, 1 faint ring	134 K	Hydrogen and helium
Uranus	Outer planet	51,118.0 km	Gas	11 faint rings	76 K	Hydrogen and helium
Neptune	Outer planet	49,532.0 km	Gas	4 faint rings	73 K	Hydrogen and helium
Pluto	Outer planet	2,274.0 km	Unknown		38–63 K	Probably nitrogen

than if they had merely read the material. Proactive teachers incorporate all of the literacy domains when creating lesson plans that will enhance the linguistic capacities of CLD students. This allows students to communicate for real social and academic purposes.

Teachers can make activities meaningful for all students by first considering the levels of English proficiency represented in their classroom and then adapting assignments accordingly. For example, when creating writing assignments in which students practice writing persuasive, descriptive, chronological event, or compare/contrast paragraphs, effective teachers differentiate between the expectations they have for newcomer students and those they have for students with greater proficiency in English. Although the content remains the same, extra scaffolding, such as that illustrated in Figure 8.4, is provided to accommodate the needs of students who are still in the early stages of acquiring English language skills.

Meaningful Activities: In Practice   Ms. Nygaard structures the activities in her classes to create authentic opportunities for all students to use oral and written language to communicate for both social and academic purposes. A few examples include learning logs, a postcard activity that deals with the planets' characteristics, and a planet colony project. The learning logs give students a place to record their ideas, understandings, new vocabulary, and language structures. Such logs enhance students' capacities for metacognitive learning and encourage students to put their thoughts into words and use their languages for their own purposes and in their own ways. As the students learn about the planets, they are also encouraged to be creative and apply their new knowledge through the planet postcard activity. For this activity, the students create a postcard that describes what they see and their experiences as they "visit" each planet. Such postcards emphasize personal relevancy and provide opportunities for experiential and constructivist learning. As a final project, students work together in small groups to develop a colony on a planet of their choice. The only requirement is that their colony designs must provide the necessary accommodations to sustain human life.

Instruction

Once a teacher has completed preparation by deciding on content objectives, language objectives, content concepts, supplementary materials, adaptations, and meaningful activities, she or he determines how to deliver instruction to help all students meet the language and content objectives. The manner in which a teacher delivers instruction, the second critical aspect of the SIOP model, is guided by indicators that are grouped into the following six categories: building background, comprehensible input, strategies, interaction, practice and application, and lesson delivery (refer to Figure 8.3). SIOP lessons that include these categories of indicators provide the necessary support to promote academic success and language development for all students (Echevarria et al., 2000). These categories do not occur in any specific order. Rather, they are interwoven throughout a lesson.

Building Background

Effective instruction using the SIOP model of sheltered instruction accommodates both the differential learning needs of CLD students and the assets they bring to the classroom. One of the most overlooked of the five categories of accommodative instruction is building background. Building background is necessary for the instruction of CLD students for several reasons. First, CLD students' prior knowledge greatly affects their ability to understand new information. If CLD students have already been exposed to the concepts discussed in the text, their comprehension is much greater than if the concepts are completely unfamiliar (García, 1991; Jimenez, 1997). In addition, instruction that helps CLD students connect new

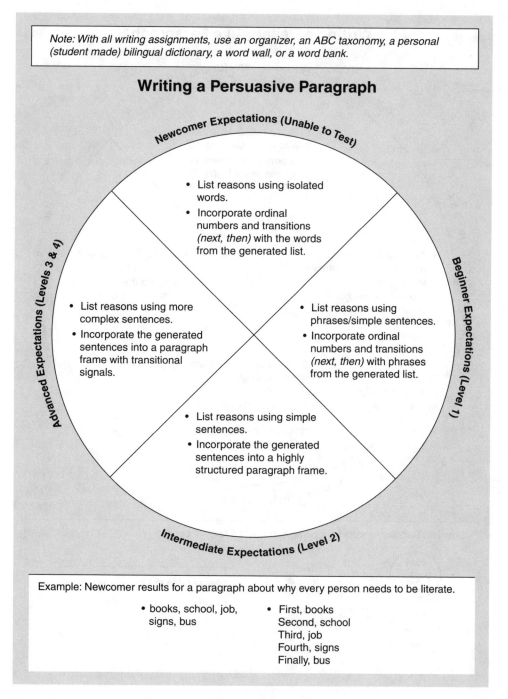

Note: With all writing assignments, use an organizer, an ABC taxonomy, a personal (student made) bilingual dictionary, a word wall, or a word bank.

Writing a Persuasive Paragraph

Newcomer Expectations (Unable to Test)

- List reasons using isolated words.
- Incorporate ordinal numbers and transitions *(next, then)* with the words from the generated list.

Beginner Expectations (Level 1)

- List reasons using phrases/simple sentences.
- Incorporate ordinal numbers and transitions *(next, then)* with phrases from the generated list.

Advanced Expectations (Levels 3 & 4)

- List reasons using more complex sentences.
- Incorporate the generated sentences into a paragraph frame with transitional signals.

Intermediate Expectations (Level 2)

- List reasons using simple sentences.
- Incorporate the generated sentences into a highly structured paragraph frame.

Example: Newcomer results for a paragraph about why every person needs to be literate.

- books, school, job, signs, bus

- First, books
  Second, school
  Third, job
  Fourth, signs
  Finally, bus

■ **figure 8.4**   Adapting Writing Assignments

(continued)

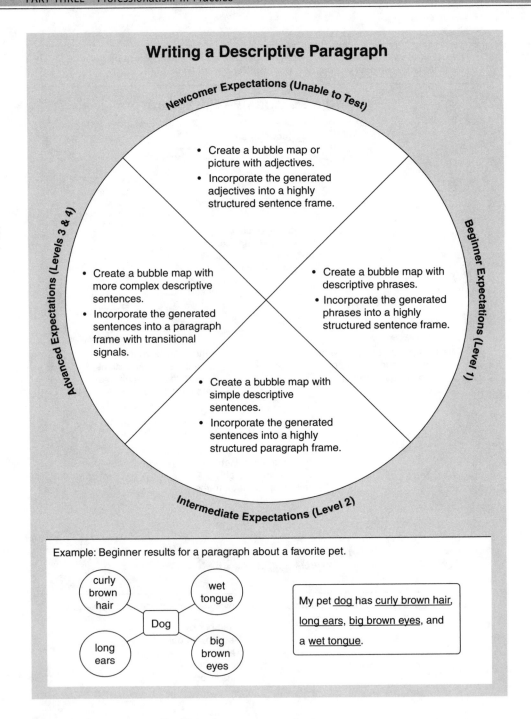

Writing a Descriptive Paragraph

Newcomer Expectations (Unable to Test)

- Create a bubble map or picture with adjectives.
- Incorporate the generated adjectives into a highly structured sentence frame.

Advanced Expectations (Levels 3 & 4)

- Create a bubble map with more complex descriptive sentences.
- Incorporate the generated sentences into a paragraph frame with transitional signals.

Beginner Expectations (Level 1)

- Create a bubble map with descriptive phrases.
- Incorporate the generated phrases into a highly structured sentence frame.

- Create a bubble map with simple descriptive sentences.
- Incorporate the generated sentences into a highly structured paragraph frame.

Intermediate Expectations (Level 2)

Example: Beginner results for a paragraph about a favorite pet.

curly brown hair   wet tongue   Dog   long ears   big brown eyes

My pet <u>dog</u> has <u>curly brown hair</u>, <u>long ears</u>, <u>big brown eyes</u>, and a <u>wet tongue</u>.

■ **f i g u r e   8 . 4**   Continued

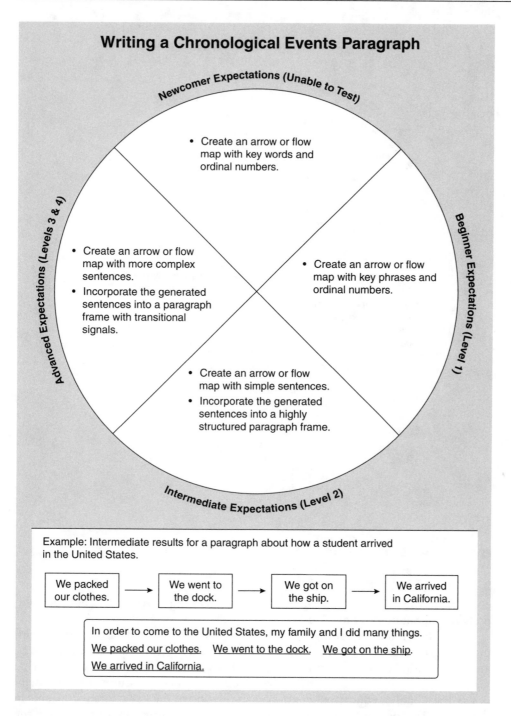

Writing a Chronological Events Paragraph

Newcomer Expectations (Unable to Test)

- Create an arrow or flow map with key words and ordinal numbers.

Beginner Expectations (Level 1)

- Create an arrow or flow map with key phrases and ordinal numbers.

Advanced Expectations (Levels 3 & 4)

- Create an arrow or flow map with more complex sentences.
- Incorporate the generated sentences into a paragraph frame with transitional signals.

Intermediate Expectations (Level 2)

- Create an arrow or flow map with simple sentences.
- Incorporate the generated sentences into a highly structured paragraph frame.

Example: Intermediate results for a paragraph about how a student arrived in the United States.

| We packed our clothes. | → | We went to the dock. | → | We got on the ship. | → | We arrived in California. |

In order to come to the United States, my family and I did many things. <u>We packed our clothes.</u> <u>We went to the dock.</u> <u>We got on the ship.</u> <u>We arrived in California.</u>

■ **figure 8.4** Continued

(continued)

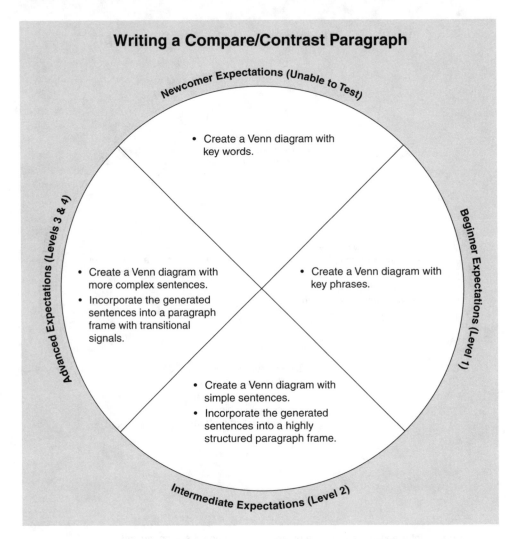

figure 8.4 Continued

concepts to their prior life and learning experiences improves their language comprehension (Saunders et al., 1999).

The SIOP model encourages teachers to consider three indicators when building background: students' life experiences, students' prior learning experiences, and key vocabulary (Echevarria et al., 2000). When building background during instruction, effective teachers always begin lessons by helping students evoke memories of personal or educational experiences relating to the key content concepts in the lesson. This points to the importance of the teacher's prior understanding of the students' experiential and learning backgrounds, which should be obtained

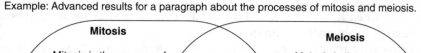

Example: Advanced results for a paragraph about the processes of mitosis and meiosis.

Mitosis

- Mitosis is the process of cell division.
- The four main phases each occurs once.
- Mitosis takes place in various types of animal cells.
- The result is two daughter cells.

- The process involves division.
- The four main phases are prophase, anaphase, metaphase, and telephase.

Meiosis

- Meiosis is the process of nuclear division.
- The four main phases each occurs twice.
- Meiosis only takes place in the sex cells of animals.
- The result is four daughter cells.

Mitosis and meiosis are each biological processes that <u>involve division</u> and <u>the four main phases of prophase, anaphase, metaphase, and telephase</u>. However, there are many differences that distinguish mitosis from meiosis. For example, mitosis <u>is the process of cell division</u>. <u>The four main phases each occurs once</u>. <u>Mitosis takes place in various types of animal cells</u>. <u>The result is two daughter cells</u>. In comparison, meiosis <u>is the process of nuclear division</u>. <u>The four main phases each occurs twice</u>. <u>Meiosis only takes place in the sex cells of animals</u>. <u>The result is four daughter cells</u>. Together, both processes enable species of animals to continue in existence.

■ **figure 8.4**   Continued

through preassessment (see Chapter 5). By encouraging students to tap into their prior experiences, teachers help them make connections between what they already know and what they are going to learn. These connections create a constructivist context for understanding new concepts. In addition, knowledge of students' backgrounds enables teachers to build into instruction the scaffolding that CLD students need to accomplish the lesson objectives (Echevarria et al., 2000). Consequently, including culturally familiar perspectives, materials, and themes as an integral part of the grade-level curriculum not only shows respect for and validation of different cultures and points of view but also promotes academic achievement for all students in culturally rich classrooms.

Key content vocabulary is another essential indicator of effectiveness in building background using the SIOP model. Emphasizing key vocabulary helps CLD students connect what they know to new words in the target language. Vocabulary knowledge is a crucial component of literacy development for CLD students (García, 1991; Perez, 2002). Furthermore, vocabulary knowledge forms a major component of cognitive academic language proficiency (Cummins, 2001a). Yet the sort of vocabulary development encouraged by the SIOP model is not the traditional instruction that often focuses on dictionary skills and the memorization of definitions. Rather, Echevarria et al. (2000) advocate for a more meaning-based set of vocabulary development techniques.

Students acquire new words best when they encounter words several times in meaningful contexts (Stahl & Fairbanks, 1986). For example, although it is important for CLD students to see the specific words in the text as they appear, it is also helpful if they can hear the words in a paraphrased sentence or have the words explained to them through synonyms or antonyms. Concept definition maps, similar to the one depicted in Figure 8.5, and cloze sentences, like those shown in Figure 8.6, are examples of other tools that teachers can use to provide students with additional contexts through which they can develop their understanding of key vocabulary terms. CLD students also benefit from instruction that teaches them to consider cognates in discerning the meaning of unfamiliar words (Hancin-Bhatt & Nagy, 1994; Jimenez, 1997; Jimenez, García, & Pearson, 1996). Figure 8.7 provides examples of cognates related to cell biology.

■ **figure 8.5** Civil War
Concept Definition Map

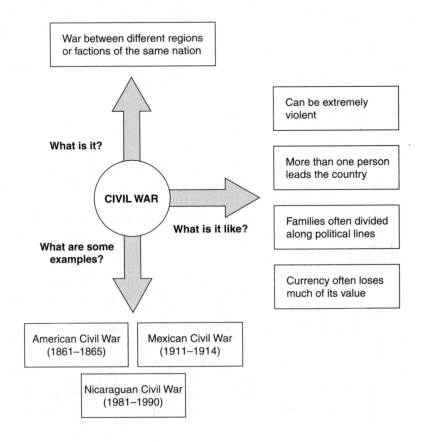

During a _____, two or more individuals attempt to lead the people of a country. *(civil war)*

■ **figure 8.6** Civil War Cloze Sentences

In times of civil war, the possession of natural resources such as gold and silver are extremely important because the _____ of a country often becomes worthless. *(currency)*

Those who are displeased with the actions of their government and decide to fight against the nation's leaders are often referred to as _____. *(rebels)*

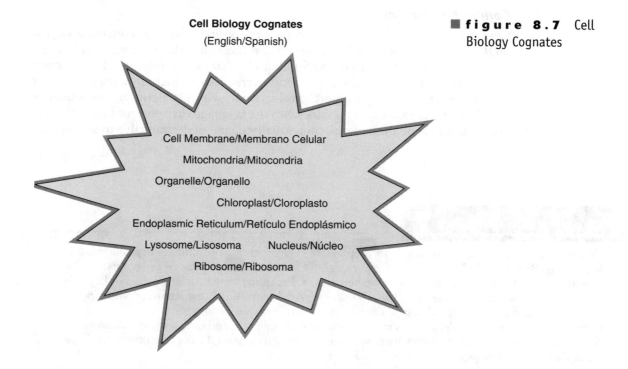

Cell Biology Cognates

(English/Spanish)

Cell Membrane/Membrano Celular

Mitochondria/Mitocondria

Organelle/Organello

Chloroplast/Cloroplasto

Endoplasmic Reticulum/Retículo Endoplásmico

Lysosome/Lisosoma   Nucleus/Núcleo

Ribosome/Ribosoma

■ **figure 8.7** Cell Biology Cognates

Building Background: In Practice Throughout her lessons, Ms. Nygaard incorporates the SIOP indicators that are pertinent to building background. She helps her students connect what they are learning to their life experiences and what they already know. She also emphasizes key vocabulary. One activity she often uses with her students is a picture preview. When starting a unit or beginning to read a new text, she displays a picture that is related to the main content concepts that will be covered. For instance, in the solar system unit she displays a diagram of the solar system.

When creating the pictures, Ms. Nygaard often copies and pastes pictures from the Internet into a word-processing document. Then she prints the picture on an overhead transparency. Each student writes about the picture in his or her most meaningful language. She encourages the students to write what they know about the topic, what the picture reminds them of, and a personal experience related to the picture. Then the students get into collaborative groups and label copies of the picture with the English vocabulary words they think might relate to the unit. Finally, the groups share their words with the class as Ms. Nygaard records them on the transparency. During the discussion, she elicits any critical vocabulary words the students do not mention and she stretches students to explain how the words relate to the topic.

Comprehensible Input

Comprehensible input is a second category of accommodative instruction using the SIOP variation of sheltered instruction. Providing comprehensible input to learners is one of the many features of the SIOP model that distinguishes SIOP instruction from instruction one would see in a nonsheltered lesson taught by a master teacher (Echevarria et al., 2000). Comprehensible input, which is a critical component of second language instruction, occurs when the language environment makes the second language more meaningful, contextualized, and understandable to second lan-

theory *into Practice*

Sheltered instruction traces its origin to Stephen Krashen's (1985) input hypothesis *i + 1*. Krashen argues that language is acquired in a developmental sequence when students receive abundant comprehensible input. When messages that contain new information are comprehensible, learners move a little beyond their current level of competence. Krashen states that when students are given comprehensible input they move from their actual development level *(i)* to their next level of development *(+1)*. The input hypothesis is often called the *i + 1* theory.

Academic content often tends to become more abstract and complex for CLD students in the higher grade levels. Therefore, it is even more crucial to provide adaptations such as:

• Previewing key content vocabulary in the first and second languages.

• Highlighting or outlining key concepts.
• Gesturing to emphasize key points.
• Providing time for clarification of key concepts in the first language with a peer or paraprofessional.
• Simplifying and modifying the academic language used during instruction.

■ *What does this imply for secondary educators who wish to create an effective classroom climate that bolsters the CLD student's capacity for i + 1? In what other ways can teachers enhance the comprehensibility of their instruction? How can elementary teachers create a classroom environment that is responsive to the academic needs of CLD students?*

guage learners (Cummins, 2001b; Krashen, 1991). For example, a person who does not speak Spanish may not understand the phrase *En sus libros de ciencia, vayan a la pagina cuarenta y dos.* However, if the person speaking the phrase picks up a science book, turns to page 42, shows the class page 42 while pointing to the number on the page, and then praises students who are opening their science books and turning to page 42, the non-Spanish speaker may have received sufficient comprehensible input to understand what the person was saying in Spanish.

The comprehensible input category of the SIOP model consists of the following three indicators of accommodative instruction: appropriate speech, techniques to clarify content concepts, and clear explanations of academic tasks. Teachers provide comprehensible input to CLD students by modifying their speech through guarded vocabulary and supporting the meaning of what they are saying by using nonverbal cues. When modifying their speech, SIOP teachers speak naturally, but they enunciate their words, simplify sentence structure, speak a little more slowly, emphasize key information, and pause momentarily between sentences or main ideas to provide CLD students time to create meaning.

In order for language development to occur in an English language environment, CLD students need enough contextual cues to make the language meaningful (Cummins, 2001a). Therefore, as they are discussing content concepts, SIOP teachers use gestures, pictures, objects, role playing, video clips, modeling, manipulatives, and demonstrations to help CLD students understand what they are saying (Echevarria et al., 2000).

Effective teachers communicate to CLD students exactly what they need to do to accomplish academic tasks. This explanation of academic tasks to be accomplished might take the form of modeling procedures or posting checklists in simple English or pictures. However, even when using techniques for providing comprehensible input, effective SIOP teachers frequently check for student understanding (Echevarria et al., 2000).

Comprehensible Input: In Practice Ms. Nygaard uses many nonverbal cues to support language use in her classroom. As previously described, she uses pictorial word walls, pictures, displays, graphic organizers, and videos. In this lesson, she is also using realia and demonstrations to support the meaning of text as she reads the grade-level text with her students. For example, as the students talk about the dryness of Mars (dried lakebeds, dry hydrothermal spring), they can examine labeled boxes of dry and wet sand. The students also have a labeled box of rocks they can refer to as they talk about Mars' rocky terrain. As they read through the text, Ms. Nygaard points out key features (such as craters) using overhead projector transparencies that display labeled pictures of Mars.

Then, after the students discuss the meanings of *rotation, orbit, day,* and *year,* the class goes out into the hallway and the students have a chance to "practice" the words with their bodies. In this role-play, one student is the sun and another student is a planet. The planet student orbits the sun when Ms. Nygaard says "orbit" and rotates when Ms. Nygaard says "rotate." They act out the words *year* and *day* in the same manner.

Strategies

As depicted in Figure 8.3, strategies is a third category of accommodative instruction using the SIOP variation of sheltered instruction. Attention to the following indicators is necessary to achieve instruction that effectively incorporates this category: opportunities for students to use strategies, use of a variety of question types (especially those that promote higher-order thinking skills), and scaffolding techniques. If CLD students are to develop CALP in the second language, the comprehensible input that teachers provide must move students beyond surface-level comprehension of words to form a deep understanding and knowledge base (Cummins, 2001a). However, while teachers can help students understand language and content by providing comprehensible input, students can learn to take a more active role in constructing their own meaning through opportunities to use, practice, and develop learning strategies.

In addition to explicitly teaching CLD students to apply learning strategies toward the construction of meaning, teachers can promote the cognitive development of CLD students through the ways in which they structure lessons. When teachers ask questions that provoke higher-order thinking and provide students with the scaffolding (support) they need to answer the questions, the students are able to develop conceptual understandings at a much more cognitively complex level (Echevarria et al., 2000). Asking a variety of questions, including those designed to provoke higher-order thinking, is a critical feature of accommodative instruction using the SIOP model. Some teachers believe that CLD students are incapable of higher-order thinking in English. Lessons that simply focus on learning basic English often deny CLD students the opportunity to obtain the cognitively rich curriculum they need (Echevarria et al., 2000). Rather than focusing primarily on lower-level thinking skills, such as repeating memorized facts, CLD students need to be able to practice comprehension, application, analysis, synthesis, and evaluation of new information (Bloom, 1956; Diaz-Rico & Weed, 2002).

Nonetheless, teachers cannot expect students to venture into higher-order thinking about new material unless the instruction regarding that material is appropriately scaffolded. The SIOP model uses both verbal and procedural scaffolding to support students as they attempt higher-order thinking. During verbal scaffolding, SIOP teachers orally guide students through the thought processes necessary to apply higher-order thinking to new concepts and information. A teacher first presents a problem to the students. Then she or he thinks aloud to demonstrate how to solve the problem. In effect, a teacher verbally opens up his or her brain so that students can "see" how an expert learner would approach the task. The teacher describes how he or she would approach the problem and verbalizes the internal dialogue running through his or her mind while solving the problem.

Procedural scaffolding involves organizing instruction so that lessons within a unit build on one another and become increasingly complex at the cognitive level. Effective teachers organize lessons to progress from presenting a new content concept to modeling its actual application. The next critical step is to provide students with guided practice in applying the new information. Finally, after students have received the instructional support they need to feel more confident about their understanding of new material and its practical application, effective SIOP teachers provide students opportunities to apply the new concept independently (Echevarria et al., 2000).

Strategies: In Practice   Ms. Nygaard knows that proficient readers make predictions about content and meaning before and during reading (Clay, 1991; Fountas & Pinnell, 1996). Therefore, she explains to her class the importance of making predictions. She prompts the students to think of a mystery or suspense television show or movie they have watched. She instructs the students to discuss with a partner the story line and how they tried to guess what was going to happen next. Each pair then shares some examples with the class.

Ms. Nygaard continues by explaining to the students that good readers collect "clues" from what they are reading and what they know in order to make good predictions about the reading material. She displays a transparency copy of the grade-level science text on the overhead projector. Ms. Nygaard begins by pointing out some of the pictures and words in bold print. Guiding them to make connections between contextual clues and predictions, she asks the students what they think the topic might be. The students then list these clues in their learning logs. Ms. Nygaard further prompts the students to offer suggestions of other clues from the text that are found in diagrams, tables, and section headings. The students discuss and record these clues.

Next, using their clues as evidence, the students predict what the text might say. Ms. Nygaard explains to the students that good detectives add to or change their ideas when they collect new clues. Therefore, as they read along in their texts, students add new clues and revise their predictions. After this activity, Ms. Nygaard debriefs the students on how and why they used the strategy, and the students discuss what effect it had on their understanding. After practicing this prediction strategy several times as a class over several days, the students practice the strategy in small groups, and eventually they are able to use the strategy independently.

Interaction

Accommodative, SIOP-based instruction for CLD students also involves the category of interaction. Any good teacher knows that students cannot learn what they do not practice. Therefore, if students are going to develop CALP in a second language, they must have frequent opportunities to practice language use in academic settings (Thomas & Collier, 2002). Social interaction will help students develop social language, but this use of language does little to promote a student's language development for cognitive and academic purposes. In a SIOP lesson, instruction should minimize teacher-centered lecturing and maximize student interaction with teachers and other students (Echevarria et al., 2000). The interaction category of the SIOP model incorporates the following four indicators of effective instruction: discussion and in-depth responses about concepts, sufficient response wait time, appropriate grouping configurations, and clarification of lesson material in L1.

Sometimes when students are not proficient in English, they respond to discussions with brief answers. SIOP teachers become skilled at asking probing follow-up questions that require CLD students to elaborate on their responses. Teachers use this opportunity to ask questions that push CLD students into higher-order thinking. By using prompts similar to the following examples, teachers ask the students to explain their answers: *Tell me more about . . . ; Why do you think . . . ; What connections can you make between . . . ; How does X relate to what you know . . . ; How would you change . . . ; What if . . . ; What would you recommend . . .* Having students elaborate on their answers guides them to use more complex thought processes as well as complex language structures and vocabulary (Echevarria et al., 2000). However, when teachers ask students to respond to questions, especially higher-order thinking questions, it is imperative that teachers allow students sufficient time to process the question, think about the concept or issue, and develop a response.

When students work in collaborative groups, teachers have the perfect opportunity to walk around the classroom, discuss projects with small groups of students, and challenge the students' understandings of the key content concepts. Small groups provide CLD students with a safe context in which to stretch a bit beyond their comfort level of comprehension and language usage toward their potential level, which is characterized by a deep conceptual understanding of the material and more advanced language proficiency (Vygotsky, 1978). In arranging collaborative groups for lessons, teachers need to consider the grouping configurations that will best match the content and language objectives of a lesson and the characteristics of the students. For example, effective teachers consider the ability of students to work independently with the new content and language concepts. If the students are beginning a unit, they may need a lot of support, so whole-class or small-group instruction might be most appropriate. If the students have some proficiency with the content and language, they may need less support. In such situations, a teacher might consider having students work with a partner or independently (Echevarria et al., 2000).

Grouping students by first language is another consideration. When beginning a unit, a teacher might consider putting students in same-language groups so that the CLD students can work in their first language when making connections between prior knowledge and key content concepts. CLD students need to be able to use the native language, even in school settings where English is the primary language of instruction. Students who have the opportunity to use their first language to discuss second language text have greater second language reading comprehension than students who do not make use of their first languages to help create meaning (García, 1998; Jimenez, 1997; Jimenez et al., 1996; Saunders et al., 1999).

Additionally, CLD students need opportunities to use English to negotiate meaning and solve complex problems so that they can develop their CALP in English (Cummins, 2001a). Therefore, as students progress through a unit and acquire new language structures, vocabulary, and critical content understandings, it is essential that they practice delving into more cognitively complex tasks using English. In this case, mixed-language groups encourage students to use English to solve problems together.

Teachers might also consider second language proficiency when grouping students. However, it is important to keep in mind that while grouping students by second language proficiency can be useful for some lessons, students generally benefit more from participating in mixed language proficiency groups. When students are grouped, or tracked, by proficiency level for extended periods of time, teachers tend to hold students with less English language proficiency to lower expectations. As a result, these students are more likely to participate in a cognitively, linguistically, and academically poor curriculum (Thomas & Collier, 2002). Heterogeneous grouping is beneficial to all students. More proficient students can serve as good linguistic models and give less proficient students the comprehensible input they need to understand difficult concepts. Questions posed by less proficient students can challenge more proficient students to clarify their understandings of content and language concepts.

Interaction: In Practice   Ms. Nygaard uses student collaborative groups throughout her lessons. The group work activities provide students with opportunities to interact in a constructivist environment and enable her to provide more individualized attention to her students. The students' cumulative project, in which they create a colony on a planet, is a good example of how she facilitates student interaction in her classroom. Ms. Nygaard arranges the groups so that language groups are mixed. She wants students to use English to negotiate meaning, but she pairs CLD students together who speak the same native language (a less English proficient student with a more English proficient student) to encourage more project participation by students who are less English proficient. In this way, the more English proficient student can clarify information and concepts for the less English proficient peer, if necessary.

In these groups, students ask and answer questions, assemble key information, and bring together their different ideas to come to consensus. Through such interaction, the students' use of dialogue goes far beyond a BICS level. While the students work together to design their colonies, Ms. Nygaard circulates from group to group. She challenges the students' thinking by questioning *why* and *what if*. She tries to guide students to revise their own understandings rather than simply telling them the "right" answer. She wants her students to think for themselves and develop their own solutions.

Practice and Application

As illustrated in Figure 8.3, a fifth category of accommodative instruction using the SIOP variation of the sheltered instruction method is practice and application. In order for CLD students to internalize new concepts and language with the deep understanding necessary for the development of CALP, instruction needs to incorporate the following three indicators of this category: hands-on materials and manipulatives, activities requiring students to apply knowledge of content and language, and activities that use all domains of language. It is essential that CLD students be active participants in real uses of language and content concepts (Cummins, 2001a; Echevarria et al., 2000). To be actively involved in instruction, students can conduct experiments, create models, role-play historical and literary events, take action on social issues, write bilingual books, and more.

As previously discussed, students' learning is enhanced if new information and concepts are relevant to them. It is through the physical and mental manipulation of information that students are able to make the content material pertinent to their personal lives. Students who are passive learners (listening to a teacher or reading a text as a primary source of information) rather than active learners (manipulating information to create personal meaning) may not have sufficient opportunity to create deep personal meaning with new content and language concepts. Knowing about a subject such as polynomials or prejudice is not sufficient; students must come to think and communicate like a mathematician or a social scientist if they are going to become proficient in a particular subject domain such as math or science (Costa & Liebmann, 1997).

Additionally, CLD students must extensively practice the use of academic language (reading, writing, speaking, and listening) in academic contexts if they are to acquire the ability to use English as a tool for learning. The four literacy domains (listening, speaking, reading, and writing) are interdependent—development in one area facilitates development in another (Genesee, 1999). For example, CLD students who have opportunities for in-depth discussion with teachers and peers concerning text they have read in English have greater reading comprehension skills than students who do not have as many opportunities to discuss readings (Saunders et al., 1999). Furthermore, students who read extensively have much better writing and grammar usage skills than those students who do not (Alexander, 1986; Elly, 1991; Nagy, Herman, & Anderson, 1985; Polak & Krashen, 1988). Because academic language is more cognitively and structurally complex than social language, students will only develop high levels of second language proficiency if they engage in language use for academic purposes (Cummins, 1991, 2001b; Thomas & Collier, 2002).

Practice and Application: In Practice Ms. Nygaard uses the cumulative project, in which the students design their own colonies, to help her students practice and apply the language and content concepts from the solar system unit. The students synthesize and analyze what they have learned about the characteristics of a planet and the unique characteristics of Earth that have allowed for the creation and sustenance of life. Then they apply that information to create an inhabitable colony on another planet. This activity affords students the opportunity to integrate their voices into the content. It also pushes them to understand the material and its implications on a much deeper level than that achieved when students are merely required to regurgitate information back to their teacher on a test.

Lesson Delivery

Lesson delivery is a sixth category of accommodative instruction grounded in the SIOP model of sheltered instruction. This category emphasizes that teachers incorporate the following four indicators into their lessons: support of content objectives, support of language objectives, appropriate engagement of students, and appropriate pacing. The lesson delivery category of the SIOP model is designed to help teachers examine whether they have actually met content and language objectives, evaluate the effectiveness of the lesson in actively engaging students, and determine if the pacing of the lesson matched the students' academic and language proficiency levels.

Effective SIOP teachers explicitly state and display a lesson's content and language objectives so that all students know the purpose of a lesson, the key ideas they need to learn, and the tasks they need to be able to accomplish with the information (Echevarria et al., 2000). Explicit knowledge of lesson objectives helps both teachers and students assess how the students are progressing throughout the lesson toward meeting the objectives. Displayed objectives also serve as a tool with which students can refocus on the content concepts if their attention momentarily drifts away from the lesson.

In order to maximize the time students spend on task, proactive teachers deliver lessons in a manner that keeps students actively engaged. SIOP lessons with well-developed opportunities for interaction and hands-on activities encourage students to be actively engaged in instruction. Teachers must be careful to ensure that student engagement is centered on activities that help students meet content and language objectives. Activities that do not align with lesson objectives but engage students simply because they are fun should not be a part of a SIOP lesson (Echevarria et al., 2000).

Finally, teachers should make sure that the pacing of a lesson accommodates students' prior knowledge bases and content or language proficiencies. Prior knowledge development activities can serve as a preassessment from which teachers can gather information about students' areas of strength and inexperience concerning a particular topic for study. Effective teachers use this information to develop appropriate pacing for lessons. Such teachers realize that students will be at various levels of preparedness to engage in a new topic. Therefore, these teachers use scaffolding to help bridge the gap between students who have more experience and students who have less experience with the lesson topic (Echevarria et al., 2000). SIOP teachers frequently check for student understanding and revise the pace of their lessons accordingly. They use collaborative student learning time to provide individual students the support they need.

Lesson Delivery: In Practice   Ms. Nygaard knows that a good lesson plan means nothing if the actual implementation fails to respond to the needs of the students. Consequently, she begins every lesson by reading through the content and language objectives, which she has written on poster board with brightly colored markers. Throughout the lessons and units, she constantly reflects on whether the students are actively engaged in the learning process and in making progress toward attaining the objectives. Ms. Nygaard subsequently adjusts her instruction to go into more or less detail and to emphasize areas of concern. When the class finishes an activity, she prompts the students to share various ways in which they feel the activity has helped them create stronger understandings of the content concepts.

Review and Assessment

Review and assessment is an aspect of professional practice that is essential to the effectiveness of any method used with CLD students, and accordingly it is a third critical aspect of the SIOP variation of the sheltered instruction method (see Figure 8.3). Echevarria et al. (2000) combine notions of review and assessment because they believe that teaching, reviewing, providing feedback to students, and assessing should be a cycle that runs throughout a SIOP lesson. In considering review and assessment, SIOP teachers make sure they incorporate the following four indicators in the lesson: review of key vocabulary, review of content concepts, ongoing feedback to students regarding language production and the application of new content concepts, and formal and informal assessment of student progress toward attaining content and language objectives. Then they use the information they gather from the review and assessment cycle to revise lesson plans to ensure that students meet content and language objectives.

Review and Assessment: In Practice

Ms. Nygaard provides her students with positive feedback throughout the lesson. She knows that her students desire her approval and want to succeed. Therefore, she tries to monitor the ways she reacts to her students' responses to review questions. In addition to clarifying concepts and explaining misunderstandings, Ms. Nygaard emphasizes the correct aspects of answers. She also models correct language usage by rephrasing the students' responses as she incorporates them into her verbal feedback.

As mentioned earlier, Ms. Nygaard encourages her students to make extensive use of learning logs. In these logs, the students write for themselves. They record their ongoing development of understanding regarding key concepts and language. Students use these learning logs to reflect on and assess their own learning. They determine how they are progressing and what they still need to master. Ms. Nygaard also reviews her students' learning logs to gain a better understanding of where the students are in their language and concept development. Using the learning logs helps her make better instructional decisions when revising her lesson plans in response to her students' progress.

During the five minutes she specifically sets aside for review at the end of each lesson, Ms. Nygaard asks a few students to summarize what the class has learned about specific content concepts. She then encourages students to share any discoveries they made during the lesson that were particularly intriguing or surprising. Additionally, she prompts students to discuss any ways in which they will use what they learned in their daily lives.

Closing Thoughts on the SIOP Model of Sheltered Instruction

Recently, Echevarria et al. (2002) developed SIOP institutes and modules for school educators. These modules emphasize implementation of SIOP as an eight-component model for sheltered instruction, involving the following components:

- Preparation
- Building background
- Comprehensible input
- Strategies
- Interaction
- Practice and application
- Lesson delivery
- Review and assessment

Therefore, the SIOP variation of the sheltered instruction method can be understood as composed of three critical aspects or eight components, according to the structure depicted in Figure 8.8. Regardless of whether teachers implement SIOP emphasizing its three critical aspects or its eight components, the model provides educators a rigorous and field-tested framework for sheltered instruction that appropriately accommodates the differential learning needs of CLD students. Teachers can then evaluate the effectiveness of their implementation of SIOP using the thirty indicators of the model's protocol (Echevarria et al., 2000). Each of the thirty indicators is specified as a bullet in Figure 8.3.

Through their use of the sheltered instruction observation protocol variation of the sheltered instruction method, effective teachers are able to enhance the success of CLD students. Such teachers use the indicators of the SIOP model to focus on the key elements of lesson preparation, instruction, and review and assessment that help CLD students develop both their academic and language skills. SIOP teachers provide all students with an affirming environment in which they can share their individual talents and cultures and work together to create new knowledge.

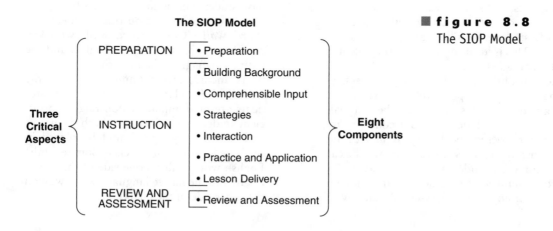

figure 8.8
The SIOP Model

tips for practice

Note: The following tips for practice are provided according to each of the eight components of the sheltered instruction observation protocol. Most tips listed are applicable to either elementary or secondary educators.

Preparation

1. In order to both familiarize CLD students with and maintain a focus on the relevancy of the content and language objectives of a lesson:
   - Ensure that content and language objectives are written or posted in a location easily visible to students. Ask students to volunteer to read the objectives aloud.
   - Use language that clarifies and simplifies the objectives that may be difficult for students to understand. For example, explain to students that *compare and contrast* means to discuss ways in which ideas or items are alike and different.

2. Select content-area concepts that are at the appropriate academic grade-level for students. It is important to continually challenge CLD students with grade-level content material. Adaptations to text for multiple learning styles can result in a more thorough understanding of content concepts. Content can be adapted to meet the varying student levels of language proficiency in the following ways:
   - Before presenting a concept or lesson from the textbook, highlight the key vocabulary, concepts, and summary statements.
   - Tape-record key portions or entire texts for CLD students to follow along with as they read. This is ideal for use at learning centers at any grade level.
   - Rewrite difficult text by looking for passages that are the most powerful in conveying the main ideas. That is, summarize the text making sure to include important concepts and content-specific vocabulary in shorter, linguistically simpler sentences that will be easier for CLD students to comprehend. The exact number of sentences used is not important; however, it is essential that key in-formation is retained and content is not watered down.
   - Create study guides that are modified for the language proficiencies of CLD students. These study guides might include questions, important statements, and summaries of the text. Also, adapt exercises and activities related to the lesson according to the varying language proficiencies among students. For example, ask more language proficient CLD students to write a short, three-paragraph essay on a key concept. Modify the same activity even further for less language proficient CLD students by asking them to list words or create five sentences that describe the concept.

3. Provide supplementary materials and activities to help students better comprehend new concepts, make clearer connections with the content, and learn new vocabulary related to a lesson. Educators may find the following tools effective:
   - *Graphic Organizers:* Before reading content text, prepare a graphic organizer for CLD students (e.g., T-charts, Venn diagrams, time lines).
   - *Hands-On Manipulatives and Realia:* Provide real-life objects that help students make connections from content concepts to their own experiences. For example, when studying a unit on nutrition, bring in food labels or have students bring in food labels from their own homes to analyze nutrition content.
   - *Word Walls:* Create word walls with key content vocabulary in both English and the native language of the majority of CLD students. Include pictures and symbols on the word wall for clarification. If the CLD students are predominantly non-English proficient students, word walls in both the native and second language should be placed in separate locations of the classroom (e.g., the English word wall on one side of the chalkboard and the native language word wall on the other side of the chalkboard).

Building Background

1. Create meaningful connections between the existing knowledge and personal experiences of CLD students and the content concepts to be taught. Foster the relevant connections through:

   - *Picture Walks:* Before reading a content-specific text, "walk" the students through the reading selection by skimming through the text and looking at visuals provided. The visuals highlighted might include time lines, pictures, graphs, and more. Additionally, encourage students to take note of boldface vocabulary words found along this "walk" in order to familiarize and introduce them to content-specific vocabulary.

   - *Picture Prompts:* Use "picture prompts" to help students connect prior knowledge to what they are studying. For example, when teaching the concept of a "democracy," you might begin a lesson by showing a picture of the Statue of Liberty as well as international icons representing freedom that are relevant to your students' cultural backgrounds. Examples from other countries include the India Gate/Red Fort in India and the Dove in Mexico. Give students five minutes to write what they know about the pictures or what thoughts the pictures prompt. More linguistically proficient students can write sentences or even a paragraph. Those new to the second language can write words related to the picture that they know in English. Have a class discussion about what the students wrote. Call on some of the less proficient students first to make sure they have a chance to share.

   - *ABC Taxonomy:* This provides vocabulary development in the first and second languages and is also a tool that can be used for assessing the prior knowledge that CLD students bring to the classroom. Supply CLD students with a piece of paper that has the alphabet listed letter by letter down the left-hand column. In collaborative groups, round-robin style, students will brainstorm words related to the current topic using each letter of the alphabet. Encourage students to generate at least one word for each letter of the alphabet. For example, when studying the theme of transportation, CLD students might begin their lists with A = airplane, automobile, *autobus;* B = boat, bus, *barco;* C = car, carriage, *carro, coche,* etc. As an ongoing process, students can constantly add words to the master class list.

   - Ask CLD students to list five things they know about the theme or concept of focus. Students not quite proficient in English may write in the native language or draw pictures related to the topic (use paraprofessionals or parent volunteers as translators).

Comprehensible Input

1. Modify speech patterns and language use to accommodate the proficiency levels of CLD students and provide clarity of content through the following:

   - Speak clearly and slowly using plenty of gestures. Avoid unnecessary jargon or idioms that may cause confusion.

   - Paraphrase and repeat key concepts.

   - Use cognates to help students make connections between their native language and English. This is most effective when used for the Romance languages such as Spanish, French, Italian, and Portuguese.

2. Academic tasks can be further clarified for CLD students when the following techniques are used:

   - Create personalized vocabulary notebooks for each content class. The notebooks will include new content words related to the unit currently being studied. The words selected by the student may be written in the native language as well as in English. These resource "dictionaries" can be in any chosen format that is conducive to knowledge construction.

   - Present and model instructions in a clear, step-by-step manner using a visual to guide students through the process. For example, a simple outline on the board that lists step 1, step 2, and step 3 procedures can be a predictable "life saver" for the CLD student (such activities also enhance procedural knowledge).

   - Ask a student volunteer to summarize instructions in his or her own words and perhaps in the native language of your CLD students.

- Encourage proficient CLD speakers to clarify directions for those CLD students who are not as proficient in the second language.

3. Use a variety of scaffolding techniques for clarifying concepts. Such scaffolding will enable teachers to check for student understanding and should gradually move students from teacher dependence to independence in learning. For example:
   - Rather than correcting student errors as the student speaks, model the correct way to say something by paraphrasing what the student has said using appropriate English. For example, when Gina says, "Spider, ants, and flies is all insects," reply with, "Yes, you're right. Spiders, ants, and flies are all insects."
   - During explanation or reading, restate, emphasize, or explain terms that may be unfamiliar or difficult for CLD students (e.g., "After these three difficult days, the family was famished—extremely hungry or starving—and knew they could not carry on like this much longer.").

Strategies

1. Provide general guidance in the use of learning strategies to help CLD students understand, study, and retain information. These strategies become the tools that students can continually use to become independent, active learners. The following suggestions may help CLD students attain this goal:
   - *Think-Alouds:* Model think-alouds to help students understand the processes you use to better understand content concepts. Encourage students to exercise the same think-alouds as they practice different learning strategies.
   - *Questioning:* Provide questions that target higher levels of thinking while still simplifying language. For example, instead of asking, "Do we depend on rain forests for our survival?" ask a higher-level question such as, "Why are we dependent on the rain forest for survival on Earth?"
   - *Word Sorts:* Have students categorize words according to meaning, structure, word endings, or sounds. For example, students can make a list of all words from a unit ending in

"ion" (e.g., *revolution, taxation, solution*) or "sion" (e.g., *tension, mission, vision*).
   - *Directed Reading–Thinking Activities:* Before CLD students read a text, ask them to predict what will happen. Stop periodically to ask for confirmation, revisions, or additional predictions as the class reads the text orally or silently in pairs or as a group. For example, Ms. Brooks is reading *The Little Prince* (de Saint-Exupéry, 2000) with her seventh-grade students. As they read, she stops to ask, "What do you think will happen next? Why? What clues are provided to help you figure this out?"

Interaction

1. Keep in mind the following when pairing CLD students or forming groups for successful collaborative interaction:
   - The linguistic and academic abilities of each student within each group
   - The content and language objectives of the current lesson
   - Particular personality conflicts that may arise
   - The advantages to be gained by maximizing more academically and linguistically capable peers
2. The following tips may be helpful for beneficial interaction among CLD students:
   - If possible, occasionally group CLD students with the same native languages. A group peer can clarify new concepts as well as relate prior knowledge in the first language to the current topic introduced in the second language.
   - Frequently, group students of mixed language proficiencies. Structure activities to encourage more proficient peers to help peers new to the second language understand concepts and learn new vocabulary. For instance, ask students to read a text and generate ten key sentences as a collaborative group using a write-around, which is writing in a round-robin style with everyone taking a turn. The more proficient students will provide clarification of needed information such as directions, concepts, and writing in the first language for CLD students new to the second language.

- Use a variety of strategies to group students. The duration of the groups can be decided by the teacher (e.g., weekly, bimonthly, semester; by thematic unit).
- Regulate and vary wait time as needed for CLD students to process questions and formulate answers according to their levels of second language proficiency.

Practice and Application

1. CLD students need to consistently practice and apply the interdependent literacy domains of listening, speaking, reading, and writing throughout the day. In this way, they will become more independent thinkers and learners, and the acquisition of knowledge and language will occur more successfully. Implement the following to effectively encourage practice and application for the acquisition of knowledge and language:
   - Provide CLD students with a fill-in-the-blank note outline that is partially completed. This is a cloze activity in which vocabulary is taught in context by leaving out the key term of a sentence and having students fill it in. This will help students take notes as a lesson progresses.
   - Structure writing activities that focus on format by creating passages like the following: I believe that a good friend must have three important qualities. First, _____. Second, _____. Finally, _____. If a person does not have these three qualities, he or she may not be a good friend.
   - Read aloud to your students or have your students read aloud in pairs. Then have them write about or answer questions from what they heard. Post the questions to be asked on the board or an overhead so that all students can refer to them as they read. The questions should include those that promote higher-order thinking skills as well as basic knowledge. Students may also be tape-recorded as they read so they can listen to it later. For example, students could read about rain forests on the web and record their findings on a graphic organizer to share with group members orally. Then they could listen and

compare and contrast their input and the information that other group members have found. Be aware of the language proficiencies of CLD students in their ability to understand what is being read orally, as well as of those asked to read; be careful not to force non-English proficient students into producing language before they are ready. Find more comfortable ways for them to express the information requested.
- Have students design and create their own trade books in order to demonstrate mastery of key concepts and content vocabulary. They can share their books aloud in pairs, in groups, or with the entire class.
- Ask CLD students to explain a process to a peer in their cooperative learning group using newly learned vocabulary. Keep in mind the language proficiencies represented, as CLD students who are not yet highly proficient in L2 (English) may need to explain concepts in the native language.

Lesson Delivery

1. To support content and language objectives during the lesson, adapt the pace of the lesson according to the ability levels of the CLD students, and engage students for the majority of the time (90 to 100 percent):
   - Use a variety of activities such as games, discovery learning, and inquiry tasks.
   - Consistently use and practice the academic vocabulary throughout the class period or school day. This will help link it to real-life experiences and also help CLD students become familiar with and comfortable using the vocabulary.
   - Create engaging and meaningful activities for students that are directly related to the language and content objectives of the lesson. For example, during a math lesson in which the content objective is that students understand a geometric theorem, have CLD students work in collaborative groups to apply the content knowledge through the writing of a song, which is the language objective.
   - Observe the progress of CLD students throughout a lesson and take anecdotal

notes. Make modifications through pacing, reteaching, and enriching the content and language according to the needs of students.

- Lead students in reading a paragraph from a selection. First, read the paragraph aloud by individual words, phrases, or sentences to concentrate on key vocabulary and main points. Then have students repeat what is read orally (echo) as a choral group. This activity will help your CLD students remember key points and vocabulary and improve their sight vocabulary.

Review and Assessment

1. Review and assessment throughout the instructional process helps to identify those CLD students who need additional instruction as well as those who are ready to move on. To be assured of student understanding and retention of content concepts and key vocabulary:

   - Use a variety of methods for eliciting group responses that are sensitive to student needs and aid in the determination of student comprehension levels. A few may include pencils up to agree/pencils down to disagree, number cards numbered 0 to 5 to indicate answers to questions or statements with multiple-choice responses, or dry-erase response pads for written responses.

- Introduce and model academic tasks throughout the lessons and units so that CLD students are less anxious about "school talk." For example, CLD students who will be involved in literary discussions may need to review what the word *discussion* means as well as what it means to "share ideas." This will also provide a format for understanding the processes of asking and answering questions.

- Plan a consistent time at the end of every class period to evaluate the extent to which students have understood key concepts and key terms. This can be done by attaching sticky notes to a clipboard and making anecdotal notes on students throughout the class period.

- As needed, modify and simplify the language of the assessment tool used for the various language proficiencies represented. For instance, when creating an assessment for a heterogeneously language proficient class ranging from non-English proficient (NEP) to fluent English proficient (FEP), think about having:

  —NEP students draw the known information with an accompanying description in the native language, or use the known English vocabulary to describe the drawing.

  —FEP students draw the known information with a written paragraph in English describing the drawing.

■ key theories and concepts

actual development	hands-on	SIOP instruction
adaptation of content	language proficiency	SIOP model of the sheltered
building background	level playing field	method
cloze sentences	meaningful activities	SIOP preparation
cognates	more capable peer	SIOP review and assessment
content and language objectives	potential development	social interaction
content concepts	practice and application	standards of best practice with
cooperative learning	scaffolding	CLD students
core curriculum	SDAIE	supplementary materials
differential learning and transition	sheltered instruction	TESOL
needs	sheltered method of	visuals
effective instruction	instruction	zone of proximal development
guarded vocabulary	SIOP indicators	(ZPD)

■ professional conversations on practice

1. This chapter explores the academic and career potentials that are possible when CLD students receive the accommodative instruction they require to be successful in public school. Discuss the ways in which the perspective of a level playing field often denies CLD students the appropriate instructional accommodations they require to address their differential learning and transition needs.

2. Despite the many variations of the sheltered instruction method that have evolved over time,

themes are common to this accommodative instruction for CLD students. Discuss each of these themes of sheltered instruction and the ways in which each is beneficial for CLD students.

3. The SIOP model of the sheltered instruction method is defined by three aspects and eight components. Discuss how a teacher should undertake the evaluation of his or her effectiveness in using the SIOP model with CLD students.

■ questions for review and reflection

1. What are the five components of preparation according to instruction that is delivered using the SIOP model?

2. In what ways are content and language objectives integrated into a SIOP lesson?

3. In what ways is the adaptation of content beneficial for CLD students who are taught according to a SIOP lesson?

4. What, according to the SIOP model of the sheltered method, is meant by the term *meaningful activities* (be specific)?

5. What are the six components of instruction when it is delivered according to the SIOP model of sheltered instruction?

6. List and discuss at least three ways teachers can build background among CLD students as part of a SIOP lesson. Why is building background important?

7. In what ways does the SIOP model target comprehensible input (be specific)?

8. What is the role of interaction in a SIOP lesson?

9. Differentiate lesson delivery in a SIOP lesson from traditional grade-level lesson delivery. In what ways is the former beneficial for CLD students?

10. In what ways do the thirty SIOP indicators enhance instruction delivered according to the SIOP model of the sheltered method?

suggested activities

Preservice Teachers

1. Sonia, a ten-year-old CLD student from Ecuador, arrived in the United States three months ago and has had no formal schooling in her native country. Choose two components of the SIOP model and elaborate on how you will meet her needs within the heterogeneous classroom by means of the thorough implementation of these two components. For example, if you choose the comprehensible input component, through what techniques can you

ensure that she understands the key concepts in a specific content area?

2. Observe a classroom teacher with CLD students. Choose two components from the SIOP method on which to focus for this observation. For example, observe lesson delivery and watch how he or she implements and carries out the language objectives clearly, how much time students are engaged during the class period, and how he or she paces the lesson to the ability level of the students. Watch for innovative ways

in which he or she is accommodating the CLD student consistent with the component emphasized. In what ways is his or her teaching consistent with what you have learned about the SIOP method? What alternative strategies and techniques might the teacher have used to target the chosen component of the SIOP method?

3. Based on what you have learned from your previous observation of an educator serving CLD students and your knowledge of the SIOP method, what are the implications for *your* future classroom?

In-Service Teachers

1. Review the eight components of the SIOP method and reflect on your classroom instruction.
   - In what two or more components of your instruction do you find your strengths in meeting the needs of your CLD students?
   - In what two components of your instruction do you find improvement needed to meet the needs of your CLD students? How can these areas of improvement be addressed to more effectively meet the needs of students in your classroom?

2. Reflect on a concept in a content area that has been of particular difficulty to teach. Target that area through the following activity:
   - Implement the use of student learning logs for one week. Through such logs, students

write and reflect on what they have learned. For instance, if the targeted area is word problems in math, a log might begin with: "Today I learned three ways to solve word problems." Subsequently, the students will write about the three ways while reflecting on the processes learned. Adapt these logs as needed for academic and language proficiency, noting that they may also include illustrations of a concept, diagrams with labeled parts, poems, outlines, graphic organizers, and more.
   - What gains have your CLD students made in this content area after this first week of using learning logs?
   - Can they articulate key concepts and content vocabulary more readily? Why?
   - What frustrations are you encountering and how can these be overcome?
   - Think about the CLD population in your classroom. List two areas of need specific to each CLD student that can be addressed effectively using the SIOP method. For example, if you have a non-English proficient student schooled in his first language, you can provide material in his native language or ask a proficient bilingual peer to preview the lesson and then review for a few minutes after a lesson for clarification of content (comprehensible input).

assessment tips and strategies

The following assessment tips and strategies are drawn from the content of Chapter 8.

Assessment

Review and assessment is the third critical aspect of the SIOP model. The information gathered from the review and assessment cycle is used to revise lesson plans and to ensure that students are meeting content and language objectives. Multifaceted assessments, which can be formal or informal, can be used to evaluate process and product, with a process em-

phasis on portfolios, running records, and anecdotal records.

Assessment Tips
- The review and assessment aspect of the SIOP model includes the following four indicators:
  —Review of key vocabulary
  —Review of content concepts
  —Ongoing feedback to students regarding language production and the application of new content concepts

—Formal and informal assessment of student progress toward attaining content and language objectives
- Learning logs enhance students' metacognitive learning and encourage students to put their thoughts into words and to use their language for their own purposes in their own ways.
- Informal multifaceted assessments determine the general level of understanding in the class.
- Formal multifaceted assessments help educators plan lessons to enhance the students' levels of understanding.

Assessment Strategies
- Use a variety of methods to elicit group responses to assess comprehension levels:
  —Pencils up means agree/pencils down means disagree.
  —Dry-erase response pads for written responses.
  —Numbered note cards that indicate multiple responses.
- Use learning logs as a type of multifaceted assessment in which students can:
  —Record their ideas.
  —Write down their understandings.
  —Record their new vocabulary and language structures.
- Informal multifaceted assessments include observations and verbal questioning.
- Formal multifaceted assessments include:
  —Tests
  —Quizzes
  —Projects

The information provided in this chapter, will help the educator to:

- Discuss the relationship between the CALLA method and the cognitive approach.
- Discuss four types of learning strategies associated with the cognitive approach.
- Describe the foundations and development of the CALLA method.
- Describe each of the five phases of the CALLA method.
- Describe appropriate professional actions in the preparation phase of CALLA instruction.
- Summarize the role of visual and hands-on materials in the presentation phase of the CALLA instructional sequence.
- Explain why the practice phase of CALLA is more student-centered than the preparation or presentation phases.
- Explain why student self-assessment is critical to the evaluation phase of CALLA instruction.
- Discuss why the expansion phase of CALLA emphasizes that students reflect on the relevancy of content to their personal lives.
- Discuss professional guidelines for choosing among learning strategies when teaching CLD students according to the CALLA method.
- Specify reasons for teaching learning strategies that apply to multiple contexts.

The CALLA Method of Instruction

I have found it useful to think of learning as the extensions of one's ability to make explicit and elaborate (to spell out), contextualize (to make associations within a frame of reference), validate (to establish the truth or authenticity of an assertion) and/or act (to perform) upon some aspect of one's engagement with the world.

—Jack Mezirow, *Transformative Dimensions of Adult Learning*

critical standards *Guiding Chapter Content*

TESOL/NCATE teacher standards reflect professional consensus on standards for the quality teaching of pre-K–12 CLD students. Additionally, the CEEE Guiding Principles and their accompanying indicators serve as a framework to assist practitioners, policymakers, and clients as they collaborate to enhance academic enrichment and language acquisition among CLD students. Therefore, in order to help educators understand how they might appropriately target and address national professional teaching standards in practice, we have designed the content of this chapter to reflect the following standards.

TESOL ESL Standards for P–12 Teacher Education Programs

TESOL ESL—Domain 1: Language. Candidates know, understand, and use the major concepts, theories, and research related to the nature and acquisition of language to construct learning environments that support ESOL [CLD] students' language and literacy development and content-area achievement. (p. 1)

- **Standard 1.a. Describing language.** Candidates demonstrate understanding of languages as a system and demonstrate a high level of competence in helping ESOL students acquire and use English in listening, speaking, reading, and writing for both social and academic purposes. (p. 2)

  1a.6. Demonstrate ability to help ESOL students develop social and academic language skills in English. (p. 5)

TESOL ESL—Domain 3: Planning, Implementing, and Managing Instruction. Candidates know, understand, and are able to use standards-based practices and strategies related to planning, implementing, and management of ESL instruction, including classroom organization, teaching strategies for developing and integrating language skills, and choosing and adapting classroom resources. (p. 21)

- **Standard 3.a. Planning for standards-based ESL and content instruction.** Candidates know, understand, and apply concepts, research, and best practices to plan classroom instruction in a supportive learning environment for ESOL students. Candidates serve as effective English language models as they plan the classroom for multilevel classrooms with learners from diverse backgrounds using standards-based ESL and content curriculum. (p. 21)

  3.a.3. Plan students' learning experiences based on assessment of language proficiency and prior knowledge. (p. 23)

Note: All TESOL/NCATE standards are cited from TESOL (2001). All Guiding Principles are cited from Center for Equity and Excellence in Education (1996).

- **Standard 3.c. Using resources effectively in ESL and content instruction.** Candidates are familiar with a wide range of standards-based materials, resources, and technologies and choose, adapt, and use them in effective ESL and content teaching. (p. 26)

  3.c.3. Employ appropriate variety of materials for language learning, including books, visual aids, props, and realia. (p. 27)

TESOL ESL—Domain 4: Assessment. Candidates understand issues of assessment and use assessment measures that are standards based as they relate to ESOL students. (p. 30)

- **Standard 4.c. Classroom-based assessment for ESL.** Candidates know and use a variety of classroom and performance-based assessment tools that are standards based to inform instruction. (p. 30)

  4.c.2. Use various instruments and techniques to assess content-area learning (e.g., math, science, social studies) for ESOL learners at varying levels of language and literacy development. (p. 36)

CEEE Guiding Principles

Guiding Principle # 4: Limited English proficient students receive instruction that builds on their previous education and cognitive abilities and that reflects their language proficiency levels.

4.6 Teachers identify and design comprehensible instruction that is appropriate to limited English proficient students' developmental levels as well as to their stages of first and second language acquisition.

4.8 Teachers use instructional materials and resources that support English language learners in the classroom (e.g., properly translated native language materials, English language materials controlled for linguistic complexity).

4.11 All teachers understand and value the linguistic backgrounds and cultural heritages of their students' families and use this information to enrich classroom instruction and to facilitate limited English proficient students' learning of academic content. (p. 8)

Cognitive methods share many of the same characteristics as the communicative methods, but they take instruction a step further to include components that stem from recent research on second language acquisition and cognitive development. Specifically, cognitive methods place a greater emphasis on the explicit teaching of higher-order thinking skills, the social/affective dynamics of learning, and the development of students' metacognitive awareness. Although some educators may believe that young children are not developmentally ready for complex thought processes, even first graders can develop metacognitive awareness (Chamot & El-Dinary, 2000). The cognitive-developmental view argues that children are active thinkers and hypothesizers, and it concludes that higher-order thinking activities are necessary to stimulate children's active and higher-level thinking skills (Piaget & Inhelder, 1969). Furthermore, intrinsic motivation among students arises from basic human needs for competence, autonomy, and the sense of belonging (Deci & Ryan, 1985). Thus, to promote the best avenue for the acquisition of knowledge and language with the English language learner, activities need to include higher-order thinking activities that challenge and are relevant to the student.

Extensive, explicit instruction in applying learning strategies to facilitate CLD student cognitive development also differentiates the cognitive approach from other approaches. Ellen Bialystok (2001), an internationally renowned expert on second language acquisition and cognition, describes the role of learning strategies:

> The conclusion that general cognitive processes are at the very center of language acquisition is inescapable. It is not only adults past some punitive critical period who must resort to using brute learning strategies to acquire language, but so must children at every age and at every stage of language acquisition. (p. 88)

As a foundation for understanding methods that are grounded in the cognitive approach, we share in this chapter some of the findings of research on second language acquisition and the explicit instruction of learning strategies. We also present related teaching strategies and techniques that educators have used to translate these findings into practice.

■ Cognitive Methods and Learning Strategies

Some educators may argue that they will not be able to meet the needs of their native-English-speaking students if they are required to spend extra time providing specialized instruction for CLD students. In reality, *all* students need encouragement, guidance, and practice in building their capacities to apply learning strategies. Many native-English-speaking children also struggle with reading, writing, and using higher-order thinking skills. As research shows, explicit instruction in applying learning strategies benefits not only CLD students but also native-English-speaking children (Clay, 1991; Rosenshine, Meister, & Chapman, 1996; Stevens, Slavin, & Farnish, 1991). However, while all students benefit from this type of differentiated instruction, CLD students are not likely to succeed academically without it.

Moreover, effective teachers integrate strategy instruction with content-area instruction rather than using drill-oriented worksheets on thinking skills as a separate component of the curriculum. As research indicates, students require extensive practice over extended periods to learn to apply learning strategies effectively (Nist & Simpson, 1990; Pressley, 1995). If teachers spend a large amount of instructional time focusing on workbook drills related to thinking skills, they neglect the content curriculum. Yet, if strategy instruction is a key aspect of content instruction, teachers can use course materials as the context of strategy instruction, which results in a much more efficient use of instructional time.

Cognitive methods emphasize three main categories of learning strategies: cognitive, metacognitive, and social/affective strategies. However, recent research on learning strategies used by CLD students demonstrates that these students use some unique strategies that fall under a fourth category—crosslinguistic strategies (García, 1998; Jimenez, García, & Pearson, 1996). Cognitive strategies involve the mental or physical manipulation of information. These strategies include classification, linking new information to prior knowledge, and summarizing (Chamot & O'Malley, 1994).

Metacognitive strategies incorporate three domains: awareness of one's own cognitive abilities, the ability to discern the difficulty of a task, and knowing how and when to use specific strategies (Flavell & Wellman, 1977). This awareness of the learning process involves (a) deciding how to approach a task, (b) self-monitoring of understanding and producing language, and (c) self-assessment of how well one is attaining cognitive, academic, and linguistic objectives. Specific metacognitive strategies include skimming for information, monitoring comprehension and production, and reflecting on what one has learned (Chamot & O'Malley, 1994).

Social/affective strategies involve the use of socially mediated learning and lowering one's own affective filter. In socially mediated learning, CLD students interact with one another in order to better understand content and to develop language skills naturally. In classrooms that focus on socially mediated learning, students work collaboratively to solve problems. This student-centered time allows students to negotiate meaning with their teachers and with other students by asking for more information and clarifying misconceptions. Using affective strategies such as positive self-talk encourages students to lower their affective filters. Instead of telling themselves, *I can't do this,* or *I'll never understand anything,* students tell themselves they can succeed using self-talk such as *I can do this if I break it down into smaller steps,* or *I will understand more in a few months. Language learning takes time* (Chamot & O'Malley, 1994).

Crosslinguistic Strategies

Crosslinguistic strategies constitute the most recently researched area of CLD student strategy use. Because the use of learning strategies with CLD students evolved from research on learning strategy use by monolingual students, research on crosslinguistic strategies has until recently been neglected. This lack of focus on crosslinguistic strategies for second language learners has, in a way, denied the power and legitimacy of a child's first language as well as a critical part of the child's identity. Students who have learned two or more languages have unique resources for negotiating meaning. For example, bilingual students are often able to *code switch,* which means that they sometimes use both languages in the same conversation to express themselves.

Bilingual students also frequently use a second strategy, *translation,* but the effectiveness of the strategy depends on its use. García (1998) found that when successful bilingual students translated text, they paraphrased meaning, whereas less successful language learners tended to translate text word for word. Additionally, García, as well as other researchers, has found that bilingual students benefit from recognizing cognates and using them to construct meaning in the second language (García, 1998; Jimenez, 1997; Jimenez et al., 1996). However, bilingual students may gain an advantage from explicit instruction in using cognates as a reading comprehension strategy (García, 1998). Finally, bilingual students who understand that reading in all languages is a similar process and that the strategies they use to negotiate meaning in one language can be applied to negotiating meaning in the second language, tend to be more successful language learners (Jimenez, 1997; Jimenez et al., 1996). Figure 9.1 compares the strategy use of more successful language learners with that of less successful language learners, as evidenced in the literature (Chamot & El-Dinary, 2000; Jimenez et al., 1996). For a more comprehensive description of learning strategies and the cognitive approach, see Chapters 2 and 6.

■ Cognitive Teaching Methods for Instructing CLD Students

Research on second language acquisition and cognitive development in the 1980s and 1990s led to the specification of a cognitive approach to teaching CLD students. The most well-known method arising from this research is the cognitive academic language learning approach, or CALLA, a teaching method developed by Anna Uhl Chamot and Michael O'Malley (1994). Extensive field-testing has created a body of research supporting the effectiveness of the CALLA method (Chamot, 1995; Chamot & El-Dinary, 1999, 2000; Chamot & O'Malley, 1996). The following section provides an overview of the CALLA instructional method.

More successful language learners

1. Are more likely to rely on background knowledge (inferences, predictions, elaborations).
2. Tend to focus more on metacognitive strategies.
3. Are more flexible at adapting strategy use to fit with a particular task; more flexible in strategy use.
4. Tend to use multiple strategies to resolve situations.
5. Tend to view comprehension holistically; an unknown word does not hinder comprehension.
6. Often use more complex strategies more appropriately.
7. Usually focus on meaning.

All students benefit from explicit strategy instruction.

Less successful language learners

1. Are more likely to use phonetic decoding.
2. Tend to focus on cognitive strategies when they use strategies.
3. Are more likely to use strategies that are ineffective for a task; are less flexible in strategy use.
4. Tend to use only one strategy to resolve a situation.
5. Use fewer strategies than more successful language learners.
6. View comprehension discretely; get stuck on a word; comprehension is lost in the details.
7. Tend to focus more on form or structure.

■ **figure 9.1** CLD Students and Learning Strategies

The CALLA Method

The CALLA method was developed from the research on learning strategy use among CLD students (O'Malley & Chamot, 1990; O'Malley, Chamot, Stewner-Manzanares, Russo, & Küpper, 1985a, 1985b; Wenden & Rubin, 1987; Paris & Winograd, 1990). During the 1980s, researchers became interested in and began examining learning strategy use by CLD students. Many interviewed CLD students who were identified by their teachers as successful learners to determine which strategies the students used to comprehend and acquire the second language. They found that the students identified as more successful learners were aware of the strategies they employed to learn the new language. The researchers used the information gathered to create an inventory of language strategies and their applications as used by more successful language learners (O'Malley et al., 1985a).

Later, researchers created studies to discover if the strategies applied by more successful language learners could be explicitly taught to less successful language learners. They found that these strategies could, in fact, be explicitly taught and that less successful language learners who learned to use the new strategies became better language learners (O'Malley et al., 1985b). In subsequent studies, researchers found that more successful language learners used a greater number of strategies and selected more appropriate strategies for a given task than less successful language learners (O'Malley, Chamot, & Küpper, 1989). These studies, in addition to the work of other researchers such as Cummins, Collier, and Thomas, compelled Chamot and O'Malley to create the CALLA method in order to provide educators a framework from which to operate when helping CLD students to enhance CALP development (Chamot & O'Malley, 1994).

Chamot and O'Malley designed the CALLA method to provide intermediate CLD students with (a) grade-level-appropriate cognitive and academic instruction, (b) instruction that promotes second language development (reading, writing, speaking, and listening) in content areas, and (c) instruction that focuses on explicit instruction in using learning strategies (Chamot, 1995). Consequently, CALLA lessons include content, language, and learning strategy objectives. Although Chamot and O'Malley (1994) originally recommended CALLA for intermediate CLD students, research on its implementation has shown that the method is also effective with beginning CLD students, as well as with native-English-speaking students, in developing higher-order thinking and literacy skills (Chamot, 1995; Montes, 2002).

CALLA and Learning Strategy Instruction

The CALLA method focuses on explicitly teaching CLD students to understand and tactically apply metacognitive, cognitive, and social/affective strategies (Chamot & O'Malley, 1994). Table 9.1 (page 304) offers a synopsis of sample descriptions, potential benefits, and research foundations for the three types of learning strategies emphasized by the CALLA method. Four foundational beliefs form the basis of explicit learning strategy instruction according to the CALLA method:

- *Active learners are better learners.* Students who organize and synthesize new information and actively relate it to existing knowledge should have more cognitive linkages to assist comprehension and recall than students who approach each new task by simple rote repetition.
- *Strategies can be learned.* Students who are taught to use strategies and who are guided through positive experiences in which such strategies are applied will learn more effectively than students who have no experience with learning strategies.
- *Academic language learning is more effective with learning strategies.* Learning academic language in content areas among ESL students should follow the same principles that govern reading and problem solving among native speakers of English.
- *Learning strategies transfer to new tasks.* Learning strategies will be used by students on new tasks that are similar to the learning activities on which they were initially instructed to use learning strategies. Transfer will be facilitated with metacognitive training. (Chamot & O'Malley, 1994, pp. 59–60)

These foundations suggest that it is possible to improve CLD student achievement and language acquisition through a variety of instructional actions explicitly designed to focus learning. Specifically, such actions focus learning on active participation, strategy development and use, and capacity building for the transfer of strategies learned across subject areas.

The Five Phases of the CALLA Instructional Method

Lessons designed from the perspective of the CALLA method follow a specific five-phase instructional sequence: preparation, presentation, practice, evaluation, and expansion. This sequence provides scaffolding for students as they progress through the phases by gradually shifting from student dependence on the teacher to employ strategies and content concepts to the student's independent ability to apply the declarative and procedural knowledge he or she has learned (Chamot & O'Malley, 1994). The following sections of this chapter describe how to teach content and strategies in each phase of the CALLA instructional sequence.

For the purposes of illustration, an example from the hypothetical Mrs. Reddy's first-grade mathematics lesson accompanies each phase of CALLA instruction. Her first-grade class is located in a rural community. The class includes CLD and native-English-speaking students. The CLD students' stages of second language acquisition range from the preproduction to the intermediate fluency stages of English language proficiency (see Chapter 3 for a description of the stages of SLA). The languages of the class include Bosnian, Spanish, and English. Mrs. Reddy has chosen to use the CALLA method in her class because she knows that although all of her students benefit from explicit instruction in and modeling of learning strategies, without this kind of differentiated instruction, her CLD students are not likely to succeed academically.

■ **table 9.1**   Selected Learning Strategies Emphasized by the Methods of the Cognitive Approach: Descriptions, Benefits, and Research Foundations

	METACOGNITIVE		
Strategy	**Strategy Description**	**Benefits of Strategy for CLD Students**	**Research Base**
Graphic organizers (e.g., KWL charts and other organizational planning)	K—Ask the CLD student what he or she knows about the topic. W—Ask the CLD student what he or she wants to know about the topic. L—At the end of the lesson, ask the CLD student what he or she learned from the lesson.	By asking the CLD student what he or she knows about the topic, the teacher is engaging the CLD student's background knowledge and is preassessing. By asking what the student wants to know, the teacher is actively engaging the CLD student in the learning process. Finally, when the teacher asks the student what he or she has learned, comprehension is being assessed and reinforced.	Armbruster, Anderson, & Meyer, 1991; Gordon & Rennie, 1987
Self-monitoring	The CLD student monitors his or her use of strategies.	By engaging in the active monitoring of the use of strategies in learning, the CLD student is able to assess and refine strategies in practice that will enhance comprehension and capacity building across subject areas.	Anderson, 2002; Bialystok, 1981; Miller, Giovenco, & Rentiers, 1987; Payne & Manning, 1992

	COGNITIVE		
Strategy	**Strategy Description**	**Benefits of Strategy for CLD Students**	**Research Base**
Elaboration of background knowledge	The CLD student is able to draw on background knowledge and prior experiences to make meaningful connections to the lesson.	The teacher implements research-based classroom activities to activate and build on CLD student's prior knowledge as a basis for constructivist connections to new learning.	Au, 1980; Spires, Gallini, & Riggsbee, 1992
Predicting/ making inferences	The CLD student anticipates what is coming in the text or lesson by making predictions based on contextual cues.	Predicting and making inferences encourages CLD students to use context to construct meaning.	Carr, Dewitz, & Patberg, 1983; Jimenez, 1997

■ **t a b l e   9 . 1**   Continued

SOCIAL AFFECTIVE			
Strategy	**Strategy Description**	**Benefits of Strategy for CLD Students**	**Research Base**
Questioning for clarification	The CLD student asks questions to elaborate on material or verify comprehension, thereby reducing anxiety.	Ongoing questioning and reflection on content enables the CLD student to continually evaluate his or her comprehension of new concepts/content and recognize the progress that she or he is making.	Jimenez, 1997; Muñiz-Swicegood, 1994
Cooperative learning	The CLD student works with peers to complete activities and share information, thereby maximizing social and communicative interaction in the learning process.	Vygotsky (1978) has argued that comprehension is enhanced when the student is able to work cooperatively with his or her peers to build and foster a deeper level of understanding, especially when he or she learns from a more capable peer.	Vygotsky, 1978; Moll, 1990

t h e o r y *into Practice*

Effective teachers target development among CLD students in each dimension of the CLD student biography: sociocultural, cognitive, academic, and linguistic. Development in the cognitive dimension is often the most neglected in the classroom. Therefore, it is often highly beneficial for educators to provide explicit instruction in learning strategies to empower students as problem solvers and lifelong learners. CLD students benefit from explicit instruction that targets the nature and uses of metacognitive, cognitive, and social affective learning strategies. The CALLA method (Chamot & O'Malley, 1994) is a highly effective way to provide this instruction. Once learning strategies are acquired, they are no longer simply something students can recite back to the teacher. The strategies become tools students can apply effectively without excessive deliberation.

■ *What are the developmental implications of learning strategy instruction for your practice as an elementary or secondary educator of CLD students? In what ways might you incorporate and explicitly teach learning strategies along with effective instruction for CLD students?*

The Preparation Phase The preparation phase of the CALLA method primarily emphasizes students' prior knowledge and experiences (Chamot & O'Malley, 1994). This phase is the cornerstone of the entire learning experience because the relevance of new concepts and language to a student's prior knowledge and experiences is a crucial factor in long-term memory retention (Jensen, 1996). In other words, students will only understand and remember new concepts and language if they can relate new information to what they already know. Unfortunately, students do not always make these critical connections independently (thus the importance of historical relevancy). Accordingly, effective CALLA teachers start new learning experiences by helping their students establish connections between prior knowledge and key content concepts, language, and strategy applications.

The preparation phase of the CALLA method emphasizes the concepts, language, and thought processes that will allow students to attain the lesson's content, language, and learning strategy objectives. Consequently, when planning the lesson's objectives it is important that the language of the objectives reflect the higher-order thinking that is a targeted outcome of the lesson. The verbs depicted in Figure 9.2 are categorized according to the levels of Bloom's taxonomy of educational objectives (Bloom, 1956) and can help educators develop objectives that adequately guide students to the appropriate levels of cognitive engagement. The cognitive levels of Bloom's taxonomy, listed in order of increasing complexity, are as follows: knowledge, comprehension, application, analysis, synthesis, and evaluation.

Within the preparation phase of the CALLA instructional sequence, the teacher provides the students with an overview of the lesson's theme and objectives in order to give them a general idea of what they will learn and why the concepts and skills are important. Next, the teacher guides students through hands-on and visual activities that promote reflection on how the students' personal and educational experiences relate to these new concepts, strategies, and skills. This reflection also assists the teacher and students in identifying areas of student inexperience and misunderstanding. The teacher can then use his or her knowledge of student inexperience, as well as knowledge of students' strengths and assets, to sculpt the lesson to the specific cognitive, academic, and linguistic needs of the students in the class. Table 9.2 provides a brief summary of research ideas from the literature (Amaral, Garrison, & Klentschy, 2002; Anstrom, 1998a, 1998b, 1999a, 1999b; Chamot, Dale, O'Malley, & Spanos, 1992; Chamot & O'Malley, 1994; García, 1998; Kober, n.d.; Short, 1993b) as well as from the authors regarding many ways in which teachers can help CLD students overcome the challenges they often face when building knowledge in the content areas.

The essence of the preparation phase is to help students discover what they already know. The *what* in CALLA lessons includes facts, concepts, language, skills, and learning strategies. An effective CALLA teacher escorts students through a process of self-examination and brainstorming designed to uncover prior knowledge and experiences related to the topic at hand. Students can make these connections together as a class, in small groups, or with a partner. When educators fail to help students make these connections, the presentation of new information to students will be less effective because students are less likely to know how the new information relates to their existing knowledge base.

Evaluation

A focus on judging the personal value or usefulness of given information/topics

Evaluate, judge, assess, reflect, appraise

Synthesis

A focus on integrating prior knowledge and experiences with new information to create a new conceptual understanding

Hypothesize, synthesize, integrate, design a new..., formulate

Analysis

A focus on understanding the relationship between facts/concepts and how the facts/concepts are organized within the topic

Categorize, relate, distinguish relevant from irrelevant information, conclude, identify assumptions, support conclusions with evidence

Application

A focus on making generalizations using information related to the topic

Apply, predict, relate, demonstrate, solve

Comprehension

A focus on understanding the information related to the topic

Translate, interpret, infer, generalize, summarize, estimate

Knowledge

A focus on factual recall regarding the topic

Recall, define, recite, recognize, describe, tell

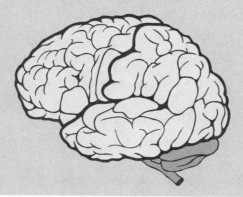

■ **figure 9.2** Action Verbs Describing Each Level of Bloom's Taxonomy

■ **t a b l e   9 . 2**   Challenges and Accommodations for CLD Students in the Classroom

Content Area	Vocabulary/Structures	Cognition	Culturally Unfamiliar Topics
Language Arts	Colloquial language Dialects Archaic language English character names Academic syntax Metaphors Idioms Introductory prepositional phrases Personification	Reading/writing strategies Irony Symbols Sequence of events Foreshadowing and flashback Character analysis Motive Mood Tone Theme	Settings Story patterns/frameworks Cultural values Belief systems Discourse patterns (circular versus linear) Point of view Allusions specific to a particular culture

Recommendations for Promoting CLD Student Success	Select literature that reflects the identity of your CLD students. Use folktales and myths that have their origin in the cultures of your students. Select literature written by authors from underrepresented groups. Use graphic organizers (e.g., semantic maps and webs, storyboards, clusters, matrices, Venn diagrams). Use student journals. Encourage predictions about the content or conclusions of a work. Surface background knowledge through prereading activities (e.g., agree/disagree statements) Encourage multiple viewpoints and interpretations. Offer a writing program that emphasizes a balance of fluency, clarity, and correctness. Have students/teacher read parts of the texts out loud to enhance the speaking (inflection, pronunciation, and more) and listening skills of the students. Incorporate activities that challenge students to clarify their thoughts and think critically about the material (e.g., compare different versions of the Cinderella tale).

■ **table 9.2**   Continued

Content Area	Vocabulary/Structures	Cognition	Culturally Unfamiliar Topics
Mathematics	Homophones (e.g., *sum/some*) Technical terms (e.g., *exponent, quotient*) Common terms used in new ways (e.g., *mean, product*) Symbols Multiple words or phrases indicate the same mathematical operation Passive voice for questions and statements Typical syntax often reversed Comparatives Superlatives	"If . . . then . . ." statements Abstract concepts and representational nature of math	New information that clashes with previously acquired methods of notation and problem solving Culture-specific symbols Word problems drawn from unfamiliar situations

Recommendations for Promoting CLD Student Success	Use practical application problems to help beginning CLD students acquire computation skills. Incorporate explicit teaching of metacognitive strategies (e.g., self-monitoring, self-evaluation, planning how to solve various types of problems). Instruct students on the sequence of steps that should be used to solve problems. Use authentic problems and real-life situations (avoid those that accentuate class distinctions). Incorporate explicit instruction of the mathematical language related to the concepts you cover. Have students use journals to clarify ideas, justify rationales, summarize ideas, connect concepts, review material, and express frustrations, accomplishments, and discoveries. Engage students by using a variety of methods such as cooperative learning, direct instruction, computer-assisted learning, and guided discovery. Connect concepts to the background knowledge of your students by asking them to write their own word problems. Find out how your students mentally manipulate and organize content information by encouraging them to explain their problem-solving process.

(continued)

■ **table 9.2**   Continued

Content Area	Vocabulary/Structures	Cognition	Culturally Unfamiliar Topics
Science	Technical terms (e.g., *catalyst*) Common terms with new meanings (e.g., *table, mass, solid*) Homophones (e.g., *cell/sell*) Connecting words for argumentation Passive voice Clauses	Abstract thought Reading for specific, detailed information Making inferences Forming hypotheses Cause and effect relationships Creating and defending an argument Classification	Topics tied to geographical locations and resources (e.g., boreal forest, water purification)

Recommendations for Promoting CLD Student Success	Develop instruction that emphasizes a focused, in-depth study of the major principles and unanswered questions related to a concept rather than a broad overview of general information. Use inquiry-based instruction; formulate questions to guide students and model the process. Discuss misconceptions and confusion that students may initially have about science concepts. Contextualize new terms using hands-on activities. Use a word wall for key terms (use separate word walls for different languages). Repeat or paraphrase difficult processes and concepts. Allow students to use bilingual learning logs for brainstorming, recording questions, and describing observations. Incorporate field trips to local businesses. Ask students to collaboratively collect data through investigations, research, or interviews and then report to the rest of the class. Have students work in pairs or teams (maximize use of more capable peers). Allow students to choose from a list of projects to complete. Focus on the correct aspects of student responses rather than on the errors. Adapt materials by adding flowcharts, pictures, more background information, and sequence words such as *first* and *next*. Provide students with a unit organizer.

■ **t a b l e   9 . 2**   Continued

Content Area	Vocabulary/Structures	Cognition	Culturally Unfamiliar Topics
Social Studies	Abstract terms (e.g., *liberty*)	Cause and effect relationships	Topics tied to democracy (e.g., voting)
	Culturally connotative meanings (e.g., *justice*)	Comparison and contrast	Famous people from American history (e.g., Abraham Lincoln)
	Complex sentence structure and use of past-tense verbs	Generalization and example	Geographical places of import (e.g., Plymouth)
	Prevalence of referent terms (e.g., *it, them*)	Chronology	
		Reading for specific details	
	Conjunctions and words that imply causation (e.g., *as a result, so*)	Historical narratives	
		Multiple points of view	
	Historical present tense	Analysis and interpretation of historical events and patterns	
		Reading maps, time lines, and globes	
		Making inferences	

Recommendations for Promoting CLD Student Success	Promote a thorough, in-depth understanding of topics by using units and periodically revisiting and embellishing on old material.
	Use prereading and prewriting activities to surface the background knowledge of your students.
	Incorporate community and parental involvement.
	Invite guest speakers (especially those from the community).
	Have students conduct and share the results of interviews.
	Encourage students to share past experiences that relate to the topics being covered.
	Motivate students by having them role-play important historical figures.
	Use historical artifacts and encourage students to bring items from home.
	Use graphic organizers (e.g., semantic maps and webs, storyboards, clusters, matrices, Venn diagrams).

■ **Voices from the Field**

Graphic Organizers for Secondary Classrooms

"Graphic organizers are important for students to organize concepts. ELL [CLD] adolescents especially need to see what they have learned and how to gather information into useful approaches. One of the biggest differences between adolescents and elementary students is the attitude of approach. For example, it usually works to ask elementary students, 'What do you want to learn?' in a K-W-L chart. Whereas, adolescents need to be asked, 'What does your teacher expect you to learn?' This feedback is useful for making adjustments based on the students' needs and attitudes to make graphic organizers more effective. Graphic organizers are especially effective when students have the opportunity to work on them in pairs or groups. This is so critical for ELL students when considering that most high school English books lack visuals.

Another motivational aspect for adolescents is to see growth from one graphic organizer to the

next. In my English IV class, ELL students track their growth in vocabulary as words move into categories of increasing familiarity and usage. Without this activity, students are often unaware of successful growth. I can also use this information for alternative planning for each unit. As the usage becomes more familiar, I can increase the complexity and change the settings of the usage, so that students can make new connections and apply prior learning to new situations. When ELL students become excited about making connections to things they already know, discipline problems usually disappear and teaching and learning is a joyful experience for everyone."

■ *Tom Ressler, high school ESOL instructor, Kansas City, MO*

The Preparation Phase: In Practice   Mrs. Reddy prepares her students for a lesson on measurement conversion by previewing the following content, language, and learning strategy objectives:

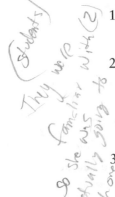

1. Content objectives
   a. Students will identify fractions as part of a whole.
   b. Students will illustrate halves and fourths.
2. Language objectives
   a. Students will say the names of their favorite foods in English.
   b. Students will write the names of their favorite foods in English.
   c. Students will listen and respond to members of their collaborative groups.
   d. Students will read or identify the initial sounds of the written words for their favorite foods.
3. Learning strategy objectives
   a. Students will relate new information to their prior knowledge and experiences.
   b. Students will work collaboratively with other students to solve problems.
   c. Students will assess the quality and accuracy of their own work.

Mrs. Reddy first chose content objectives from her school district's first-grade mathematics curriculum framework (for more information regarding using content standards as a guide to planning instruction, refer to Chapter 6). Then she determined three learning strategy objectives that students would need to accomplish the content objectives. She made sure to include a cognitive, a social/affective, and a metacognitive strategy. Mrs. Reddy knows that she should focus on only one new strategy at a time, so she chose the collaborative learning and prior knowledge elaboration for two of the strategies because her students already have extensive experience in applying those strategies in multiple contexts. Self-assessment was the new focus strategy. Finally, Mrs. Reddy examined the lesson's content and learning strategy objectives for natural ways to emphasize language use. Then she incorporated reading, writing, speaking, and listening objectives into her lesson plans.

Mrs. Reddy uses a wall chart checklist with the objectives listed in simplified language as a reference throughout the lesson. For example, instead of saying, "Students will illustrate halves and fourths," the checklist says, "I can draw one-half" and "I can draw one-fourth." This wall chart becomes an important part of student learning as they learn the art of self-assessment. Each student gets a personal copy of the wall chart on a piece of paper.

As Mrs. Reddy begins the lesson, she emphasizes to the students that they will be using their prior knowledge of sharing food with others as a way of understanding fractions. In collaborative groups of four students, the students discuss the foods they like to eat and share with others. Then, on a piece of butcher paper, they draw pictures of their favorite foods that are easy to share. After making their drawings, the students write the names of the foods to the best of their abilities. The students write at least the initial sounds for most of the food words. Many groups also include some ending sounds as well. Mrs. Reddy circulates around the room providing assistance to students as necessary, giving students feedback on their work, and informally assessing their progress.

As the students finish writing the food words to the best of their abilities, Mrs. Reddy points to the lesson objectives wall chart. She asks students, "Did you write the first sound for each food word? If you say *yes,* draw a smiley face next to this sentence on your paper," as she points to the sentence on the wall chart and holds up a self-assessment paper. Then she reads and draws a smile next to the sentence that says, "I can write the first sound of my food words." She walks around the room, assessing whether the students understand the self-assessment checklist.

The students share their responses as Mrs. Reddy writes the words on an overhead transparency. She saves this list to make a pictorial word wall for all the food words. She gives the list to Bosnian- and Spanish-speaking parent volunteers so that they can make word wall cards in Bosnian and Spanish. She goes through the same self-assessment procedure using the lesson objectives wall chart, only this time the students indicate whether they have said the names of their favorite foods in English.

Next, Mrs. Reddy asks each student to choose a partner. Each pair of students gets one candy bar. Mrs. Reddy tells them to unwrap the candy bar as she unwraps hers. She tells the students not to eat the candy bar until she tells them it is okay.

Then she puts her hand over her mouth and shakes her head *no* to ensure that everyone understands not to eat the candy bar. She tells them to break the candy bar into two pieces so that they can share it with each other. Subsequently, the class discusses whether the students divided each candy bar into two pieces of the same size or of different sizes. Most of the pairs divided the candy bar into two equal parts because they thought that having equal parts was the fairest way to divide. Mrs. Reddy explains that fractions are dividing something into pieces that are all the same size. She guides the students through the self-assessment procedure using the lesson objectives wall chart. This time the students indicate if they met one of the language objectives by speaking with and listening to their partners.

The Presentation Phase In the presentation phase of the CALLA method, the teacher usually begins by presenting information supporting what he or she says using visual or hands-on materials and uncomplicated language (guarded vocabulary). During this presentation, the teacher frequently checks for student understanding of key concepts and clarifies any misunderstandings. After the students demonstrate at least a basic understanding of key concepts, the teacher introduces and guides students through the written text for the lesson as the students practice asking questions to clarify any confusion (Chamot & O'Malley, 1994).

The foundation for a well-planned presentation phase is making new information meaningful to students. Throughout this phase, the teacher should frequently demonstrate how the new information relates to and builds on students' prior knowledge and experiences. Because CLD students who are learning English may not understand new concepts when they are presented orally, an effective

---

Are You Aware?

Are you aware that the CALLA method can be effectively used with preliterate upper elementary and secondary students? For a variety of reasons, such students have typically experienced interrupted or inconsistent schooling and exhibit poor literacy skills in their native language. For these students, the CALLA method recommends preassessing and building on what prior knowledge students do possess. Such students often possess considerable knowledge at the practical level and an oral literacy tradition in their native language. For example, rural CLD students may demonstrate knowledge of agricultural practices and weather that can be used and elaborated on to teach science concepts such as photosynthesis and the water cycle. Similarly, a student's knowledge of folklore and stories can be used as a foundation for reading instruction.

Using the CALLA method (Chamot & O'Malley, 1994), literacy skills should be first taught and, ideally, addressed in the student's native language. Bilingual paraprofessionals, parents or caregivers, and more capable CLD peers are invaluable in this regard. Once the student has learned to read and write in his or her native language, these literacy skills will quickly transfer to L2 (English). If district or school logistics require that initial literacy development be targeted in L2 (English), then *The CALLA Handbook* (Chamot & O'Malley, 1994) provides a variety of strategies that can be used to assist CLD students as they target literacy development in a language they speak imperfectly.

teacher in a culturally rich classroom surrounds students with pictures, objects, demonstrations, and so forth to support the meaning of what he or she is explaining. Furthermore, an effective CALLA teacher models, or demonstrates, the skills and strategies that he or she expects the students to know and apply as a result of the lesson. In bringing closure to this phase of the CALLA instruction, she or he discusses how, why, and when to use the skills and apply the strategies.

The Presentation Phase: In Practice Mrs. Reddy and the class discuss the drawings the students made the previous day. Each group of students takes turns holding up their illustrations. Mrs. Reddy asks them to point out some of the foods that lend themselves to illustrating one whole (e.g., pizza, candy bars, pies). Then the students illustrate some of these foods on the chalkboard. Mrs. Reddy shows them how to divide the whole food into two equal parts, emphasizing that they are halves, and then into four equal parts, emphasizing that they are fourths.

Mrs. Reddy shows the students a large laminated picture of a pizza. Then she asks the students if they have ever eaten pizza before. All of the students have eaten pizza during lunch in the school cafeteria. She asks them if they eat the whole pizza all by themselves (as she holds up the picture of the whole pizza in one hand), or if they eat one piece at a time, and she holds up a picture of a slice of pizza that is one-fourth of a whole pizza. The students all indicate that they eat the piece of pizza. Mrs. Reddy passes out to each student one cutout picture of a piece of pizza that is one-fourth of a whole. The students get into groups of four. Then Mrs. Reddy guides the discussion toward what a "whole" pizza looks like and verbally compares it to what a "part" of a pizza looks like.

Each group also gets a picture of a whole pizza that is the same size as four of the pictures of pizza pieces. The students practice making whole pizzas out of their pieces and dividing their whole pizza into four parts. She explains to students that today they are learning about *fractions*. A fraction is part of a whole. For example, a pizza that does not have any pieces missing is one whole pizza. A pizza that has some pieces missing has only a fraction or a part of the pizza left for people to eat. Mrs. Reddy explains to the students that fractions help people show how to break up whole candy bars, pizzas, or pies into equal pieces to share with friends. Mrs. Reddy and the students discuss and the students self-assess, using the self-assessment checklist, their use of making fractions from wholes and putting fractions together to make wholes.

The Practice Phase The third or practice phase of the CALLA instructional sequence is much more student-centered than previous phases. In this phase, students collaborate in hands-on activities to practice applying new concepts, language, and strategies. Each activity is designed to provide students the practice they need to attain content, language, and learning strategy objectives. Through scaffolding, the teacher provides more support in the beginning and less support as students become more adept at applying what they are learning.

CLD students need a supportive environment in which to experiment during the practice phase. Students will be working with new information, language, and strategies, so they will make mistakes. During this phase, teacher support is critical. The students do not have enough practice and skill to apply new understandings independently, and their understandings may be naive at this point. Consequently, an effective CALLA teacher will use this time to work with collaborative groups to provide additional modeling when necessary, use questioning to guide students into deeper understandings, and clarify misunderstandings. Teachers can use this time to tailor small-group instruction to the individual needs of the students.

The Practice Phase: In Practice Mrs. Reddy tells the students to form groups once again. She gives each of them a fresh piece of butcher paper, and each student draws a line down the middle of the butcher paper. On one side of the butcher paper, the students draw some of the foods from their original drawings. On the other side of the line, they illustrate what the foods look like when half of the portion originally drawn is missing. Then Mrs. Reddy asks her students to examine the illustrations on each side of their paper and discuss the difference between the parts and the wholes. The students conclude that the items on one side show foods that are whole and the items on the other side show foods that are a fraction or a part of a whole.

Mrs. Reddy models the fraction one-half by drawing a circle or pizza on the chalkboard and dividing it into two equal parts. Then she shades in one of the two parts. Next she does the same with a rectangle or candy bar. Under each illustration, she writes "½." She asks the students how many pieces are in the whole pizza or candy bar. They respond, "Two." She explains that when writing a fraction, they should put the whole number on the bottom of the horizontal line. Then she erases half of both the candy bar and the pizza. She asks the students how many pieces are left. The students reply, "One." Mrs. Reddy explains that when writing a fraction, they should put the number of pieces on top of the line.

Next Mrs. Reddy models the fraction one-fourth by drawing a circle and dividing it into four equal parts. She explains to the students that the size and shape of the pizza or candy bar does not change, but the number of pieces you cut them into can change. In this case, they would cut their pizza and candy bar into four equal pieces. If the students have three friends instead of one, they would make four pieces because two pieces would not be enough for four friends. She tells the students that the pieces are called fourths because there are four pieces. Mrs. Reddy shades in one out of the four parts. Then she does the same with a rectangle and she writes "¼" next to each illustration.

The students form collaborative groups. Mrs. Reddy tells them to make their own halves and fourths on the other side of their butcher paper. Each group presents its fractions to the other groups. Mrs. Reddy leads the students through the process of self-assessment using the lesson objectives wall chart.

Working in small groups throughout the lesson helps the CLD students feel more comfortable with the concept of fractions. A common language of terms such as *fractions, halves,* and *fourths* should become easier for CLD students to engage in as they progress through the lesson. Furthermore, using the technique of cutting commonly known foods into equal pieces and actually sharing candy bars allows students to relate the content knowledge to what they already know and engage in some hands-on learning at the same time.

The Evaluation Phase The fourth or evaluation phase of the CALLA method provides students the opportunity to reflect on their own learning. In many models of teaching and learning, teachers tend to be the primary assessors. However, in the CALLA method, students become important assessors of their own work. Developing higher-order thinking skills is a major focus of CALLA, and self-assessment is a critical metacognitive strategy (Chamot & O'Malley, 1994). If students are to understand themselves as learners and take responsibility for their own learning, then they must learn to examine the quality of their own work and determine whether they are achieving lesson objectives. This process of self-assessment is critical to becoming a lifelong, self-directed learner (Murry, 1996; Murry & Herrera, 1999).

For CLD students who are not accustomed to evaluating themselves, this phase can be particularly difficult. Students need to see others evaluating themselves. They benefit from discussion of the essentials of a quality project or assignment. They need practice evaluating work together. Examples of exemplary work and collaborative, student-created rubrics help students develop the discernment needed to effectively evaluate their own thinking and performance. Eventually, after much modeling and practice, students are able to evaluate their understanding of lesson objectives, as well as the quality of their classroom products.

The Evaluation Phase: In Practice Mrs. Reddy uses both group and self-assessment in the evaluation phase of CALLA. The lesson on fractions ends with the students commenting on one another's fraction sheets with illustrations, a form of peer evaluation. Then Mrs. Reddy leads the students through a review of the entire self-assessment checklist as the students discuss the objectives they thought were easy and the objectives they thought were difficult for them. Mrs. Reddy explains to the students that knowing what they can do well and what is difficult for them is important because such knowledge will help them decide what they should practice. Mrs. Reddy reteaches the objectives that the students said were still difficult.

The Expansion Phase In the fifth or expansion phase of the CALLA instructional sequence, students integrate the new knowledge they are gaining with their existing knowledge base. Students reflect on the relevance of information to what they have experienced and learned in the past and how they can apply it to tasks or to their own lives (Chamot & O'Malley, 1994). This phase stimulates students to take possession of the new knowledge as their own. To successfully take possession of this new knowledge, students may need to reflect on the ways in which their previous understandings need to be revised in order to incorporate them into what they are learning (Chamot & O'Malley, 1994).

In this phase, the teacher leads students to reflect on how the new knowledge they have learned can be applied in various situations in their lives or in the world in general. Then the students choose (or are assigned) an activity that will allow them to apply the new knowledge for personal meaning (Chamot & O'Malley, 1994). Encouraging students to apply new knowledge to meaningful activities facilitates the process of integrating the new knowledge into students' existing conceptual understandings.

The Expansion Phase: In Practice   For homework the students are asked to illustrate and write two fractions that represent two ways they use fractions at home. For example, if a student shares a twin Popsicle with a sibling, the student can represent his or her portion with a fraction. Another example could use family members. Maybe a student has four family members living at home. In this case, the student could represent the fraction of the family present in the house when his or her mother is home alone. When the students return with their home fractions, they show their fractions to the class and explain how they see fractions in their lives.

Choosing Learning Strategies with CALLA: Suggestions

Chamot and O'Malley (1994) offer several suggestions for choosing and teaching learning strategies:

- Align strategies with content and language objectives.
- Teach one or two related strategies at a time.
- Teach strategies using manageable tasks.
- Select research-supported strategies.
- Focus on strategies that students can use in many different classes.

These suggestions for choosing learning strategies will promote effective strategy instruction because they make the strategies more relevant to students and can lower their affective filters. Each of these suggestions for choosing and teaching learning strategies is explored more comprehensively in the following sections.

Aligning Learning Strategies   First, Chamot and O'Malley (1994) recommend that the strategies taught align with content and language objectives relevant to the lesson or unit theme. A teacher should choose strategies that help students develop the communication and thinking skills necessary to successfully comprehend a situation and complete a task independently. Ideally, content, language, and thinking strategy objectives describe content-specific declarative and procedural knowledge that students need to think and communicate like a person proficient in the field. For example, a mathematics student needs to learn to understand, apply, and communicate information like a mathematician. Therefore, learning strategies that allow the student to understand, apply, and communicate knowledge related to the lesson objectives should be the natural choice in selecting strategies to be taught explicitly during a particular unit.

Aligning Learning Strategies: In Practice   Effective teachers of the CALLA method choose learning strategies that students will need in order to independently demonstrate proficiency in both language and content objectives. For example, Mrs. Huang, a ninth-grade biology teacher, decides to focus on classification as a strategy for a unit covering the biological classification system (i.e., kingdom, phylum, class, order, family, genus, and species). She wants her students to understand how particular sets of characteristics can distinguish one group of organisms from another. In another example, Mr. Mambo, an eighth-grade social studies teacher, chooses the monitoring of listening and reading comprehension as a natural strategy for a reading- and video-based lesson on how the writings of Gandhi influenced the views of Dr. Martin Luther King Jr. regarding nonviolent resistance. He knows that his students will become more independent learners in his class if they learn to recognize when they do not comprehend oral or written language and learn to take corrective steps in order to create meaning. Both Mrs. Huang and Mr. Mambo choose strategies that students will need to use in order to think and communicate in English like experts in their content areas.

Beginning with Limited Learning Strategies   In teaching, according to the guidelines of the CALLA method, educators should begin explicit strategy instruction with one strategy or two closely related strategies. Students need to concentrate intensively on understanding and applying one or two strategies in multiple ways in various situations. They need to become adept at using current strategies before learning to use additional strategies. Furthermore, learning a few strategies at a time helps students gain confidence in their abilities to learn and apply strategies (Chamot & O'Malley, 1994). Many teachers underestimate the amount of time and effort needed for students to acquire new understandings and skills. Sometimes adults do not understand that concepts that often seem obvious to them are more difficult for students who have not yet learned the material. For those students who have not had the modeling and practice necessary to learn a new concept or skill, the *obvious* may not be so obvious.

Beginning with Limited Learning Strategies: In Practice   Miss Chen, a high school literature teacher, knows that if she chooses several strategies on which to focus, her students may feel overwhelmed and not learn any of the strategies thoroughly because their attention is divided. However, if she chooses one or two strategies, students can concentrate on learning to apply the strategies in many different ways and in many different situations. Miss Chen also realizes that literature can be a difficult class for many of her CLD students because the meaning of writing reflects an author's culture. Keeping the culture-specific nature of literature in mind, Miss Chen chooses literature for her class that was written by authors from many different cultures. Consequently, students, and sometimes even Miss Chen, may not have the necessary experiential or educational background to understand the true meaning of the literature.

Miss Chen chooses to teach her students to use their prior knowledge as a strategy for creating meaning as one of her first strategies of the school year. Because she has such a culturally rich classroom, her students can serve as cultural informants for one another. For example, the Dominican students in Miss Chen's class help the other students in their collaborative groups to understand their cultural insights regarding the Dominican Republic before, during, and after reading *How the García Girls Lost Their Accents* (Alvarez, 1991), a collection of vignettes about sisters who emigrate from the Dominican Republic to the United States. As the Dominican students serve as cultural informants, the other students share how their own experiences relate to the issues presented in the story.

Maximizing Manageable Tasks   Another suggestion for teaching strategies according to the CALLA method involves choosing a manageable task. For initial strategy instruction, teachers should choose material that has familiar information and language (Chamot & O'Malley, 1994). If the material is too difficult, the students

dilemmas *of Practice*

Mr. Maxwell has been teaching U.S. and world history in high school for the past ten years. In recent years, he has experienced a dramatic increase in the number of students who speak languages other than English at home. Mr. Maxwell is well aware that there is little support for the first languages represented by his CLD students. His CLD students are failing with strategies and techniques that he feels are successful with other grade- level students, such as answering questions at the end of the chapter, reading, and filling out worksheets. With the variety of English proficiencies represented in his classroom, he is frustrated in meeting the content standards set for his courses, particularly with his CLD students.

■ *What should Mr. Maxwell do? Conceptual development in history and social studies classes calls for the thoughtful and active participation of students. The implementation of activities involving learning strategies that stress the necessary academic language are encouraged. It is important that Mr. Maxwell first preassesses the background knowledge of his CLD students and then focus his strategies on making connections to this background knowledge.*

One way to do this would be the use of interviews, conducted by the CLD students, designed to ascertain family history informa-

tion. The histories can then be placed on preconstructed time lines containing relevant information from the chapter being studied. Mr. Maxwell can also provide a video about which the students can discuss and freewrite about any personal associations they may find. The use of realia and visuals such as maps, time lines, globes, photos, documentation, and so on is essential in his class. He may also want to try role playing or reenactments to assess the CLD students' comprehension levels, focusing on particular concepts in the history lesson.

Mr. Maxwell needs to consistently implement activities that are specific to the academic language of history, because the students will later be asked to listen, read, discuss, write, and make presentations regarding the information. Finally, Mr. Maxwell needs to provide opportunities for his students to engage in higher-order thinking activities in which his CLD students can demonstrate and apply what they have learned. Such opportunities are especially valuable in allowing students to relate the lesson to their cultural experiences and their personal lives. He should encourage students to compare and contrast themes in history with their own lives and families so that CLD students will connect with the information he is covering.

will not be able to concentrate as much on understanding and applying the strategy because they will also have to struggle with unfamiliar content and language. As students become more skillful at applying the new strategy, the teacher can support them as they use the strategy on less familiar topics or tasks using some unfamiliar language. Therefore, effective teachers who use the CALLA method teach learning strategies by maximizing manageable tasks.

Maximizing Manageable Tasks: In Practice Ms. Nguyen, a fourth-grade teacher, wants to teach her students to monitor their reading comprehension, so she chooses a manageable task to introduce the new strategy. She knows that encountering a large amount of new information while learning a new strategy might overwhelm her students. She decides to teach the students to monitor their reading comprehension using text that concerns a familiar topic and that contains many words her students already know. She chooses *Cam Jansen and the Mystery of the Dinosaur Bones* (Adler, 1997) because the book is written just below the fourth-grade level, the class has just finished a unit on dinosaurs, and the students have listened to other Cam Jansen mysteries as read-aloud books in the third grade. Choosing such a text will allow her students to concentrate on learning the strategy because they will not have too many aspects of reading on which to focus. As the students become more skilled in using the new strategy, Ms. Nguyen will lead them through learning to monitor their reading comprehension on less familiar topics and with more difficult text.

Maximizing Research In selecting strategies to teach students, a teacher should look for strategies supported by either content-specific strategy research (e.g., mathematical strategies, reading strategies) or the growing body of research on CLD students (Chamot & O'Malley, 1994). Because learning strategy instruction has become a popular topic in education, many different print and electronic sources recommend teaching students various learning strategies. However, in choosing a strategy, teachers should make certain that the strategy facilitates academic, cognitive, and linguistic development among CLD students. Many such research-based strategies are listed in Table 9.1.

Maximizing Research: In Practice In his search to find appropriate, research-supported learning strategies, Mr. Diomande, a fifth-grade teacher, has read journal articles about how more successful language learners paraphrase rather than directly translate text for understanding. He decides he is going to explicitly teach the paraphrasing strategy to his students. He begins by explaining that readers who paraphrase, rather than directly translate, tend to understand text better. Next he displays a story on the overhead projector. The class reads a small part of the story together. Then Mr. Diomande covers the text and models paraphrasing by retelling the story in his own words. He asks the students to write in their first languages what the story said. The students share their responses. The process is repeated, except this time the students provide a paraphrase as a class. After practicing as a whole class, students practice in groups, then in pairs, and finally independently.

Focusing on Contexts Effective CALLA teachers prioritize the teaching of strategies by focusing on strategies that students can use in many different contexts (Chamot & O'Malley, 1994). If students can apply a strategy in many different classes, they are more likely to employ the strategy and reap its benefits. Consequently, teaching students highly applicable strategies rather than context-specific strategies is more likely to affect CLD student achievement. For example, students would benefit from learning to monitor their comprehension because they could apply the strategy in all content areas. When students monitor their reading comprehension in a science class, they ensure that they are discerning and comprehending the key facts and understanding the important concepts. However, in a literature class the same students monitor their reading comprehension by attending to various points of view, character development, plot analysis, themes, and symbolism. Teachers must keep in mind, however, that teaching students to employ a strategy in one circumstance does not mean that the students will recognize the strategy application in other contexts. Furthermore, in developing the procedural and conditional knowledge of applying learning strategies, students benefit from practice in applying the strategies in different contexts (Mayer, 1996; Pressley, 1995). Therefore, teachers who effectively use the CALLA method provide students with modeling of and opportunities to practice the same strategy in many different content contexts (Chamot & O'Malley, 1994).

Focusing on Contexts: In Practice Mr. Ibarra, a seventh-grade health teacher, wants to teach his CLD students strategies they can use not only in his class but also in other classes. He collaborates with the seventh-grade team of teachers to choose a strategy that all the seventh-grade teachers will emphasize over the next few weeks. The team decides to focus on the metacognitive strategy of questioning for clarification. Through the health lessons, Mr. Ibarra models asking questions for clarification by thinking aloud as if he were a student. Then he asks students to ask their own questions. On an index card, the students write interesting pieces of information they learned and a question they still have at the end of each lesson. Mr. Ibarra uses selected questions as an introduction to the next day's lesson.

Closure

Through the preparation, presentation, practice, evaluation, and expansion phases of the CALLA instructional sequence, effective educators enable students to develop their understandings of learning strategies, content, and language. CALLA's particular emphasis on the explicit instruction of learning strategies assists educators as they guide students to improve their capacities for critical thinking and independent learning. The CALLA method was developed from a strong research base in second language acquisition and cognitive development. Nearly a decade of research on implementation of the method has demonstrated its effectiveness in helping students acquire second languages (Chamot, 1995; Chamot & El-Dinary, 2000; Montes, 2002). As a result of its robust research base and nationwide implementation, the CALLA method is perhaps the most well-known method of the cognitive approach to appropriate accommodative instruction for CLD students.

tips for practice

Note: Tips for practice are listed according to each of the three main categories of learning strategies essential for CLD student success and independent learning.

Tips for Implementing Cognitive Strategies

1. Allow time for the use of reference materials. The use of resources such as textbooks, dictionaries, and encyclopedias will help students make cognitive connections with the information you are providing. The Internet can also be used to help students make real-world connections to the topics being discussed.

2. Provide CLD students with an outline of the content concepts to be discussed in the lesson. Also, provide the students time and opportunities to follow along and make notes on the outline. This will give the students an idea of the important information relating to the concepts they should note and learn.

3. Read aloud information regarding the new concept to be learned. The students will summarize the information heard. Discuss the new information as a whole class or in smaller groups, with the CLD students grouped according to language and proficiency level. The students will discuss the information and then record the summary in written form.

4. Use imagery to illustrate a concept or strategy. Have the students close their eyes and visualize the concept at hand. Then ask them to draw a picture of the concept being studied. Finally, ask student volunteers to explain the concept using their pictures.

5. The list-group-label strategy can be used to present vocabulary and concepts before reading in order to activate prior knowledge, stimulate thinking, and set purposes for learning. With this strategy, CLD students typically work in heterogeneous groups to categorize a set of words related to the content being studied. This will provide a foundation for use later when the students encounter the words in the lesson. The teacher can provide a list of words related to the topic or provide the topic and have the students brainstorm words they associate with the topic.

6. Provide a story map that includes the setting, characters, problems, and key events leading to the solution and conclusion of the problem. Students will use the story map as a graphical representation of the story's narrative structure. It can also be used to illustrate hierarchical and sequential relationships (see Figure 9.3).

7. Provide an opportunity for students to make predictions concerning the concept of focus. Predicting allows students to use the limited information provided to guess meanings or predict information to come later in the lesson. Prediction will use prior knowledge to increase student comprehension of new concepts. Assessment is focused on the ability of the CLD student to speculate, hypothesize, and draw conclusions based on the information provided before the actual lesson.

Tips for Implementing Social/Affective Strategies

1. Provide extra time and opportunities for CLD students to ask clarifying questions when new concepts are introduced. Rephrase or adjust language use to suit proficiency levels for each CLD student. Questioning for clarification will help ensure students' understanding of the concepts as well as encourage CLD student participation. CLD students will be more willing to contribute to classroom discussion if they feel comfortable with and confident about the new concepts.

2. Model self-questioning techniques to check for understanding while reading aloud. Ask questions such as, "Is this making sense to me?" or "Do I understand this?" Self-questioning will help CLD students comprehend new content concepts. At the same time, the CLD students will be able to draw on prior knowledge in order to clarify the information. When the CLD student is able to personally clarify information, his or her anxiety level goes down and he

■ **figure 9.3** Story Map:
Because of Winn-Dixie

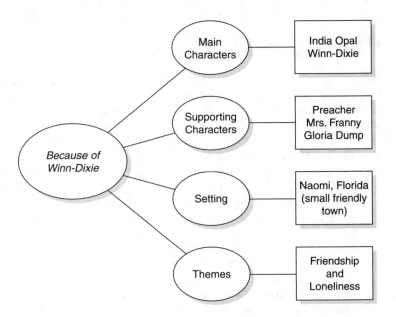

or she is more comfortable answering questions posed by the teacher.

3. Encourage CLD students to talk themselves through new material or challenging tasks. Self-talk is a strategy in which the CLD student uses positive statements to reassure himself or herself that he or she will understand and complete each assignment. This strategy will aid students by reducing the anxiety level felt when discussing new concepts.

4. Provide opportunities for CLD students to work in heterogeneous cooperative groups to complete an activity. Small groups allow CLD students to feel more comfortable about using the second language while still being challenged to learn and comprehend the lesson. Cooperative groups allow all students to pool information to enhance understanding, solve problems, and get feedback for clarification.

Tips for Implementing Metacognitive Strategies

1. Prepare an anticipation guide that will engage students in discussion of the new concept to be learned by posting declarative statements such

as, "Isaac Newton developed the theory of gravity," or "The Pythagorean theorem states that $a^2 + b^2 = c^2$." Discussion can be conducted in groups or as a whole. The statements are to be revisited after reading about the topic to ensure the development and accuracy of student interpretation.

2. Brainstorming is a practice that is useful for students during the first phase of a new lesson, so teachers often use brainstorming when introducing a new content concept. Brainstorming can engage, prepare, and direct student understanding of the new concepts. This strategy also allows for creativity and idea development without immediate evaluation or critique by the instructor or peers. Each student will first list words he or she associates with the information provided by the teacher. All ideas are recorded so that everyone can view them. This strategy can be completed as a class, as a group, or by an individual. Brainstorming is a good strategy for the development of story ideas for writing assignments.

3. Mnemonics such as rhyming or acronyms can be used to facilitate the learning of new concept

terms. For example, "King Phillip Crossed Over From Germany to Spain" is a tool for learning the biological classification system (kingdom, phylum, class, order, family, genus, and species).

4. Talking aloud during the introduction of new concepts illustrates the strategy of talking about thinking. This strategy, if first introduced by the teacher, also builds vocabulary and demonstrates the sort of thinking processes that students will need as the discussion of the topic continues. The teacher will read aloud as an introduction to the topic. He or she will pause in order to clarify meaning, connect prior knowledge, make comparisons and contrast, and discuss areas that might cause confusion. An example might be interpreting a short story or poem such as Robert Frost's "The Road Not Taken."

5. Encourage students to keep a learning log or journal throughout the academic year. The log allows for reflection on what has been learned.

As illustrated in Figure 9.4, the log needs to consist of information the student has acquired, misconceptions, inaccuracies, or problems he or she experienced concerning concepts covered.

6. An organizational planner can be used to introduce and guide discussions of content concepts to be learned. An outline of the material to be learned, along with a list of priorities explaining estimated time requirements, organization of materials, and schedule procedures, helps CLD students focus on the objectives of the lesson. Developing a plan before beginning any task will help reduce CLD student anxiety and ensure the task will be completed (see Table 9.3)

7. Provide time in the discussion of new concepts to check for understanding. This can be accomplished by grouping or pairing students. If students work in pairs, one student talks through a problem, describing her or his thinking processes. The partner listens and asks questions to help clarify thinking.

■ key theories and concepts

active learners	expansion phase of CALLA	preparation phase of CALLA
CALLA method	higher-order thinking skills	presentation phase of CALLA
code switching	language and content objectives	self-talk
cognitive approach	manageable tasks	social/affective learning strategies
cognitive learning strategies	metacognition	
crosslinguistic learning strategies	metacognitive learning strategies	
evaluation phase of CALLA	practice phase of CALLA	

■ professional conversations on practice

1. This chapter explores the grounding of the CALLA method in the cognitive approach. Discuss the foundations and tenets of the cognitive approach. In what ways is the cognitive approach applicable to the differential learning and adjustment needs of CLD students?

2. This chapter discusses recent research on crosslinguistic strategies used by CLD students. Some of these strategies, such as code switching, are considered by some educators to be indicators of a lack of language acquisition in either L1 or L2. Discuss why such assumptions arise and ways in which they should be addressed by effective professional educators of CLD students?

3. For CLD students, learning strategies should be aligned with content and language objectives. Discuss why this is so and why both types of objectives should be targeted simultaneously with CLD students.

■ **figure 9.4**   Example of a Student Learning Log Entry

	Gabriel Coronado 8th Grade Science
	Learning Strategies:
28 Aug 2003	
	1. Brainstorming—the teacher told us to make a list of words that
	go with the topic she gave us. We are studying the planets.
	My group will find words about the planet Saturn. I liked my
	group, because they helped me understand where the rings
	come from.
17 Sept 2003	
	2. Mnemonics—are words we can make up out of other words about
	the lesson we are learning to help us remember. Like ROY G
	BIV to help us remember the order of colors in the light
	spectrum. R means Red, O means Orange, Y means Yellow,
	G means Green, B means Blue, I means Indigo, and V means
	Violet. I always thought that light was white. I learned why the
	sky is blue and grass is green.
7 Oct 2003	
	3. Prediction—is when we guess what is going to happen when we
	do an experiment in class. Mrs. Smith asked me what I thought
	would happen with the air pressure experiment. I told her that
	nothing would happen to the can because it's metal. She put some
	water in an empty coke can and heated the can till the water
	boiled. Then she turned the can over in a tub with cold water.
	The coke can was crushed like someone stepped on it!!
	I was wrong about nothing happening to the can. I like to do
	experiments.

■ **questions for review and reflection**

1. What is metacognition? In what ways can a capacity for metacognition enhance the academic performance of CLD students?

2. In what ways would you describe the crosslinguistic strategy of translation?

3. Why is language learning more effective with strategy instruction?

4. What are at least three guidelines for choosing among learning strategies, according to the CALLA method?

■ **t a b l e   9 . 3**   Organizational Planner for the Lewis and Clark Transcontinental Expedition

Brainstorm a list of supplies needed for transcontinental travel.

Divide list into items that will need to be transported and items that can be found or collected along the way.	Transported Items	Collected Items

Narrow list down to the (10–20) most important *transportable* items. (Remember the keelboat dimensions are 55 feet long and 8 feet wide.)

Defend/justify choices Why did you choose to bring these items along?

Estimate the quantity of each item that would be needed to supply a group of 33 men.

Compare your list to the actual list of supplies taken by Lewis and Clark.	Classroom List	Lewis & Clark's List

Summarize the importance of the items purchased by Lewis and Clark.

5. In what ways can a teacher maximize manageable tasks in selecting learning strategies?

6. Among the five phases of the CALLA instructional sequence, which phases are not student-centered? Why?

7. What teacher actions are appropriate in conducting frequent checks for understanding as part of the presentation phase of CALLA instruction?

8. What types of activities for CLD students are appropriate in the practice phase of CALLA instruction? Why?

9. What teaching strategies help CLD students cope with the difficulties of applying learning strategies in the practice phase of CALLA instruction?

10. In what ways might the evaluation phase of CALLA instruction prove difficult for CLD students?

11. The expansion phase of the CALLA instructional sequence encourages CLD students to take possession of new knowledge. In what ways is this objective especially important for CLD students?

12. In what ways can a teacher increase the likelihood that CLD students will be able to transfer learning strategies to different contexts?

13. As discussed in this chapter, research has indicated that students who learn to use learning strategies improve their ability to construct meaning. What reasons might account for this finding?

14. What specific outcomes do CLD students typically gain from learning social/affective strategies?

suggested activities

Preservice Teachers

1. Observe a grade-level elementary or secondary classroom in which CLD students are instructed. Identify which (if any) learning strategies discussed in this chapter are evident in the teacher's method(s) of classroom instruction.
   - Metacognitive
   - Cognitive
   - Social/affective

   For each strategy observed, discuss the way it aided comprehension or critical thinking for CLD students in the classroom. If no strategies were observed, discuss ways in which each type of strategy could have aided comprehensibility for CLD students.

2. Imagine that you are an educator for an agriculture education class, a heterogeneous class grouped according to ability, with several CLD students of varying proficiency levels. What strategies are well suited to meet the needs of *all* the students? Justify your answers with examples and reasons for effectiveness.

3. Select a lesson in a teacher's edition of a content-area textbook. Modify this lesson (using the strategies found in this chapter as a framework) so that the lesson content more appropriately encourages higher-order thinking for CLD students and is more comprehensible.

In-Service Teachers

1. Adapt a content-area lesson that may prove to be a challenge for CLD students by:
   - Providing an outline to be completed as the lesson is presented.
   - Asking students to write one-sentence summaries for each of the top five key concepts.
   - Prompting students to draw key concepts beside each key concept summary.
   - Providing an opportunity for students to work in heterogeneous groups and explain the key concepts to one another.

   Discuss the following: What worked? What was a challenge? How will you address this challenge in the future?

2. To review key concepts in a content area, encourage students to state or write outcome sentences in a learning log, such as "I learned . . ."; "I was surprised . . ."; "I

think . . ." and then share with their group or with the class. Observe the specific ways in which outcome sentences about content concepts aid students' learning, retention, and higher-order thinking.

3. (Social Studies) Before reading about a particular event in history, arrange students in small groups of three or four and have them list on paper at least five reasons why they think this particular event occurred. For example, they can list five reasons why they think people moved west in the 1800s. Students then post their lists and compare the themes they have in common in order to make a prediction. Students then write in their social studies journals, "I predict the most common reason why people moved west in the 1800s was _____." Then ask them to write and respond to the following, "If I lived in the 1800s, I would or would not move west because _____." These may be done as a heterogeneous collaborative group activity as well. After the lesson, ask the students to revisit these statements in their groups to see if some learners want to change their response. If students do want to alter their response, they must provide a logical justification. Compare and contrast student responses and justifications for change.

assessment tips and strategies

The following assessment tips and strategies are drawn from the content of Chapter 9.

ASSESSMENT

The CALLA method emphasizes various types of assessment in the preparation, presentation, and evaluation phases of instruction. The findings from these assessments are used to plan instruction that builds on the knowledge and experiences that CLD students bring to the classroom. Such assessments also enable teachers to clarify any misunderstandings the students might have regarding lesson concepts, as well as determine which aspects of the lesson need to be re-covered to ensure student understanding.

Assessment Tips

- It is important to first preassess the background knowledge of CLD students and then focus strategies on making connections to this background knowledge.
- Provide time in the discussion of new concepts to check for understanding.
- Question the students for clarification to ensure comprehension and encourage student participation.

- Encourage students to use self-questioning techniques to assess their own understanding as they read.
- Use both group and self-assessment of student work.

Assessment Strategies

- To check for understanding, teachers can observe students as they discuss content concepts in groups or pairs.
- When CLD students are asking clarifying questions, rephrase or adjust language to suit the proficiency level of each student.
- While reading aloud, model for students the self-questioning techniques that are helpful for assessing one's comprehension of written material.
- When using group assessment, teachers can ask students to give one another feedback on individual work.
- Students can be prompted to self-assess their understanding of the lesson material by reviewing the content, language, and learning strategy objectives of the lesson.

The information provided in this chapter will help the educator to:

- Differentiate among at least three nationally recognized standards of best practice with CLD students.

- Describe the foundations of the TESOL/NCATE standards and the Guiding Principles for best practice with CLD students and families.

- Explain the relationship among self-assessment, critical reflection, and refinement of practice.

- Describe the four key facets of a platform for best practice with CLD students.

- Self-assess current teaching practices as they relate to nationally recognized standards of best practice.

Achieving Standards-Driven Professional Practice

The range of what we think and do
is limited by what we fail to notice.
And because we fail to notice
there is little we can do
to change
until we notice how failing to notice
shapes our thoughts and deeds.

—R. D. Laing, *Knots: Selected Works of R. D. Laing, Volume Seven*

chapter outline

Nationally Recognized Standards for Teachers of CLD Students

Standards-Driven Reflection on Professional Practice

Conclusion: Setting Goals for Professional Development

critical standards *Guiding Chapter Content*

TESOL/NCATE teacher standards reflect professional consensus on standards for the quality teaching of pre-K–12 CLD students. Additionally, the CEEE Guiding Principles and their accompanying indicators serve as a framework to assist practitioners, policymakers, and clients as they collaborate to enhance academic enrichment and language acquisition among CLD students. Therefore, in order to help educators understand how they might appropriately target and address national professional teaching standards in practice, we have designed the content of this chapter to reflect the following standards.

TESOL ESL Standards for P–12 Teacher Education Programs

TESOL ESL—Domain 3: Planning, Implementing, and Managing Instruction. Candidates know, understand, and are able to use standards-based practices and strategies related to planning, implementing, and management of ESL and content instruction, including classroom organization, teaching strategies for developing and integrating language skills, and choosing and adapting classroom resources. (p. 21)

- **Standard 3.a. Planning for standards-based ESL and content instruction.** Candidates know, understand, and apply concepts, research, and best practices to plan classroom instruction in a supportive learning environment for ESOL students. Candidates serve as effective English models as they plan the classroom for multilevel classrooms with learners from diverse backgrounds using standards-based ESL and content curriculum. (p. 21)

  3.a.1. Plan standards-based ESL and content instruction.

- **Standard 3.c. Using resources effectively in ESL and content instruction.** Candidates are familiar with a wide range of standards-based materials, resources, and technologies and choose, adapt, and use them in effective ESL and content teaching. (p. 21)

  3.c.1. Select and use culturally responsive, age appropriate, and linguistically accessible materials. (p. 27)

Note: All TESOL/NCATE standards are cited from TESOL (2001). All Guiding Principles are cited from Center for Equity and Excellence in Education (1996).

TESOL ESL—Domain 5: Professionalism. Candidates demonstrate knowledge of the history of ESL teaching. Candidates keep current with new instructional techniques, research results, advances in ESL field, and public policy issues. Candidates use such information to reflect upon and improve their instructional practices. Candidates provide support and advocate for ESOL students and their families and work collaboratively to improve the learning environment. (p. 38)

- **Standards 5.b. Partnerships and advocacy.** Candidates serve as professional resources, advocate for English language learners, and build partnerships with students' families. (p. 40)

    5.b.1. Advocate and serve as language resources for students and families in their schools and communities. (p. 40)

CEEE Guiding Principles

Guiding Principle #4: Limited English proficient students receive instruction that builds on their previous education and cognitive abilities and that reflects their language proficiency levels. (p. 8)

4.1 School districts take into consideration the whole profile of a student, including language/cultural background, native language literacy, and appropriate and valid student assessment data, when making decisions about the placement and provision of services to limited English proficient students. (p. 8)

4.6 Teachers identify and design comprehensible instruction that is appropriate to limited English proficient students' developmental levels as well as to their stages of first and second language acquisition. (p. 8)

4.9 Teachers use instructional approaches, such as cooperative learning and experiential learning, that are sensitive to the multiple experiences of learners and that address different learning and performance modes. (p. 8)

The first nine chapters of this text provide both theoretical and practical information on the appropriate instructional accommodation of culturally and linguistically diverse (CLD) students. By design the content of each of these chapters is aligned with nationally recognized teaching standards that guide educators toward effective practice for CLD students.

In this chapter, we explore ways that educators can maximize nationally recognized standards of best practice to enhance the effectiveness of their efforts to appropriately accommodate the CLD student. Teachers do not begin a teaching career as master teachers. Fundamentally, the process of developing effective practice begins with awareness. Often educators fail to notice and investigate critical issues because they are unaware that the issues are relevant. Throughout this text, we attempt to increase awareness regarding issues that affect the education of CLD students. A review of national teaching standards can also build this awareness by providing educators with knowledge of what students should be able to do and by outlining research-based instructional practice for helping students meet language and content standards. After reviewing several national teaching standards relating to the education of CLD students, this chapter promotes teacher self-awareness by discussing ways in which educators can appropriately engage in the evaluation of prior instructional planning and implementation. These evaluation processes use national teaching standards as touchstones of comparison.

Before you begin reading the following sections of this chapter, take some time to reflect on and write about the ways in which your CLD students are performing in your classroom. You may want to use the following questions as a guide:

- In general, how well do my CLD students perform in my class?
- What are my CLD students' strengths?
- What are the pivotal challenges (sociocultural, academic, cognitive, linguistic) for my CLD students?
- Do my CLD students perform as well academically as my native-English-speaking students?
- Do my CLD students participate in class as much as my native-English-speaking students?

However, the most important questions to ask yourself are:

- Where do my CLD students want to be in one week, one month, one year, twenty years?
- How will I assess my professional practice as a way of ensuring that I am appropriately accommodating and supporting my CLD students in reaching their academic goals?

■ Nationally Recognized Standards for Teachers of CLD Students

Quality standards for professional practice embody the research on effective teaching practices for CLD students. Such standards translate theory and research into what accommodative, effective, and reflective practice looks like from a practitioner's point of view. Professional standards provide consistency in teacher education and offer teachers a framework for effective practice. These standards can provide teachers with the impetus and understanding to go beyond good teaching to encourage both personal and professional growth toward excellence. Educators can use these standards as a means of articulating effective practice strategies and premises and of defending their own effective practice vis-à-vis the critiques of colleagues, administrators, and policymakers who may not understand the process of second language acquisition and the realities of teaching CLD students.

Over the years, educators have noted the development of a variety of professional standards. Professional consensus provides the foundation for some sets of standards, whereas others are built on educational theory and research. A combination of educational theory, research, and professional consensus grounds only a limited group of comprehensive standards. Most recently, a few nationally recognized entities have developed professional standards for practice to accommodate the unique and multidimensional needs of CLD students.

dilemmas *of Practice*

Mrs. Espinoza is a first-year language arts teacher at an urban junior high school. The school district has a diverse student population, including students recently arrived from Mexico, Africa, Asia, Indonesia, and Vietnam, as well as native-English-speaking students. She has had numerous courses in professional practice and methodologies of classroom teaching and instruction. However, Mrs. Espinoza has been asked by the administration to make accommodations for the diverse needs of the students in her classroom by aligning her professional practice with nationally recognized standards of best practice, such as the TESOL/NCATE standards (TESOL, 2001). Panic has struck because she does not know how to begin aligning her practice with best practice standards for CLD students while still targeting the language arts standards in her state.

■ *What should Mrs. Espinoza do? The process of accommodation necessarily involves understanding quality standards for effective practice in diverse educational environments. Therefore, a review of the standards for effective practice with CLD students will open the door for Mrs. Espinoza to modify her practice with CLD students in the classroom. She should seek out research-based ways to adapt her classroom practice to ensure the academic success of CLD students.*

We have conducted an analysis of national teaching standards for professional practice with CLD students and found that the conception of effective teaching practice for CLD students is comparatively consistent across the various sets of standards, whether the standards are research-based, professional consensus–based, or a combination of both. The following organizations have developed professional standards of appropriate practice for educators who serve the needs of culturally and linguistically diverse student populations:

- The National Board for Professional Teaching Standards (NBPTS)
- Center for Research on Education, Diversity & Excellence (CREDE)
- Teachers of English to Speakers of Other Languages (TESOL)
- The Center for Equity and Excellence in Education (CEEE)

For highlights of each of these sets of standards, see Table 10.1.

NBPTS Standards

The National Board for Professional Teaching Standards, a project funded by the U.S. Department of Education and the National Science Foundation, used findings from educational research to create rigorous professional teaching standards. The goal of NBPTS is to enhance the content-area achievement of all students. As a result of the increasing numbers of CLD students in public school classrooms, NBPTS established English as a New Language standards to define quality practice in twelve areas of professional practice that address CLD student learning (NBPTS, 1998). These comprehensive standards emphasize teacher awareness of students'

Professional Standards	Summaries/Highlights
NBPTS National Board for Professional Teaching Standards	This project was funded in part with the grants from the U.S. Department of Education and the National Science Foundation. The standards lay the foundation for the English as a New Language certificate. They represent a professional consensus on the critical aspects of practice that distinguish accomplished teachers. The standards incorporate essential knowledge, skills, dispositions, and commitments that allow teachers to practice at a high level: • *Knowledge of students* • *Knowledge of language and language development* • *Knowledge of culture and diversity* • *Knowledge of subject matter* • *Meaningful learning* • *Multiple paths to knowledge* • *Instructional resources* • *Learning environment* • *Assessment* • *Reflective practice* • *Linkages with families* • *Professional leadership*
Unique Features:	Grounded in theory and has a fundamental philosophical foundation Professional consensus
CREDE Center for Research on Education, Diversity & Excellence, University of California, Santa Cruz	This center was funded by the U.S. Department of Education to create the Standards for Effective Pedagogy and Learning through CREDE research and through an extensive analysis of the research and development literature on education and diversity. The standards represent recommendations on which the literature is in agreement, across all cultural, racial, and linguistic groups in the United States, all age levels, and all subject matters. Thus, they express the principles of effective pedagogy for all students. CREDE's research and development is based on a sociocultural framework that is sensitive to diverse cultures and languages but powerful enough to identify the great commonalities that unite people. The research consensus can be expressed as five standards: • *Joint Productive Activity—Teacher and Students Producing Together* • *Language Development—Developing Language and Literacy Across the Curriculum* • *Contextualization—Making Meaning: Connecting School to Students' Lives* • *Challenging Activities—Teaching Complex Thinking* • *Instructional Conversation—Teaching through Conversation*
Unique Features:	Grounded on a sociocultural framework Based on 30 research projects under 6 programmatic strands (experimental, quasi-experimental, qualitative, and consensus-based)
TESOL Teachers of English to Speakers of Other Languages	A project that was completed and approved by the TESOL board of directors and the National Council for the Accreditation of Teacher Education (NCATE) in 2001 for use in accrediting ESL teacher preparation programs in the United States. The standards are expressed as five domains:

(continued)

■ **t a b l e   1 0 . 1**   Continued

Professional Standards	Summaries/Highlights
(TESOL Board of Educators & the National Council for the Accreditation of Teacher Education)	• *Language—describing language, language acquisition, and development* • *Culture—nature and role of culture, cultural groups and identity, interrelationship between language and culture* • *Planning and Managing Instruction—planning for ESL instruction, managing ESL instruction, managing content instruction for ESL learners, using resources effectively in ESL instruction* • *Assessment—issues of assessment for ESL, language proficiency assessment, classroom-based assessment for ESL* • *Professionalism—ESL research and history, partnerships and advocacy, professional development and collaboration*
Unique Features:	Professional consensus Includes performance indicators Includes rubrics for meeting the standards (self-evaluation)
CEEE Guiding Principles Center for Equity and Excellence in Education	The Evaluation Assistance Center East of the CEEE is funded by the U.S. Department of Education's Office of English Language Acquisition. This is a national initiative conducted by George Washington University, which created the six overarching Guiding Principles to capture the essence of the conditions of an optimal environment for the education of second language learners. The six Guiding Principles represent best practices based on research and serves as a framework to assist practitioners, policymakers, and clients: • *Principle I: Limited English proficient students are held to the same high expectations of learning established for all students.* • *Principle II: Limited English proficient students develop full receptive and productive proficiencies in English in the domains of listening, speaking, reading, and writing, consistent with expectations for all students.* • *Principle III: Limited English proficient students are taught challenging content to enable them to meet performance standards in all content areas, including reading and language arts, mathematics, social studies, science, the fine arts, health, and physical education consistent with those for all students.* • *Principle IV: Limited English proficient students receive instruction that builds on their previous education and cognitive abilities and that reflects their language proficiency levels.* • *Principle V: Limited English proficient students are evaluated with appropriate and valid assessments that are aligned to state and local standards and that take into account the language acquisition stages and cultural background of the students.* • *Principle VI: The academic success of limited English proficient students is a responsibility shared by all educators, the family, and the community.*
Unique Features:	Grounded in educational research on second language acquisition Professional consensus Includes indicators for policymakers, practitioners, and clients Includes Guiding Principles checklists for meeting the standards (self-evaluation, observation, auditing course content for preservice teachers and current teachers)

languages and cultures, meaningful learning environments, authentic assessments, strong home–school collaboration, and content-appropriate pedagogy.

CREDE Standards

The Center for Research on Education, Diversity & Excellence of the University of California, Santa Cruz, as funded by the U.S. Department of Education, has created the Standards for Effective Pedagogy and Learning through extensive analysis of the research and development literature in education and diversity. The five broad standards encompass the commonalities among research on effective instruction, content-area instruction, and multicultural education across all age, cultural, ethnic, and linguistic groups in the United States (Dalton, 1998). These five broad standards express the principles of effective pedagogy for all students, including CLD students. These standards are not prescriptive; instead, they serve as philosophical statements that suggest standards toward which teachers can align their practices.

TESOL/NCATE Standards

The National Council for the Accreditation of Teacher Education (NCATE) and the board of directors of the National Teachers of English to Speakers of Other Languages organization collaboratively developed their pre-K–12 ESL teacher standards (TESOL, 2001). These standards encompass five domains: professionalism, language, culture, instruction, and assessment. The standards aspire to provide consistency in teacher education programs across the United States by describing and specifying the competencies that ESL teachers need to demonstrate in professional practice. Additionally, various best practice indicators specify different levels of attainment for each competency. The ESL teacher standards differ from content teacher standards in that the former acknowledge the central role of language in the academic achievement of CLD students and highlight the multidimensional learning styles, instructional needs, and assessment issues of learners who are developing proficiency in English.

CEEE Guiding Principles

The Center for Equity and Excellence in Education, through a project funded by the Office of Bilingual Education and Minority Language Affairs (OBEMLA) (now OELA), synthesized the findings of theory and research on appropriate educational practices for CLD students. This synthesis was used to develop the comprehensive Guiding Principles for professional practice with CLD students (Center for Equity and Excellence in Education, 1996). These six Guiding Principles serve as a framework to assist practitioners, policymakers, and clients. Two key aspects of the Guiding Principles distinguish them from other professional standards for CLD students. First, the Guiding Principles are accompanied by an extensive list of over sixty indicators for effective practice. Second, the Guiding Principles are written to uniquely address the roles and responsibilities of the practitioner, policymaker, and client.

■ Standards-Driven Reflection on Professional Practice

After a review and analysis of all the previously mentioned sets of standards, we chose two sets of standards to guide the content of this text: the TESOL/NCATE teacher standards (TESOL, 2001) and the Guiding Principles (Center for Equity and Excellence in Education, 1996). We chose these standards for several reasons. First, the Guiding Principles were found to be the most theory and research grounded, comprehensive, practice-driven, specified through quality indicators, and applicable to a broad base of educational practice. By targeting all levels of the educational system, the organization of the principles and indicators underscores the interconnectedness of the issues and the systemic nature of successful collaborations to enhance academic enrichment and language acquisition among CLD students.

Second, TESOL is the national professional organization for ESL educators, and NCATE is a national accreditation agency for teacher education programs. The TESOL/NCATE standards developed for pre-K–12 ESL teachers reflect professional consensus on standards for the quality teaching of CLD students. Moreover, the TESOL/NCATE standards are consistent with the other national professional teaching standards and include performance indicators and rubrics that help educators effectively target the standards in practice.

Whether you are a content-area or second language acquisition specialist, the likelihood that you will encounter cultural and linguistic diversity within your professional practice increases almost daily. Therefore, this chapter is designed to assist you in building connections between what you have learned about appropriate programming and instruction for CLD students and the recommendations of nationally recognized teaching standards. To simplify the process, only the TESOL/NCATE pre-K–12 teaching standards are used to illustrate ways in which practice can be effectively tied to standards.

Benchmarks of Effective Practice

Effective practice is not characterized by a one-size-fits-all formula. Methods and strategies that are successfully used with some school populations do not work well with others. Additionally, the site-specific dynamics of a particular school or classroom are constantly changing from one year to the next. It is, therefore, unrealistic to think that teacher efforts, which constitute effective practice for a given population at a given point in time, will be equally effective in situations in which one or both of these variables differ. A more practical way to ensure that students are receiving quality education is to incorporate the three benchmarks of effective practice: self-assessment, critical reflection, and the refinement of practice.

Despite the learning nature of the teaching profession, teacher evaluation tends to flow from an administrator to a teacher, a situation that places the teacher in a passive role in the assessment process. This model of assessment does little to effect change in teaching practice (Danielson & McGreal, 2000). Accordingly, we place a high priority on the active participation of the educator in the learning process that is required for a teacher to be a reflective practitioner in educational settings with diverse student populations. Self-assessment is an empowering benchmark in becoming a constructivist learner–teacher.

After self-assessing current practices, effective educators critically reflect on the changes in ideology, perspectives, and attitudes that typically emerge before change in instructional practice can be realized. One goal of this text is to foster an understanding of the research on the process of change in transforming one's own educational practice in ways that enhance the academic achievement and transitional successes of CLD students. As professional educators, we must all understand how our teaching practice affects the achievement of every student we teach, including CLD students.

theory *into Practice*

Mezirow (1991) described the self-reflective process a learner must go through to transform his or her own perspectives. Explained in terms of teaching CLD students, these steps include:

1. Acknowledging that at least some CLD students are not faring well in one's classroom.
2. Identifying the similarities and differences between one's current teaching practice and what research says is effective teaching practice for CLD students.
3. Challenging one's beliefs about the potential of discrepancies between one's own practice and current theory- and research-based practice.
4. Recognizing that other educators face similar dilemmas of practice.
5. Seeking out new research-based teaching methods from the professional literature and knowledgeable colleagues.
6. Gathering as much information about the new theory- and research-based teaching methods as possible.
7. Understanding how and why certain methods are more effective with certain CLD students than others.
8. Creating an implementation plan for using a new method.
9. Experimenting with and refining the implementation of the new method.
10. Implementing the new research-based method as the foundation of one's professional practice.
11. Evaluating the outcomes of implementation and refining professional practice based on the feedback gained.

To this end, Mezirow (1985, 1991) concluded that effective professional development must begin and end with an acknowledgement of the importance of critically reflective dialogue and discourse.

■ *In what ways can educators incorporate reflection and critical reflection in their professional practice? How might educators use technology to gather information and resources concerning research- and theory-based practices for CLD students? In what ways might collaboration with colleagues enhance the process of appropriately accommodating the differential learning and transition needs of CLD students?*

However, simply determining the strengths and weaknesses of one's practice is not enough. If a teacher believes there are areas for growth in his or her professional practice, then action must be taken if students are to reach higher levels of achievement. After critically reflecting on the discrepancies between what they are currently doing and what they predict will be more effective with their students, proactive teachers make efforts to refine classroom practices. Such teachers also realize the necessity of collaborating with colleagues and staying informed about current research. Research-based methods, strategies, and techniques that colleagues are successfully using may provide valuable insight concerning ways instruction can be modified to better meet the needs of CLD students.

Master teachers also know that the benchmarks of effective practice—self-assessment, critical reflection, and practice refinement—do not occur just once or twice each year. Rather, evidence of these benchmarks is apparent throughout an effective educator's professional practice. Master teachers are constantly self-assessing their practice as it relates to standards of best practice, critically reflecting on ways in which their practice could better reflect the existing research and educational theory, and refining their practice to provide students with the best education possible.

Key Facets of a Platform for Best Practice with CLD Students

To assist the educator with the process of self-assessment, the subsequent sections of this chapter focus on the following key facets of a platform for best practice with CLD students (Herrera & Murry, 1999):

1. *Language development and learning dynamics*
2. *Sociopolitical and sociocultural realities*
3. *Planning, implementing, and managing instruction*
4. *Professionalism, reflection, and evaluation of practice*

Because this text emphasizes methodological issues relating to the education of CLD students, each of these facets, and discussions of each, focus on the ways in which standards relate to methodological issues rather than issues of human assessment. Although standards of best practice with CLD students typically address other related issues, such additional challenges are beyond the scope of this text.

As you proceed through each of the self-assessment sections, answer the reflection questions as a source of evidence for the evaluation of your teaching practice. Remember, evidence is factual information, not opinion. You want to collect evidence that includes but is not limited to (a) factual descriptions of your actions, (b) factual descriptions of your students' actions, (c) measurable outcomes such as grades and test scores, (d) quotations from lesson plans, (e) CLD student classroom documentation and samples of student work, (f) parent contact logs, and (g) professional development logs. Once you have gathered your evidence, determine which levels of professional performance best describe your current teaching practice under each rubric topic. Allow considerable time for the review in the follow-

f a l l a c i e s AND f a c t s

Mr. Diaz is an eleventh-grade English teacher at a rural midwestern high school. On a weekly basis, Mr. Diaz reads to the students a list of vocabulary words for SAT preparation. Then he asks the students to write down the weekly list of vocabulary words and define them. For homework the students are required to write sentences using each word appropriately. Mr. Diaz is becoming frustrated with his CLD students who are doing poorly on the weekly vocabulary tests. He posts the vocabulary tests with perfect scores, thinking he will be able to motivate the struggling students.

Fallacy: Vocabulary-focused instruction, in which students write and define words, is an effective way to promote second language acquisition.

Fact: Vocabulary that is acquired in isolation is rarely stored in long-term memory. This drill-and-practice type of activity does not promote second language acquisition effectively because there are no meaningful connections made with the words. Moreover, when CLD students do not find success in their work, their affective filter is often raised and their motivation level decreases. The most effective way to develop second language acquisition is through the instruction of content. Language is acquired through activities that promote listening, speaking, reading, and writing. For example, Mr. Diaz could select vocabulary words from a novel that is of high interest to his CLD students. Because the students find relevancy in the novel, the affective filter is lowered and motivation to learn vocabulary is increased. Another way for Mr. Diaz to make vocabulary more meaningful would be to plan with other content-area teachers who share the same students. They could decide which themes would motivate students and at the same time offer the necessary vocabulary to be acquired. Such professional accommodations are among many constructivist ways to make learning more relevant and meaningful for CLD students.

ing sections, for thinking about the self-reflection questions, and for then self-assessing your practice using the rubrics provided.

Facet 1: Language Development and Learning Dynamics

Language is a critical aspect of instruction. Language is the primary means for communicating information, as well as a foundation of a person's thought processes (Vygotsky, 1962). Language and a teacher's beliefs about second language acquisition become critical issues of instruction when teaching CLD students. For example, if a teacher believes that second language learners are incapable of content-area instruction because of limited English proficiency, then that teacher will not provide CLD students with the content-based language instruction they need to develop high levels of academic language proficiency. Consequently, CLD students may be unfairly excluded from educational opportunities that are available to other students and may not experience academic success to their full potential.

Conversely, a master teacher of CLD students knows how to negotiate meaning using as many situational, nonlanguage supports as possible in order to provide CLD students with a wide range of content-based material from which to construct meaning. Additionally, a master teacher of CLD students understands the levels of language proficiencies that each student brings to the educational experiences and adapts language and instruction accordingly. Finally, master teachers of CLD students are adept at using various instructional materials and groupings of students to promote first and second language acquisition as well as content-related conceptual development.

Consider the following TESOL/NCATE standard when reflecting on your knowledge base concerning learning and language learning, as well as the potential impact on instruction:

> Candidates know, understand, and use the major concepts, theories, and research related to the nature and acquisition of language to construct learning environments that support ESOL (CLD) students' language and literacy development and content area achievement. (TESOL, 2001, p. 1)

Step 1: If you are unsure of the ways in which your knowledge of, or perspectives on, second language acquisition will affect your instruction of CLD students, you are encouraged to refer to the chapters in this text that most significantly address language issues. Chapters 1 through 3 address the dynamic interaction between a CLD student's sociocultural realities and his or her cognitive, academic, and linguistic growth. Chapter 3 stresses the linguistic dimension of the CLD student biography. Chapters 7 through 9 provide a menu of contemporary teaching methods designed for CLD students. These methods are designed to develop both language proficiency and content-area knowledge among CLD students. Some key questions to ask yourself include:

- How do I define learning and language learning?
- In what ways does my knowledge of first and second language acquisition influence my classroom instruction?
- In what ways does my knowledge of CLD students' levels of second language proficiency influence my instructional planning?
- In what ways does my knowledge of the BICS–CALP distinction influence the programmatic decisions and recommendations I make for CLD students?
- What roles do social and academic language play in my classroom?
- How do I plan for CALP development in a student's first and second languages?
- In what ways does my classroom environment foster first and second language acquisition?
- What role does a student's first language play in my classroom?
- In what ways do I support a student's first and second language literacy development?
- How do I provide comprehensible input to CLD students?

Step 2: Your answers to the previous questions provide evidence for assessing your teaching practice. Using Figure 10.1 as a guide, write down your responses to the reflection questions on the right-hand side of the T-chart.

■ **figure 10.1**   Language Development and Learning Dynamics Chart

Research-Based Teaching Practice	My Teaching Practice
Example:	Example:
• Jimenez, García, and Pearson (1996) found that CLD students benefit from explicit instruction in recognizing and applying learning strategies.	• I often teach reading strategy recognition and use the directed reading–thinking activity (DR-TA) which involves using predictions to guide reading.
• Jimenez, García, and Pearson (1996) found that CLD students benefit from using crosslinguistic transfer strategies (bilingual strategies).	• I do not promote student use of the native language when I teach reading strategies.

For any differences between what research indicates is good teaching practice and what you are currently doing, explain why you are choosing your alternative teaching practices.

Step 3: Refer to Chapters 3, 7, 8, and 9 to collect evidence about what educational researchers have described as research-based teaching practice.

Step 4: Write the evidence you collect regarding research-based teaching practice on the left side of the T-chart.

Step 5: Compare how you currently address language development in your professional practice with that which research indicates is effective teaching practice. If you locate any discrepancy or difference between what research defines as good teaching practice and the ways in which you currently practice, explain what has led you to choose your current teaching practices.

Step 6: Finally, use the evidence you have gathered from the teaching practice T-chart to rate yourself using the rubric of Table 10.2.

■ t a b l e   1 0 . 2   Language Development and Learning Dynamics Rubric

	LEVEL OF PERFORMANCE			
Element	**Unsatisfactory**	**Basic**	**Proficient**	**Distinguished**
I understand the critical concepts specific to the curriculum I teach and the implications of pedagogy on language acquisition and learning for students acquiring English.	I do not understand the critical concepts specific to the curriculum I teach as they relate to implications of pedagogy on language acquisition and learning for students acquiring English.	I have a basic understanding of the critical concepts specific to the curriculum I teach and the implications of pedagogy on language acquisition and learning for students acquiring English.	I have a solid understanding of the critical concepts specific to the curriculum I teach and the implications of pedagogy on language acquisition and learning for students acquiring English.	I have an extensive understanding of the critical concepts specific to the curriculum and the implications of pedagogy on language acquisition and learning for students acquiring English.
I design instruction based on my understanding of students' linguistic, cultural, and learning needs.	I design instruction that does not take into account an understanding of students' linguistic, cultural, and learning needs.	I design instruction based on basic knowledge of students' linguistic, cultural, and learning needs.	I design instruction based on solid knowledge of students' linguistic, cultural, and learning needs.	I design instruction based on extensive and thorough knowledge of students' linguistic, cultural, and learning needs.
I select instructional goals and objectives consistent with the linguistic abilities and learning processes of my CLD students.	My instructional goals and objectives are not consistent with the linguistic abilities and learning processes of my CLD students.	My instructional goals and objectives are somewhat consistent with the linguistic abilities and learning processes of my CLD students.	My instructional goals and objectives are consistent with the linguistic abilities and learning processes of my CLD students.	My instructional goals and objectives are highly consistent and aligned with the linguistic abilities and learning processes of my CLD students.
I select resources consistent with the content, linguistic characteristics, and instructional goals and objectives for my CLD students.	I do not select resources consistent with the content, linguistic characteristics, and instructional goals and objectives for my CLD students.	I seldom select resources consistent with the content, linguistic characteristics, and instructional goals and objectives for my CLD students.	I select resources that are generally consistent with the content, linguistic characteristics, and instructional goals and objectives for my CLD students.	I select resources that are highly consistent with the content, linguistic characteristics, and instructional goals and objectives for my CLD students.

Source: Adapted for use with CLD students from Danielson (1996).

Facet 2: Sociopolitical and Sociocultural Realities

As Haim Ginott (1993) once said, "To reach a child's mind a teacher must first capture his heart. Only if a child feels right can he think right" (p. 57). Culture is the heart of student perspectives, expectations, motivations, and evaluations. Indeed, culture lies at the center of the CLD student biography. Integral to engaging and motivating the CLD student is the consideration of his or her sociocultural realities. Failure to consider a student's sociocultural realities can deny the child equitable access to educational opportunities. Instruction that does not build on the student's culture-based socialization and address the sociocultural realities particular to the learner can negatively affect that student's cognitive, academic, and linguistic development.

Previous chapters emphasized the importance of comprehensible input in the learning processes of CLD students. Providing CLD students with comprehensible input goes beyond merely helping them understand the literal meaning of information to making the information relevant to these students (Cummins, 2000, 2001b). Cognitive research supports the importance of making students' cultures an integral part of instruction. In fact, the relevancy of information to a student is a prerequisite to the storage of that information in long-term memory (Jensen, 1996; Sousa, 1995). Consequently, instruction that does not maximize the socialization experiences of a CLD student in a particular culture will do little to promote learning and academic excellence.

A caring connection between students and teachers is also crucial to both content and language learning. Content and language learning are shared experiences between students and the teacher. As the CLD student learns about the language and culture of the teacher, the teacher learns about the language and culture of the student, even if the teacher is not proficient in the student's native language. A master teacher conveys the importance of native language development by promoting the use of the native language in collaborative learning groups, encouraging students to write in their native languages, and providing native language materials whenever feasible.

Language use and curricular content both convey the educator's explicit and underlying perspectives on students' languages and cultures. In a classroom in which language and content learning is transmitted only from teacher to student, students have few opportunities to explore their prior knowledge and experiences in relation to content-area concepts. Such teacher-centered environments require students to abandon their cultures and languages in order to be accepted and succeed in the school environment (Cummins, 2000). Students in these situations enjoy few opportunities to explore their own identities and ways of personal expression. As a consequence, CLD students are less likely to develop a deep, personal understanding of the course content or the ability to express a profound understanding of key concepts in the target language. In other words, they fail to develop CALP (Cummins, 2001b).

The following TESOL/NCATE domain of best practice demonstrates the expectation for the integration of cultural knowledge into professional teaching practice:

> Candidates know, understand, and use the major concepts, theories, and research related to the nature and structure of culture to construct learning environments that

support ESOL (CLD) students' language and literacy development and content area achievement. (TESOL, 2001, p. 15)

Step 1: As you consider this teaching standard and the following reflection questions, you might want to refer to the chapters in this text that best emphasize sociocultural issues. Chapter 1 highlights the ways in which a CLD student's sociocultural realities affect her or his academic, cognitive, and linguistic development. In Chapters 7, 8, and 9, the teaching methods presented discuss culture in the form of prior knowledge connections. Consider the role of students' cultures in your professional practice as you reflect on the following questions:

- For planning and instruction, how do I use the knowledge, skills, and experiences that CLD students bring to my classroom?
- In what ways do I gather and use information regarding students' primary cultures, home environments, communities, and languages?
- In what ways does my instruction affect students' affective filter?
- In what ways do my instructional materials reflect the lives, experiences, cultures, and languages of all students?
- In what ways do I use the prior knowledge, experiences, and native languages of CLD students to enrich instruction for all students?
- How do I address the stages of acculturation that CLD students tend to experience?
- In what ways does my instruction support my students' ethnic identities?
- In what ways do I facilitate or promote social and academic interaction between my CLD students and my native-English-speaking students?

Step 2: Your answers to the previous questions provide evidence for assessing your teaching practice. Using Figure 10.2, write your responses to the reflection questions on the right-hand side of the T-chart.

Step 3: Refer to Chapters 1, 7, 8, and 9 to collect evidence regarding research-based teaching practice.

Step 4: Write the evidence you collect regarding research-based teaching practice on the left side of the T-chart.

Step 5: Compare how you currently address culture in your professional practice with what the research indicates is accommodative teaching practice. For any difference that exists between your current teaching practices and those that research indicates are good teaching practices explain what has prompted you to choose your current teaching practices.

Step 6: Finally, use the evidence you have gathered from the teaching practice T-chart to rate yourself using the rubric of Table 10.3.

Facet 3: Planning, Implementing, and Managing Instruction

Professional educators who are beginning the process of instructional planning for a culturally and linguistically rich setting first consider the sociocultural realities of

■ **figure 10.2**   Sociopolitical and Sociocultural Realities Chart

Research-Based Teaching Practice	My Teaching Practice
Example: • C. Collier (1987) found that teachers' lack of understanding regarding the influences of the acculturation process was often responsible for the overreferral of CLD students to special education.	Example: • I have referred a much larger percentage of my CLD students than my native-English-speaking students for special education evaluation.

For any differences between what research indicates is good teaching practice and what you are currently doing, explain why you are choosing your alternative teaching practices.

CLD students: their prior life experiences, their families, their communities, the school climate, and the school culture. Additionally, they formally or informally preassess students' language proficiencies, educational backgrounds, preferred learning styles, levels of cognitive development, personal interests, areas of strength, and areas of inexperience. CLD student characteristics drive the instructional planning process for these students.

Once the process of preinstructional student assessment has been thoughtfully addressed, knowledge gained from this process is combined with the professional educator's philosophies and perspectives concerning critical issues. For example, the educator should consider questions such as the following: What are my perspectives regarding the ways in which CLD students learn most effectively? What is my worldview on the nature of best practice for second language acquisition? When discerning personal philosophies and perspectives, the professional educator relies on his or her knowledge of educational research regarding CLD students, as well as insight gained through reflection on his or her professional experience. An educator's understanding of and ongoing reflection on her or his perspectives as they relate to

■ **table 10.3** Sociopolitical and Sociocultural Realities Rubric

Element	LEVEL OF PERFORMANCE			
	Unsatisfactory	**Basic**	**Proficient**	**Distinguished**
I consider my students' linguistic, cultural, academic, and cognitive needs when deciding instructional procedures in my classroom.	I do not consider my students' linguistic, cultural, academic, and cognitive needs when deciding instructional procedures in my classroom.	I partially consider my students' linguistic, cultural, academic, and cognitive needs when deciding instructional procedures in my classroom.	I frequently consider my students' linguistic, cultural, academic, and cognitive needs when deciding instructional procedures in my classroom.	I regularly consider my students' linguistic, cultural, academic, and cognitive needs when deciding instructional procedures in my classroom.
I establish a learning environment in which expectations for achievement are high regardless of linguistic abilities and academic backgrounds of students.	I do not establish a learning environment in which expectations for achievement are high regardless of linguistic abilities and academic backgrounds of students.	I generally establish a learning environment in which expectations for achievement are high regardless of linguistic abilities and academic backgrounds of students.	I always establish a learning environment in which expectations for achievement are high regardless of linguistic abilities and academic backgrounds of students.	I consistently and positively establish a learning environment in which expectations for achievement are high regardless of linguistic abilities and academic backgrounds of students.
I respect and acknowledge my students' cultures and native languages in supporting a risk-free environment.	I do not respect and acknowledge my students' cultures and native languages.	I often respect and acknowledge my students' cultures and native languages in supporting a risk-free environment.	I always respect and acknowledge my students' cultures and native languages in supporting a risk-free environment.	I positively and sensitively respect and acknowledge my students' cultures and native languages in supporting a risk-free environment.
I recognize and accept unique interaction styles, values, religions, and worldviews of different cultures represented in my classroom.	I do not recognize and accept unique interaction styles, values, religions, and worldviews of different cultures represented in my classroom.	I seldom recognize and accept unique interaction styles, values, religions, and worldviews of different cultures represented in my classroom.	I frequently recognize and accept unique interaction styles, values, religions, and worldviews of different cultures represented in my classroom.	I consistently and sensitively recognize and accept unique interaction styles, values, religions, and worldviews of different cultures represented in my classroom.

Source: Adapted for use with CLD students from Danielson (1996).

personal and instructional contexts contribute to the successful implementation of site-specific methods and strategies for the instruction of CLD students.

When proactively planning instruction for CLD students, professional educators turn to local, state, and national language and content standards. In order to receive an equitable education, CLD students deserve to be held to the same standards as all other students. However, instructional approaches that appropriately account for the differential learning and transition needs of CLD students provide them with superior support in attaining these content standards. Backward mapping can guide standards-based instructional planning (Mitchell, Willis, & Chicago Teachers' Union Quest Center, 1995; Wiggins & McTighe, 1998). In backward mapping, educators identify learning goals and plan instruction to ensure that CLD students can achieve the goals. Wiggins and McTighe (1998) delineate three stages in their backward design process:

1. Identify desired results.
2. Determine acceptable evidence.
3. Plan learning experiences and instruction.

The desired results of stage 1 of the process are national content and second language standards (e.g., the TESOL standards for CLD students) (TESOL, 1997). In choosing student standards, professional educators ask themselves, "Which knowledge bases and skills do my CLD students need to attain grade-level content and language proficiencies?"

In determining acceptable evidence, educators design assessments that measure levels of attainment of the targeted standards. These assessments can be both formal, such as tests, quizzes, and projects, and informal, such as observations and verbal questioning to determine the general level of understanding in the class. During this stage of the planning process, professional educators ask themselves, "What formal and informal assessments can be used to measure CLD student understanding and incremental progress? In what purposive ways can my CLD students express what they have learned?"

Finally, educators who use the backward design process plan learning experiences and instruction through which CLD students can gain the knowledge and skills needed to achieve the target standards. Key questions at this point in the learning process include: "Which learning experiences will give my CLD students the knowledge and skills they need to reach the goals of this lesson? What materials and resources can be developed or adapted to make learning more meaningful? In what ways can instruction be modified or differentiated to ensure that CLD students are able to match or exceed the target standards for this unit?"

The following domain descriptor from the TESOL/NCATE teacher standards applies to the planning, implementation, and management of instruction for CLD students:

Candidates know, understand, and are able to use standards-based practices and strategies related to the planning, implementation, and management of ESL and content instruction, including classroom organization, teaching strategies for developing and integrating language skills, and choosing and adapting classroom resources. (TESOL, 2001, p. 21)

Step 1: In considering this standard and the following reflection questions, you may want to refer to the chapters in this text that best address the planning, implementation, and management of instruction for CLD students. Chapter 6 addresses approaches, methods, strategies, and techniques and provides the theoretical and research-based foundation for understanding the teaching methods discussed in Chapters 7 through 9. Chapter 7 introduces the integrated content-based method, Chapter 8 discusses the method of sheltered instruction, and Chapter 9 provides an overview of the CALLA method. Because all of the contemporary methods presented in this text are grounded in a strong research base, educators can confidently choose from any one of the methods discussed in Chapters 7 through 9 as a means of organizing and presenting instruction. The following questions should guide you as you reflect on your professional practice in terms of this key facet of a platform for best practice with CLD students:

- Do I know the national, state, and local teaching standards and benchmarks for my content area, as well as those that apply to the appropriate instruction of CLD students?
- In what ways do I use national, state, and local content and second language teaching standards and benchmarks as I plan instruction?
- Which instructional method do I use to teach my CLD students? What is the research basis or rationale underlying my chosen method?
- How do I select the most appropriate strategies and techniques to differentiate instruction for students with varying levels of English and native language proficiency?
- In what ways does my instruction build on the preferred learning styles of my CLD students?
- To what extent are my CLD students actively involved in classroom instruction?
- In what ways do I support my CLD students in reaching grade-appropriate content standards?
- How and to what extent do I integrate language and content-area instruction?
- What kinds of opportunities and support do I provide for my CLD students as they develop their speaking, listening, reading, and writing skills in my class?
- What kinds of supplementary materials do I use in my class to support the cognitive, academic, and linguistic development of my CLD students?
- In what specific ways do I ensure that my CLD students have access to the same challenging curriculum as other students?

Step 2: Your answers to the previous questions provide evidence for assessing your teaching practice. Using Figure 10.3, write your responses to the reflection questions on the right-hand side of the T-chart.

■ **f i g u r e   1 0 . 3**   Planning, Implementing, and Managing Instruction Chart

Research-Based Teaching Practice	My Teaching Practice
Example: • Lessons that include both language and content objectives facilitate a CLD student's academic and linguistic development.	Example: • My lessons always have both language and content objectives.

For any differences between what research indicates is good teaching practice and what you are currently doing, explain why you are choosing your alternative teaching practices.

Step 3: Refer to Chapters 6 through 9 to collect evidence about what educational researchers have said regarding research-based teaching practice.

Step 4: Write the evidence you collect regarding research-based teaching practice on the left side of the T-chart.

Step 5: Compare how you currently address planning, implementing, and managing instruction in your professional practice with what the research indicates is effective accommodative teaching practice. For any difference between what research indicates is good teaching practice and what you currently do in practice, explain what has led you to choose your current teaching practices.

Step 6: Finally, use the evidence you have gathered from the teaching practice T-chart to rate yourself using the rubric of Table 10.4.

■ table 10.4 Planning, Implementing, and Managing Instruction Rubric

	LEVEL OF PERFORMANCE			
Element	**Unsatisfactory**	**Basic**	**Proficient**	**Distinguished**
The content and instruction in my classroom is designed to maximize student engagement and learning.	The content and instruction in my classroom does not maximize student engagement and learning.	The content and instruction in my classroom is seldom designed to maximize student engagement and learning.	The content and instruction in my classroom is usually designed to maximize student engagement and learning.	The content and instruction in my classroom is always designed to maximize student engagement and learning.
I understand the academic and linguistic needs of my students and provide flexibility and responsiveness during lesson delivery.	I do not take into account the academic and linguistic needs of my students, and my instruction does not provide flexibility and responsiveness during lesson delivery.	I seldom take into account the academic and linguistic needs of my students and provide flexibility and responsiveness during lesson delivery.	I frequently take into account the academic and linguistic needs of my students and often provide flexibility and responsiveness during lesson delivery.	I consistently and extensively take into account the academic and linguistic needs of my students and provide high levels of flexibility and responsiveness during lesson delivery.
I adjust questioning and discussion techniques to maximize student participation based on linguistic abilities.	I do not adjust my questioning and discussion techniques according to students' linguistic abilities.	I seldom adjust my questioning and discussion techniques to maximize student participation based on linguistic abilities.	I generally adjust questioning and discussion techniques to maximize student participation based on linguistic abilities.	I consistently and efficiently adjust questioning and discussion techniques to maximize student participation based on linguistic abilities.
I use multiple modes of communicating and facilitating feedback to ensure CLD students' understanding of expectations and lesson objectives.	I do not communicate and provide feedback to ensure CLD students' understanding of expectations and lesson objectives.	I often communicate and facilitate my feedback in a way that ensures CLD students' understanding of expectations and lesson objectives.	I always use multiple modes of communicating and facilitating feedback to ensure CLD students' understanding of expectations and lesson objectives.	I efficiently and sensitively use multiple modes of communicating and facilitating feedback to ensure CLD students' understanding of expectations and lesson objectives.

Source: Adapted for use with CLD students from Danielson (1996).

Facet 4: Professionalism, Reflection, and Evaluation of Practice

Recently, signs of a new trend have emerged. This trend redefines and reconceptualizes the educator as an adult learner who is capable of ongoing, self-directed, and critically reflective practice. Educators are more frequently asking questions about the students they serve and are often successful in developing instructional plans that are better aligned with the needs of the CLD students they serve. Given the diversity of the languages and cultures represented in today's classrooms, as well as the individuality of the educators working in such classrooms, no one method or model can successfully address all challenges in all classrooms. Indeed, the educator's knowledge of theory, the history of second language instruction, current research, and site-specific practice dynamics combined with the knowledge gained from preinstructional student assessments should determine which approach, methods, and strategies will be implemented in a particular classroom or school setting.

Self-directed, culturally conscious, profession-oriented educators are in the best position to undertake informed and authentic decision making that accommodates the complexity of practice settings and diverse student populations. Darling-Hammond (1986) provides a useful description of profession-oriented practice:

> In a more professional conception of teaching, teachers plan, conduct, and evaluate their work both individually and collectively. Teachers analyze the needs of their students, assess resources available, take the school district's goals into account, and decide on their instructional strategies. (p. 532)

Given this new conception of teaching, teacher self-evaluation becomes largely an organized effort to implement teaching standards in a professional approach to practice.

Four key indicators characterize this profession-oriented approach to educational practice (Shanker, 1985). First, professional educators align their practice with national teaching standards. Additionally, they read journals and practitioners' texts and participate in conferences to ground themselves in the constantly evolving professional knowledge base. Furthermore, collaborative relationships with colleagues characterize the interactions of these educators. Finally, professionals act in the informed best interest of the learners in their classrooms and schools. They become true advocates for the needs of their students at the local, state, or national levels.

TESOL/NCATE teaching standards define professionalism in the following manner:

> Candidates demonstrate knowledge of the history of ESL teaching. Candidates keep current with new instructional techniques, research results, advances in the ESL field, and public policy issues. Candidates use such information to reflect on and improve their instructional practices. Candidates provide support and advocate for ESOL (CLD) students and their families and work collaboratively to improve the learning environment. (TESOL, 2001, p. 38)

Are You Aware? A number of professional organizations and publications address the following four key facets of a platform for best practice with CLD students discussed in this chapter: *language development and learning dynamics; sociopolitical and sociocultural realities; planning, implementation, and managing instruction*; and *professionalism, reflection, and evaluation of practice*. Included below are professional organizations and journals that may or may not be specific to CLD students but that are relevant to CLD students. These resources promote best practices among teachers as well as increased student academic achievement.

- The National Association for Bilingual Education (NABE) advocates for the differential needs of CLD students and emphasizes the importance of providing all children with access to a quality education. Publication: *Bilingual Research Journal*.
- Teachers of English to Speakers of Other Languages (TESOL) articulates and advances standards for professional preparation, continuing education, and student programs. It advocates teaching English to speakers of other languages to help them foster effective communication in diverse settings while respecting individuals' first language rights. Publications: *TESOL Quarterly; Essential Teacher*.
- The National Association for Multicultural Education (NAME) strives to bring together professionals from diverse disciplines who have a professional interest in multicultural education. Publication: *Multicultural Perspectives*.
- The International Reading Association (IRA) promotes high levels of literacy for all students and cooperates with NCATE to accredit programs in reading for institutions and states. Publications: *Standards for Reading; The Reading Teacher (RT); The Journal of Adolescent & Adult Literacy (JAAL); Reading Research Quarterly (RRQ)*.

Step 1: In considering this standard and the following reflection questions, you may want to refer to the chapters in this text that best address professional practice with CLD students and reflection on that practice. Chapter 4 discusses research regarding the effectiveness of various program models. Chapter 5 explores the following areas of educator readiness that are needed to deliver mutually accommodative instruction: critical reflection, CLD students and families, environment, curriculum, programming, instruction, application, and advocacy. As you reflect on your professional capacities, consider the following questions:

- Which journals, texts, and other materials have I read lately about teaching CLD students?
- In what ways have I been involved in shaping local, state, or national guidelines, curriculum, or policy regarding CLD students?
- In what ways am I applying in practice what I have been learning about teaching CLD students?
- How do I involve the family members of my CLD students as well as community members in my classroom practice and in the school environment?
- In what ways do I share what I am learning about teaching CLD students with colleagues in my school or state?

- To what extent and in what ways do I collaborate with my colleagues to provide CLD students with appropriate educational services?
- In what ways have I changed my professional practice as a result of getting to know my students, reading professional literature, collaborating with my colleagues, participating in workshops or graduate classes, and reflecting on my teaching practice?
- How do I become actively involved in advocating for the rights of my CLD students and families?
- What role does social justice play in my professional practice and in my curriculum?

Step 2: Your answers to the previous questions provide evidence for assessing your teaching practice. Using Figure 10.4, write your responses to the reflection questions on the right-hand side of the T-chart.

Step 3: Refer to Chapters 4 and 5 to collect evidence concerning research-based teaching practice.

Step 4: Write the evidence you collect regarding research-based teaching practice on the left side of the T-chart.

Step 5: Compare how you currently address professionalism in your professional practice with what research indicates is effective teaching practice. For any difference between what research indicates is good teaching practice and what you currently do, explain what has prompted you to choose your current teaching practices.

Step 6: Finally, use the evidence you have gathered from the teaching practice T-chart to rate yourself using the rubric of Table 10.5.

■ Conclusion: Setting Goals for Professional Development

As you read this chapter, you should be assessing your professional practice in terms of current research and national teaching standards.

- How did you rate yourself?
- Were you honest with yourself?
- What surprised you?
- Did you confirm what you already knew about your professional practice?
- Was self-assessment uncomfortable? Why or why not?
- In what ways did you critically reflect on your self-assessments?
- In what ways will you refine your practice as a result of applying the benchmarks of self-assessment, critical reflection, and refinement of practice?

At this point in your self-assessment process, you should reexamine your responses to the reflection questions, the T-charts, and the rubrics to discern your areas of

■ **figure 10.4**   Professionalism, Reflection, and Evaluation of Practice Chart

Research-Based Teaching Practice	My Teaching Practice
Example: • Adult or teacher reflection involves building a capacity for surfacing assumptions and testing the validity of those assumptions (Murry, 1996).	Example: • As I read through this textbook, I actively compared what I am doing in my classroom to what the research indicates I should be doing, but I didn't try to identify my underlying assumptions regarding teaching CLD students.

For any differences between what research indicates is good teaching practice and what you are currently doing, explain why you are choosing your alternative teaching practices.

strength and your areas for growth. Then, using Table 10.6, choose two to three areas in which you have the most potential for growth. Use the table to write goals, list potential resources, decide on actions, and determine expected outcomes. In this manner, you can maximize Table 10.6 as a guide to your ongoing professional development.

Fullan (2001) has summarized the necessary conditions for change in a teacher's professional practice. Specifically, he discussed the importance of changing personal perspectives on teaching, using new instructional materials, and participating in professional development designed to support change in practice. However, all of these essential elements, as they relate to the education of CLD students, may or may not be readily available in one's teaching environment. If new instructional materials and professional development opportunities for educating CLD students are not readily available, then the teacher must rely on his or her own research and volition. Consider the ways in which you might (a) build your knowledge base through reading professional literature, (b) collaborate with other

■ **table 10.5**   Professionalism, Reflection, and Evaluation of Practice Rubric

Element	LEVEL OF PERFORMANCE			
	Unsatisfactory	**Basic**	**Proficient**	**Distinguished**
I reflect on the multidimensional educational needs of my CLD students and take action to ensure academic success.	I do not reflect on the multidimensional educational needs of my CLD students and do not take action to ensure academic success.	I seldom reflect on the multidimensional educational needs of my CLD students and sometimes take action to ensure academic success.	I generally reflect on the multidimensional educational needs of my CLD students and often take action to ensure academic success.	I regularly reflect on the multidimensional educational needs of my CLD students and regularly take action to ensure academic success.
I communicate in a language the parents understand and pursue nontraditional ways of ensuring participation in their child's education.	I do not communicate in a language parents understand and pursue few ways of ensuring participation in their child's education.	I seldom communicate in a language the parents understand and pursue few nontraditional ways of ensuring participation in their child's education.	I regularly communicate in a language the parents understand and often pursue nontraditional ways of ensuring participation in their child's education.	I regularly and consistently communicate in a language the parents understand and sensitively pursue nontraditional ways of ensuring participation in their child's education.
I look for ways to share my knowledge of CLD students and their needs with colleagues and district administrators to ensure equity in access to high-quality education.	I do not share my knowledge of CLD students and their needs with colleagues and district administrators.	I sometimes share my knowledge of CLD students and their needs with colleagues and district administrators to ensure equity in access to high-quality education.	I frequently share my knowledge of CLD students and their needs with colleagues and district administrators to ensure equity in access to high-quality education.	I consistently and efficiently share my knowledge of CLD students and their needs with colleagues and district administrators to ensure equity in access to high-quality education.
I recognize the need to continue enhancing my professional knowledge and its role in advocacy and decision making.	I do not consider the need to enhance my professional knowledge and its role in advocacy and decision making.	I sometimes consider the importance of enhancing my professional knowledge and its role in advocacy and decision making.	I frequently recognize the need to continue enhancing my professional knowledge and its role in advocacy and decision making.	I consistently and regularly recognize the need to continue enhancing my professional knowledge and its role in advocacy and decision making.

Source: Adapted for use with CLD students from Danielson (1996).

■ **t a b l e 1 0 . 6** Setting Goals for Professional Development

Perceived Area(s) of Growth	Related Goals	Potential Resources	Actions	Expected Outcomes
Example: Using CLD students' first languages as a resource	Example: CLD students in my classroom will use their native languages as a resource for understanding classroom instruction and texts.	Example: • Bilingual peers • Bilingual para-professionals • Parents • Siblings • Native language texts/materials • Teachers using the native languages of students for instruction • Professional books and journals	Example: 1. Read journal articles and talk to experienced teachers about providing students with native language support. 2. Encourage my students to use their native languages in more capable peer or collaborative group activities that emphasize literacy and connections to prior knowledge. 3. Teach my students to recognize and use cognates to enhance their understanding of content. 4. Use bilingual paraprofessionals or others to work on developing content understanding in the native language of the student, rather than translating homework. 5. Gather content-related texts in the languages represented in my classroom.	Example: 1. CLD students will increase their reading comprehension and content understanding as measured by a minimum of one letter grade higher average in my class. 2. CLD student active involvement in classroom instruction will increase by 50 percent.

educators to advise and coach one another, (c) focus on your relative strengths to discuss with students how your teaching affects their learning, (d) make better use of or adapt available resources, and (e) gather new resources. This process of professional growth should not occur in isolation. Create a relationship of mutual support with other educators who are progressing through the same self-reflective process.

Now that you know what research-defined effective practice for CLD students entails, how will you share that information with students, parents, colleagues, administrators, and policymakers? What are you going to do to become a self-directed learner and make the necessary changes in your professional practice? In what ways are you going to address inappropriate teaching practices in your school? As Howard Zinn (2002) has so astutely observed, "You can't be neutral on a moving train" (p. i). We challenge you to move forward using what you have learned to initiate and sustain the change process in your own professional practice, encourage and support changes in the practice of other educators, and advocate for educational policies and practices that ensure equitable access to high-quality education for all CLD students.

tips for practice

Note: Tips for practice are listed according to each of the four key facets of a platform for best practice with CLD students.

If you would like more information on *language development and learning dynamics* as they relate to CLD students, the following books will further your professional development in this area:

1. August, D., & Hakuta, K. (1997). *Improving schooling for language-minority children: A research agenda.* Washington, DC: National Academy Press.

   This book summarizes recent educational research on second language acquisition for CLD students as it relates to classroom practice.

2. Bialystok, E., & Hakuta, K. (1995). *In other words: The science and psychology of second-language acquisition.* New York: Basic Books.

   This book explains second language acquisition from multiple perspectives: linguistics, biology, psychology, anthropology, and sociology. It conveys key concepts in second language acquisition in an easily accessible manner.

3. De la Luz Reyes, M., & Halcón, J. (2001). *The best for our children: Critical perspectives on literacy for Latino students.* New York: Teachers College Press.

   This book provides tips for literacy instruction for CLD students; teaching CLD students with learning disabilities; making literacy culturally relevant for CLD students; helping CLD students to develop critical literacy; and involving parents in CLD students' literacy development.

If you would like more information on the *sociopolitical and sociocultural realities* of practice as they relate to CLD students, the following books will further your professional development in this area:

1. Cummins, J. (2001). *Language, power, and pedagogy: Bilingual children caught in the crossfire.* Philadelphia: Multilingual Matters.

   This book explains how the sociopolitical realities of U.S. society affect the education of CLD students and provides a framework for addressing these realities through classroom instruction.

2. Darling-Hammond, L., French, J., & García-Lopez, S. (2002). *Learning to teach for social justice*. New York: Teachers College Press.

   This book describes ways in which teachers can lead students to identify and challenge cultural assumptions; restructure curriculum to examine topics from multiple points of view and challenge students to take action on social issues; promote respect and inclusion of all students within a classroom; encourage students to graduate from high school; and build community.

3. Tse, L. (2001). *Why don't they learn English? Separating fact from fallacy in the U.S. language debate*. New York: Teachers College Press.

   This book dispels misconceptions regarding language use and learning in the United States.

If you would like more information on *planning, implementing, and managing instruction* as they relate to CLD students, the following books will further your professional development in this area:

1. Brinton, D., Snow, M., & Wesche, M. (2003). *Content-based second language instruction: Michigan classics*. Ann Arbor: University of Michigan Press.

   This book provides an in-depth description of integrated content-based instruction.

2. Chamot, A., & O'Malley, J. M. (1994). *The CALLA handbook: Implementing the cognitive academic language learning approach*. Boston: Longman.

   This book provides an in-depth description of the CALLA method and its use in a variety of instructional settings.

3. Echevarria, J., Vogt, M., & Short, D. (2000). *Making content comprehensible for English language learners*. Boston: Allyn and Bacon.

   This book provides an in-depth description of the SIOP model of sheltered instruction.

If you would like more information on *professionalism, reflection, and evaluation of practice* as they relate to CLD students, the following books will further your professional development in this area:

1. Danielson, C. (1996). *Enhancing professional practice: A framework for teaching*. Alexandria, VA: Association for Supervision and Curriculum Development.

   This book provides an extensive description of effective teaching practice as well as a teacher assessment tool that addresses effective teaching from multiple perspectives.

2. Fullan, M. (2001). *The new meaning of educational change* (3rd ed.). New York: Teachers College Press.

   This book provides an in-depth discussion of the educational change process and makes suggestions for initiating, implementing, and sustaining educational change.

3. Miramontes, O., Nadeau, A., & Commins, N. (1997). *Restructuring schools for linguistic diversity: Linking decision making to effective programs*. New York: Teachers College Press.

   This book offers a decision-making framework for developing and implementing instructional programming for CLD students.

4. Vavrus, M. (2002). *Transforming the multicultural education of teachers: Theory, research, and practice*. New York: Teachers College Press.

   This book gives recommendations for addressing the sociopolitical and multicultural realities of professional practice with diverse student populations. Vavrus goes beyond the celebration mentality of multicultural education to pose difficult but necessary questions to move teachers and teacher educators to a transformative view of multicultural education.

■ key theories and concepts

advocacy
benchmarks of effective practice

CREDE standards
critical reflection

evidence
Guiding Principles

key facets of a platform for best practice	NBPTS standards	refinement of practice
language development	planning, implementing, managing	self-assessment
learning dynamics	professionalism, reflection, evaluation	sociopolitical and sociocultural realities
maximizing standards		TESOL/NCATE standards

■ professional conversations on practice

1. This chapter demonstrates the ways in which school educators can achieve standards-driven professional practice with CLD students and families by maximizing self-assessment, critical reflection, and refinements to practice. Discuss the critical importance of standards-driven professional practice and at least three beneficial outcomes that are possible from targeting this level of practice.

2. This chapter serves as the evaluation component of Part III of this text. Discuss the following: (a) the rationale behind the organization of this text in relation to professional practice with CLD students, and (b) the role this chapter plays in that organization.

■ questions for review and reflection

1. In what specific ways can a school educator maximize standards of best practice with CLD students?

2. What are the origins and general purposes of at least two nationally recognized sets of standards for best practice with CLD students?

3. What are the benchmarks of effective practice with CLD students, as discussed in this chapter? In what ways do these benchmarks target standards-driven reflection on professional practice?

4. What role does a teacher's perspectives on content and language learning play in instructional planning?

5. In what specific ways is practice enhanced when it is well grounded in theory and research?

6. In what ways would you define evidence in teaching?

7. In what ways can the use of backward planning enhance instruction?

8. In what ways do the CEEE Guiding Principles and the TESOL/NCATE standards for professional practice with CLD students compare and contrast?

9. What are some questions the professional should ask in deciding his or her perspectives on learning and language learning?

10. What is the role of a caring connection between the CLD student and his or her teacher in professional practice?

suggested activities

Preservice Teachers

1. Compare and contrast the four key facets of a platform for best practice with CLD students. Discuss the implications of each facet for providing CLD students with a high-quality education.

2. Chapter 10 discusses the benefits of aligning classroom pedagogy and process planning with

standards. When choosing standards that promote CLD student excellence, it is important to consider how you can address each of the four key facets identified in this chapter. Therefore, obtain a set of state or district standards and analyze the standards using the guiding questions below.

In the case of theory- and research-based support, consider the following:
- Are the standards based on cited sources of research and theory?
- How current are the sources cited?
- Are the sources derived from robust analyses of theory and rigorous research applicable to CLD students?
- What is the quality of research that supports the standards, and how applicable is that research to the differential learning and adjustment needs of CLD students in your region?

In the case of cross-cultural sensitivity, consider the following:
- Do the standards control for biases regarding culture and ethnicity?
- Do the standards consider important information related to culture and ethnicity?
- Do the standards demonstrate inclusive perspectives on culture and ethnicity?
- Do the standards promote diversity, multiculturalism, and cross-cultural affirmation in the school and in the classroom?
- Do the standards support student acculturation without assimilation?

In the case of the extent to which standards can be directly connected to classroom practice, consider the following:
- Can you make direct connections between the standards and your educational practice?
- Can you make a strong connection between the standards and the student populations represented in your school?

- Are specific indicators of best practice incorporated into the standards?
- Can language and content objectives be aligned with the standards?

In the case of advocacy and leadership, consider the following:
- Do the standards promote advocacy for appropriate programming, differentiated classroom instruction, and CLD student accommodation?
- Do the standards support and encourage ongoing CALP development in L1 for CLD students?
- Do the standards encourage teacher leadership in the school, district, community, and region?
- Do the standards support collaboration among educators in appropriate accommodations for CLD students and families?
- Do the standards endorse ongoing professional development, especially that which better prepares teachers, administrators, and staff for the differential learning, language learning, and transitional needs of CLD students?

In-Service Teachers

1. In a collaborative group, compare and contrast the four key facets of a platform for best practice with CLD students and discuss the feasibility of implementing each of these key facets in your professional practice. Then, as a group, create a lesson plan that reflects elements of each key facet and implement it with CLD students. Assess the effectiveness of the lesson plan as a collaborative group.

2. As a collaborative group, select one of the four key facets and an element within that facet. Discuss what evidence you would collect as a group to demonstrate attainment of the highest level of performance.

Selected Examples of Activities That Are Specific to Sociocultural, Academic, Cognitive, and Linguistic Growth among Mexican American Students

Because the overwhelming majority of CLD students are Spanish dominant and because many of these are Mexican American students, this appendix provides examples of classroom activities that are specific to the background experiences and growth needs of these students. These activities are organized according to those applicable to elementary, middle, and high school. Within each of these categories, the activities are further subdivided according to those that apply to language arts, mathematics, and social studies.

■ Elementary School

1. Mathematics: Ask students to talk about their experiences at the *mercado* (market) in Mexico, in either Spanish or English (ask a paraprofessional, community volunteer, or more capable peer to translate as necessary). Have students draw their favorite items to buy at the *mercado* (especially items not typically available in your region of the United States). (*Note:* Students may be familiar with terms other than *mercado*, such as *colmado*.) Discuss with students a fair price to attach to their favorite items in U.S. currency based on their prior experiences. For example, if they have, in their prior experience, purchased a mango for 8 pesos and there are roughly 8 pesos to the dollar at this time, then the item would cost one U.S. dollar. Then ask students to select U.S. coins from a classroom box that will enable them to purchase two of their favorite items with the least amount of coins. Allow students to experiment in a meaningful and constructivist way with various coin combinations to arrive at the optimal mathematical solution.

2. Mathematics: Heterogeneously group students by language and mathematical capabilities. For any non-English-speaking (NES) students, ensure that a more capable Spanish-speaking peer is also in that group (as feasible). Ask students to use the Internet to research the role of mariachi bands and music in Mexican culture. Have Mexican American students share their experiences with mariachi bands with the group in L1 or L2 (collaborate with paraprofessionals or more capable peers to translate as needed). Provide students with opportunities to listen to mariachi music that you have acquired through local sources or the Internet.

Discuss the ways in which many mariachi bands include as many as twelve members, each of whom may sing or play a different musical instrument. Have students locate pictures of mariachi bands on the Internet. Ask them to print these photographs (black-and-white or color) and cut pictures to form their own twelve-member mariachi band. Have students collaborate to solve each of the following mathematical challenges involving fractions and their mariachi band: (a) If your mariachi band has been performing for several hours and 1/2 of the band decides to take a break of ten minutes, what fraction of the band is left to perform and how many band members remain? (b) If 2/3 of your twelve-member mariachi band perform in the restaurant and 1/3 performs on the patio, how many band members are on the patio? (c) If 1/6 of your complete mariachi band is featured in the performance of a particular song, how many band members are not featured and what fraction of the band is not featured?

3. **Language Arts:** Use modified preview-view-review (Kole, 2003) to explore a big book text available in both Spanish and English (e.g., *Cómo Nació el Arco Iris* [Ada, 1999]). First use a paraprofessional, parent volunteer, or community liaison to *preview* the story in Spanish, using the big book for illustration. Discuss difficult vocabulary that may inhibit understanding in Spanish. Second, *view* or read the book to the students in English, again maximizing the big book illustrations to establish context. Third, *review* the book in Spanish to clarify any misunderstandings among students.

4. **Language Arts:** Each week of the school year, encourage bilingual literacy development by conducting a Friday Free Day. During a designated time on this day, students are *free* to write about whatever they wish, in whatever language they are comfortable. Collaborate with paraprofessionals, parent volunteers, community members, or more capable peers to translate any passage written in Spanish by your Mexican American students. Encourage *freewriting* and *creative spelling*. Maximize the writing of your Mexican American students as informal preassessment and assessment of important information, including level of acculturation, literacy development in Spanish, prior schooling or academic experiences, interests and motivators, and so forth. Provide nonthreatening feedback on students' writing samples, especially feedback that is intentionally designed to encourage their future writing efforts in purposive directions. Periodically engage Mexican American students in encouraging dialogue about their writing and other academic interests based on the areas of curiosity they have demonstrated in their writing samples (collaborate with a translator as needed).

5. **Social Studies:** As a means of reinforcing a lesson on direction in geography, provide cooperative groups of students with a blank map of Mexico. Ask the groups to identify north, south, east, and west on the blank map, as well as borders and coasts. Use student records or notes from prior preassessments of Mexican American students to focus the activity on particular cities or geographic regions in Mexico (e.g., border cities, ports, mountainous regions) with which they are familiar. Ask groups of students to identify a northern border town, a

western beach town, an eastern port, or a southern mountainous region with which they are familiar. Ask Mexican American students to share their prior experiences with the group's selected town or region of Mexico. Then provide each group with a map of Mexico (e.g., from a travel atlas). Ask each group to discuss the direction they would proceed in traveling from their selected town or region to (a) Mexico City, (b) the United States, and (c) Guatemala.

6. Social Studies: Schedule a Special Day once a month throughout the school year. On this day, allow rotating students to present to or share with the class anything about the geography, lifestyles, culture, or history of their background. Encourage all students, especially the Mexican American students, to invite parents, extended family members, or community members to share with the class as part of the presentation. Permit students or guests to share in Spanish or English by collaborating with more capable peers, paraprofessionals, or community members to translate as needed. Encourage students also to share artifacts, documents, or maps, and copy them for the class as feasible. Use these presentations as foci for discussions about commonalities and differences across cultures, the value of bilingualism, the importance of parental involvement, and more. Each month of the school year, create a bulletin board on which highlights from students' presentations are posted for the class and guests to review and discuss.

■ Middle School

1. Mathematics: Heterogeneously group students by language and mathematical capabilities. For any NES students, ensure that a more capable Spanish-speaking peer is also in that group (as feasible). Ask students to plan a trip from Mexico City to at least two major sites of pyramids in Mexico (i.e., they will visit two sites in one trip from Mexico City). Allow students to maximize the Internet in locating pyramid sites (e.g., Tulum) and in selecting the locations to which they wish to travel. Provide the groups with a map of Mexico that appropriately simplifies distances to potential sites (according to the mathematical and geographical capabilities represented among students), but post those distances in kilometers. Ask students to highlight their best route from Mexico City to the two sites and rationalize their choice in L1 or in L2 (collaborate with community volunteers, paraprofessionals, or more capable peers to translate as needed). Students should then calculate the distance from Mexico City to the final site, via the first pyramid site, using their selected routes. This distance should be calculated in kilometers. Then ask students to determine the total distance traveled on their trip, in miles, using the conversion 1 kilometer = 0.6213712 miles. Finally, have groups compare their routes and trips. During this process, students should determine who had the longest and shortest trips (in miles) and estimate the driving time for each of those routes.

2. Language Arts: Ask students to form into cooperative learning groups, the members of which have mixed second language abilities. Provide a miniature Mexican flag or a large illustration of the flag to each group. Have the group discuss in

L1 or L2 what each of the figures and colors of the flag symbolize. If group members are unsure of these connotations, ask them to discuss what the flag symbolizes for each of the members of the group. Based on these discussions, ask each student to individually write in L1 or L2 (or type at the computer) what the flag means to her or him. As necessary, ask more capable peers, parent volunteers, or paraprofessionals to translate passages written in Spanish.

3. **Social Studies:** Ask students to individually identify with a particular state in Mexico in which they have lived or have an abiding interest (e.g., Tamaulipas). Then cooperatively group students (to the extent feasible) by the state or region (which might encompass two or more neighboring states) with which they have identified. Ask students to collaboratively identify a state of common interest for discussion and research as a group. Ask students to discuss and focus on the following: (a) What is the main industry or source of employment in that state of Mexico? (b) What are the major population centers and their density in that state? (c) What aspects of culture are unique to that state (e.g., styles of living, foods, celebrations, etc.)? First, ask students to discuss and answer the questions from their own experiences. Then ask students to fill the knowledge gaps they identify by using the classroom library, school library, or the Internet. Finally, ask groups to develop a brief presentation that explores answers to each of the questions. Offer them options for presentation format, such as a board meeting, drama, or PowerPoint.

4. **Social Studies:** Discuss with the class the concept of a passport. Obtain a passport from a friend or use graphics from a book or the Internet to illustrate the concept. Discuss with the class what is typically included and not included in a passport. Explore what someone from a new country who wanted to be your friend might want to know about you and whether such information would be included in a typical passport. Create an assignment in which each student in the class develops a Learning Passport. In this passport, they will include a picture, their full name, their country of origin, the region of the country in which they were born, information about their family and extended family, information about their culture, information about their key learning interests, information about what they interpret to be their strengths and weaknesses as learners, and information about what occupation they hope to pursue as an adult. Students will also include in their passport one teacher section for each period of the typical school day. Students should develop their Learning Passports as a foldout brochure on word-processing software, and they should keep a copy on disk. Mexican American students should be encouraged to develop bilingual, two-part passports with the aid of a paraprofessional, community volunteer, or more capable peer. Once the format and student sections of the brochure are complete, students should meet in heterogeneous learning groups to share their passports and discuss what they learned from each. Next, students should share their Learning Passports and associated disks with their various teachers on a once per quarter basis. In the appropriate teacher section of the passports, teachers should update the disk to include those methods, strategies, and techniques of instruction that are proving effective for this student. The teacher should then return the reprinted brochure and disk to the stu-

dent. Students can periodically update their own Learning Passports and share them with parents and extended family members. Teachers can learn from the student and other teachers in the building (a) what the student brings to the classroom that can be elaborated on in classroom instruction, (b) what interests or motivates the student, and (c) what methods, strategies, and techniques have proven effective with the student.

■ High School

1. Mathematics: Discuss with students ways in which to figure out the time required to travel between cities at a given rate of speed. Ask students to form in cooperative learning groups, the members of which have mixed second language abilities. Provide the groups with maps of Mexico or Puerto Rico. Ask students to select three cities in Mexico or Puerto Rico that are at least thirty-five miles distant from one another. Tell students that they will be taking a road trip from the first city, to the second, to the third, without stopping for gasoline. Ask them to first determine the distances between their selected cities from the map. Then ask them to derive an average speed for the car based on their knowledge of the region, terrain, and traffic. Next, ask them to deliberate, collaborate, and determine the amount of time required to reach each of the two destinations (e.g., time from city one to two, time from city two to three, and total time from city one to three). Ask each group to briefly present their findings (in L1 or L2) and the methods they used to arrive at each solution (collaborate with paraprofessionals, parent volunteers, or more capable peers for translations). After these presentations, conduct a whole-class discussion of this exercise with an emphasis on applications to other types of mathematical challenges (allow NES students to respond in L1 as necessary). For algebra students, also ask them to construct a word problem from their exercise, with answers already calculated. Discuss the ways in which word problems in algebra can be reframed by students into more culturally and experientially meaningful problems for their solution.

2. Language Arts: Teach the concept of Spanish–English cognates to a class of students. Have heterogeneous groups of Spanish- and English-dominant students research (using the Internet or the library) which Spanish–English cognates are useful in the following subject areas: mathematics, science, and history. After the groups have developed their lists for each subject area, ask them to research, for each subject area, the hypothesis that increasingly technical terms are more likely to prove cognates. Finally, ask each group to (a) present their cognate lists to the class, (b) discuss the findings of their research regarding the hypothesis, and (c) discuss their explanation of findings regarding the hypothesis and potential implications for second language acquisition.

3. Social Studies: Heterogeneously group students by language ability and prowess in social studies or history. Have students use library and Internet resources to compare presidents. Ask them to identify one president from the history of Mexico and one from the history of the United States who were similar in background, philosophy, management style, foreign policy, and so forth. Have the students develop one or more graphics that illustrate these similarities (e.g., T-chart, web, table). Discuss the notion of culture and the ways in which a person learns a particular culture. Ask the students to research and develop a bulleted summary of reasons why these two presidents are similar despite the fact that each was socialized to a different culture. Have each group present or discuss their graphic and their summary. Highlight discussions that explore the ways in which cultures are similar.

ABC taxonomy   A tool that is used for the development of vocabulary in the first and second languages and for the assessment of students' prior knowledge. An ABC taxonomy consists of a piece of paper on which the alphabet is listed down the left-hand side. For each letter, students generate words related to the current topic.

adaptation   A means or path to acculturation in which the individual learns a new culture while retaining the best of his or her primary culture. This process is preferred to the **assimilation** method of acculturation in which the individual is prompted to relinquish his or her primary culture (and often language) as he or she learns another.

affective filter   Controls the extent to which an individual internalizes input by converting it into learning. It has been compared to a defense mechanism because if it is raised it may negatively influence language acquisition, academic success, and classroom behavior and action.

approach   The philosophical orientation to instruction that serves as a guide for choosing among methods considered consistent with the tenets of the theory and research that ground the philosophy.

assimilation   A means or path to acculturation in which the individual is prompted to relinquish his or her primary culture (and often language) as he or she learns another. This process contrasts with the more preferred method of acculturation, **adaptation,** in which the individual learns a new culture while retaining the best of his or her primary culture.

brokering   A means by which two parties of different languages or cultures communicate with each other through the mediation of a third party, often a CLD student.

caregiver speech   A means of communication in which an adult modifies his or her language to make the information comprehensible for a child. Modification efforts to accommodate

the child include adjusting vocabulary, simplifying sentences, and incorporating modeling and rephrasing. See also **motherese.**

cognate   A word in one language, the form and definition of which resemble a word in a different language (e.g., *animals* [English] and *animales* [Spanish]).

communicative competence   The ability of an individual to comprehend incoming messages and effectively communicate responses in ways that are appropriate for a given situation.

comprehensible input   New language information that an individual is able to understand because efforts have been made to draw on the individual's cognitive and linguistic abilities as well as to accommodate his or her cognitive and linguistic needs.

concurrent translation   An ineffective manner of delivering instruction in which everything is stated twice, once in English (L2) and once in the native language (L1).

conditional knowledge   The comprehension of *when, why,* or *where* to use information, capacities, and skills.

creative spelling   The product of an individual's attempt to spell an unfamiliar word using her or his cumulative knowledge regarding a language.

declarative knowledge   The information that constitutes *what* an individual knows or can declare as related to a topic.

discourse   A communication of oral or written language that occurs within a context in ways that directly influence the manner in which the individual constructs and expresses his or her thoughts and ideas.

elaboration   The process of building on prior knowledge as a basis for learning new concepts.

foreigner talk   A means of communication in which a native English speaker modifies his or her language to accommodate the needs of a non-native English speaker by talking at a slower pace, reducing the complexity of sentences, avoiding contractions, expanding phrases, and incorporating other modifications to enhance the comprehension of the non-native English speaker.

fundamental attribution error   The inclination of an individual to apply a different set of criteria to others than to himself or herself when making judgments; also when the shortcomings of others are perceived as a result of internal factors while the individual's own shortcomings are perceived as a result of external, circumstantial factors (also referred to as *blaming the victim*).

grade-level classroom   A classroom designed to accommodate the needs of native-English-speaking students who are generally expected to have roughly equivalent levels of background academic knowledge that is considered appropriate for their age.

guarded vocabulary   Language in which the speaker makes a conscious effort to enunciate words, simplify sentence structure, speak a little more slowly, emphasize key information, and pause momentarily between sentences and main ideas.

interference hypothesis   An outdated notion not supported by research that suggests that L1 capacities drastically interfere with L2 acquisition.

invented spelling   The product of an individual's attempt to spell a word that he or she does not already know how to spell, using her or his cumulative knowledge regarding a language.

joinfostering   The process by which a grade-level teacher of a linguistically diverse classroom population promotes two-way communication and the social integration of all students within the classroom.

language brokering   A means by which two parties of different languages communicate with each other through the mediation of a third party, often a CLD student.

manipulatives   Tangible, hands-on materials such as Cuisenaire rods, counters, felt boards, beakers, and scales that enable students to practice skills and explore new concepts in contextualized and meaningful ways.

meritocracy   A system in which the upward mobility of an individual is almost solely determined by his or her individual efforts because it is assumed that the educational system treats all students the same. This notion is built on the premise of equality versus equity as well as the false notion of a level playing field and is, therefore, detrimental to the success of CLD students in school.

method   A body of philosophically grounded and purposively integrated strategies and techniques that constitutes one translation of an approach in professional practice.

morpheme   The smallest unit of language that carries meaning. For instance, the word *talked* comprises two morphemes, *talk* and *-ed*.

Bound morphemes—morphemes that cannot stand alone within a sentence and must be attached to other morphemes (e.g., *-ed*).

Free morphemes—morphemes that can stand alone as a word within a sentence (e.g., *talk*).

morphology   The study of how words are formed, including aspects such as compounds, derivations, and so forth.

motherese   A means of communication in which an adult modifies his or her language to make the information comprehensible for a child. Efforts to accommodate the child include adjusting vocabulary, simplifying sentences, and incorporating modeling and rephrasing. See **caregiver speech.**

non-English speaker (NES)   An individual who has little or no proficiency in the English language. The preferred term is *CLD* because the *N* in NES highlights a deficit rather than an asset.

paralinguistics   The study of behaviors that contribute to linguistic communication, such as body movements and voice pitch, duration, tone, and loudness.

phoneme   The smallest unit of sound that conveys a distinction in meaning during speech production. For instance, the *s* in *song* is a phoneme.

phonology   The study of sounds in speech, including their distribution and pronunciation.

pragmatics   The study of the use of language in the context of social and related interactions.

procedural knowledge   An individual's understanding of *how* to use information to exercise a capacity or to sequence actions as a skill.

reductionism   The educational approach used in teaching content knowledge that involves breaking the curriculum into subjects, allotting each subject a specific period of time, and emphasizing basic skills and concepts rather than holistic learning. This term also refers to an occidental tradition of reducing complex concepts and tasks to their simplest component units for purposes of study, understanding, or pedagogy.

reification   The treatment of concepts, ideas, societal tendencies, states of affairs, and so forth as permanent, concrete, and inherently right.

scaffolding   The use of supporting aids and activities that enable the student to perform tasks that would otherwise be too complex for his or her abilities.

semantics   The study of linguistic meaning.

socialization   The total of one's prior experiences and interpersonal, cultural, and cross-cultural interactions that influence one's attitudes, beliefs, values, skills, understandings, and knowledge.

social justice   The equity of access to opportunities and resources for all people, regardless of perspectives on race, ethnicity, language, gender, religion, sexual orientation, physical and mental ability, SES status, or social class.

strategy   A collection of philosophically grounded and functionally related techniques that serves as an implementation component of an instructional method.

syntax   The manner in which words and other structural elements of language are arranged to construct the sentences of a language.

target language   The language around which instruction for second language acquisition is designed.

technique   Specific actions or action sequences that have been designed to achieve a defined, strategic objective.

threshold hypothesis   The proposition that an individual must reach a certain level of proficiency in the primary language to ensure that developmentally appropriate cognitive abilities are acquired and that the bilingual abilities of the individual can be used to enhance cognitive growth.

transitional signal   A word or phrase in writing that cues an individual to the fact that a change in direction, thought, or topic is going to occur.

word bank   A collection of words that are related to a particular topic and that can serve as choices to be used to complete an activity.

Acton, W. R., & de Félix, J. W. (1986). Acculturation and mind. In J. M. Valdés (Ed.), *Culture bound* (pp. 20–32). New York: Cambridge University Press.

Ada, A. F. (1999). *Cómo nació el arco iris* [How the rainbow was born]. Miami: Santillana USA.

Adams, M. J. (1990). *Beginning to read: Thinking and learning about print*. Cambridge, MA: MIT Press.

Adler, D. A. (1997). *Cam Jansen and the mystery of the dinosaur bones*. New York: Puffin Books.

Akmajian, A., Demers, R. A., Farmer, A. K., & Harnish, R. M. (1995). *Linguistics: An introduction to language and communication* (4th ed.). Cambridge, MA: MIT Press.

Alexander, F. (1986). *California assessment program: Annual report*. Sacramento: California State Department of Education.

Alexander, K., Alexander, M. D., & Alexander, D. (2000). *American public school law* (5th ed.). Belmont, CA: Wadsworth.

Alvarez, J. (1991). *How the García girls lost their accents*. Chapel Hill, NC: Algonquin Books.

Amaral, O., Garrison, L., & Klentschy, M. (2002). Helping English learners increase achievement through inquiry-based science instruction. *Bilingual Research Journal, 26*(2), 213–239.

American Association for Employment in Education (AAEE). (2001). *Educator supply and demand in the United States: Executive Summary.* Columbus, OH: Author.

American Psychological Association Board of Educational Affairs (APA). (1995). *Learner-centered psychological principles: A framework for school redesign and reform* [Online]. Available at www.apa.org/ed/lcp.html.

Anderson, J. R. (1983). *The architecture of cognition.* Cambridge, MA: Harvard University Press.

Anderson, N. J. (1999). *Exploring second language reading: Issues and strategies.* Boston: Heinle & Heinle.

Anderson, N. J. (2002). *The role of metacognition in second language teaching and learning.* Washington, DC: ERIC Clearinghouse on Languages and Linguistics. (ERIC Digest No. EDO-FL-01-10)

Angell, V. (1997). *Teachers as researchers.* Retrieved February 22, 2003, from www.suu.edu/faculty/angell/Comprehension/teacher.researchers.htm.

Anstrom, K. (1998a). *Preparing secondary education teachers to work with English language learners: English language arts* (NCBE Resource Collection Series No. 10). Washington, DC: National Clearinghouse for Bilingual Education. Retrieved January 13, 2003, from www.ncela.gwu.edu/ncbepubs/resource/ells/language.htm.

Anstrom, K. (1998b). *Preparing secondary education teachers to work with English language learners: Science* (NCBE Resource Collection Series No. 11). Washington, DC: National Clearinghouse for Bilingual Education. Retrieved October 23, 2002, from www.ncela.gwu.edu/ncbepubs/resource/ells/science.htm.

Anstrom, K. (1999a). *Preparing secondary education teachers to work with English language learners: Mathematics* (NCBE Resource Collection Series No. 14). Washington, DC: National Clearinghouse for Bilingual Education. Retrieved January 13, 2003, from www.ncela.gwu.edu/ncbepubs/resource/ells/math.htm.

Anstrom, K. (1999b). *Preparing secondary education teachers to work with English language learners: Social studies* (NCBE Resource Collection Series No. 13). Washington, DC: National Clearinghouse for Bilingual Education. Retrieved January 13, 2003, from www.ncela.gwu.edu/ncbepubs/resource/ells/social.htm.

Anthony, E. M. (1963). Approach, method, and technique. *English Language Teaching, 17,* 63–67.

Anthony, E. M., & Norris, W. E. (1969). *Method in language teaching.* ERIC focus report on teaching of foreign languages No. 8. New York: Modern Language Association of America. (ERIC Document Reproduction Service No. ED031984)

Appiah, K. A., & Gates, H. L. (1997). *The dictionary of global culture.* New York: Knopf.

Armbruster, B., Anderson, T., & Meyer, J. (1991). Improving content-area reading using instructional graphics. *Reading Research Quarterly, 26*(4), 393–416.

Au, K. (1980). Participation structures in a reading lesson with Hawaiian children. *Anthropology and Education Quarterly, 11,* 91–115.

Au, K. (2000). A multicultural perspective on policies for improving literacy achievement: Equity and excellence. In M. Kamil, P. Mosenthal, P. D. Pearson,

& R. Barr (Eds.), *Handbook of reading research: Volume III* (pp. 835–851). Mahwah, NJ: Lawrence Erlbaum.

Au, K. H., & Carroll, J. H. (1997). Improving literacy achievement through a constructivist approach: The KEEP Demonstration Classroom Project. *Elementary School Journal, 97,* 203–221.

August, D., & Hakuta, K. (Eds.). (1997). *Improving schooling for language-minority children: A research agenda.* Washington, DC: National Academy Press.

Awh, E., & Jonides, J. (1998). Spatial selective attention and spatial working memory. In R. Parasuraman (Ed.), *The attentive brain* (pp. 353–380). Cambridge, MA: MIT Press.

Baca, L., & Cervantes, H. (1998). *The bilingual special education interface.* Upper Saddle River, NJ: Merrill.

Baddeley, A. D. (1986). *Working memory.* Oxford, UK: Clarendon Press.

Baker, C., & Freebody, P. (1988). Talk around text: Construction of textual and teacher authority in classroom discourse. In S. de Castell, A. Like, & C. Luke (Eds.), *Language, authority, and criticism: Readings on the school textbook* (pp. 111–132). London: Falmer.

Banich, M. T. (1997). *Neuropsychology: The neural bases of mental function.* Boston: Houghton-Mifflin.

Banks, J. (1993). Approaches to multicultural curriculum reform. In J. A. Banks & C. A. M. Banks (Eds.), *Multicultural education: Issues and perspectives* (2nd ed., pp. 195–214). Boston: Allyn and Bacon.

Bastian, A., Fruchter, N., Gittell, M., Greer, C., & Hoskins, K. (1986). *Choosing equality.* Philadelphia: Temple University Press.

Beck, S. (n.d.). *Considerations, notes, accommodations & adaptations for English language learning (ELL)/limited English proficient (LEP) students in mainstream classrooms.* Retrieved February 24, 2003, from www2.gasou.edu/facstaff/salbeck/ELL-LEP.html.

Bennett, C. I. (1999). *Comprehensive multicultural education: Theory and practice* (4th ed.). Boston: Allyn and Bacon.

Berlak, H. (1999). Standards and the control of knowledge [Electronic version]. *Rethinking Schools, 13*(3).

Bialystok, E. (1981). The role of conscious strategies in second language proficiency. *Modern Language Journal, 65,* 24–35.

Bialystok, E. (1990a). *Communication strategies.* Cambridge, MA: Basil Blackwell.

Bialystok, E. (1990b). The dangers of dichotomy: A reply to Hulstijn. *Applied Linguistics, 11,* 46–52.

Bialystok, E. (2001). *Bilingualism in development: Language, literacy, & cognition.* New York: Cambridge University Press.

Bilingual Education Act of 1968, Pub. L. No. 90-247, 81 Stat. 816 (1968).

Blair, R. (Ed.). (1982). *Innovative approaches to language teaching.* Rowley, MA: Newbury House.

Bley-Vroman, R. (1988). The fundamental character of foreign language learning. In W. Rutherford & M. Sharwood-Smith (Eds.), *Grammar and second language teaching: A book of readings* (pp. 19–30). New York: Newbury House/Harper & Row.

Bloom, B. (1956). *Taxonomy of educational objectives: The classification of educational goals: Handbook I, cognitive domain.* New York: Longman.

Boyd, V. (1992). *School context: Bridge or barrier to change.* SEDL's Leadership for Change Project. Retrieved October 15, 2002, from www.sedl.org/change/school/welcome.html.

Brinton, D. M., Snow, M. A., & Wesche, M. B. (1989). *Content-based second language instruction.* New York: Newbury House.

Brisk, M. E. (1981). Language policies in American education. *Journal of Education, 163*(1), 3–15.

Broderbund. (2003). Reader Rabbit: Learn to read with phonics 1st & 2nd grade [Computer software]. Novato, CA: Author.

Brooks, N. (1960). *Language and language learning: Theory and practice.* New York: Harcourt, Brace & World.

Brown, H. D. (1986). Learning a second culture. In J. M. Valdes (Ed.), *Culture bound* (pp. 33–48). New York: Cambridge University Press.

Brown, H. D. (1987). *Principles of language learning and teaching* (2nd ed.). Englewood Cliffs, NJ: Prentice Hall.

Brown, H. D. (1992). Sociocultural factors in teaching language minority students. In P. A. Richard-Amato & M. A. Snow (Eds.), *The multicultural classsroom: Readings for content-area teachers* (pp. 73–92). White Plains, NY: Longman.

Brown, H. D. (1994). *Principles of language learning and teaching* (3rd ed.). Englewood Cliffs, NJ: Prentice Hall.

Burns, M. (1993). *Mathematics: Assessing understanding.* White Plains, NY: Cuisenaire Company of America.

Butler, D., & Winne, P. (1995). Feedback and self-regulated learning: A theoretical synthesis. *Review of Educational Research, 65,* 245–281.

Buxton, C. (1999). Designing a model-based methodology for science instruction: Lessons from a bilingual classroom [Electronic version]. *Bilingual Research Journal, 23*(2–3). Retrieved November 12, 2002, from http://brj.asu.edu/v2323/articles/art4.html.

Cahill, L., Prins, B., Weber, M., & McGaugh, J. (1994). Adrenergic activation and memory for emotional events. *Nature, 371,* 702–704.

Caine, R. N., & Caine, G. (1991). *Making connections: Teaching and the human brain.* Alexandria, VA: Association of Supervision and Curriculum Development.

Calderón, M., Tinajero, J., & Hertz-Lazarowitz, R. (1992). Adopting cooperative integrated reading and composition to meet the needs of bilingual students. *The Journal of Educational Issues of Language Minority Students, 10,* 79–106.

California State Department of Education. (1994). *Building bilingual instruction: Putting the pieces together.* Sacramento, CA: Bilingual Education Office.

Canale, M. (1983). From communicative competence to communicative language pedagogy. In J. Richards & R. Schmidt (Eds.), *Language and communication* (pp. 2–27). New York: Longman.

Cantoni-Harvey, G. (1987). *Content-area language instruction: Approaches and strategies.* Reading, MA: Addison-Wesley.

Carr, E., Dewitz, P., & Patberg, J. (1983). The effect of inference training on children's comprehension of expository text. *Journal of Reading Behavior, 15*(3), 1–18.

Carrera, J. W. (1989). *Immigrant students: Their legal right of access to public schools.* Boston: National Coalition of Advocates for Students.

Castañeda v. Pickard, 648 F.2d 989 (5th Cir. 1981).

Cazden, C. (1977). Language, literacy and literature. *The National Elementary Principal, 57*(1), 40–52.

Cazden, C. B. (1979). Curriculum/language contexts for bilingual education. In E. J. Briere (Ed.), *Language development in a bilingual setting* (pp. 129–138). Los Angeles: California State University, National Dissemination and Assessment Center. (ERIC Document Reproduction Service No. ED224661)

Center for Advanced Research on Language Acquisition (CARLA). (n.d.). *Why content-based instruction?* University of Minnesota. Retrieved September 16, 2002, from http://carla.acad.umn.edu/CBI.html.

Center for Equity and Excellence in Education. (1996). *Promoting excellence: Ensuring academic success for limited English proficient students.* Arlington, VA: Author.

Chambers, J., & Parrish, T. (1992). *Meeting the challenge of diversity: An evaluation of programs for pupils with limited proficiency in English: Vol. 4. Cost of programs and services for LEP students.* Berkeley, CA: BW Associates.

Chamot, A. U. (1985, December). Guidelines for implementing a content-based English language development program. *NCBE Forum, 8*(6), 2.

Chamot, A. (1995). Implementing the cognitive academic language learning approach: CALLA in Arlington, Virginia. *Bilingual Research Journal, 19*(3–4), 379–394.

Chamot, A. U., Dale, M., O'Malley, J. M., & Spanos, G. (1992). Learning and problem solving strategies of ESL students. *Bilingual Research Journal, 16*(3–4), 1–33.

Chamot, A., & El-Dinary, P. (1999). Children's learning strategies in language immersion classrooms. *The Modern Language Journal, 83,* 319–338. Retrieved October 24, 2002, from WilsonSelectPlus database.

Chamot, A. U., & El-Dinary, P. B. (2000). *Children's learning strategies in language immersion classrooms.* Washington, DC: National Capital Language Resource Center. (ERIC Document Reproduction Service No. ED445518)

Chamot, A. U., & O'Malley, J. M. (1994). *The CALLA handbook: Implementing the cognitive academic language learning approach.* Reading, MA: Addison-Wesley.

Chamot, A., & O'Malley, J. (1996). The cognitive academic language learning approach: A model for linguistically diverse classrooms. *The Elementary School Journal, 96,* 259–273.

Chi, M. T. H., de Leeuw, N., Chiu, M. H., & LaVancher, C. (1994). Eliciting self-explanations improves conceptual understanding, *Cognitive Science, 18,* 439–477.

Chomsky, N. (1966). Linguistic theory. In R. G. Mead, Jr. (Ed.), *Northeast conference on the teaching of foreign languages: Reports of the working committees* (pp. 43–49). New York: MLA Materials Center.

Chomsky, N. (1986). *Knowledge of language: Its nature, origin, and use.* New York: Praeger.

Christian, D. (1994). *Two-way bilingual education: Students learning through two languages* (Educational Practice Rep. No. 12). Washington, DC, and Santa Cruz, CA: National Center for Cultural Diversity and Second Language Learning.

Clay, M. (1991). *Becoming literate: The construction of inner control*. Portsmouth, NH: Heinemann.

Clegg, J. (Ed.). (1996). *Mainstreaming ESL: Case studies in integrating ESL students into the mainstream curriculum*. Clevedon, UK: Multilingual Matters.

Cobb, P. (1994). Where is the mind? Constructivist and sociocultural perspectives on mathematical development. *Educational Researcher, 23*(7), 13–20.

Cohen, E. G. (1986). *Designing groupwork: Strategies for the heterogeneous classroom*. New York: Teachers College Press.

Cohen, A. D. (1998). *Strategies in learning and using a second language*. Harlow Essex, UK: Longman.

Collier, C. (1987). Comparison of acculturation and education characteristics of referred and nonreferred culturally and linguistically different children. In L. M. Malare (Ed.), *NABE theory, research and application: Selected papers* (pp. 183–195). Buffalo: State University of New York.

Collier, V. P. (1987). The age and rate of acquisition of second language for academic purposes. *TESOL Quarterly, 21*, 617–641.

Collier, V. P. (1988, April). *The effect of age on acquisition of a second language for school*. Washington, DC: National Clearinghouse for Bilingual Education.

Collier, V. P. (1989a). *Academic achievement, attitudes, and occupations among graduates of two-way bilingual classes*. Paper presented at the annual meeting of the American Educational Research Association, San Francisco, CA.

Collier, V. P. (1989b). How long? A synthesis of research on academic achievement in a second language. *TESOL Quarterly, 23*, 509–531.

Collier, V. P. (1992). A synthesis of studies examining long-term language minority student data on academic achievement. *Bilingual Research Journal, 16*(1–2), 187–212.

Collier, V. P. (1995a). *Acquiring a second language for school*. Washington, DC: National Clearinghouse for Bilingual Education.

Collier, V. P. (1995b). *Promoting academic success for ESL students: Understanding second language acquisition for school*. Elizabeth: New Jersey Teachers of English to Speakers of Other Languages-Bilingual Educators.

Collier, V. P., & Thomas, W. P. (1988). *Acquisition of cognitive-academic second language proficiency: A six-year study*. Paper presented at the annual meeting of the American Educational Research Association, New Orleans, LA.

Collier, V. P., & Thomas, W. P. (1989). How quickly can immigrants become proficient in school English? *Journal of Educational Issues of Language Minority Students, 5*, 26–38.

Cooper, J. D. (1986). *Improving reading comprehension*. Boston: Houghton Mifflin.

Costa, A., & Liebmann, R. (1997). *Envisioning process as content: Towards a Renaissance community*. Thousand Oaks, CA: Corwin Press.

Council of Chief State School Officers (CCSSO). (1992). *Recommendations for improving the assessment and monitoring of students with limited English proficiency*. Washington, DC: Author.

Crandall, J., Spanos, G., Christian, D., Simich-Dudgeon, C., & Willetts, K. (1987). Integrating language and content instruction for language minority students. *NCBE Teacher Resource Guide Series*. Retrieved March 5, 2003, from www.ncela.gwu.edu/ncbepubs/classics/trg/04integrating.htm.

Crandall, M. (1998). Bilingual education: Policy worth pursuing. *The High School Magazine, 6*(2), 44.

Crawford, J. (1992a). *Hold your tongue: Bilingualism and the politics of "English only."* Reading, MA: Addison-Wesley.

Crawford, J. (1992b). What's behind official English? In J. Crawford (Ed.), *Language loyalties: A source book on the Official English controversy* (pp. 171–177). Chicago: University of Chicago Press.

Crawford, J. (1995). *Bilingual education: History, politics, theory, and practice* (3rd ed.). Los Angeles: Bilingual Educational Services.

Crawford, J. (1997). *Best evidence: Research foundations of the Bilingual Education Act*. Washington, DC: National Clearinghouse for Bilingual Education. Online at www.ncbe.gwu.edu/ncbepubs/reports/bestevidence/.

Crawford, J. (1999). *Bilingual education: History, politics, theory, and practice* (4th ed.). Los Angeles: Bilingual Educational Services.

Crawford, J. (2000). *At war with diversity: U.S. language policy in an age of anxiety*. Clevedon, UK: Multilingual Matters.

Cresswell, J. W. (1994). *Research design: Qualitative and quantitative approaches.* Thousand Oaks, CA: Sage.

Cummins, J. (1979). Linguistic interdependence and the educational development of bilingual children. *Review of Educational Research, 49*(2), 222–251.

Cummins, J. (1981). The role of primary language development in promoting educational success for language minority students. In C. F. Leyba (Ed.), *Schooling and language minority students: A theoretical framework* (pp. 3–49). Los Angeles: Evaluation, Dissemination and Assessment Center, CSULA.

Cummins, J. (1989). Language and affect: Bilingual students at home and at school. *Language Arts, 66,* 29–43.

Cummins, J. (1991). Interdependence of first- and second-language proficiency in bilingual children. In E. Bialystok (Ed.), *Language processing in bilingual children* (pp. 70–89). Cambridge, UK: Cambridge University Press.

Cummins, J. (1992). Bilingual education and English immersion: The Ramírez report in theoretical perspective. *Bilingual Research Journal, 16*(1–2), 91–104.

Cummins, J. (1994). Primary language instruction and the education of language minority students. In C. F. Leyba (Ed.), *Schooling and language minority students: A theoretical framework* (2nd ed., pp. 3–46). Los Angeles: California State University, National Evaluation, Dissemination and Assessment Center.

Cummins, J. (1996). *Negotiating identities: Education for empowerment in a diverse society.* Los Angeles: California Association for Bilingual Education.

Cummins, J. (1998). Language issues and educational change. In A. Hargreaves, A. Lieberman, M. Fullan, & D. Hopkins (Eds.), *International handbook of educational change* (pp. 440–459). Dordrecht, Netherlands: Kluwer Academic.

Cummins, J. (1999). *BICS and CALP: Clarifying the distinction.* (ERIC Document Reproduction Service No. ED438551)

Cummins, J. (2000). "This place nurtures my spirit": Creating contexts of empowerment in linguistically diverse schools. In R. Phillipson (Ed.), *Rights to language: Equity, power and education* (pp. 249–258). Mawah, NJ: Lawrence Erlbaum.

Cummins, J. (2001a). Instructional conditions for trilingual development. *International Journal of Bilingual Education and Bilingualism, 4*(1), 61–75.

Cummins, J. (2001b). *Language, power, and pedagogy: Bilingual children in the crossfire.* Philadelphia: Multilingual Matters.

Cummins, J., & Swain, M. (1986). *Bilingualism in education.* New York: Longman.

Cunningham, P. M., Moor, S. A., Cunningham, J. W., & Moore, D. W. (1995). *Reading and writing in elementary classrooms: Strategies and observations* (3rd ed). White Plains, NY: Longman.

Curtain, H. (1995). *Helena Curtain: Integrating language and content instruction* [Video]. Manoa: University of Hawaii, NFLRC Second Language Teaching and Curriculum Center.

Curtain, H., & Haas, M. (1995). *Integrating foreign language and content instruction in grades K–8.* Washington, DC: ERIC Clearinghouse on Languages and Linguistics. (ERIC Digest No. EDO-FL-95–07.) Retrieved February 19, 2003, from www.cal.org/ericcll/digest/int-for-k8.html.

Curtain, H., & Pesola, C. A. (1994). *Languages and children, making the match* (2nd ed.). New York: Longman.

Cushner, K., McClelland, A., & Safford, P. (2000). *Human diversity in education: An integrative approach* (3rd ed.). Boston: McGraw-Hill.

Dalton, S. S. (1998). *Pedagogy matters: Standards for effective teaching practice* (Research Report No. 4). Santa Cruz: University of California, Center for Research on Education, Diversity & Excellence.

Danielson, C. (1996). *Enhancing professional practice: A framework for teaching.* Alexandria, VA: Association for Supervision and Curriculum Development.

Danielson, C., & McGreal, T. L. (2000). *Teacher evaluation: To enhance professional practice.* Alexandria, VA: Association for Supervision and Curriculum Development.

Darling-Hammond, L. (1986). A proposal for evaluation in the teaching profession. *Elementary School Journal, 86*(4), 531–551.

Darling-Hammond, L. (1992, November). Reframing the school reform agenda. *The School Administrator,* 22–27.

Deci, E. L., & Ryan, R. M. (1985). *Intrinsic motivation and self-determination in human behavior.* New York: Plenum.

de Lopez, M., & Montalvo-Cisneros, M. (1986). Developing community support for second language programs. *Foreign Language Annals, 19*(6), 529–531.

de Saint-Exupéry, A. (2000). *The little prince* (R. Howard, Trans.). San Diego, CA: Harcourt.

Delgado-Gaitán, C. (1989). Classroom literacy activity for Spanish-speaking students. *Linguistics and Education, 1,* 285–297.

Delpit, L. (1995). *Other people's children: Cultural conflicts in the classroom.* New York: New Press.

Derry, S. J. (1999). A fish called peer learning: Searching for common themes. In M. O'Donnell & A. King (Eds.), *Cognitive perspectives on peer learning* (pp. 197–211). Mahwah, NJ: Lawrence Erlbaum.

Díaz, S., Moll, L. C., & Mehan, H. (1986). Sociocultural resources in instruction: A context-specific approach. In Bilingual Education Office, California Department of Education (Ed.), *Beyond language: Social and cultural factors in schooling language minority students* (pp. 187–230). Los Angeles: Evaluation, Dissemination, and Assessment Center, California State University.

Diaz-Rico, L. T., & Weed, K. Z. (2002). *The crosscultural, language, and academic development handbook: A complete K–12 reference guide* (2nd ed.). Boston: Allyn and Bacon.

Dilworth, M. E., & Brown, C. E. (2001). Consider the difference: Teaching and learning in culturally rich schools. In V. Richardson (Ed.), *Handbook of research on teaching* (4th ed., pp. 643–667). Washington, DC: American Educational Research Association.

Dolson, D. P., & Mayer, J. (1992). Longitudinal study of three program models for language-minority students: A critical examination of reported findings. *Bilingual Research Journal, 16*(1–2), 105–157.

Donato, R. (1997). *The other struggle for equal schools: Mexican Americans during the civil rights era.* Albany: State University of New York Press.

Duffy, G. G., Roehler, L. R., & Mason, J. (1984). *Comprehension instruction: Perspective and suggestions.* New York: Longman.

Dulay, H., & Burt, M. (1977). Remarks on creativity in language acquisition. In M. Burt, H. Dulay, & M. Finocchiaro (Eds.), *Viewpoints on English as a second language* (pp. 95–126). New York: Regents.

Dulay, H., Burt, M., & Krashen, S. (1982). *Language two.* Oxford, UK: Oxford University Press.

Duncan, S., & DeAvila, E. (1979). Bilingualism and cognition: Some recent findings. *NABE Journal, 4*(1), 15–50.

Earl, L., & LeMahieu, P. (1997). Rethinking assessment and accountability. In A. Hargreaves (Ed.), *Rethinking educational change with heart and mind* (pp. 149–168). The 1997 ASCD Yearbook. Alexandria, VA: Association for Supervision and Curriculum Development.

Echevarria, J., & Graves, A. (2003). *Sheltered content instruction: Teaching English-language learners with diverse abilities* (2nd ed.). Boston: Pearson Education.

Echevarria, J., & Short, D. (2001). *Selected findings from the CREDE SIOP research project.* Center for Applied Linguistics. Retrieved December 20, 2002, from www.cal.org/crede/si.htm.

Echevarria, J., Vogt, M., & Short, D. J. (2000). *Making content comprehensible for English language learners: The SIOP Model.* Boston: Allyn and Bacon.

Echevarria, J., Vogt, M., & Short, D. J. (2002, June). *SIOP training of trainers institute.* Symposium conducted at California State University, Long Beach, CA.

Edelsky, C. (1982). Writing in a bilingual program: The relation of L1 and L2 texts. *TESOL Quarterly, 16,* 211–228.

Education Watch. (1996). *The Education Trust: Community data guide.* Washington, DC: Author.

Ehren, B. J., & Gildroy, P. G. (2000). Background knowledge (Module IV, Lesson 1). In B. J. Ehren (Ed.), *Building background knowledge for reading comprehension* [Online]. Lawrence: The University of Kansas, Center for Research on Learning. Retrieved March 7, 2003, from http://itc.gsu.edu/academymodules/a304/support/xpages/a304b0_20400.html.

Elly, W. (1991). Acquiring literacy in a second language: The effect of book-based programs. *Language Learning, 41,* 375–411.

Elman, J., Bates, E. A., Johnson, M., Karmiloff-Smith, A., Parisi, D., & Plunkett, K. (1997). *Rethinking innateness.* Cambridge, MA: MIT Press.

Enright, D., & McCloskey, M. (1988). *Integrating English: Developing English language and literacy in the multilingual classroom.* Reading, MA: Addison-Wesley.

Escamilla, K. (1994). The sociolinguistic environment of a bilingual school: A case study introduction. *Bilingual Research Journal, 18,* 21–48.

Escamilla, K. (1999). The false dichotomy between ESL and transitional bilingual education programs: Issues that challenge all of us. *Educational Considerations, 26*(2), 1–6.

Escamilla, K. (2000). Teaching literacy in Spanish. In J. Tinajero & R. DeVillar (Eds.), *The power of two languages.* New York: Macmillan/ McGraw-Hill.

Fairfield Language Technologies. (2000). The Rosetta Stone Level I, Classroom Edition (Version 1.5.5S/2.3.8S) [Computer software]. Harrisonburg, VA: Author.

Faltis, C. (1986). Initial cross-lingual reading transfer in bilingual second grade classrooms. In E. García & B. Flores (Eds.), *Language and literacy research in bilingual education* (pp. 145–157). Tempe: Arizona State University Press.

Faltis, C. J., & Hudelson, S. J. (1998). *Bilingual education in elementary and secondary school communities: Toward understanding and caring.* Boston: Allyn and Bacon.

Feinberg, R. C. (2000). Newcomer schools: Salvation or segregated oblivion for immigrant students. *Theory into Practice, 39*(4), 220–227. Retrieved October 14, 2002, from WilsonSelectPlus database.

Félix-Ortiz, M., Newcomb, M. D., & Myers, H. (1994). A multidimensional measure of cultural identity for Latino and Latina adolescents. *Hispanic Journal of Behavioral Science, 16*(2), 99–115.

Fern, V., Anstrom, K., & Silcox, B. (1994). Active learning and the limited English proficient student. National Clearinghouse for Bilingual Education. *Directions in Language and Education, 1*(2). Retrieved February 24, 2003, from www.ncela.gwu.edu/ncbepubs/directions/02.htm.

Festinger, L. (1957). *A theory of cognitive dissonance.* Stanford, CA: Stanford University Press.

Fine, M. (1991). *Framing dropouts: Notes on the politics of an urban public high school.* Albany: State University of New York Press.

Fitzgerald, J. (1995). English-as-a-second-language learners' cognitive reading processes: A review of research in the United States. *Review of Educational Research, 65,* 145–190.

Flavell, J. H. (1979). Metacognition and cognitive monitoring: A new area of cognitive-developmental inquiry. *American Psychologist, 34,* 906–911.

Flavell, J., & Wellman, T. (1977). Metamemory. In R. Kail & J. Hagen (Eds.), *Perspectives on the development of memory and cognition* (pp. 3–33). Hillsdale, NJ: Lawrence Erlbaum.

Flores, B., Cousin, P. T., & Díaz, E. (1991). Critiquing and transforming the deficit myths about learning, language and culture. *Language Arts, 68*(5), 369–379.

Florida, R., Cushing, R., & Gates, G. (2002). When social capital stifles innovation. *Harvard Business Review, 80*(8), 20.

Fountas, I., & Pinnell, G. (1996). *Guided reading: Good first teaching for all children.* Portsmouth, NH: Heinemann.

Freeman, D. E., & Freeman, Y. S. (2001). *Between worlds: Access to second language acquisition* (2nd ed.). Portsmouth, NH: Heinemann.

Freeman, D. E., Freeman, Y. S., & Mercuri, S. (2002). *Closing the achievement gap.* Portsmouth, NH: Heinemann.

Freeman, W. (1995). *Society of brains.* Hillsdale, NJ: Lawrence Erlbaum.

Freeman, Y. S., & Freeman, D. E. (1992). *Whole language for second language learners.* Portsmouth, NH: Heinemann.

Freeman, Y. S., & Freeman, D. E. (1998). *ESL/EFL teaching: Principles for success.* Portsmouth, NH: Heinemann.

Freire, P. (1970). *Pedagogy of the oppressed.* New York: Herder and Herder.

Fullan, M. (2001). *The new meaning of educational change* (3rd ed.). New York: Teachers College, Columbia University.

Gagné, E. D. (1985). *The cognitive psychology of school learning.* Boston: Little, Brown.

Garbe, D. G. (1985). Mathematics vocabulary and the culturally different student. *Arithmetic Teacher, 33*(22), 29–42.

Garcia, E. (1996). Preparing instructional professionals for linguistically and culturally diverse students. In J. Sikula, T. Buttery, & E. Guyton (Eds.), *Handbook of research on teacher education* (2nd ed., pp. 802–813). New York: Macmillan.

García, G. (1991). Factors influencing the English reading test performance of Spanish-speaking Hispanic children. *Reading Research Quarterly, 26*(4), 371–392.

García, G. E. (1998). Mexican-American bilingual students' metacognitive reading strategies: What's transferred, unique, problematic? *National Reading Conference Yearbook, 47,* 253–263.

García, G. E. (2000). Bilingual children's reading. In M. Kamil, P. Mosenthal, P. D. Pearson, & R. Barr (Eds.), *Handbook of reading research: Volume III* (pp. 813–834). Mahwah, NJ: Lawrence Erlbaum.

García-Castañón, J. (1994). Training Hmong refugee students. In G. D. Spindler & L. Spindler (Eds.), *Pathways to cultural awareness: Cultural therapy with teachers and students* (pp. 197–219). Thousand Oaks, CA: Corwin Press.

Gardner, J. E., & Wissick, C. A. (2002). Enhancing thematic units using the World Wide Web: Tools and strategies for students with mild disabilities. *JSET E-Journal, 17*(1). Retrieved February 19, 2003, from http://jset.unlv.edu/17.1T/tgardner/first.html.

Gattegno, C. (1982). Much language and little vocabulary. In R. Blair (Ed.), *Innovative approaches to language teaching* (pp. 273–292). Rowley, MA: Newbury House.

Gault, A., & Murphy, J. (1987). The implications of high expectations for bilingual students. *Journal of Educational Equity and Leadership, 7*(8), 301–317.

Gay, G. (2000). *Culturally responsive teaching: Theory, research, & practice.* New York: Teachers College Press.

General Accounting Office (GAO). (1987). *Bilingual education: A new look at the research evidence* (Report No. PEMD-87-12BR). Washington, DC: U.S. General Accounting Office.

Genesee, F. (1983). Bilingual education for majority language children: The immersion experiments in review. *Applied Psycholinguistics, 4,* 1–46.

Genesee, F. (1987). *Learning through two languages: Studies of immersion and bilingual education.* Cambridge, MA: Newbury House.

Genesee, F. (1994). *Integrating language and content: Lessons from immersion* (Educational Practice Report No. 11). Santa Cruz, CA, and Washington, DC: National Center for Research on Cultural Diversity and Second Language Learning. Retrieved March 5, 2003, from www.ncela.gwu.edu/miscpubs/ncrcdsll/epr11.htm.

Genesee, F. (1998). Content-based language instruction (introduction to Chapter 5). In M. Met (Ed.), *Critical issues in early second language learning* (pp. 103–105). Reading, MA: Scott Foresman-Addison Wesley.

Genesee, F. (1999). *Program alternatives for linguistically diverse students.* Washington, DC, and Santa Cruz, CA: Center for Research on Education, Diversity & Excellence.

Genesee, F. (2000). *Brain research: Implications for second language learning.* Washington, DC: ERIC Clearinghouse on Languages and Linguistics.

(ERIC Digest No. EDO-FL-00-12.) Retrieved March 6, 2003, from www.cal.org/ericcll/digest/0012brain.html.

Gersten, R. (1996). Literacy instruction for language-minority students: The transition years. *Elementary School Journal, 96,* 227–244.

Ghosn, I. K. (2002). Four good reasons to use literature in the primary school ELT. *English Language Teaching Journal, 56*(2), 172–179.

Gibson, Margaret A. (1995). Perspectives on acculturation and school performance. *IAMME Bulletin, 20*(2), 1, 10, 11, 16.

Gilhooly, K. J., Logie, R. H., Wetherick, N. E., & Wynn, V. (1993). Working memory and strategies in syllogistic-reasoning tasks. *Memory and Cognition, 21,* 115–124.

Ginott, H. (1993). *Teacher and child.* New York: Macmillan.

Gleason, H. A. (1961). *An introduction to descriptive linguistics* (Rev. ed.). New York: Holt, Rinehart & Winston.

Glenn, C., & LaLyre, I. (1991). Integrated bilingual education in the USA. In K. Jaspaert & S. Kroon (Eds.), *Ethnic minority languages and education* (pp. 37–55). Amsterdam: Swets and Zeitlinger.

Goldenberg, C., & Gallimore, R. (1991). Local knowledge, research knowledge, and educational change: A case study of early Spanish reading improvement. *Educational Researcher, 20*(8), 2–14.

Goldman, C., & O'Shea, C. (1990). A culture for change. *Educational Leadership, 47*(8), 41–43.

Goldstein, L. (1999). The relational zone: The role of caring relationships in the co-construction of the mind. *American Educational Research Journal, 36*(3), 647–673.

Gonzalez, G. A. (2002, June). *A total integrated language approach.* Elementary strand session presented at the second annual CLD Education Institute, Wichita, KS.

Goodlad, J. I. (1990). Common schools for the common weal: Reconciling self-interest with the common good. In J. I. Goodlad & P. Keating (Eds.), *Access to knowledge: An agenda for our nation's schools* (pp. 1–21). New York: College Entrance Examination Board.

Gordon, C., & Rennie, B. (1987). Restructuring content schemata: An intervention study. *Reading Research and Instruction, 26*(3), 162–188.

Grabe, W., & Stoller, F. L. (1997). Content-based instruction: Research foundations. In M. A. Snow & D. M. Brinton (Eds.), *The content-based class-*

room: *Perspectives on integrating language and content* (pp. 5–21). White Plains, NY: Longman.

Grasha, A. F. (1990). The naturalistic approach to learning styles. *College Teaching, 38*(3), 106–113.

Gray, W. S., & Leary, B. E. (1935). *What makes a book readable?* Chicago: University of Chicago Press.

Haas, M. (2000). *Thematic, communicative language teaching in the K–8 classroom.* Washington, DC: ERIC Clearinghouse on Languages and Linguistics. (ERIC Digest No. EDO-FL-00-04.) Retrieved February 19, 2003, from www.cal.org/ericcll/digest/0004thematic.html.

Hacking, I. (2000). *The social construction of what?* Cambridge, MA: Harvard University Press.

Hamayan, E. (1994). Language development of low literacy students. In F. Genesee (Ed.), *Educating second language children* (pp. 166–199). Cambridge, UK: Cambridge University Press.

Hancin-Bhatt, B., & Nagy, W. (1994). Lexical transfer and second language morphological development. *Applied Psycholinguistics, 15,* 289–310.

Hanson-Smith, E. (1997). *Technology in the classroom: Practice and promise in the 21st century.* Alexandria, VA: Teachers of English to Speakers of Other Languages.

Hargreaves, A., & Fullan, M. (1998). *What's worth fighting for out there?* New York: Teachers College Press.

Henderson, R., & Landesman, E. (1992). *Mathematics and middle school students of Mexican descent: The effects of thematically integrated instruction.* Santa Cruz, CA: The National Center for Research on Cultural Diversity and Language Learning.

Herrera, S. (1996). The meaning perspectives teachers hold regarding their Mexican American students: An ethnographic case study. *Dissertation Abstracts International, 56*(12), 4643. [CD-ROM]. Abstract from: ProQuest File: Dissertations Abstracts Item: AAC 9610795.

Herrera, S. (2001). *Classroom strategies for the English language learner: A practical guide for accelerating language and literacy development.* Manhattan, KS: The MASTER Teacher.

Herrera, S., & Fanning, R. (1999). Preparing today's teachers for tomorrow's children. *Educational Considerations, 26*(2), 40–43.

Herrera, S., & Murry, K. G. (1999). In the aftermath of Unz. *Bilingual Research Journal, 23*(2–3), 113–132.

Hertz-Lazarowitz, R., & Calderón, M. (1993). *Children's writing about learning in the Bilingual Cooperative Integrated Reading and Composition (BCIRC) Project.* Baltimore, MD: Johns Hopkins University, Center for Research on Effective Schooling for Disadvantaged Students.

Howatt, A. (1984). *A history of English language teaching.* Oxford, UK: Oxford University Press.

Hudelson, S., & Serna, I. (1994). Beginning literacy in English in a whole-language bilingual program. In A. Flurkey & R. Meyer (Eds.), *Under the whole language umbrella: Many cultures, many voices* (pp. 278–294). Urbana, IL: National Council of Teachers of English.

Hymes, D. (1972). On communicative competence. In J. B. Pride & J. Holmes (Eds.), *Sociolinguistics* (pp. 269–293). Harmondsworth, UK: Penguin.

Jensen, E. (1996). *Brain-based learning.* Del Mar, CA: Turning Point.

Jimenez, R. (1994). Understanding and promoting the reading comprehension of bilingual students. *Bilingual Research Journal, 18,* 99–119.

Jimenez, R. (1997). The strategic reading abilities and potential of five low-literacy Latina/o readers in middle school. *Reading Research Quarterly, 32,* 224–243.

Jimenez, R., García, G. E., & Pearson, P. (1996). The reading strategies of bilingual Latina/o students who are successful English readers: Opportunities and obstacles. *Reading Research Quarterly, 31,* 90–112.

Johnson, K. (1996). *Language teaching and skill learning.* Oxford, UK: Blackwell.

Just, M. A., & Carpenter, P. A. (1992). A capacity theory of comprehension: Individual differences in working memory. *Psychological Review, 99,* 122–149.

Kagan, S. (1986). Cooperative learning and sociocultural factors in schooling. In *Beyond language: Social and cultural factors in schooling language minority students* (pp. 231–298). Los Angeles: Evaluation, Dissemination and Assessment Center, California State University.

Kameenui, E., & Carnine, D. (1998). *Effective teaching strategies that accommodate diverse learners.* Upper Saddle River, NJ: Prentice Hall.

Kang, H-W., Kuehn, P., & Herrell, A. (1996). The Hmong literacy project: Parents working to preserve the past and ensure the future. *The Journal of Educational Issues of Language Minority Students, 16.* Online at www.ncbe.gwu.edu/miscpubs/jeilms/vol16/jeilms1602.htm.

Kelly, L. (1976). *25 centuries of language teaching.* Rowley, MA: Newbury House.

Kessler, C., & Quinn, M. (1980). Positive effects of bilingualism on science problem-solving abilities. In J. Alatis (Ed.), *Current issues in bilingual education* (pp. 61–74). Washington, DC: Georgetown University.

Kim, K., & Hirsch, J. (1997, July). Distinct cortical areas associated with native and second languages. *Nature, 388,* 171.

Kloss, H. (1997). *The American bilingual tradition.* Rowley, MA: Newbury House.

Kober, N. (n.d.). What special problems do LEP students face in science? What can teachers and schools do [Electronic version]? *EDTALK: What we know about mathematics teaching and learning, 32–33.* Retrieved January 8, 2003, from http://enc.org/topics/equity/articles/document.shtm?input=ENC-111335-1335.

Kole, N. (2003). *Native-language supported reading instruction: A VALID framework.* Unpublished doctoral dissertation, Kansas State University, Manhattan.

Krashen, S. D. (1981). *Second language acquisition and second language learning.* London: Pergamon Press.

Krashen, S. (1982). *Principles and practice in second language acquisition.* Oxford, UK: Pergamon Press.

Krashen, S. (1985). *The input hypothesis: Issues and implications.* London: Longman.

Krashen, S. (1991). Bilingual education and second language acquisition theory. In C. F. Leyba (Ed.), *Schooling and language minority students: A theoretical framework* (pp. 51–79). Los Angeles, CA: Evaluation, Dissemination and Assessment Center, CSULA.

Krashen, S. (1996). *Under attack: The case against bilingual education.* Culver City, CA: Language Education Associates.

Krashen, S. (2000). *Has whole language failed?* University of Southern California Rossier School of Education. Retrieved November 15, 2002, from www.usc.edu/dept/education/CMMR/text/Krashen_WholeLang.html.

Krashen, S., & Terrell, T. (1983). *The natural approach: Language acquisition in the classroom.* Englewood Cliffs, NJ: Prentice Hall.

Kroll, L. R. (1998). Cognitive principles applied to the development of literacy. In N. M. Lambert & B. L. McCombs (Eds.), *How students learn: Reforming schools through learner-centered education* (pp. 113–142). Washington, DC: American Psychological Association.

Kukla, A. (2000). *Social constructivism and the philosophy of science.* London: Routledge.

Kurzweil Educational Systems. (2002). Kurzweil 3000 [computer software]. Bedford, MA: Author.

Ladson-Billings, G. (1995). Toward a theory of culturally relevant pedagogy. *American Educational Research Journal, 32*(3), 465–491.

Laing, R. D. (1999). *Knots: Selected works of R. D. Laing* (Vol. 7). New York: Routledge.

Lanauze, M., & Snow, C. (1989). The relation between first and second language writing skills: Evidence from Puerto Rican elementary school children in bilingual programs. *Linguistics and Education, 1,* 323–339.

Lantolf, J. P., & Appel, G. (Eds.). (1996). *Vygotskian approaches to second language research.* Norwood, NJ: Ablex.

Lau v. Nichols, 414 U.S. 563 (1974).

Leibowitz, A. H. (1971). *Educational policy and political acceptance: The imposition of English as the language of instruction in American schools.* Washington, DC: Center for Applied Linguistics.

Leone, B., & Cisneros, R. (Eds.). (1995). Special issue on the ESL component of bilingual education in practice. *Bilingual Research Journal, 19*(3–4).

Lieberman, A., & Grolnick, M. (1997). Networks, reform and the professional development of teachers. In A. Hargreaves (Ed.), *Rethinking educational change with heart and mind* (pp. 192–215). The 1997 ASCD Yearbook. Alexandria, VA: Association for Supervision and Curriculum Development.

Leinhardt, G. (1992). What research on learning tells us about teaching. *Educational Leadership, 49*(7), 20–25.

Lessow-Hurley, J. (1990). *The foundations of dual language instruction.* White Plains, NY: Longman.

Lightbrown, P., & Spada, N. (1993). *How languages are learned.* Oxford, UK: Oxford University Press.

Lindholm, K. (1990). Bilingual immersion education: Criteria for program development. In A. M. Padilla, H. H. Fairchild, & C. M. Valdez (Eds.), *Bilingual education: Issues and strategies* (pp. 91–105). Newbury Park, CA: Sage.

Lindholm, K. (1992). Two-way bilingual/immersion education: Theory, conceptual issues, and pedagogical implications. In R. Padilla & A. Benavides (Eds.), *Critical perspectives in bilingual education research* (pp. 195–220). Tucson, AZ: Bilingual Review/Press.

Linquanti, R. (1999). *Fostering academic success for English language learners: What do we know?* Retrieved September 16, 2002, from www.wested. org/policy/pubs/fostering/adv_conc.htm.

Livingston, J. A. (1997). *Metacognition: An overview.* Retrieved March 8, 2003, from www.gse.buffalo. edu/fas/shuell/cep564/Metacog.htm.

Loxterman, J., Beck, I., & McKeown, M. (1994). The effects of thinking aloud during reading on students' comprehension of more or less coherent text. *Reading Research Quarterly, 29,* 353–368.

Lozanov, G. (1982). Suggestology and suggestopedia: Theory and practice. In R. Blair (Ed.), *Innovative approaches to language teaching* (pp. 146–159). Rowley, MA: Newbury House.

Lucas, T. (1999). Promoting secondary school transitions for immigrant adolescents. *High School Magazine, 6*(4), 40–41.

Lucas, T., Henze, R., & Donato, R. (1990). Promoting the success of Latino language-minority students: An exploratory study of six high schools. *Harvard Educational Review, 60,* 315–340.

Massachusetts Institute of Technology (MIT). (1990). *Education that works: An action plan for the education of minorities.* Cambridge, MA: Author.

Mayer, R. (1996). Learning strategies for making sense out of expository text: The SOI model for guiding three cognitive processes in knowledge construction. *Educational Psychology Review, 8,* 357–371.

Mayer, R. E. (1998). Cognitive theory for education: What teachers need to know. In N. M. Lambert & B. L. McCombs (Eds.), *How students learn: Reforming schools through learner-centered education* (pp. 353–377). Washington, DC: American Psychological Association.

McGroarty, M. (1989). The benefits of cooperative learning arrangements in second language instruction. *NABE Journal, 13*(2), 127–143.

McLaren, P. (1998). *Life in schools: An introduction to critical pedagogy in the foundations of education* (3rd ed.). New York: Longman.

McLaughlin, B. (1990). Conscious versus unconscious learning. *TESOL Quarterly, 24,* 617–634.

McLaughlin, B. (1995). *Fostering second language learning in young children* (Educational Practice Report No. 14). Santa Cruz, CA, and Washington, DC: National Center for Research on Cultural Diversity and Second Language Learning.

McNeil, J. D. (1984). *Reading comprehension: New directions for classroom practice.* Glenview, IL: Scott, Foresman.

McNeil, L. (2000a). *Contradictions of school reform: Educational costs of standardized testing.* New York: Routledge.

McNeil, L. (2000b). The educational costs of standardization [Electronic version]. *Rethinking Schools, 14*(4). Retrieved April 14, 2003, from www.rethinkingschools.org/archive/14_04/tex144. shtml.

Medina, S. (1995). K–6 bilingual programs in the Los Angeles metropolitan area. *Bilingual Research Journal, 19*(3–4), 629–640.

Met, M. (1991). Learning language through content: Learning content through language. *Foreign Language Annals, 24*(4), 281–295.

Mettetal, G., & Cowen, P. (2000). Assessing learning through classroom research: The Supporting Teachers as Researchers Project [Electronic version]. *Classroom Leadership, 3*(8). Retrieved February 22, 2003, from www.ascd.org/readingroom/ classlead/0005/1may00.html.

Meyer, L. M. (2000). Barriers to meaningful instruction for English learners. *Theory into Practice, 39*(4), 228–236. Retrieved October 15, 2002, from WilsonSelectPlus database.

Mezirow, J. (1975). *Education for perspective transformation: Women's re-entry programs in community colleges.* New York: Center for Adult Education, Teachers College, Columbia University.

Mezirow, J. (1985). A critical theory of self-directed learning. In S. Brookfield (Ed.), *Self-directed learning: From theory to practice* (pp. 17–30). New directions for continuing education No. 25. San Francisco: Jossey-Bass.

Mezirow, J. (1991). *Transformative dimensions of adult learning.* San Francisco: Jossey-Bass.

Miller, G., Giovenco, A., & Rentiers, K. (1987). Fostering comprehension monitoring in below average readers through self-instruction training. *Journal of Reading Behavior, 19*(4), 379–394.

Minicucci, C. (1996). *Learning science and English: How school reform advances scientific learning for limited English proficient middle school students.* Santa Cruz, CA: National Center for Research on Cultural Diversity and Language Learning.

Mish, F. C., et al. (Eds.). (2001). *Merriam-Webster's collegiate dictionary* (10th ed.). Springfield, MA: Merriam-Webster.

Mitchell, R., Willis, M., & Chicago Teachers' Union Quest Center. (1995). *Learning in overdrive.* Golden, CO: North American Press.

Mohan, B. A. (1986). *Language and content.* Reading, MA: Addison-Wesley.

Mohan, B. (1990). Integration of language and content. In *Proceedings of the first research symposium on limited English proficient students' issues* (pp. 113–160). Washington, DC: U.S. Department of Education, Office of Bilingual Education and Minority Languages Affairs.

Moll, L. C. (Ed.). (1990). *Vygotsky and education: Instructional implications and applications of sociocultural psychology.* New York: Cambridge University Press.

Moll, L. C., Amanti, D. N., & Gonzalez, N. (1992). Funds of knowledge for teaching: Using a qualitative approach to connect homes and classrooms. *Theory into Practice, 31,* 132–141.

Montes, F. (2002). Enhancing content areas through a cognitive academic language learning collaborative in South Texas. *Bilingual Research Journal, 26*(3), 697–716.

Mora, J. K. (2002). *Debunking the English-only ideology: Bilingual educators are not the enemy.* Retrieved August 7, 2003, from http://coe.sdsu.edu/people/jmora/Prop227/EngOnly.htm.

Morris, R. W. (1975). Linguistic problems encountered by contemporary curriculum projects in mathematics. In E. Jacobsen (Ed.), *Interactions between linguistics and mathematical education: Final report of the symposium sponsored by UNESCO, CEDO and ICMI, Nairobi, Kenya, September 1–11, 1974* (UNESCO Report No. ED-74/CONF.808, pp. 25–52). Paris: United Nations Educational, Scientific and Cultural Organization.

Morrow, L. M., Pressley, M., Smith, J. K., & Smith, M. (1997). The effect of a literature-based program integrated into literacy and science instruction with children from diverse backgrounds. *Reading Research Quarterly, 32,* 54–76.

Moshman, D., Glover, J. A., & Bruning, R. H. (1987). *Developmental psychology.* Boston: Little, Brown.

Muñiz-Swicegood, M. (1994). The effects of metacognitive reading strategy training on the reading performance and student reading analysis strategies of third grade bilingual students. *Bilingual Research Journal, 18,* 83–97.

Murry, K. (1996). Reflective-transformative professional development predicated upon critical reflection and enabled by a school–university partnership: A microethnographic case study. *Dissertation Abstracts International, 56*(12), 4643. [CD-ROM]. Abstract from: ProQuest File: Dissertations Abstracts Item: AAC 9610795.

Murry, K. (1998). Diversity-driven program innovation in higher education: An incremental approach. *Continuing Higher Education Review, 62,* 119–126.

Murry, K., & Herrera, S. (1999). CLASSIC impacts: A qualitative study of ESL/BLED programming. *Educational Considerations, 26*(2), 11–18.

Nagy, W., García, G., Durgunoglu, A., & Hacin-Bhatt, B. (1993). Spanish–English bilingual children's use and recognition of cognates in English reading. *Journal of Reading Behavior, 25*(3), 241–259.

Nagy, W., Herman, P., & Anderson, R. (1985). Learning words from context. *Reading Research Quarterly, 23,* 414–440.

National Board for Professional Teaching Standards (NBPTS). (1998). *English as a new language standards.* Arlington, VA: Author.

National Center for Education Statistics (NCES). (1997). *1993–94 schools and staffing survey: A profile of policies and practices for limited English proficient students: Screening methods, program support, and teacher training.* Washington, DC: U.S. Department of Education, Office of Educational Research and Improvement.

National Center for Education Statistics (NCES). (2002a). *Schools and staffing survey, 1999–2000: Overview of the data for public, private, public charter, and Bureau of Indian Affairs elementary and secondary schools* (NCES 2002-13). Washington, DC: U.S. Department of Education. Available at http://nces.ed.gov/pubsearch/pubs info.asp?pubid=2002313.

National Center for Education Statistics (NCES). (2002b). *U.S. Department of Education's survey of the states' limited English proficient students and available educational programs and service, 1989–90 through 1999–2000 summary reports.* Supplemented by state publications (1998–99 data) and enrollment totals from NCES. Retrieved August 7, 2003, from www.ncela.gwu.edu/ncbepubs/reports/state-data/2000/list.htm.

National Reading Panel. (2000). *Teaching children to read: An evidence-based assessment of the scientific research literature on reading and its implications for reading instruction.* National Institute of Child Health and Human Development. Retrieved April 14, 2003, from www.nichd.nih. gov/publications/nrp/smallbook.htm.

New York State Department of Education. (2002). *Key issues in bilingual special education work paper #5*. Retrieved November 12, 2002, from www. vesid.nysed.gov/lsn/bilingual/trainingmodules05rr. pdf.

Newell, A. (1990). *Unified theories of cognition*. Cambridge, MA: Harvard University Press.

Ney, J., & Pearson, B. A. (1990). Connectionism as a model of language learning: Parallels in foreign language teaching. *Modern Language Journal, 74*, 474–482.

Nieto, S. (1992). *Affirming diversity: The sociopolitical context of multicultural education*. New York: Longman.

Nieto, S. (1999). Critical multicultural education and students' perspectives. In S. May (Ed.), *Critical multiculturalism: Rethinking multicultural and antiracist education* (pp. 191–215). Philadelphia: Falmer Press.

Ninio, A., & Bruner, J. (1978). The achievement and antecedents of labeling. *Child Language, 5*, 1–15.

Nist, S., & Simpson, M. (1990). The effect of PLAE upon students' test performance and metacognitive awareness. In J. Zutell & S. McCormick (Eds.), *Literacy, theory, and research: Analyses from multiple paradigms: Thirty-ninth yearbook of the National Reading Conference* (pp. 321–328). Chicago: National Reading Conference.

Ochs, E., & Schieffelin, G. G. (1984). Language acquisition and socialization: Three developmental stories and their implications. In R. Shweder & R. LeVine (Eds.), *Culture theory: Essays on mind, self, and emotion* (pp. 276–322). Cambridge, MA: Cambridge University Press.

Oller, J. W. Jr. (Ed.). (1993). *Methods that work: Ideas for literacy and language teachers* (2nd ed.). Boston: Heinle & Heinle.

Olsen, L. (1988). *Crossing the schoolhouse border* (California Tomorrow Policy Research Report). San Francisco: California Tomorrow.

O'Malley, J. M., & Chamot, A. U. (1990). *Learning strategies in second language acquisition*. New York: Cambridge University Press.

O'Malley, J., Chamot, A., & Küpper, L. (1989). Listening comprehension strategies in second language acquisition. *Applied Linguistics, 10*(4), 418–437.

O'Malley, J., Chamot, A., Stewner-Manzanares, G., Russo, R., & Küpper, L. (1985a). Learning strategies used by beginning and intermediate ESL students. *Language Learning, 35*, 21–46.

O'Malley, J., Chamot, A., Stewner-Manzanares, G., Russo, R., & Küpper, L. (1985b). Learning strategy applications with students of English as a second language. *TESOL Quarterly, 19*, 285–296.

Orasanu, J. (Ed.). (1986). *Reading comprehension: From research to practice*. Hillsdale, NJ: Lawrence Erlbaum.

Ovando, C., & Collier, V. (1998). *Bilingual and ESL classrooms: Teaching in multicultural contexts* (2nd ed.). Boston: McGraw-Hill.

Ovando, C. J., Collier, V. P., Combs, M. C. (2003). *Bilingual and ESL classrooms: Teaching in multicultural contexts* (3rd ed.). New York: McGraw-Hill.

Oxford, R. (1989). Use of language learning strategies: A synthesis of studies with implications for strategy training. *System, 17*(2), 235–247.

Padilla, A. M., & Gonzalez, R. (2001). Academic performance of immigrant and U.S.-born Mexican heritage students: Effects of schooling in Mexico and bilingual/English language instruction. *American Educational Research Journal, 38*(3), 727–742.

Padrón, Y. (1992). The effect of strategy instruction on bilingual students' cognitive strategy use in reading. *Bilingual Research Journal, 16*(3), 35–51.

Palincsar, A., & Brown, A. (1984). Reciprocal teaching of comprehension-fostering and monitoring activities. *Cognition and Instruction, 1*, 117–175.

Pally, M. (1994). Lingua franca: Film and video in second language acquisition. *NABE News, 18*(3), 11–13, 17, 34.

Palmer, H. E., & Palmer, D. (1925). *English through actions*. London: Longman Green.

Paris, S. G., & Winograd, P. (1990). How metacognition can promote academic learning and instruction. In B. F. Jones & L. Idol (Eds.), *Dimensions of thinking and cognitive instruction* (pp. 15–51). Hillsdale, NJ: Lawrence Erlbaum.

Parker, D. (1997). *An untapped gold mine: Parent support for language and literacy development*. Ballard & Tighe. Retrieved February 24, 2003, from www.ballard-tighe.com/Ballard-Tighe/Source/ CommunityHTML/IdeasOfExcellence/idea9.htm.

Patterson, J. L., Purkey, S. C., & Parker, J. V. (1986). *Productive school systems for a nonrational world*. Alexandria, VA: Association for Supervision and Curriculum Development.

Payne, B., & Manning, B. (1992). Basal reader instruction: Effects of comprehension monitoring training on reading comprehension, strategy use and attitude. *Reading Research and Instruction, 32*(1), 29–38.

Pearson, P. D. (1984). *Twenty years of research in reading comprehension: The contents of school-based literacy.* New York: Random House.

Pease-Alvarez, L., & Hakuta, K. (1992). Enriching our views of bilingualism and bilingual education. *Educational Researcher, 21*(2), 4–6.

Peregoy, S., & Boyle, O. (2000). English learners reading English: What we know, what we need to know. *Theory into Practice, 39,* 237–247. Retrieved October 24, 2002, from WilsonSelectPlus database.

Peregoy, S. F., & Boyle, O. F. (2001). *Reading, writing, and learning in ESL: A resource book for K–12 teachers* (3rd ed.). New York: Longman.

Perez, D. (2002). *Comprender: Comprehension: Orchestrating meaning and purpose for reading English among newly developing English language readers.* Unpublished doctoral dissertation, Kansas State University, Manhattan.

Perez, B., & Torres-Guzman, M. (2002). *Learning in two worlds: An integrated Spanish/English biliteracy approach* (3rd ed.). Boston: Allyn and Bacon.

Pesola, C. A. D. (1995). *Background, design, and evaluation of a conceptual framework for FLES curriculum.* Unpublished doctoral dissertation, University of Minnesota, Minneapolis.

Phelan, P., Davidson, A. L., & Yu, H. C. (1993). Students' multiple worlds: Navigating the borders of family, peer, and school cultures. In P. Phelan & A. L. Davidson (Eds.), *Renegotiating cultural diversity in American schools* (pp. 52–88). New York: Teachers College Press.

Piaget, J., & Inhelder, B. (1969). *The psychology of the child* (H. Weaver, Trans.). New York: Basic Books.

Plyler v. Doe, 457 U.S. 202, 102 S.Ct. 2382 (1982).

Polak, J., & Krashen, S. (1988). Do we need to teach spelling? The relationship between spelling and vocabulary reading among community college ESL students. *TESOL Quarterly, 22,* 141–146.

Porter, R. P. (1990). *Forked tongue: The politics of bilingual education.* New York: Basic Books.

Pressley, M. (1995). More about the development of self-regulation: Complex, long-term, and thoroughly social. *Educational Psychologist, 4,* 1–32.

Purcell-Gates, V. (1996). Process teaching with direct instruction and feedback in a university-based clinic. In E. McIntyre & M. Pressley (Eds.), *Balanced instruction: Strategies and skills in whole language* (pp. 107–127). Norwood, MA: Christopher-Gordon.

Ramírez, J. D. (1992). Executive summary. *Bilingual Research Journal, 16*(1–2), 1–62.

Ramírez, J. D., Yuen, S. D., Ramey, D. R., & Pasta, D. J. (1991). *Final report: Longitudinal study of structured English immersion strategy, early-exit and late-exit transitional bilingual education programs for language-minority children* (Vols. I and II). San Mateo, CA: Aguirre International.

Reyes, M., de la Luz, M., & Halcón, J. J. (Eds.). (2001). *The best for our children: Critical perspectives on literacy for Latino students.* New York: Teachers College Press.

Richard-Amato, P. A. (1996). *Making it happen: Interaction in the second language classroom: From theory to practice* (2nd ed.). White Plains, NY: Longman.

Richards, J. C. (1983). Listening comprehension: Approach, design, procedure. *TESOL Quarterly, 17,* 219–240.

Richards, J. C., & Rodgers, T. (1982). Method: Approach, design, procedure. *TESOL Quarterly, 16,* 153–168.

Roberts, R., Phinney, J., Romero, A., & Chen, Y. W. (1996). *The cross-cultural structure of adolescent ethnic identity.* Paper presented at the meeting of the Society for Research on Adolescence, Boston, MA.

Rodriguez, D., Parmar, R. S., & Signer, B. R. (2001). Fourth-grade culturally and linguistically diverse exceptional students' concepts of number line. *Exceptional Children, 67*(2), 199–210. Retrieved November 13, 2002, from WilsonSelectPlus database.

Rohac, R. (2000, May). S.D.A.I.E.—Specially Designed Academic Instruction in English. *ELT Newsletter.* Retrieved February 20, 2003, from www.eltnewsletter.com/back/May2000/art112000.shtml.

Rosebery, A. S., Warren, B., & Conant, F. R. (1992). Appropriate scientific discourse: Findings from language minority classrooms. *The Journal of the Learning Sciences, 2*(1), 61–94.

Rosenshine, B., Meister, C., & Chapman, S. (1996). Teaching students to generate questions: A review of the intervention studies. *Review of Educational Research, 66*(2), 181–221.

Routman, R. (1996). *Literacy at the crossroads: Crucial talk about reading, writing, and other teaching dilemmas.* Portsmouth, NH: Heinemann.

Ruddell, M. R. (1997). *Teaching content reading and writing* (2nd ed.). Boston: Allyn and Bacon.

Russell, S. (2002). *Specially designed academic instruction in English (SDAIE).* California State University, Dominguez Hills School of Education. Retrieved November 5, 2002, from www.pda.calstate.edu/arco/SDAIE.pdf.

Samway, K. D., & McKeon, D. (1999). *Myths and realities: Best practices for language minority students.* Portsmouth, NH: Heinemann.

Sasser, L. (1992). Teaching literature to language minority students. In P. A. Richard-Amato & M. A. Snow (Eds.), *The multicultural classroom: Readings for content-area teachers* (pp. 300–315). White Plains, NY: Longman.

Saunders, W., & Goldenberg, C. (1999). *The effects of instructional conversations and literature logs on the story comprehension and thematic understanding of English proficient and limited English proficient students* (Research Rep. No. 6). Washington, DC, and Santa Cruz, CA: Center for Research on Education, Diversity & Excellence.

Saunders, W., O'Brien, G., Lennon, D., & McLean, J. (1999). *Successful transition into mainstream English: Effective strategies for studying literature.* Center for Research on Education, Diversity & Excellence. Retrieved December 9, 2002, from www.cal.org/crede/PUBS/edpractice/EPR2.pdf.

Sautter, R. C. (1994). *Who are today's city kids? Beyond the "deficit model."* Retrieved October 31, 2002, from www.ncrel.org/sdrs/cityschl/city1_1a.htm.

Saville-Troike, M. (1984). What really matters in second language learning for academic achievement? *TESOL Quarterly, 18*(2), 199–219.

Scarcella, R. C. (1990). *Teaching language minority students in the multicultural classroom.* Englewood Cliffs, NJ: Prentice Hall Regents.

Scherer, M. (2000). Perspectives/not by tests alone. *Educational Leadership, 57*(5), 5.

Schieffelin, B. B., & Eisenberg, A. (1984). Cultural variation in children's conversations. In R. L. Schiefelbusch & J. Pickar (Eds.), *The acquisition of communicative competence* (pp. 377–420). Baltimore, MD: University Park Press.

Scholastic. (2000). WiggleWorks: Scholastic beginning literacy system (Version 3.0) [Computer software]. New York: Author.

Searle, J. R. (1995). *The construction of social reality.* New York: Free Press.

Senge, P. (1997). Preface to A. Costa and R. Liebmann. In *Envisioning process as content: Toward a Renaissance curriculum.* Thousand Oaks, CA: Corwin Press.

Shanker, A. (1985). *Being a professional.* Presentation to the National Press Club, Washington, DC.

Sheppard, K. (1995). *Content-ESL across the USA* (Volume I, Technical Report). Washington, DC: National Clearinghouse for Bilingual Education.

Shepard, L. A. (1997). *Measuring achievement: What does it mean to test for robust understanding?* Princeton, NJ: Policy Information Center, Educational Testing Service.

Short, D. J. (1991). *Integrating language and content instruction: Strategies and techniques* (NCBE Program Information Guide Series No. 7). Washington, DC: National Clearinghouse for Bilingual Education. Retrieved March 13, 2003, from www.ncela.gwu.edu/ncbepubs/pigs/pig7.htm.

Short, D. J. (1993a). Assessing integrated language and content instruction. *TESOL Quarterly, 27*(4), 627–656.

Short, D. J. (1993b). *Integrating language and culture in middle school American history classes* (Educational Practice Report No. 8). National Center for Research on Cultural Diversity and Second Language Learning. Retrieved January 9, 2003, from www.ncela.gwu.edu/miscpubs/ncrcds11/epr8.htm.

Short, D., & Boyson, B. (1998). *Secondary newcomer programs in the U.S. 1997–98 supplement.* Washington, DC, and Santa Cruz, CA: Center for Research on Education, Diversity & Excellence.

Shuell, T. J. (1986). Cognitive conceptions of learning. *Review of Educational Research, 56,* 411–436.

Slavin, R. (1983). When does cooperative learning increase student achievement? *Psychological Bulletin, 94*(3), 429–445.

Slavin, R. E. (1995). *Cooperative learning: Theory, research, and practice* (2nd ed.). Boston: Allyn and Bacon.

Snow, C., Arlman-Rupp, A., Hassing, Y., Jobse, J., Joosten, J., & Yorster, J. (1976). Mothers' speech in three social classes. *Journal of Psycholinguistic Research, 5,* 1–20.

Snow, C. E., Burns, M. S., & Griffin, P. (Eds.). (1998). *Preventing reading difficulties in young children.* Washington, DC: National Academy Press.

Soto, G. (2000). The marble champ. In *Reading: Fantastic voyage* (pp. 269–280). Glenview, IL: Scott Foresman.

Sousa, D. A. (1995). *How the brain learns*. Reston, VA: National Association of Secondary School Principals.

Spires, H., Gallini, J., & Riggsbee, J. (1992). Effects of schema-based and text structure-based cues on expository prose comprehension in fourth graders. *Journal of Experimental Education, 60*(4), 307–320.

Stahl, S., & Fairbanks, M. (1986). The effects of vocabulary instruction: A model-based meta-analysis. *Review of Educational Research, 56,* 72–110.

Stanovich, K. E. (1986). Matthew effects in reading: Some consequences of individual differences in the acquisition of literacy. *Reading Research Quarterly, 21,* 360–406.

Stevens, C. (2002, October 28). Verdict still out on programs. *USA Today.* Retrieved November 4, 2002, from www.usatoday.com/news/opinion/editorials/2002-10-28-edit_x.htm.

Stevens, R., Slavin, R., & Farnish, A. (1991). The effects of cooperative learning and direct instruction in reading comprehension strategies on main idea identification. *Journal of Educational Psychology, 83*(1), 8–16.

Strain, J. (1986). Method: Design-procedure versus method-technique. *System, 14*(3), 287–294.

Strevens, P. (1980). *Teaching English as an international language.* Oxford, UK: Pergamon.

Swain, M., & Lapkin, S. (1982). *Evaluating bilingual education: A Canadian case study.* Clevedon, UK: Multilingual Matters.

Swain, M., & Lapkin, S. (1991). Additive bilingualism and French immersion education: The roles of language and proficiency and literacy. In A. Reynolds (Ed.), *Bilingualism, multiculturalism, and second language learning: The McGill conference in honour of Wallace E. Lambert* (pp. 203–216). Hillsdale, NJ: Lawrence Erlbaum.

Teachers of English to Speakers of Other Languages (TESOL). (1997). *ESL standards for pre-K–12 students.* Alexandria, VA: Author.

Teachers of English to Speakers of Other Languages (TESOL). (2001). *TESOL ESL standards for P–12 teacher education programs.* Retrieved February 18, 2003, from www.tesol.org/pdfs/aboutassoc/ncatestds.pdf.

Teachers of English to Speakers of Other Languages (TESOL). (n.d.). *The ESL standards for pre-K–12 students, appendix A: Access brochure—The TESOL standards: Ensuring access to quality educational experiences for language minority students.* Retrieved February 26, 2003, from www.tesol.org/assoc/k12standards/it/11.html.

Teitelbaum, H., & Hiller, R. J. (1977). Bilingual education: The legal mandate. *Harvard Educational Review, 47,* 138–170.

Terrell, T. (1991). The natural approach in bilingual education. In C. Leyba (Ed.), *Schooling and language minority students: A theoretical framework.* Los Angeles: Evaluation, Dissemination and Assessment Center.

Terrell, T., Egasses, J., & Voge, W. (1982). Techniques for a more natural approach to second language acquisition and learning. In R. Blair (Ed.), *Innovative approaches to language teaching* (pp. 174–175). Rowley, MA: Newbury House.

Terrisse, S. (2001). Does your organization's gene pool need to make a bigger splash? Workplace diversity and its impact on creativity. *Public Relations Quarterly, 46*(1), 30.

Tharp, R. (1989, February). Psychocultural variables and constants: Effects on teaching and learning in schools. *American Psychologist, 44*(2), 349–359.

Thomas, W. P. (1992). An analysis of the research methodology of the Ramírez study. *Bilingual Research Journal, 16*(1–2), 213–245.

Thomas, W. P. (1994). *The Cognitive Academic Language Learning Approach project for mathematics.* Fairfax, VA: Center for Bilingual/Multicultural/ESL Education, George Mason University.

Thomas, W., & Collier, V. (1995). Language-minority student achievement and program effectiveness studies support native language development. *NABE News, 18*(8), 5, 12.

Thomas, W. P., & Collier, V. P. (1997). *School effectiveness for language minority students* (NCBE Resource Collection Series No. 9). Washington, DC: National Clearinghouse for Bilingual Education. Retrieved October 7, 2002, from www.ncela.gwu.edu/ncbepubs/resource/effectiveness.

Thomas, W. P., & Collier, V. P. (1999). Accelerated schooling for English language learners. *Educational Leadership, 56*(7), 46–49.

Thomas, W. P., & Collier, V. P. (2002). *A national study of school effectiveness for language minority students' long-term academic achievement.* Santa Cruz, CA: Center for Research on Education, Diversity & Excellence. Retrieved February

5, 2003, from www.crede.ucsc.edu/research/llaa/1.1_final.html.

Tinajero, J. V., & Ada, A. F. (Eds.). (1993). *The power of two languages: Literacy and biliteracy for Spanish-speaking students*. New York: Macmillan.

Tinajero, J. V., Calderón, M. E., & Hertz-Lazarowitz, R. (1993). Cooperative learning strategies: Bilingual classroom applications. In J. V. Tinajero & A. F. Ada (Eds.), *The power of two languages: Literacy and biliteracy for Spanish-speaking students* (pp. 241–253). New York: Macmillan.

Trifonovitch, G. (1977). Culture learning—culture teaching. *Educational Perspectives, 16*(4), 18–22.

Trueba, H. T. (1994). Reflections on alternative visions of schooling. *Anthropology & Education Quarterly, 25,* 376–393.

U.S. Census Bureau. (2000). *QT-02 profile of selected social characteristics: 2000* [Electronic version]. Washington, DC: Author. Retrieved November 22, 2002, from http://factfindercensus.gov/servlet/QTTable?ds_name=D&geo_id=D&qr_name=ACS_C2SS_EST_G00_QT02&_lang=en.

U.S. Department of Education (USDE). (2002). *Survey of the states' limited English proficient students & available educational programs and services 1999–2000 summary report.* Washington, DC: National Clearinghouse for English Language Acquisition and Language Instruction Educational Programs.

U.S. English. (1990, May 21). The door to opportunity. *Roll Call.*

Valdes, G. (1996). *Con respeto: Bridging the distance between culturally diverse families and schools: An ethnographic portrait.* New York: Teachers College Press.

Valdes, G. (1997). The teaching of Spanish to bilingual Spanish-speaking students: Outstanding issues and unanswered questions. In M. C. Colombi & F. X. Alarcon (Eds.), *La ensenanza del espanol a hispanohablantes: Praxis y teoria* (pp. 93–101). Boston: Houghton Mifflin.

Valdez, L., & Steiner, S. (Eds.). (1972). *Aztlán: An anthology of Mexican American literature.* New York: Vintage Books.

Vavrus, M. (2002). *Transforming the multicultural education of teachers: Theory, research, and practice.* New York: Teachers College Press.

Veeder, K., & Tramutt, J. (2000). Strengthening literacy in both languages in grades 2–5. In N. Cloud, F. Genesee, & E. Hamayan (Eds.), *Dual language*

instruction: A handbook for enriched education (p. 91). Boston: Heinle and Heinle.

Vernez, G., & Abrahamese, A. (1996). *How immigrants fare in U.S. education.* Santa Monica, CA: Rand.

Vygotsky, L. S. (1962). *Thought and language.* Cambridge, MA: MIT Press.

Vygotsky, L. S. (1978). *Mind in society: The development of higher psychological processes.* Cambridge, MA: Harvard University Press.

Walqui, A. (2000). *Access and engagement: Program design and instructional approaches for immigrant students in secondary school.* Center for Applied Linguistics. McHenry, IL: Delta Systems.

Walsh, E. (1989). *Mouse paint.* San Diego, CA: Voyager Books.

Weedon, C. (1993). Teachers as researchers [Electronic version]. *Research in Education, 53.* The SCRE Centre. Retrieved February 22, 2003, from www.scre.ac.uk/rie/nl53weedon.html.

Wenden, A., & Rubin, J. (Eds.). (1987). *Learner strategies in language learning.* Englewood Cliffs, NJ: Prentice Hall.

Wertsch, J. (1991). *Voices of the mind: A sociocultural approach to mediated action.* Cambridge, MA: Harvard University Press.

Whorf, B. (1956). Science and linguistics. In J. B. Carroll (Ed.), *Language, thought, and reality: Selected writings of Benjamin Lee Whorf* (pp. 207–219). Cambridge, MA: MIT Press.

Wiggins, G., & McTighe, J. (1998). *Understanding by design.* Alexandria, VA: Association for Supervision and Curriculum Development.

Williams-Morris, R. S. (1996). Racism and children's health: Issues in development. *Ethnicity and Disease, 6,* 69–82.

Willig, A. C. (1981). The effectiveness of bilingual education: Review of a report. *National Association for Bilingual Education Journal, 6*(2–3), 1–20.

Willig, A. C. (1985). A meta-analysis of selected studies on the effectiveness of bilingual education. *Review of Educational Research, 55,* 269–317.

Wittrock, M. C. (1998). Cognition and subject matter learning. In N. M. Lambert & B. L. McCombs (Eds.), *How students learn: Reforming schools through learner-centered education* (pp. 143–152). Washington, DC: American Psychological Association.

Wong Fillmore, L. (1991). Second language learning in children: A model of language learning in social context. In E. Bialystok (Ed.), *Language processing in bilingual children* (pp. 49–69). Cambridge, MA: Cambridge University Press.

Wong Fillmore, L., & Valadez, C. (1986). Teaching bilingual learners. In M. C. Wittrock (Ed.), *Handbook of research on teaching* (3rd ed., pp. 648–685). New York: Longman.

Young, K. M., & Leinhardt, G. (1996). *Writing from primary documents: A way of knowing in history* (Tech. Rep. No. CLIP-96-01). Pittsburgh, PA: University of Pittsburgh, Learning Research and Development Center.

Zimmerman, B. J. (1990). Self-regulated learning and academic achievement: An overview. *Educational Psychologist, 25*(1), 3–17.

Zinn, H. (2002). *You can't be neutral on a moving train: A personal history of our times.* Uckfield, East Sussex, UK: Beacon Press.

Sheltered method of instruction *(continued)*
  nature of, 251–252
  sheltered instruction, 251–259
  SIOP (sheltered instruction observation protocol), 10, 188, 251, 252–253, 261–287, 292
  specially designed academic instruction in English (SDAIE), 10, 252–253, 259, 261
  variations on, 252–257
Silent period, 70, 76
Silent way, 185
SIOP (sheltered instruction observation protocol), 10, 188, 251, 252–253, 261–287
  closing thoughts on, 286–287
  development of, 262
  instruction in, 270–285
  preparation for, 263–270, 288
  review and assessment in, 286, 292
Social affective learning strategies, 43, 44, 300, 302, 305, 323–324
Socialization, 35, 130–131, 199
Social studies
  challenges and accommodations for CLD students, 311
  guarded vocabulary in, 256
  linguistic and academic development in, 19
Sociocultural dimension, 12–26, 117–119, 213–214
  challenges of, 13–19
  implications for classroom and school practice, 24–26
  interrelationship between cognitive dimension and, 37
  processes of, 14, 19–24
  of student biography, 12–13
  tips for practice, 26–27
Sociocultural processes, 14, 19–24
Sociolinguistic competence, 64–65
Sociopolitical and sociocultural realities, in platform for best practice, 345–346, 347, 348
Specially designed academic instruction of English (SDAIE), 10, 252–253, 259, 261
Speech, print correspondence to, 77–78
Spiraling curriculum, 114
Stages of second language acquisition, 64–65, 70–76
Standards
  of academic achievement, 145–146
  for teachers. *See* Standards-driven professional practice; TESOL/NCATE teacher standards

Standards-driven professional practice, 330–359
  benchmarks of effective practice, 338–340
  facets of platform for best practice, 340–355, 359–360
  nationally recognized standards for teachers, 333–338
  setting goals for professional practice, 355–359
Strategic competence, 65, 68
Strategies, 303
  consistency of, 169, 171, 172–173
  in SIOP variation of sheltered instruction, 280–281, 290
Structured immersion programs, 115
Student-centered perspective, 190, 216
Subject-area domains. *See also specific subject areas*
  academic language development in, 51–53
Subtractive bilingualism, 101–102
Suggestopedia, 187
Summative assessment, 238–239, 240–241
Supplementary materials, 267
SUP (separate underlying proficiency), 10, 99–102, 107–108

Teachers. *See also* Standards-driven professional practice; Tips for practice
  dilemmas of practice, 20, 42, 76, 102, 148, 198, 215, 258, 320, 334
  effective, 263–264, 305, 338–340
  expectations for student learning, 4
  preparation for CLD students, 4, 6
  reflective, 24–26, 44–45, 130–134
Teachers of English to Speakers of Other Languages (TESOL), 146–147, 188, 260, 354
Teaching to the test, 47–48
Technique, consistency of, 169, 171, 173
Television, 42
TESOL/NCATE teacher standards, 334, 335–336, 337, 338, 342, 345–346, 349–350, 353
  Domain 1: Language, 3, 31, 59–60, 95, 167, 207, 297
  Domain 2: Culture, 3–4, 125
  Domain 3: Planning, Implementing and Managing Instruction, 31–32, 249–250, 297–298, 331
  Domain 4: Assessment, 250, 298
  Domain 5: Professionalism, 126, 167–168, 332
Texas, 5, 12
Thematic units, 209